ISBN-13: 978-0-7387-3759-1

Cover design by Ellen Lawson
Cover images: iStockphoto.com/2407241/©nicoolay;
Celestial©DigitalStock
Designed by Susan Van Sant
Edited by Aaron Lawrence and Ed Day

A special thanks to Phoebe Aina Allen for astrological proofreading.

Astrological calculations compiled and programmed by Rique Pottenger based on the earlier work of Neil F. Michelsen. Re-use is prohibited.

Published by
LLEWELLYN WORLDWIDE LTD.
2143 Wooddale Drive
Woodbury, MN 55125-2989

Printed in the United States of America

Table of Contents

Mercury Retrograde 2017

	DATE	ET	PT			DATE	ET	PT
Mercury Retrograde	12/19/16	**5:55 am**	2:55 am	—	Mercury Direct	1/8/17	**4:43 am**	1:43 am
Mercury Retrograde	4/9	**7:14 pm**	4:14 pm	—	Mercury Direct	5/3	**12:33 pm**	9:33 am
Mercury Retrograde	8/12	**9:00 pm**	6:00 pm	—	Mercury Direct	9/5	**7:29 am**	4:29 am
Mercury Retrograde	12/2		11:34 pm	—	Mercury Direct	12/22	**8:51 pm**	5:51 pm
Mercury Retrograde	12/3	**2:34 am**		—	Mercury Direct	12/22	**8:51 pm**	5:51 pm

Moon Void-of-Course 2017

Times are listed in Eastern Time in this table only. All other information in the *Pocket Planner* is listed in both Eastern Time and Pacific Time. Refer to "Time Zone Conversions" on page 7 for changing to other time zones. Note: All times are corrected for daylight saving time.

Last Aspect		Moon Enters New Sign			Last Aspect		Moon Enters New Sign			Last Aspect		Moon Enters New Sign		
Date	Time	Date	Sign	Time	Date	Time	Date	Sign	Time	Date	Time	Date	Sign	Time
JANUARY					**FEBRUARY**					**MARCH**				
2	2:59 am	2	♓	4:57 am	2	11:50 am	2	♉	8:50 pm	1	9:18 pm	2	♉	2:43 am
4	11:14 am	4	♈	11:20 am	4	5:42 pm	4	♊	11:44 pm	3	10:20 am	4	♊	5:05 am
6	1:41 pm	6	♉	3:18 pm	6	5:53 pm	7	♋	2:03 am	6	3:22 am	6	♋	7:54 am
7	9:23 pm	8	♊	5:06 pm	8	5:00 pm	9	♌	4:41 am	8	9:59 am	8	♌	11:45 am
10	4:38 pm	10	♋	5:49 pm	11	12:52 am	11	♍	8:52 am	10	12:06 pm	10	♍	5:07 pm
12	6:34 am	12	♌	7:08 pm	13	7:36 am	13	♎	3:43 pm	12	10:36 pm	13	♎	1:28 am
14	10:17 am	14	♍	10:52 pm	15	8:54 pm	16	♏	1:41 am	15	6:05 am	15	♏	11:11 am
17	1:09 am	17	♎	6:16 am	17	2:38 pm	18	♐	1:52 pm	17	5:56 pm	17	♐	11:00 pm
19	3:55 am	19	♏	5:09 pm	20	6:37 pm	21	♑	2:08 am	20	6:37 am	20	♑	11:31 am
21	8:24 pm	22	♐	5:45 am	22	10:24 pm	23	♒	12:17 pm	22	9:20 am	22	♒	10:28 pm
24	12:33 pm	24	♑	5:43 pm	25	1:11 pm	25	♓	7:24 pm	25	1:56 am	25	♓	6:06 am
27	2:18 am	27	♒	3:37 am	27	6:08 pm	27	♈	11:52 pm	27	6:19 am	27	♈	10:11 am
29	12:52 am	29	♓	11:10 am						29	8:07 am	29	♉	11:48 am
31	12:36 pm	31	♈	4:46 pm						30	7:12 pm	31	♊	12:40 pm

Moon Void-of-Course 2017 (cont.)

APRIL

Last Aspect Date	Last Aspect Time	Moon Enters New Sign Date	Sign	Time
2	10:43 am	2	♋	2:27 pm
4	4:45 pm	4	♌	6:13 pm
6	8:16 pm	7	♍	12:20 am
9	4:21 am	9	♎	8:34 am
11	2:19 pm	11	♏	6:42 pm
14	12:18 am	14	♐	6:27 am
16	2:26 pm	16	♑	7:05 pm
19	5:57 am	19	♒	6:52 am
21	2:23 pm	21	♓	3:43 pm
23	5:34 pm	23	♈	8:32 pm
25	5:53 pm	25	♉	9:56 pm
27	9:18 pm	27	♊	9:39 pm
29	5:28 pm	29	♋	9:48 pm

MAY

Last Aspect Date	Last Aspect Time	Moon Enters New Sign Date	Sign	Time
1	4:23 pm	2	♌	12:12 am
4	12:35 am	4	♍	5:47 am
6	8:42 am	6	♎	2:20 pm
8	6:59 pm	9	♏	1:01 am
10	5:42 pm	11	♐	12:59 pm
13	10:14 pm	14	♑	1:37 am
16	6:22 am	16	♒	1:50 pm
18	8:33 pm	18	♓	11:52 pm
20	11:39 pm	21	♈	6:10 am
23	2:59 am	23	♉	8:33 am
24	3:08 pm	25	♊	8:15 am
27	2:18 am	27	♋	7:25 am
29	2:59 am	29	♌	8:12 am
31	7:14 am	31	♍	12:16 pm

JUNE

Last Aspect Date	Last Aspect Time	Moon Enters New Sign Date	Sign	Time
2	5:48 pm	2	♎	8:04 pm
5	4:57 am	5	♏	6:46 am
6	8:35 pm	7	♐	6:59 pm
10	2:20 am	10	♑	7:36 am
12	2:45 pm	12	♒	7:45 pm
15	1:40 am	15	♓	6:17 am
17	7:33 am	17	♈	1:55 pm
19	3:42 pm	19	♉	5:53 pm
21	12:26 am	21	♊	6:44 pm
23	2:45 pm	23	♋	6:07 pm
25	2:44 pm	25	♌	6:06 pm
27	5:12 pm	27	♍	8:41 pm
29	4:35 pm	30	♎	3:02 am

JULY

Last Aspect Date	Last Aspect Time	Moon Enters New Sign Date	Sign	Time
2	9:16 am	2	♏	12:59 pm
4	9:34 pm	5	♐	1:08 am
7	10:12 am	7	♑	1:45 pm
9	10:12 pm	10	♒	1:35 am
12	8:40 am	12	♓	11:51 am
14	1:00 pm	14	♈	7:52 pm
16	10:19 pm	17	♉	1:04 am
19	2:11 am	19	♊	3:31 am
21	1:41 am	21	♋	4:09 am
23	2:05 am	23	♌	4:34 am
25	5:22 am	25	♍	6:32 am
27	2:31 am	27	♎	11:37 am
29	5:30 pm	29	♏	8:23 pm
31	7:10 am	8/1	♐	8:01 am

AUGUST

Last Aspect Date	Last Aspect Time	Moon Enters New Sign Date	Sign	Time
7/31	7:10 am	1	♐	8:01 am
3	5:38 pm	3	♑	8:37 pm
6	5:22 am	6	♒	8:15 am
8	3:07 pm	8	♓	5:56 pm
10	9:38 am	11	♈	1:22 am
13	4:01 am	13	♉	6:40 am
14	9:15 pm	15	♊	10:06 am
17	9:38 am	17	♋	12:13 pm
19	11:17 am	19	♌	1:55 pm
21	2:30 pm	21	♍	4:25 pm
23	4:02 pm	23	♎	9:05 pm
26	1:39 am	26	♏	4:53 am
28	5:38 am	28	♐	3:48 pm
31	12:42 am	31	♑	4:18 am

SEPTEMBER

Last Aspect Date	Last Aspect Time	Moon Enters New Sign Date	Sign	Time
2	12:30 pm	2	♒	4:06 pm
5	1:15 am	5	♓	1:28 am
6	4:29 pm	7	♈	8:01 am
9	11:52 am	9	♉	12:23 pm
10	8:54 pm	11	♊	3:29 pm
13	2:35 pm	13	♋	6:12 pm
15	5:23 pm	15	♌	9:09 pm
17	8:55 pm	18	♍	12:52 am
20	1:30 am	20	♎	6:06 am
22	9:04 am	22	♏	1:40 pm
24	3:33 am	25	♐	12:01 am
27	7:08 am	27	♑	12:24 pm
29	8:14 pm	30	♒	12:40 am

OCTOBER

Last Aspect Date	Last Aspect Time	Moon Enters New Sign Date	Sign	Time
2	7:13 am	2	♓	10:26 am
4	3:19 am	4	♈	4:40 pm
6	6:38 pm	6	♉	7:56 pm
8	9:45 am	8	♊	9:44 pm
10	6:25 pm	10	♋	11:38 pm
13	12:00 am	13	♌	2:41 am
15	1:28 am	15	♍	7:19 am
17	7:27 am	17	♎	1:35 pm
19	3:12 pm	19	♏	9:41 pm
22	7:35 am	22	♐	7:57 am
24	12:44 pm	24	♑	8:12 pm
27	1:22 am	27	♒	8:59 am
29	12:22 pm	29	♓	7:46 pm
31	5:08 pm	11/1	♈	2:43 am

NOVEMBER

Last Aspect Date	Last Aspect Time	Moon Enters New Sign Date	Sign	Time
10/31	5:08 pm	1	♈	2:43 am
2	11:03 pm	3	♉	5:46 am
5	4:29 am	5	♊	5:26 am
7	5:40 am	7	♋	5:45 am
9	12:14 am	9	♌	7:29 am
11	3:55 am	11	♍	11:41 am
13	10:45 am	13	♎	6:26 pm
15	7:50 pm	16	♏	3:19 am
18	6:42 am	18	♐	1:59 pm
20	7:26 pm	21	♑	2:14 am
23	5:33 am	23	♒	3:14 pm
25	9:37 pm	26	♓	3:04 am
28	7:09 am	28	♈	11:30 am
30	1:37 pm	30	♉	3:38 pm

DECEMBER

Last Aspect Date	Last Aspect Time	Moon Enters New Sign Date	Sign	Time
1	8:53 pm	2	♊	4:21 pm
4	2:13 pm	4	♋	3:37 pm
6	12:56 pm	6	♌	3:37 pm
8	5:40 pm	8	♍	6:09 pm
10	10:02 pm	11	♎	12:01 am
13	7:27 am	13	♏	8:59 am
14	8:42 pm	15	♐	8:07 pm
18	8:10 am	18	♑	8:33 am
20	10:37 am	20	♒	9:29 pm
23	5:13 am	23	♓	9:42 am
24	9:48 pm	25	♈	7:27 pm
27	3:57 pm	28	♉	1:23 am
29	9:01 am	30	♊	3:31 am
31	6:38 pm	1/1	♋	3:10 am

How to Use the *Pocket Planner*

by Leslie Nielsen

This handy guide contains information that can be most valuable to you as you plan your daily activities. As you read through the first few pages, you can start to get a feel for how well organized this guide is.

Read the Symbol Key on the next page, which is rather like astrological shorthand. The characteristics of the planets can give you direction in planning your strategies. Much like traffic signs that signal "go," "stop," or even "caution," you can determine for yourself the most propitious time to get things done.

You'll find tables that show the dates when Mercury is retrograde (℞) or direct (D). Because Mercury deals with the exchange of information, a retrograde Mercury makes miscommunication more noticeable.

There's also a section dedicated to the times when the Moon is void-of-course (V/C). These are generally poor times to conduct business because activities begun during these times usually end badly or fail to get started. If you make an appointment during a void-of-course, you might save yourself a lot of aggravation by confirming the time and date later. The Moon is only void-of-course for 7 percent of the time when business is usually conducted during a normal workday (that is, 8:00 am to 5:00 pm). Sometimes, by waiting a matter of minutes or a few hours until the Moon has left the void-of-course phase, you have a much better chance to make action move more smoothly. Moon voids can also be used successfully to do routine activities or inner work, such as dream therapy or personal contemplation.

You'll find Moon phases, as well as each of the Moon's entries into a new sign. Times are expressed in Eastern time (in bold type) and Pacific time (in medium type). The New Moon time is generally best for beginning new activities, as the Moon is increasing in light and can offer the element of growth to our endeavors. When the Moon is Full, its illumination is greatest and we can see the results of our efforts. When it moves from the Full stage back to the New stage, it can best be used to reflect on our projects. If necessary, we can make corrections at the New Moon.

The section of "Planetary Stations" will give you the times when the planets are changing signs or direction, thereby affording us opportunities for new starts.

The ephemeris in the back of your *Pocket Planner* can be very helpful to you. As you start to work with the ephemeris, you may notice that not all planets seem to be comfortable in every sign. Think of the planets as actors, and the signs as the costumes they wear. Sometimes, costumes just itch. If you find this to be so for a certain time period, you may choose to delay your plans for a time or be more creative with the energies at hand.

As you turn to the daily pages, you'll find information about the Moon's sign, phase, and the time it changes phase. You'll find icons indicating the best days to plant and fish. Also, you will find times and dates when the planets and asteroids change sign and go either retrograde or direct, major holidays, a three-month calendar, and room to record your appointments.

This guide is a powerful tool. Make the most of it!

Symbol Key

Planets:	☉ Sun	⚳ Ceres	♄ Saturn
	☽ Moon	⚴ Pallas	⚷ Chiron
	☿ Mercury	⚵ Juno	♅ Uranus
	♀ Venus	⚶ Vesta	♆ Neptune
	♂ Mars	♃ Jupiter	♇ Pluto
Signs:	♈ Aries	♌ Leo	♐ Sagittarius
	♉ Taurus	♍ Virgo	♑ Capricorn
	♊ Gemini	♎ Libra	♒ Aquarius
	♋ Cancer	♏ Scorpio	♓ Pisces
Aspects:	☌ Conjunction (0°)	⚺ Semisextile (30°)	⚹ Sextile (60°)
	□ Square (90°)	△ Trine (120°)	
	⚻ Quincunx (150°)	☍ Opposition (180°)	
Motion:	℞ Retrograde	D Direct	
Best Days for Planting:		**Best Days for Fishing:**	

World Map of Time Zones

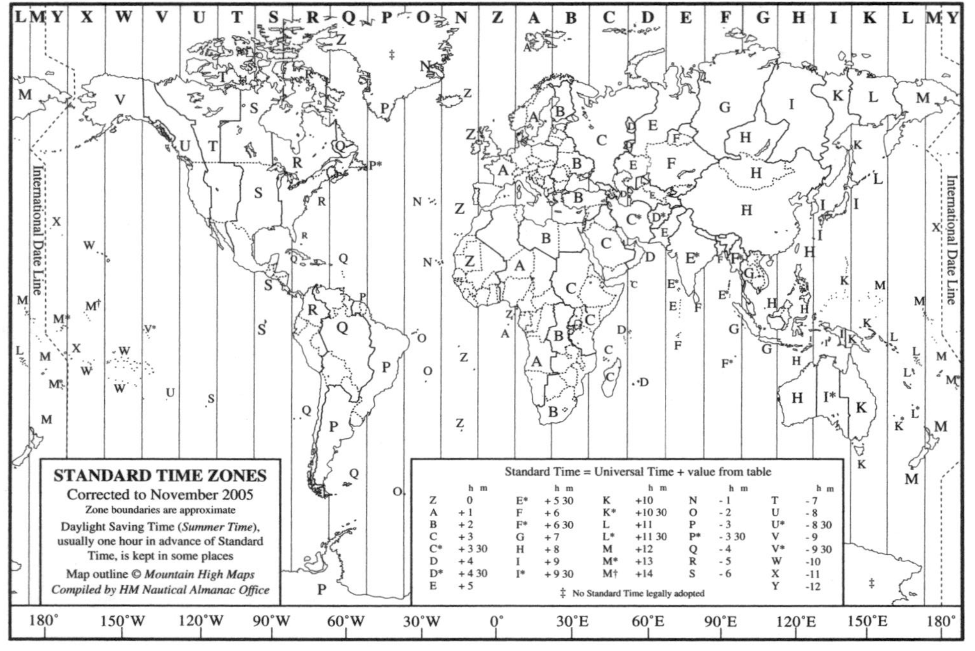
International Date Line
International Date Line
STANDARD TIME ZONES
Corrected to November 2005
Zone boundaries are approximate
Daylight Saving Time (*Summer Time*), usually one hour in advance of Standard Time, is kept in some places
Map outline © *Mountain High Maps*
Compiled by HM Nautical Almanac Office
Standard Time = Universal Time + value from table
Z 0; A +1; B +2; C +3; C* +3 30; D +4; D* +4 30; E +5
E* +5 30; F +6; F* +6 30; G +7; H +8; I +9; I* +9 30
K +10; K* +10 30; L +11; L* +11 30; M +12; M* +13; M† +14
N -1; O -2; P -3; P* -3 30; Q -4; R -5; S -6
T -7; U -8; U* -8 30; V -9; V* -9 30; W -10; X -11; Y -12
‡ No Standard Time legally adopted
180° 150°W 120°W 90°W 60°W 30°W 0° 30°E 60°E 90°E 120°E 150°E 180°

Time Zone Conversions

World Time Zones

Compared to Eastern Standard Time

( ) From Map
(S) CST/Subtract 1 hour
(R) EST
(Q) Add 1 hour
(P) Add 2 hours
(O) Add 3 hours
(N) Add 4 hours
(Z) Add 5 hours
(T) MST/Subtract 2 hours
(U) PST/Subtract 3 hours
(V) Subtract 4 hours
(W) Subtract 5 hours
(X) Subtract 6 hours

(Y) Subtract 7 hours
(A) Add 6 hours
(B) Add 7 hours
(C) Add 8 hours
(D) Add 9 hours
(E) Add 10 hours
(F) Add 11 hours
(G) Add 12 hours
(H) Add 13 hours
(I) Add 14 hours
(K) Add 15 hours
(L) Add 16 hours
(M) Add 17 hours

(C*) Add 8.5 hours
(D*) Add 9.5 hours
(E*) Add 10.5 hours
(F*) Add 11.5 hours
(I*) Add 14.5 hours
(K*) Add 15.5 hours
(L*) Add 16.5 hours
(M*) Add 18 hours
(P*) Add 2.5 hours
(U*) Subtract 3.5 hours
(V*) Subtract 4.5 hours

World Map of Time Zones is supplied by HM Nautical Almanac Office, © Center for the Central Laboratory of the Research Councils. Note: This is not an official map. Countries change their time zones as they wish.

Planetary Stations for 2017

	JAN	FEB	MAR	APR	MAY	JUN	JUL	AUG	SEP	OCT	NOV	DEC
☿	12/19 –1/8			4/9– 5/3				8/12 –9/5				12/3 –12/22
♀				3/4– 4/15								
♂												
♃				2/6–6/9								
♄						4/6–8/25						
♅										8/3–1/2/18		
♆									6/16–11/22			
♇							4/20–9/28					
⚷									7/1–12/5			
⚳												12/16– 3/19
⚴										9/11–12/17		
⚵							5/9–8/26					
⚶	12/1– 3/7/17											

30 Friday

1st ♑
☽ V/C **3:07 am** 12:07 am
☽ enters ♒ **8:29 pm** 5:29 pm

31 Saturday

1st ♒

1 Sunday

1st ♒
☽ V/C 11:59 pm

New Year's Day • Kwanzaa ends • Hanukkah ends

December 2016

S	M	T	W	T	F	S
				1	2	3
4	5	6	7	8	9	10
11	12	13	14	15	16	17
18	19	20	21	22	23	24
25	26	27	28	29	30	31

January 2017

S	M	T	W	T	F	S
1	2	3	4	5	6	7
8	9	10	11	12	13	14
15	16	17	18	19	20	21
22	23	24	25	26	27	28
29	30	31				

February 2017

S	M	T	W	T	F	S
			1	2	3	4
5	6	7	8	9	10	11
12	13	14	15	16	17	18
19	20	21	22	23	24	25
26	27	28				

2 Monday

1st ♒
☽ V/C **2:59 am**
☽ enters ♓ **4:57 am** 1:57 am
♀ enters ♓ 11:47 pm

3 Tuesday

1st ♓
♀ enters ♓ **2:47 am**

4 Wednesday

1st ♓
☿ enters ♐ **9:17 am** 6:17 am
☽ V/C **11:14 am** 8:14 am
☽ enters ♈ **11:20 am** 8:20 am

5 Thursday

1st ♈
2nd quarter **2:47 pm** 11:47 am

Eastern time in bold type
Pacific time in medium type

6 Friday

2nd ♈
☽ V/C **1:41 pm** 10:41 am
☽ enters ♉ **3:18 pm** 12:18 pm

7 Saturday

2nd ♉
☽ V/C **9:23 pm** 6:23 pm

8 Sunday

2nd ♉
☿ D **4:43 am** 1:43 am
☽ enters ♊ **5:06 pm** 2:06 pm

December 2016

S	M	T	W	T	F	S
				1	2	3
4	5	6	7	8	9	10
11	12	13	14	15	16	17
18	19	20	21	22	23	24
25	26	27	28	29	30	31

January 2017

S	M	T	W	T	F	S
1	2	3	4	5	6	7
8	9	10	11	12	13	14
15	16	17	18	19	20	21
22	23	24	25	26	27	28
29	30	31				

February 2017

S	M	T	W	T	F	S
			1	2	3	4
5	6	7	8	9	10	11
12	13	14	15	16	17	18
19	20	21	22	23	24	25
26	27	28				

9 Monday
2nd ♊

10 Tuesday
2nd ♊

⚳ enters ♋	**1:11 pm**	10:11 am
☽ V/C	**4:38 pm**	1:38 pm
☽ enters ♋	**5:49 pm**	2:49 pm

11 Wednesday
2nd ♋

12 Thursday
2nd ♋

☽ V/C	**6:34 am**	3:34 am
Full Moon	**6:34 am**	3:34 am
☿ enters ♑	**9:03 am**	6:03 am
☽ enters ♌	**7:08 pm**	4:08 pm

Eastern time in bold type
Pacific time in medium type

13 Friday

3rd ♌

14 Saturday

3rd ♌

☽ V/C **10:17 am** 7:17 am

☽ enters ♍ **10:52 pm** 7:52 pm

15 Sunday

3rd ♍

December 2016

S	M	T	W	T	F	S
				1	2	3
4	5	6	7	8	9	10
11	12	13	14	15	16	17
18	19	20	21	22	23	24
25	26	27	28	29	30	31

January 2017

S	M	T	W	T	F	S
1	2	3	4	5	6	7
8	9	10	11	12	13	14
15	16	17	18	19	20	21
22	23	24	25	26	27	28
29	30	31				

February 2017

S	M	T	W	T	F	S
			1	2	3	4
5	6	7	8	9	10	11
12	13	14	15	16	17	18
19	20	21	22	23	24	25
26	27	28				

16 Monday

3rd ♍
☽ V/C 10:09 pm

Martin Luther King Jr. Day

17 Tuesday

3rd ♍
☽ V/C **1:09 am**
☽ enters ♎ **6:16 am** 3:16 am

18 Wednesday

3rd ♎

19 Thursday

3rd ♎
☽ V/C **3:55 am** 12:55 am
☉ enters ♒ **4:24 pm** 1:24 pm
☽ enters ♏ **5:09 pm** 2:09 pm
4th quarter **5:13 pm** 2:13 pm

Sun enters Aquarius

Eastern time in bold type
Pacific time in medium type

20 Friday

4th ♏

Inauguration Day

21 Saturday

4th ♏

☽ V/C **8:24 pm** 5:24 pm

22 Sunday

4th ♏

☽ enters ♐ **5:45 am** 2:45 am

December 2016

S	M	T	W	T	F	S
				1	2	3
4	5	6	7	8	9	10
11	12	13	14	15	16	17
18	19	20	21	22	23	24
25	26	27	28	29	30	31

January 2017

S	M	T	W	T	F	S
1	2	3	4	5	6	7
8	9	10	11	12	13	14
15	16	17	18	19	20	21
22	23	24	25	26	27	28
29	30	31				

February 2017

S	M	T	W	T	F	S
			1	2	3	4
5	6	7	8	9	10	11
12	13	14	15	16	17	18
19	20	21	22	23	24	25
26	27	28				

Eastern time in bold type
Pacific time in medium type

23 Monday
4th ♐

24 Tuesday
4th ♐
☽ V/C **12:33 pm** 9:33 am
☽ enters ♑ **5:43 pm** 2:43 pm

25 Wednesday

4th ♑

26 Thursday

4th ♑
☽ V/C 11:18 pm

Eastern time in bold type
Pacific time in medium type

27 Friday

4th ♑

☽ V/C	**2:18 am**	
☽ enters ♒	**3:37 am**	12:37 am
New Moon	**7:07 pm**	4:07 pm
♂ enters ♈		9:39 pm

28 Saturday

1st ♒

♂ enters ♈	**12:39 am**	
☽ V/C		9:52 pm

Lunar New Year (Rooster)

29 Sunday

1st ♒

☽ V/C	**12:52 am**	
☽ enters ♓	**11:10 am**	8:10 am

December 2016

S	M	T	W	T	F	S
				1	2	3
4	5	6	7	8	9	10
11	12	13	14	15	16	17
18	19	20	21	22	23	24
25	26	27	28	29	30	31

January 2017

S	M	T	W	T	F	S
1	2	3	4	5	6	7
8	9	10	11	12	13	14
15	16	17	18	19	20	21
22	23	24	25	26	27	28
29	30	31				

February 2017

S	M	T	W	T	F	S
			1	2	3	4
5	6	7	8	9	10	11
12	13	14	15	16	17	18
19	20	21	22	23	24	25
26	27	28				

Eastern time in bold type
Pacific time in medium type

30 Monday

1st ♓

31 Tuesday

1st ♓

☽ V/C	**12:36 pm**	9:36 am
☽ enters ♈	**4:46 pm**	1:46 pm

1 Wednesday

1st ♈

2 Thursday

1st ♈

☽ V/C	**11:50 am**	8:50 am
☽ enters ♉	**8:50 pm**	5:50 pm
⚵ enters ♑		10:47 pm

Groundhog Day • Imbolc

Eastern time in bold type
Pacific time in medium type

3 Friday

1st ♉
⚵ enters ♑ **1:47 am**
♀ enters ♈ **10:51 am** 7:51 am
2nd quarter **11:19 pm** 8:19 pm

4 Saturday

2nd ♉
☽ V/C **5:42 pm** 2:42 pm
⚳ enters ♉ **7:17 pm** 4:17 pm
☽ enters ♊ **11:44 pm** 8:44 pm

5 Sunday

2nd ♊
♃ ℞ 10:52 pm

January 2017

S	M	T	W	T	F	S
1	2	3	4	5	6	7
8	9	10	11	12	13	14
15	16	17	18	19	20	21
22	23	24	25	26	27	28
29	30	31				

February 2017

S	M	T	W	T	F	S
			1	2	3	4
5	6	7	8	9	10	11
12	13	14	15	16	17	18
19	20	21	22	23	24	25
26	27	28				

March 2017

S	M	T	W	T	F	S
			1	2	3	4
5	6	7	8	9	10	11
12	13	14	15	16	17	18
19	20	21	22	23	24	25
26	27	28	29	30	31	

Eastern time in bold type
Pacific time in medium type

6 Monday

2nd ♊
♃ ℞ **1:52 am**
☽ V/C **5:53 pm** 2:53 pm
☽ enters ♋ 11:03 pm

7 Tuesday

2nd ♊
☽ enters ♋ **2:03 am**
☿ enters ♒ **4:35 am** 1:35 am

8 Wednesday

2nd ♋
☽ V/C **5:00 pm** 2:00 pm

9 Thursday

2nd ♋
☽ enters ♌ **4:41 am** 1:41 am

Eastern time in bold type
Pacific time in medium type

10 Friday

2nd ♌
Full Moon **7:33 pm** 4:33 pm
☽ V/C 9:52 pm

Lunar eclipse 22° ♌ 28'

11 Saturday

3rd ♌
☽ V/C **12:52 am**
☽ enters ♍ **8:52 am** 5:52 am

12 Sunday

3rd ♍

January 2017

S	M	T	W	T	F	S
1	2	3	4	5	6	7
8	9	10	11	12	13	14
15	16	17	18	19	20	21
22	23	24	25	26	27	28
29	30	31				

February 2017

S	M	T	W	T	F	S
			1	2	3	4
5	6	7	8	9	10	11
12	13	14	15	16	17	18
19	20	21	22	23	24	25
26	27	28				

March 2017

S	M	T	W	T	F	S
			1	2	3	4
5	6	7	8	9	10	11
12	13	14	15	16	17	18
19	20	21	22	23	24	25
26	27	28	29	30	31	

Eastern time in bold type
Pacific time in medium type

13 Monday

3rd ♍
☽ V/C **7:36 am** 4:36 am
☽ enters ♎ **3:43 pm** 12:43 pm

14 Tuesday

3rd ♎

Valentine's Day

15 Wednesday

3rd ♎
☽ V/C **8:54 pm** 5:54 pm
☽ enters ♏ 10:41 pm

16 Thursday

3rd ♎
☽ enters ♏ **1:41 am**

Eastern time in bold type
Pacific time in medium type

17 Friday

3rd ♏
☽ V/C **2:38 pm** 11:38 am

18 Saturday

3rd ♏
☉ enters ♓ **6:31 am** 3:31 am
☽ enters ♐ **1:52 pm** 10:52 am
4th quarter **2:33 pm** 11:33 am

Sun enters Pisces

19 Sunday

4th ♐

January 2017

S	M	T	W	T	F	S
1	2	3	4	5	6	7
8	9	10	11	12	13	14
15	16	17	18	19	20	21
22	23	24	25	26	27	28
29	30	31				

February 2017

S	M	T	W	T	F	S
			1	2	3	4
5	6	7	8	9	10	11
12	13	14	15	16	17	18
19	20	21	22	23	24	25
26	27	28				

March 2017

S	M	T	W	T	F	S
			1	2	3	4
5	6	7	8	9	10	11
12	13	14	15	16	17	18
19	20	21	22	23	24	25
26	27	28	29	30	31	

20 Monday

4th ♐
☽ V/C **6:37 pm** 3:37 pm
☽ enters ♑ 11:08 pm

Presidents' Day

21 Tuesday

4th ♐
☽ enters ♑ **2:08 am**

22 Wednesday

4th ♑
☽ V/C **10:24 pm** 7:24 pm

23 Thursday

4th ♑
☽ enters ♒ **12:17 pm** 9:17 am

Eastern time in bold type
Pacific time in medium type

24 Friday

4th ♒

25 Saturday

4th ♒

☽ V/C	**1:11 pm**	10:11 am
☿ enters ♓	**6:07 pm**	3:07 pm
☽ enters ♓	**7:24 pm**	4:24 pm

26 Sunday

4th ♓

New Moon	**9:58 am**	6:58 am

Solar eclipse 8° ♓ 12'

January 2017

S	M	T	W	T	F	S
1	2	3	4	5	6	7
8	9	10	11	12	13	14
15	16	17	18	19	20	21
22	23	24	25	26	27	28
29	30	31				

February 2017

S	M	T	W	T	F	S
			1	2	3	4
5	6	7	8	9	10	11
12	13	14	15	16	17	18
19	20	21	22	23	24	25
26	27	28				

March 2017

S	M	T	W	T	F	S
			1	2	3	4
5	6	7	8	9	10	11
12	13	14	15	16	17	18
19	20	21	22	23	24	25
26	27	28	29	30	31	

27 Monday

1st ♓
☽ V/C **6:08 pm** 3:08 pm
☽ enters ♈ **11:52 pm** 8:52 pm

28 Tuesday

1st ♈

Mardi Gras (Fat Tuesday)

1 Wednesday

1st ♈
☽ V/C **9:18 pm** 6:18 pm
☽ enters ♉ 11:43 pm

Ash Wednesday

2 Thursday

1st ♈
☽ enters ♉ **2:43 am**

Eastern time in bold type
Pacific time in medium type

3 Friday

1st ♉
☽ V/C **10:20 am** 7:20 am

4 Saturday

1st ♉
♀ ℞ **4:09 am** 1:09 am
☽ enters ♊ **5:05 am** 2:05 am

5 Sunday

1st ♊
2nd quarter **6:32 am** 3:32 am

February 2017

S	M	T	W	T	F	S
			1	2	3	4
5	6	7	8	9	10	11
12	13	14	15	16	17	18
19	20	21	22	23	24	25
26	27	28				

March 2017

S	M	T	W	T	F	S
			1	2	3	4
5	6	7	8	9	10	11
12	13	14	15	16	17	18
19	20	21	22	23	24	25
26	27	28	29	30	31	

April 2017

S	M	T	W	T	F	S
						1
2	3	4	5	6	7	8
9	10	11	12	13	14	15
16	17	18	19	20	21	22
23	24	25	26	27	28	29
30						

6 Monday

2nd ♊
☽ V/C **3:22 am** 12:22 am
☽ enters ♋ **7:54 am** 4:54 am

7 Tuesday

2nd ♋
⚶ D **4:32 am** 1:32 am

8 Wednesday

2nd ♋
☽ V/C **9:59 am** 6:59 am
☽ enters ♌ **11:45 am** 8:45 am

9 Thursday

2nd ♌
♂ enters ♉ **7:34 pm** 4:34 pm

Eastern time in bold type
Pacific time in medium type

10 Friday

2nd ♌

☽ V/C	**12:06 pm**	9:06 am
☽ enters ♍	**5:07 pm**	2:07 pm

11 Saturday

2nd ♍

12 Sunday

2nd ♍

Full Moon	**10:54 am**	7:54 am
☽ V/C	**10:36 pm**	7:36 pm
☽ enters ♎		10:28 pm

Purim

Daylight Saving Time begins at 2 am

February 2017

S	M	T	W	T	F	S
			1	2	3	4
5	6	7	8	9	10	11
12	13	14	15	16	17	18
19	20	21	22	23	24	25
26	27	28				

March 2017

S	M	T	W	T	F	S
			1	2	3	4
5	6	7	8	9	10	11
12	13	14	15	16	17	18
19	20	21	22	23	24	25
26	27	28	29	30	31	

April 2017

S	M	T	W	T	F	S
						1
2	3	4	5	6	7	8
9	10	11	12	13	14	15
16	17	18	19	20	21	22
23	24	25	26	27	28	29
30						

13 Monday
3rd ♍
☽ enters ♎ **1:28 am**
☿ enters ♈ **5:07 pm** 2:07 pm

14 Tuesday
3rd ♎

15 Wednesday
3rd ♎
☽ V/C **6:05 am** 3:05 am
☽ enters ♏ **11:11 am** 8:11 am

16 Thursday
3rd ♏

Eastern time in bold type
Pacific time in medium type

17 Friday

3rd ♏
☽ V/C **5:56 pm** 2:56 pm
☽ enters ♐ **11:00 pm** 8:00 pm

St. Patrick's Day

18 Saturday

3rd ♐

19 Sunday

3rd ♐

February 2017

S	M	T	W	T	F	S
			1	2	3	4
5	6	7	8	9	10	11
12	13	14	15	16	17	18
19	20	21	22	23	24	25
26	27	28				

March 2017

S	M	T	W	T	F	S
			1	2	3	4
5	6	7	8	9	10	11
12	13	14	15	16	17	18
19	20	21	22	23	24	25
26	27	28	29	30	31	

April 2017

S	M	T	W	T	F	S
						1
2	3	4	5	6	7	8
9	10	11	12	13	14	15
16	17	18	19	20	21	22
23	24	25	26	27	28	29
30						

Eastern time in bold type
Pacific time in medium type

20 Monday

3rd ♐
☉ enters ♈ **6:29 am** 3:29 am
☽ V/C **6:37 am** 3:37 am
☽ enters ♑ **11:31 am** 8:31 am
4th quarter **11:58 am** 8:58 am

International Astrology Day
Sun enters Aries • Ostara • Spring Equinox • 6:29 am EDT/3:29 am PDT

21 Tuesday

4th ♑

22 Wednesday

4th ♑
☽ V/C **9:20 am** 6:20 am
☽ enters ♒ **10:28 pm** 7:28 pm

23 Thursday

4th ♒

Eastern time in bold type
Pacific time in medium type

24 Friday

4th ♒
☽ V/C 10:56 pm

25 Saturday

4th ♒
☽ V/C **1:56 am**
☽ enters ♓ **6:06 am** 3:06 am

26 Sunday

4th ♓

February 2017

S	M	T	W	T	F	S
			1	2	3	4
5	6	7	8	9	10	11
12	13	14	15	16	17	18
19	20	21	22	23	24	25
26	27	28				

March 2017

S	M	T	W	T	F	S
			1	2	3	4
5	6	7	8	9	10	11
12	13	14	15	16	17	18
19	20	21	22	23	24	25
26	27	28	29	30	31	

April 2017

S	M	T	W	T	F	S
						1
2	3	4	5	6	7	8
9	10	11	12	13	14	15
16	17	18	19	20	21	22
23	24	25	26	27	28	29
30						

27 Monday

4th ♓

☽ V/C	**6:19 am**	3:19 am
☽ enters ♈	**10:11 am**	7:11 am
New Moon	**10:57 pm**	7:57 pm

28 Tuesday

1st ♈

29 Wednesday

1st ♈

☽ V/C	**8:07 am**	5:07 am
☽ enters ♉	**11:48 am**	8:48 am
⚴ enters ♈		9:47 pm

30 Thursday

1st ♉

⚴ enters ♈	**12:47 am**	
☽ V/C	**7:12 pm**	4:12 pm

Eastern time in bold type
Pacific time in medium type

31 Friday

1st ♉
☽ enters ♊ **12:40 pm** 9:40 am
☿ enters ♉ **1:31 pm** 10:31 am

1 Saturday

1st ♊

April Fools' Day (All Fools' Day—Pagan)

2 Sunday

1st ♊
☽ V/C **10:43 am** 7:43 am
☽ enters ♋ **2:27 pm** 11:27 am
♀ enters ♓ **8:25 pm** 5:25 pm

February 2017

S	M	T	W	T	F	S
			1	2	3	4
5	6	7	8	9	10	11
12	13	14	15	16	17	18
19	20	21	22	23	24	25
26	27	28				

March 2017

S	M	T	W	T	F	S
			1	2	3	4
5	6	7	8	9	10	11
12	13	14	15	16	17	18
19	20	21	22	23	24	25
26	27	28	29	30	31	

April 2017

S	M	T	W	T	F	S
						1
2	3	4	5	6	7	8
9	10	11	12	13	14	15
16	17	18	19	20	21	22
23	24	25	26	27	28	29
30						

Eastern time in bold type
Pacific time in medium type

3 Monday

1st ♋
2nd quarter **2:39 pm** 11:39 am

4 Tuesday

2nd ♋
☽ V/C **4:45 pm** 1:45 pm
☽ enters ♌ **6:13 pm** 3:13 pm

5 Wednesday

2nd ♌
♄ ℞ 10:06 pm

6 Thursday

2nd ♌
♄ ℞ **1:06 am**
☽ V/C **8:16 pm** 5:16 pm
☽ enters ♍ 9:20 pm

Eastern time in bold type
Pacific time in medium type

7 Friday

2nd ♌
☽ enters ♍ **12:20 am**

8 Saturday

2nd ♍

9 Sunday

2nd ♍

☽ V/C	**4:21 am**	1:21 am
☽ enters ♎	**8:34 am**	5:34 am
☿ ℞	**7:14 pm**	4:14 pm

Palm Sunday
Mercury retrograde until 5/3

March 2017

S	M	T	W	T	F	S
			1	2	3	4
5	6	7	8	9	10	11
12	13	14	15	16	17	18
19	20	21	22	23	24	25
26	27	28	29	30	31	

April 2017

S	M	T	W	T	F	S
						1
2	3	4	5	6	7	8
9	10	11	12	13	14	15
16	17	18	19	20	21	22
23	24	25	26	27	28	29
30						

May 2017

S	M	T	W	T	F	S
	1	2	3	4	5	6
7	8	9	10	11	12	13
14	15	16	17	18	19	20
21	22	23	24	25	26	27
28	29	30	31			

10 Monday

2nd ♎
Full Moon 11:08 pm

11 Tuesday

2nd ♎
Full Moon **2:08 am**
☽ V/C **2:19 pm** 11:19 am
☽ enters ♏ **6:42 pm** 3:42 pm

Passover begins

12 Wednesday

3rd ♏

13 Thursday

3rd ♏
☽ V/C 9:18 pm

Eastern time in bold type
Pacific time in medium type

14 Friday

3rd ♏
☽ V/C **12:18 am**
☽ enters ♐ **6:27 am** 3:27 am

Good Friday
Orthodox Good Friday

15 Saturday

3rd ♐
♀ D **6:18 am** 3:18 am

16 Sunday

3rd ♐
☽ V/C **2:26 pm** 11:26 am
☽ enters ♑ **7:05 pm** 4:05 pm

Easter
Orthodox Easter

March 2017

S	M	T	W	T	F	S
			1	2	3	4
5	6	7	8	9	10	11
12	13	14	15	16	17	18
19	20	21	22	23	24	25
26	27	28	29	30	31	

April 2017

S	M	T	W	T	F	S
						1
2	3	4	5	6	7	8
9	10	11	12	13	14	15
16	17	18	19	20	21	22
23	24	25	26	27	28	29
30						

May 2017

S	M	T	W	T	F	S
	1	2	3	4	5	6
7	8	9	10	11	12	13
14	15	16	17	18	19	20
21	22	23	24	25	26	27
28	29	30	31			

17 Monday

3rd ♑

18 Tuesday

3rd ♑

Passover ends

19 Wednesday

3rd ♑

☽ V/C **5:57 am** 2:57 am
4th quarter **5:57 am** 2:57 am
☽ enters ♒ **6:52 am** 3:52 am
☉ enters ♉ **5:27 pm** 2:27 pm

Sun enters Taurus

20 Thursday

4th ♒

♇ ℞ **8:49 am** 5:49 am
☿ enters ♈ **1:37 pm** 10:37 am

Eastern time in bold type
Pacific time in medium type

21 Friday

4th ♒

♂ enters ♊	**6:32 am**	3:32 am
☽ V/C	**2:23 pm**	11:23 am
☽ enters ♓	**3:43 pm**	12:43 pm

22 Saturday

4th ♓

Earth Day

23 Sunday

4th ♓

☽ V/C	**5:34 pm**	2:34 pm
☽ enters ♈	**8:32 pm**	5:32 pm

March 2017

S	M	T	W	T	F	S
			1	2	3	4
5	6	7	8	9	10	11
12	13	14	15	16	17	18
19	20	21	22	23	24	25
26	27	28	29	30	31	

April 2017

S	M	T	W	T	F	S
						1
2	3	4	5	6	7	8
9	10	11	12	13	14	15
16	17	18	19	20	21	22
23	24	25	26	27	28	29
30						

May 2017

S	M	T	W	T	F	S
	1	2	3	4	5	6
7	8	9	10	11	12	13
14	15	16	17	18	19	20
21	22	23	24	25	26	27
28	29	30	31			

Eastern time in bold type
Pacific time in medium type

24 Monday
4th ♈

25 Tuesday
4th ♈

☽ V/C	**5:53 pm**	2:53 pm
☽ enters ♉	**9:56 pm**	6:56 pm

26 Wednesday
4th ♉

New Moon	**8:16 am**	5:16 am

27 Thursday

1st ♉

☽ V/C	**9:18 pm**	6:18 pm
☽ enters ♊	**9:39 pm**	6:39 pm

Eastern time in bold type
Pacific time in medium type

28 Friday

1st ♊

♀ enters ♈ **9:13 am** 6:13 am

29 Saturday

1st ♊

⚳ enters ♊ **11:42 am** 8:42 am

☽ V/C **5:28 pm** 2:28 pm

☽ enters ♋ **9:48 pm** 6:48 pm

30 Sunday

1st ♋

March 2017

S	M	T	W	T	F	S
			1	2	3	4
5	6	7	8	9	10	11
12	13	14	15	16	17	18
19	20	21	22	23	24	25
26	27	28	29	30	31	

April 2017

S	M	T	W	T	F	S
						1
2	3	4	5	6	7	8
9	10	11	12	13	14	15
16	17	18	19	20	21	22
23	24	25	26	27	28	29
30						

May 2017

S	M	T	W	T	F	S
	1	2	3	4	5	6
7	8	9	10	11	12	13
14	15	16	17	18	19	20
21	22	23	24	25	26	27
28	29	30	31			

Eastern time in bold type
Pacific time in medium type

1 Monday

1st ♋

☽ V/C **4:23 pm** 1:23 pm

☽ enters ♌ 9:12 pm

Beltane

2 Tuesday

1st ♋

☽ enters ♌ **12:12 am**

⚵ enters ♌ **7:57 pm** 4:57 pm

2nd quarter **10:47 pm** 7:47 pm

3 Wednesday

2nd ♌

☿ D **12:33 pm** 9:33 am

☽ V/C 9:35 pm

4 Thursday

2nd ♌

☽ V/C **12:35 am**

☽ enters ♍ **5:47 am** 2:47 am

Eastern time in bold type
Pacific time in medium type

5 Friday

2nd ♍

Cinco de Mayo

6 Saturday

2nd ♍

☽ V/C **8:42 am** 5:42 am

☽ enters ♎ **2:20 pm** 11:20 am

7 Sunday

2nd ♎

April 2017

S	M	T	W	T	F	S
						1
2	3	4	5	6	7	8
9	10	11	12	13	14	15
16	17	18	19	20	21	22
23	24	25	26	27	28	29
30						

May 2017

S	M	T	W	T	F	S
	1	2	3	4	5	6
7	8	9	10	11	12	13
14	15	16	17	18	19	20
21	22	23	24	25	26	27
28	29	30	31			

June 2017

S	M	T	W	T	F	S
				1	2	3
4	5	6	7	8	9	10
11	12	13	14	15	16	17
18	19	20	21	22	23	24
25	26	27	28	29	30	

8 Monday

2nd ♎
☽ V/C **6:59 pm** 3:59 pm
☽ enters ♏ 10:01 pm

9 Tuesday

2nd ♎
☽ enters ♏ **1:01 am**
⚵ ℞ **7:06 pm** 4:06 pm

10 Wednesday

2nd ♏
☽ V/C **5:42 pm** 2:42 pm
Full Moon **5:42 pm** 2:42 pm

11 Thursday

3rd ♏
☽ enters ♐ **12:59 pm** 9:59 am

Eastern time in bold type
Pacific time in medium type

12 Friday
3rd ♐

13 Saturday
3rd ♐
☽ V/C **10:14 pm** 7:14 pm
☽ enters ♑ 10:37 pm

14 Sunday

3rd ♐
☽ enters ♑ **1:37 am**

Mother's Day

April 2017

S	M	T	W	T	F	S
						1
2	3	4	5	6	7	8
9	10	11	12	13	14	15
16	17	18	19	20	21	22
23	24	25	26	27	28	29
30						

May 2017

S	M	T	W	T	F	S
	1	2	3	4	5	6
7	8	9	10	11	12	13
14	15	16	17	18	19	20
21	22	23	24	25	26	27
28	29	30	31			

June 2017

S	M	T	W	T	F	S
				1	2	3
4	5	6	7	8	9	10
11	12	13	14	15	16	17
18	19	20	21	22	23	24
25	26	27	28	29	30	

15 Monday

3rd ♑

☿ enters ♉		9:07 pm

16 Tuesday

3rd ♑

☿ enters ♉	**12:07 am**	
☽ V/C	**6:22 am**	3:22 am
☽ enters ♒	**1:50 pm**	10:50 am

17 Wednesday

3rd ♒

18 Thursday

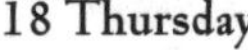

3rd ♒

☽ V/C	**8:33 pm**	5:33 pm
4th quarter	**8:33 pm**	5:33 pm
☽ enters ♓	**11:52 pm**	8:52 pm

Eastern time in bold type
Pacific time in medium type

19 Friday

4th ♓

20 Saturday

4th ♓
☉ enters ♊ **4:31 pm** 1:31 pm
☽ V/C **11:39 pm** 8:39 pm

Sun enters Gemini

21 Sunday

4th ♓
☽ enters ♈ **6:10 am** 3:10 am

April 2017

S	M	T	W	T	F	S
						1
2	3	4	5	6	7	8
9	10	11	12	13	14	15
16	17	18	19	20	21	22
23	24	25	26	27	28	29
30						

May 2017

S	M	T	W	T	F	S
	1	2	3	4	5	6
7	8	9	10	11	12	13
14	15	16	17	18	19	20
21	22	23	24	25	26	27
28	29	30	31			

June 2017

S	M	T	W	T	F	S
				1	2	3
4	5	6	7	8	9	10
11	12	13	14	15	16	17
18	19	20	21	22	23	24
25	26	27	28	29	30	

22 Monday

4th ♈
☽ V/C 11:59 pm

23 Tuesday

4th ♈
☽ V/C **2:59 am**
☽ enters ♉ **8:33 am** 5:33 am

24 Wednesday

4th ♉
☽ V/C **3:08 pm** 12:08 pm

25 Thursday

4th ♉
☽ enters ♊ **8:15 am** 5:15 am
New Moon **3:44 pm** 12:44 pm

Eastern time in bold type
Pacific time in medium type

26 Friday

1st ♊

☽ V/C 11:18 pm

27 Saturday

1st ♊

☽ V/C **2:18 am**

☽ enters ♋ **7:25 am** 4:25 am

Ramadan begins

28 Sunday

1st ♋

☽ V/C 11:59 pm

April 2017

S	M	T	W	T	F	S
						1
2	3	4	5	6	7	8
9	10	11	12	13	14	15
16	17	18	19	20	21	22
23	24	25	26	27	28	29
30						

May 2017

S	M	T	W	T	F	S
	1	2	3	4	5	6
7	8	9	10	11	12	13
14	15	16	17	18	19	20
21	22	23	24	25	26	27
28	29	30	31			

June 2017

S	M	T	W	T	F	S
				1	2	3
4	5	6	7	8	9	10
11	12	13	14	15	16	17
18	19	20	21	22	23	24
25	26	27	28	29	30	

29 Monday

1st ♋
☽ V/C **2:59 am**
☽ enters ♌ **8:12 am** 5:12 am

Memorial Day

30 Tuesday

1st ♌

31 Wednesday

1st ♌
☽ V/C **7:14 am** 4:14 am
☽ enters ♍ **12:16 pm** 9:16 am

Shavuot

1 Thursday

1st ♍
2nd quarter **8:42 am** 5:42 am

Eastern time in bold type
Pacific time in medium type

2 Friday

2nd ♍
☽ V/C **5:48 pm** 2:48 pm
☽ enters ♎ **8:04 pm** 5:04 pm

3 Saturday

2nd ♎

4 Sunday

2nd ♎
♂ enters ♋ **12:16 pm** 9:16 am

May 2017

S	M	T	W	T	F	S
	1	2	3	4	5	6
7	8	9	10	11	12	13
14	15	16	17	18	19	20
21	22	23	24	25	26	27
28	29	30	31			

June 2017

S	M	T	W	T	F	S
				1	2	3
4	5	6	7	8	9	10
11	12	13	14	15	16	17
18	19	20	21	22	23	24
25	26	27	28	29	30	

July 2017

S	M	T	W	T	F	S
						1
2	3	4	5	6	7	8
9	10	11	12	13	14	15
16	17	18	19	20	21	22
23	24	25	26	27	28	29
30	31					

5 Monday

2nd ♎
☽ V/C **4:57 am** 1:57 am
☽ enters ♏ **6:46 am** 3:46 am

6 Tuesday

2nd ♏
♀ enters ♉ **3:27 am** 12:27 am
☿ enters ♊ **6:15 pm** 3:15 pm
☽ V/C **8:35 pm** 5:35 pm

7 Wednesday

2nd ♏
☽ enters ♐ **6:59 pm** 3:59 pm

8 Thursday

2nd ♐

Eastern time in bold type
Pacific time in medium type

9 Friday

2nd ♐

Full Moon	**9:10 am**	6:10 am
♃ D	**10:03 am**	7:03 am
☽ V/C		11:20 pm

10 Saturday

3rd ♐

☽ V/C	**2:20 am**	
☽ enters ♑	**7:36 am**	4:36 am

11 Sunday

3rd ♑

May 2017

S	M	T	W	T	F	S
	1	2	3	4	5	6
7	8	9	10	11	12	13
14	15	16	17	18	19	20
21	22	23	24	25	26	27
28	29	30	31			

June 2017

S	M	T	W	T	F	S
				1	2	3
4	5	6	7	8	9	10
11	12	13	14	15	16	17
18	19	20	21	22	23	24
25	26	27	28	29	30	

July 2017

S	M	T	W	T	F	S
						1
2	3	4	5	6	7	8
9	10	11	12	13	14	15
16	17	18	19	20	21	22
23	24	25	26	27	28	29
30	31					

Eastern time in bold type
Pacific time in medium type

12 Monday

3rd ♑︎
☽ V/C **2:45 pm** 11:45 am
☽ enters ♒︎ **7:45 pm** 4:45 pm

13 Tuesday

3rd ♒︎

14 Wednesday

3rd ♒︎
☽ V/C 10:40 pm

Flag Day

15 Thursday

3rd ♒︎
☽ V/C **1:40 am**
☽ enters ♓︎ **6:17 am** 3:17 am

Eastern time in bold type
Pacific time in medium type

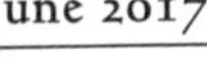

16 Friday

3rd ♓
♆ ℞ **7:09 am** 4:09 am

17 Saturday

3rd ♓
☽ V/C **7:33 am** 4:33 am
4th quarter **7:33 am** 4:33 am
☽ enters ♈ **1:55 pm** 10:55 am

18 Sunday

4th ♈

Father's Day

May 2017

S	M	T	W	T	F	S
	1	2	3	4	5	6
7	8	9	10	11	12	13
14	15	16	17	18	19	20
21	22	23	24	25	26	27
28	29	30	31			

June 2017

S	M	T	W	T	F	S
				1	2	3
4	5	6	7	8	9	10
11	12	13	14	15	16	17
18	19	20	21	22	23	24
25	26	27	28	29	30	

July 2017

S	M	T	W	T	F	S
						1
2	3	4	5	6	7	8
9	10	11	12	13	14	15
16	17	18	19	20	21	22
23	24	25	26	27	28	29
30	31					

Eastern time in bold type
Pacific time in medium type

19 Monday

4th ♈
☽ V/C **3:42 pm** 12:42 pm
☽ enters ♉ **5:53 pm** 2:53 pm

20 Tuesday

4th ♉
☉ enters ♋ 9:24 pm
☽ V/C 9:26 pm

Sun enters Cancer • Litha • Summer Solstice • 9:24 pm PDT

21 Wednesday

4th ♉
☉ enters ♋ **12:24 am**
☽ V/C **12:26 am**
☿ enters ♋ **5:57 am** 2:57 am
☽ enters ♊ **6:44 pm** 3:44 pm

Sun enters Cancer • Litha • Summer Solstice • 12:24 am EDT

22 Thursday

4th ♊

Eastern time in bold type
Pacific time in medium type

23 Friday

4th ♊
☽ V/C **2:45 pm** 11:45 am
☽ enters ♋ **6:07 pm** 3:07 pm
New Moon **10:31 pm** 7:31 pm

24 Saturday

1st ♋

25 Sunday

1st ♋
☽ V/C **2:44 pm** 11:44 am
☽ enters ♌ **6:06 pm** 3:06 pm

Ramadan ends

May 2017

S	M	T	W	T	F	S
	1	2	3	4	5	6
7	8	9	10	11	12	13
14	15	16	17	18	19	20
21	22	23	24	25	26	27
28	29	30	31			

June 2017

S	M	T	W	T	F	S
				1	2	3
4	5	6	7	8	9	10
11	12	13	14	15	16	17
18	19	20	21	22	23	24
25	26	27	28	29	30	

July 2017

S	M	T	W	T	F	S
						1
2	3	4	5	6	7	8
9	10	11	12	13	14	15
16	17	18	19	20	21	22
23	24	25	26	27	28	29
30	31					

26 Monday

1st ♌
♀ enters ♉ **10:34 pm** 7:34 pm

27 Tuesday

1st ♌
☽ V/C **5:12 pm** 2:12 pm
☽ enters ♍ **8:41 pm** 5:41 pm

28 Wednesday

1st ♍

29 Thursday

1st ♍
☽ V/C **4:35 pm** 1:35 pm

Eastern time in bold type
Pacific time in medium type

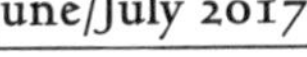

30 Friday

1st ♍
☽ enters ♎ **3:02 am** 12:02 am
2nd quarter **8:51 pm** 5:51 pm

1 Saturday

2nd ♎
⚷ ℞ **3:09 am** 12:09 am

2 Sunday

2nd ♎
☽ V/C **9:16 am** 6:16 am
☽ enters ♏ **12:59 pm** 9:59 am

May 2017

S	M	T	W	T	F	S
	1	2	3	4	5	6
7	8	9	10	11	12	13
14	15	16	17	18	19	20
21	22	23	24	25	26	27
28	29	30	31			

June 2017

S	M	T	W	T	F	S
				1	2	3
4	5	6	7	8	9	10
11	12	13	14	15	16	17
18	19	20	21	22	23	24
25	26	27	28	29	30	

July 2017

S	M	T	W	T	F	S
						1
2	3	4	5	6	7	8
9	10	11	12	13	14	15
16	17	18	19	20	21	22
23	24	25	26	27	28	29
30	31					

3 Monday

2nd ♏

4 Tuesday

2nd ♏

♀ enters ♊	**8:11 pm**	5:11 pm
☽ V/C	**9:34 pm**	6:34 pm
☽ enters ♐		10:08 pm

Independence Day

5 Wednesday

2nd ♏

☽ enters ♐	**1:08 am**	
☿ enters ♌	**8:20 pm**	5:20 pm

6 Thursday

2nd ♐

Eastern time in bold type
Pacific time in medium type

7 Friday

2nd ♐

☽ V/C	**10:12 am**	7:12 am
☽ enters ♑	**1:45 pm**	10:45 am

8 Saturday

2nd ♑

Full Moon		9:07 pm

9 Sunday

2nd ♑

Full Moon	**12:07 am**	
☽ V/C	**10:12 pm**	7:12 pm
☽ enters ♒		10:35 pm

June 2017

S	M	T	W	T	F	S
				1	2	3
4	5	6	7	8	9	10
11	12	13	14	15	16	17
18	19	20	21	22	23	24
25	26	27	28	29	30	

July 2017

S	M	T	W	T	F	S
						1
2	3	4	5	6	7	8
9	10	11	12	13	14	15
16	17	18	19	20	21	22
23	24	25	26	27	28	29
30	31					

August 2017

S	M	T	W	T	F	S
		1	2	3	4	5
6	7	8	9	10	11	12
13	14	15	16	17	18	19
20	21	22	23	24	25	26
27	28	29	30	31		

10 Monday

3rd ♑
☽ enters ♒ **1:35 am**
⚳ enters ♋ **7:47 am** 4:47 am

11 Tuesday

3rd ♒

12 Wednesday

3rd ♒
☽ V/C **8:40 am** 5:40 am
☽ enters ♓ **11:51 am** 8:51 am

13 Thursday

3rd ♓

Eastern time in bold type
Pacific time in medium type

14 Friday

3rd ♓
☽ V/C **1:00 pm** 10:00 am
☽ enters ♈ **7:52 pm** 4:52 pm

15 Saturday

3rd ♈

16 Sunday

3rd ♈
4th quarter **3:26 pm** 12:26 pm
☽ V/C **10:19 pm** 7:19 pm
☽ enters ♉ 10:04 pm

June 2017

S	M	T	W	T	F	S
				1	2	3
4	5	6	7	8	9	10
11	12	13	14	15	16	17
18	19	20	21	22	23	24
25	26	27	28	29	30	

July 2017

S	M	T	W	T	F	S
						1
2	3	4	5	6	7	8
9	10	11	12	13	14	15
16	17	18	19	20	21	22
23	24	25	26	27	28	29
30	31					

August 2017

S	M	T	W	T	F	S
		1	2	3	4	5
6	7	8	9	10	11	12
13	14	15	16	17	18	19
20	21	22	23	24	25	26
27	28	29	30	31		

Eastern time in bold type
Pacific time in medium type

17 Monday

4th ♈
☽ enters ♉ **1:04 am**
⚳ enters ♍ **7:15 pm** 4:15 pm

18 Tuesday

4th ♉
☽ V/C 11:11 pm

19 Wednesday

4th ♉
☽ V/C **2:11 am**
☽ enters ♊ **3:31 am** 12:31 am

20 Thursday

4th ♊
♂ enters ♌ **8:19 am** 5:19 am
☽ V/C 10:41 pm

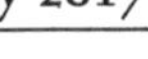

21 Friday

4th ♊
☽ V/C **1:41 am**
☽ enters ♋ **4:09 am** 1:09 am

22 Saturday

4th ♋
☉ enters ♌ **11:15 am** 8:15 am
☽ V/C 11:05 pm

Sun enters Leo

23 Sunday

4th ♋
☽ V/C **2:05 am**
☽ enters ♌ **4:34 am** 1:34 am
New Moon **5:46 am** 2:46 am

June 2017

S	M	T	W	T	F	S
				1	2	3
4	5	6	7	8	9	10
11	12	13	14	15	16	17
18	19	20	21	22	23	24
25	26	27	28	29	30	

July 2017

S	M	T	W	T	F	S
						1
2	3	4	5	6	7	8
9	10	11	12	13	14	15
16	17	18	19	20	21	22
23	24	25	26	27	28	29
30	31					

August 2017

S	M	T	W	T	F	S
		1	2	3	4	5
6	7	8	9	10	11	12
13	14	15	16	17	18	19
20	21	22	23	24	25	26
27	28	29	30	31		

24 Monday

1st ♌

25 Tuesday

1st ♌

☽ V/C	**5:22 am**	2:22 am
☽ enters ♍	**6:32 am**	3:32 am
☿ enters ♍	**7:41 pm**	4:41 pm

26 Wednesday

1st ♍

☽ V/C		11:31 pm

27 Thursday

1st ♍

☽ V/C	**2:31 am**	
☽ enters ♎	**11:37 am**	8:37 am

Eastern time in bold type
Pacific time in medium type

28 Friday

1st ♎

29 Saturday

1st ♎

☽ V/C	**5:30 pm**	2:30 pm
☽ enters ♏	**8:23 pm**	5:23 pm

30 Sunday

1st ♏

2nd quarter **11:23 am** 8:23 am

June 2017

S	M	T	W	T	F	S
				1	2	3
4	5	6	7	8	9	10
11	12	13	14	15	16	17
18	19	20	21	22	23	24
25	26	27	28	29	30	

July 2017

S	M	T	W	T	F	S
						1
2	3	4	5	6	7	8
9	10	11	12	13	14	15
16	17	18	19	20	21	22
23	24	25	26	27	28	29
30	31					

August 2017

S	M	T	W	T	F	S
		1	2	3	4	5
6	7	8	9	10	11	12
13	14	15	16	17	18	19
20	21	22	23	24	25	26
27	28	29	30	31		

Eastern time in bold type
Pacific time in medium type

31 Monday

2nd ♏
☽ V/C **7:10 am** 4:10 am
♀ enters ♋ **10:54 am** 7:54 am

1 Tuesday

2nd ♏
☽ enters ♐ **8:01 am** 5:01 am

Lammas

2 Wednesday

2nd ♐
♅ ℞ 10:31 pm

3 Thursday

2nd ♐
♅ ℞ **1:31 am**
☽ V/C **5:38 pm** 2:38 pm
☽ enters ♑ **8:37 pm** 5:37 pm

Eastern time in bold type
Pacific time in medium type

4 Friday
2nd ♑

5 Saturday
2nd ♑

6 Sunday
2nd ♑
☽ V/C **5:22 am** 2:22 am
☽ enters ♒ **8:15 am** 5:15 am

July 2017

S	M	T	W	T	F	S
						1
2	3	4	5	6	7	8
9	10	11	12	13	14	15
16	17	18	19	20	21	22
23	24	25	26	27	28	29
30	31					

August 2017

S	M	T	W	T	F	S
		1	2	3	4	5
6	7	8	9	10	11	12
13	14	15	16	17	18	19
20	21	22	23	24	25	26
27	28	29	30	31		

September 2017

S	M	T	W	T	F	S
					1	2
3	4	5	6	7	8	9
10	11	12	13	14	15	16
17	18	19	20	21	22	23
24	25	26	27	28	29	30

7 Monday

2nd ♒
Full Moon **2:11 pm** 11:11 am

Lunar eclipse 15° ♒ 25'

8 Tuesday

3rd ♒
☽ V/C **3:07 pm** 12:07 pm
☽ enters ♓ **5:56 pm** 2:56 pm

9 Wednesday

3rd ♓

10 Thursday

3rd ♓
☽ V/C **9:38 am** 6:38 am
☽ enters ♈ 10:22 pm

Eastern time in bold type
Pacific time in medium type

11 Friday

3rd ♓
☽ enters ♈ **1:22 am**

12 Saturday

3rd ♈
☿ ℞ **9:00 pm** 6:00 pm

Mercury retrograde until 9/5

13 Sunday

3rd ♈
☽ V/C **4:01 am** 1:01 am
☽ enters ♉ **6:40 am** 3:40 am

July 2017

S	M	T	W	T	F	S
						1
2	3	4	5	6	7	8
9	10	11	12	13	14	15
16	17	18	19	20	21	22
23	24	25	26	27	28	29
30	31					

August 2017

S	M	T	W	T	F	S
		1	2	3	4	5
6	7	8	9	10	11	12
13	14	15	16	17	18	19
20	21	22	23	24	25	26
27	28	29	30	31		

September 2017

S	M	T	W	T	F	S
					1	2
3	4	5	6	7	8	9
10	11	12	13	14	15	16
17	18	19	20	21	22	23
24	25	26	27	28	29	30

14 Monday

3rd ♉
☽ V/C **9:15 pm** 6:15 pm
4th quarter **9:15 pm** 6:15 pm

15 Tuesday

4th ♉
☽ enters ♊ **10:06 am** 7:06 am

16 Wednesday

4th ♊

17 Thursday

4th ♊
☽ V/C **9:38 am** 6:38 am
☽ enters ♋ **12:13 pm** 9:13 am

Eastern time in bold type
Pacific time in medium type

18 Friday

4th ♋

19 Saturday

4th ♋

☽ V/C **11:17 am** 8:17 am

☽ enters ♌ **1:55 pm** 10:55 am

20 Sunday

4th ♌

July 2017

S	M	T	W	T	F	S
						1
2	3	4	5	6	7	8
9	10	11	12	13	14	15
16	17	18	19	20	21	22
23	24	25	26	27	28	29
30	31					

August 2017

S	M	T	W	T	F	S
		1	2	3	4	5
6	7	8	9	10	11	12
13	14	15	16	17	18	19
20	21	22	23	24	25	26
27	28	29	30	31		

September 2017

S	M	T	W	T	F	S
					1	2
3	4	5	6	7	8	9
10	11	12	13	14	15	16
17	18	19	20	21	22	23
24	25	26	27	28	29	30

21 Monday

4th ♌

☽ V/C	**2:30 pm**	11:30 am
New Moon	**2:30 pm**	11:30 am
☽ enters ♍	**4:25 pm**	1:25 pm

Solar eclipse 28° ♌ 53'

22 Tuesday

1st ♍

☉ enters ♍	**6:20 pm**	3:20 pm

Sun enters Virgo

23 Wednesday

1st ♍

☽ V/C	**4:02 pm**	1:02 pm
☽ enters ♎	**9:05 pm**	6:05 pm

24 Thursday

1st ♎

Eastern time in bold type
Pacific time in medium type

25 Friday

1st ♎
♄ D **8:08 am** 5:08 am
♀ enters ♌ 9:30 pm
☽ V/C 10:39 pm

26 Saturday

1st ♎
♀ enters ♌ **12:30 am**
☽ V/C **1:39 am**
☽ enters ♏ **4:53 am** 1:53 am
⚵ D **1:14 pm** 10:14 am

27 Sunday

1st ♏

July 2017

S	M	T	W	T	F	S
						1
2	3	4	5	6	7	8
9	10	11	12	13	14	15
16	17	18	19	20	21	22
23	24	25	26	27	28	29
30	31					

August 2017

S	M	T	W	T	F	S
		1	2	3	4	5
6	7	8	9	10	11	12
13	14	15	16	17	18	19
20	21	22	23	24	25	26
27	28	29	30	31		

September 2017

S	M	T	W	T	F	S
					1	2
3	4	5	6	7	8	9
10	11	12	13	14	15	16
17	18	19	20	21	22	23
24	25	26	27	28	29	30

Eastern time in bold type
Pacific time in medium type

28 Monday

1st ♏
☽ V/C **5:38 am** 2:38 am
☽ enters ♐ **3:48 pm** 12:48 pm

29 Tuesday

1st ♐
2nd quarter **4:13 am** 1:13 am

30 Wednesday

2nd ♐
☽ V/C 9:42 pm

31 Thursday

2nd ♐
☽ V/C **12:42 am**
☽ enters ♑ **4:18 am** 1:18 am
☿ enters ♌ **11:28 am** 8:28 am

Eastern time in bold type
Pacific time in medium type

1 Friday

2nd ♑

2 Saturday

2nd ♑

☽ V/C **12:30 pm** 9:30 am

☽ enters ♒ **4:06 pm** 1:06 pm

3 Sunday

2nd ♒

August 2017

S	M	T	W	T	F	S
		1	2	3	4	5
6	7	8	9	10	11	12
13	14	15	16	17	18	19
20	21	22	23	24	25	26
27	28	29	30	31		

September 2017

S	M	T	W	T	F	S
					1	2
3	4	5	6	7	8	9
10	11	12	13	14	15	16
17	18	19	20	21	22	23
24	25	26	27	28	29	30

October 2017

S	M	T	W	T	F	S
1	2	3	4	5	6	7
8	9	10	11	12	13	14
15	16	17	18	19	20	21
22	23	24	25	26	27	28
29	30	31				

4 Monday

2nd ♒
☽ V/C 10:15 pm
☽ enters ♓ 10:28 pm

Labor Day

5 Tuesday

2nd ♒
☽ V/C **1:15 am**
☽ enters ♓ **1:28 am**
♂ enters ♍ **5:35 am** 2:35 am
☿ D **7:29 am** 4:29 am

6 Wednesday

2nd ♓
Full Moon **3:03 am** 12:03 am
☽ V/C **4:29 pm** 1:29 pm

7 Thursday

3rd ♓
☽ enters ♈ **8:01 am** 5:01 am

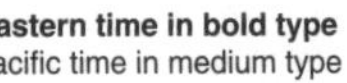
Eastern time in bold type
Pacific time in medium type

8 Friday

3rd ♈

9 Saturday

3rd ♈

☽ V/C	**11:52 am**	8:52 am
☽ enters ♉	**12:23 pm**	9:23 am
☿ enters ♍	**10:52 pm**	7:52 pm

10 Sunday

3rd ♉

☽ V/C	**8:54 pm**	5:54 pm

August 2017

S	M	T	W	T	F	S
		1	2	3	4	5
6	7	8	9	10	11	12
13	14	15	16	17	18	19
20	21	22	23	24	25	26
27	28	29	30	31		

September 2017

S	M	T	W	T	F	S
					1	2
3	4	5	6	7	8	9
10	11	12	13	14	15	16
17	18	19	20	21	22	23
24	25	26	27	28	29	30

October 2017

S	M	T	W	T	F	S
1	2	3	4	5	6	7
8	9	10	11	12	13	14
15	16	17	18	19	20	21
22	23	24	25	26	27	28
29	30	31				

Eastern time in bold type
Pacific time in medium type

11 Monday

3rd ♉
♀ ℞ **1:46 pm** 10:46 am
☽ enters ♊ **3:29 pm** 12:29 pm

12 Tuesday

3rd ♊
4th quarter 11:25 pm

13 Wednesday

3rd ♊
4th quarter **2:25 am**
☽ V/C **2:35 pm** 11:35 am
☽ enters ♋ **6:12 pm** 3:12 pm

14 Thursday

4th ♋

Eastern time in bold type
Pacific time in medium type

15 Friday

4th ♋
☽ V/C **5:23 pm** 2:23 pm
☽ enters ♌ **9:09 pm** 6:09 pm

16 Saturday

4th ♌

17 Sunday

4th ♌
☽ V/C **8:55 pm** 5:55 pm
☽ enters ♍ 9:52 pm

August 2017

S	M	T	W	T	F	S
		1	2	3	4	5
6	7	8	9	10	11	12
13	14	15	16	17	18	19
20	21	22	23	24	25	26
27	28	29	30	31		

September 2017

S	M	T	W	T	F	S
					1	2
3	4	5	6	7	8	9
10	11	12	13	14	15	16
17	18	19	20	21	22	23
24	25	26	27	28	29	30

October 2017

S	M	T	W	T	F	S
1	2	3	4	5	6	7
8	9	10	11	12	13	14
15	16	17	18	19	20	21
22	23	24	25	26	27	28
29	30	31				

18 Monday

4th ♌
☽ enters ♍ **12:52 am**
⚶ enters ♎ **3:50 am** 12:50 am

19 Tuesday

4th ♍
♀ enters ♍ **9:15 pm** 6:15 pm
☽ V/C 10:30 pm
New Moon 10:30 pm

20 Wednesday

4th ♍
☽ V/C **1:30 am**
New Moon **1:30 am**
☽ enters ♎ **6:06 am** 3:06 am

21 Thursday

1st ♎

Islamic New Year • Rosh Hashanah • UN International Day of Peace

Eastern time in bold type
Pacific time in medium type

22 Friday

1st ♎

☽ V/C	**9:04 am**	6:04 am
☽ enters ♏	**1:40 pm**	10:40 am
☉ enters ♎	**4:02 pm**	1:02 pm

Sun enters Libra • Mabon • Fall Equinox • 4:02 pm EDT/1:02 pm PDT

23 Saturday

1st ♏

⚳ enters ♌		10:45 pm

24 Sunday

1st ♏

⚳ enters ♌	**1:45 am**	
☽ V/C	**3:33 am**	12:33 am
☽ enters ♐		9:01 pm

August 2017

S	M	T	W	T	F	S
		1	2	3	4	5
6	7	8	9	10	11	12
13	14	15	16	17	18	19
20	21	22	23	24	25	26
27	28	29	30	31		

September 2017

S	M	T	W	T	F	S
					1	2
3	4	5	6	7	8	9
10	11	12	13	14	15	16
17	18	19	20	21	22	23
24	25	26	27	28	29	30

October 2017

S	M	T	W	T	F	S
1	2	3	4	5	6	7
8	9	10	11	12	13	14
15	16	17	18	19	20	21
22	23	24	25	26	27	28
29	30	31				

25 Monday

1st ♏
☽ enters ♐ **12:01 am**

26 Tuesday

1st ♐

27 Wednesday

1st ♐

☽ V/C	**7:08 am**	4:08 am
☽ enters ♑	**12:24 pm**	9:24 am
2nd quarter	**10:54 pm**	7:54 pm

28 Thursday

2nd ♑

♇ D	**3:36 pm**	12:36 pm

Eastern time in bold type
Pacific time in medium type

29 Friday

2nd ♑

☽ V/C	**8:14 pm**	5:14 pm
☿ enters ♎	**8:42 pm**	5:42 pm
☽ enters ♒		9:40 pm

30 Saturday

2nd ♑

☽ enters ♒ **12:40 am**

Yom Kippur

1 Sunday

2nd ♒

August 2017

S	M	T	W	T	F	S
		1	2	3	4	5
6	7	8	9	10	11	12
13	14	15	16	17	18	19
20	21	22	23	24	25	26
27	28	29	30	31		

September 2017

S	M	T	W	T	F	S
					1	2
3	4	5	6	7	8	9
10	11	12	13	14	15	16
17	18	19	20	21	22	23
24	25	26	27	28	29	30

October 2017

S	M	T	W	T	F	S
1	2	3	4	5	6	7
8	9	10	11	12	13	14
15	16	17	18	19	20	21
22	23	24	25	26	27	28
29	30	31				

2 Monday

2nd ♒
☽ V/C **7:13 am** 4:13 am
☽ enters ♓ **10:26 am** 7:26 am

3 Tuesday

2nd ♓

4 Wednesday

2nd ♓
☽ V/C **3:19 am** 12:19 am
☽ enters ♈ **4:40 pm** 1:40 pm

5 Thursday

2nd ♈
Full Moon **2:40 pm** 11:40 am

Sukkot begins

Eastern time in bold type
Pacific time in medium type

6 Friday

3rd ♈

☽ V/C	**6:38 pm**	3:38 pm
☽ enters ♉	**7:56 pm**	4:56 pm

7 Saturday

3rd ♉

8 Sunday

3rd ♉

☽ V/C	**9:45 am**	6:45 am
☽ enters ♊	**9:44 pm**	6:44 pm

September 2017

S	M	T	W	T	F	S
					1	2
3	4	5	6	7	8	9
10	11	12	13	14	15	16
17	18	19	20	21	22	23
24	25	26	27	28	29	30

October 2017

S	M	T	W	T	F	S
1	2	3	4	5	6	7
8	9	10	11	12	13	14
15	16	17	18	19	20	21
22	23	24	25	26	27	28
29	30	31				

November 2017

S	M	T	W	T	F	S
			1	2	3	4
5	6	7	8	9	10	11
12	13	14	15	16	17	18
19	20	21	22	23	24	25
26	27	28	29	30		

9 Monday

3rd ♊

Columbus Day • Indigenous Peoples' Day

10 Tuesday

3rd ♊

♃ enters ♏	**9:20 am**	6:20 am
☽ V/C	**6:25 pm**	3:25 pm
☽ enters ♋	**11:38 pm**	8:38 pm

11 Wednesday

3rd ♋

Sukkot ends

12 Thursday

3rd ♋

4th quarter	**8:25 am**	5:25 am
☽ V/C		9:00 pm
☽ enters ♌		11:41 pm

Eastern time in bold type
Pacific time in medium type

13 Friday

4th ♋
☽ V/C **12:00 am**
☽ enters ♌ **2:41 am**

14 Saturday

4th ♌
♀ enters ♎ **6:11 am** 3:11 am
☽ V/C 10:28 pm

15 Sunday

4th ♌
☽ V/C **1:28 am**
☽ enters ♍ **7:19 am** 4:19 am

September 2017

S	M	T	W	T	F	S
					1	2
3	4	5	6	7	8	9
10	11	12	13	14	15	16
17	18	19	20	21	22	23
24	25	26	27	28	29	30

October 2017

S	M	T	W	T	F	S
1	2	3	4	5	6	7
8	9	10	11	12	13	14
15	16	17	18	19	20	21
22	23	24	25	26	27	28
29	30	31				

November 2017

S	M	T	W	T	F	S
			1	2	3	4
5	6	7	8	9	10	11
12	13	14	15	16	17	18
19	20	21	22	23	24	25
26	27	28	29	30		

16 Monday
4th ♍

17 Tuesday
4th ♍
☿ enters ♏ **3:59 am** 12:59 am
☽ V/C **7:27 am** 4:27 am
☽ enters ♎ **1:35 pm** 10:35 am

18 Wednesday
4th ♎

19 Thursday
4th ♎
☽ V/C **3:12 pm** 12:12 pm
New Moon **3:12 pm** 12:12 pm
☽ enters ♏ **9:41 pm** 6:41 pm

Eastern time in bold type
Pacific time in medium type

20 Friday

1st ♏

21 Saturday

1st ♏

22 Sunday

1st ♏

☽ V/C	**7:35 am**	4:35 am
☽ enters ♐	**7:57 am**	4:57 am
♂ enters ♎	**2:29 pm**	11:29 am
☉ enters ♏		10:27 pm

Sun enters Scorpio

September 2017

S	M	T	W	T	F	S
					1	2
3	4	5	6	7	8	9
10	11	12	13	14	15	16
17	18	19	20	21	22	23
24	25	26	27	28	29	30

October 2017

S	M	T	W	T	F	S
1	2	3	4	5	6	7
8	9	10	11	12	13	14
15	16	17	18	19	20	21
22	23	24	25	26	27	28
29	30	31				

November 2017

S	M	T	W	T	F	S
			1	2	3	4
5	6	7	8	9	10	11
12	13	14	15	16	17	18
19	20	21	22	23	24	25
26	27	28	29	30		

Eastern time in bold type
Pacific time in medium type

23 Monday

1st ♐
☉ enters ♏ **1:27 am**

Sun enters Scorpio

24 Tuesday

1st ♐
☽ V/C **12:44 pm** 9:44 am
☽ enters ♑ **8:12 pm** 5:12 pm

25 Wednesday

1st ♑

26 Thursday

1st ♑
☽ V/C 10:22 pm

Eastern time in bold type
Pacific time in medium type

27 Friday

1st ♑

☽ V/C	**1:22 am**	
☽ enters ♒	**8:59 am**	5:59 am
2nd quarter	**6:22 pm**	3:22 pm

28 Saturday

2nd ♒

29 Sunday

2nd ♒

☽ V/C	**12:22 pm**	9:22 am
☽ enters ♓	**7:46 pm**	4:46 pm

September 2017

S	M	T	W	T	F	S
					1	2
3	4	5	6	7	8	9
10	11	12	13	14	15	16
17	18	19	20	21	22	23
24	25	26	27	28	29	30

October 2017

S	M	T	W	T	F	S
1	2	3	4	5	6	7
8	9	10	11	12	13	14
15	16	17	18	19	20	21
22	23	24	25	26	27	28
29	30	31				

November 2017

S	M	T	W	T	F	S
			1	2	3	4
5	6	7	8	9	10	11
12	13	14	15	16	17	18
19	20	21	22	23	24	25
26	27	28	29	30		

30 Monday

2nd ♓

31 Tuesday

2nd ♓

☽ V/C **5:08 pm** 2:08 pm

☽ enters ♈ 11:43 pm

Halloween/Samhain

1 Wednesday

2nd ♓

☽ enters ♈ **2:43 am**

All Saints' Day

2 Thursday

2nd ♈

☽ V/C **11:03 pm** 8:03 pm

Eastern time in bold type
Pacific time in medium type

3 Friday

2nd ♈

☽ enters ♉	**5:46 am**	2:46 am
Full Moon		10:23 pm

4 Saturday

2nd ♉

Full Moon	**1:23 am**

5 Sunday

3rd ♉

☽ V/C	**4:29 am**	1:29 am
☽ enters ♊	**5:26 am**	2:26 am
☿ enters ♐	**2:19 pm**	11:19 am

Daylight Saving Time ends at 2 am

October 2017

S	M	T	W	T	F	S
1	2	3	4	5	6	7
8	9	10	11	12	13	14
15	16	17	18	19	20	21
22	23	24	25	26	27	28
29	30	31				

November 2017

S	M	T	W	T	F	S
			1	2	3	4
5	6	7	8	9	10	11
12	13	14	15	16	17	18
19	20	21	22	23	24	25
26	27	28	29	30		

December 2017

S	M	T	W	T	F	S
					1	2
3	4	5	6	7	8	9
10	11	12	13	14	15	16
17	18	19	20	21	22	23
24	25	26	27	28	29	30
31						

6 Monday

3rd ♊

7 Tuesday

3rd ♊

☽ V/C	**5:40 am**	2:40 am
☽ enters ♋	**5:45 am**	2:45 am
♀ enters ♏	**6:38 am**	3:38 am

Election Day

8 Wednesday

3rd ♋

☽ V/C		9:14 pm

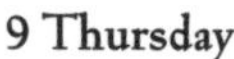

9 Thursday

3rd ♋

☽ V/C	**12:14 am**	
☽ enters ♌	**7:29 am**	4:29 am

Eastern time in bold type
Pacific time in medium type

10 Friday

3rd ♌
4th quarter **3:36 pm** 12:36 pm

11 Saturday

4th ♌
☽ V/C **3:55 am** 12:55 am
☽ enters ♍ **11:41 am** 8:41 am

Veterans Day

12 Sunday

4th ♍

October 2017

S	M	T	W	T	F	S
1	2	3	4	5	6	7
8	9	10	11	12	13	14
15	16	17	18	19	20	21
22	23	24	25	26	27	28
29	30	31				

November 2017

S	M	T	W	T	F	S
			1	2	3	4
5	6	7	8	9	10	11
12	13	14	15	16	17	18
19	20	21	22	23	24	25
26	27	28	29	30		

December 2017

S	M	T	W	T	F	S
					1	2
3	4	5	6	7	8	9
10	11	12	13	14	15	16
17	18	19	20	21	22	23
24	25	26	27	28	29	30
31						

Eastern time in bold type
Pacific time in medium type

13 Monday

4th ♍
☽ V/C **10:45 am** 7:45 am
☽ enters ♎ **6:26 pm** 3:26 pm

14 Tuesday

4th ♎

15 Wednesday

4th ♎
☽ V/C **7:50 pm** 4:50 pm
⚳ enters ♈ **9:53 pm** 6:53 pm
⚵ enters ♏ **11:16 pm** 8:16 pm

16 Thursday

4th ♎
☽ enters ♏ **3:19 am** 12:19 am

Eastern time in bold type
Pacific time in medium type

17 Friday

4th ♏

18 Saturday

4th ♏

☽ V/C	**6:42 am**	3:42 am
New Moon	**6:42 am**	3:42 am
☽ enters ♐	**1:59 pm**	10:59 am

19 Sunday

1st ♐

October 2017

S	M	T	W	T	F	S
1	2	3	4	5	6	7
8	9	10	11	12	13	14
15	16	17	18	19	20	21
22	23	24	25	26	27	28
29	30	31				

November 2017

S	M	T	W	T	F	S
			1	2	3	4
5	6	7	8	9	10	11
12	13	14	15	16	17	18
19	20	21	22	23	24	25
26	27	28	29	30		

December 2017

S	M	T	W	T	F	S
					1	2
3	4	5	6	7	8	9
10	11	12	13	14	15	16
17	18	19	20	21	22	23
24	25	26	27	28	29	30
31						

Eastern time in bold type
Pacific time in medium type

20 Monday

1st ♐
☽ V/C **7:26 pm** 4:26 pm
☽ enters ♑ 11:14 pm

21 Tuesday

1st ♐
☽ enters ♑ **2:14 am**
☉ enters ♐ **10:05 pm** 7:05 pm

Sun enters Sagittarius

22 Wednesday

1st ♑
♆ D **9:21 am** 6:21 am

23 Thursday

1st ♑
☽ V/C **5:33 am** 2:33 am
☽ enters ♒ **3:14 pm** 12:14 pm

Thanksgiving Day

Eastern time in bold type
Pacific time in medium type

24 Friday

1st ≈

25 Saturday

1st ≈
☽ V/C **9:37 pm** 6:37 pm

26 Sunday

1st ≈
☽ enters ♓ **3:04 am** 12:04 am
2nd quarter **12:03 pm** 9:03 am

October 2017

S	M	T	W	T	F	S
1	2	3	4	5	6	7
8	9	10	11	12	13	14
15	16	17	18	19	20	21
22	23	24	25	26	27	28
29	30	31				

November 2017

S	M	T	W	T	F	S
			1	2	3	4
5	6	7	8	9	10	11
12	13	14	15	16	17	18
19	20	21	22	23	24	25
26	27	28	29	30		

December 2017

S	M	T	W	T	F	S
					1	2
3	4	5	6	7	8	9
10	11	12	13	14	15	16
17	18	19	20	21	22	23
24	25	26	27	28	29	30
31						

Eastern time in bold type
Pacific time in medium type

27 Monday

2nd ♓

28 Tuesday

2nd ♓
☽ V/C **7:09 am** 4:09 am
☽ enters ♈ **11:30 am** 8:30 am

29 Wednesday

2nd ♈

30 Thursday

2nd ♈
☽ V/C **1:37 pm** 10:37 am
☽ enters ♉ **3:38 pm** 12:38 pm

Eastern time in bold type
Pacific time in medium type

1 Friday

2nd ♉
♀ enters ♐ **4:14 am** 1:14 am
☽ V/C **8:53 pm** 5:53 pm

2 Saturday

2nd ♉
☽ enters ♊ **4:21 pm** 1:21 pm
☿ ℞ 11:34 pm

Mercury retrograde until 12/22

3 Sunday

2nd ♊
☿ ℞ **2:34 am**
Full Moon **10:47 am** 7:47 am

Mercury retrograde until 12/22

November 2017

S	M	T	W	T	F	S
			1	2	3	4
5	6	7	8	9	10	11
12	13	14	15	16	17	18
19	20	21	22	23	24	25
26	27	28	29	30		

December 2017

S	M	T	W	T	F	S
					1	2
3	4	5	6	7	8	9
10	11	12	13	14	15	16
17	18	19	20	21	22	23
24	25	26	27	28	29	30
31						

January 2018

S	M	T	W	T	F	S
	1	2	3	4	5	6
7	8	9	10	11	12	13
14	15	16	17	18	19	20
21	22	23	24	25	26	27
28	29	30	31			

4 Monday

3rd ♊

☽ V/C **2:13 pm** 11:13 am

☽ enters ♋ **3:37 pm** 12:37 pm

5 Tuesday

3rd ♋

⚷ D **4:47 am** 1:47 am

6 Wednesday

3rd ♋

☽ V/C **12:56 pm** 9:56 am

☽ enters ♌ **3:37 pm** 12:37 pm

7 Thursday

3rd ♌

Eastern time in bold type
Pacific time in medium type

8 Friday

3rd ♌
☽ V/C **5:40 pm** 2:40 pm
☽ enters ♍ **6:09 pm** 3:09 pm

9 Saturday

3rd ♍
♂ enters ♏ **3:59 am** 12:59 am
4th quarter 11:51 pm

10 Sunday

3rd ♍
4th quarter **2:51 am**
☽ V/C **10:02 pm** 7:02 pm
☽ enters ♎ 9:01 pm

November 2017

S	M	T	W	T	F	S
			1	2	3	4
5	6	7	8	9	10	11
12	13	14	15	16	17	18
19	20	21	22	23	24	25
26	27	28	29	30		

December 2017

S	M	T	W	T	F	S
					1	2
3	4	5	6	7	8	9
10	11	12	13	14	15	16
17	18	19	20	21	22	23
24	25	26	27	28	29	30
31						

January 2018

S	M	T	W	T	F	S
	1	2	3	4	5	6
7	8	9	10	11	12	13
14	15	16	17	18	19	20
21	22	23	24	25	26	27
28	29	30	31			

11 Monday

4th ♍
☽ enters ♎ **12:01 am**

12 Tuesday

4th ♎

13 Wednesday

4th ♎

☽ V/C	**7:27 am**	4:27 am
☽ enters ♏	**8:59 am**	5:59 am

Hanukkah begins

14 Thursday

4th ♏

☽ V/C	**8:42 pm**	5:42 pm

Eastern time in bold type
Pacific time in medium type

15 Friday

4th ♏
☽ enters ♐ **8:07 pm** 5:07 pm

16 Saturday

4th ♐
⚵ enters ♒ **2:18 pm** 11:18 am
⚳ ℞ **5:28 pm** 2:28 pm

17 Sunday

4th ♐
☿ D **6:36 pm** 3:36 pm
New Moon 10:30 pm

November 2017

S	M	T	W	T	F	S
			1	2	3	4
5	6	7	8	9	10	11
12	13	14	15	16	17	18
19	20	21	22	23	24	25
26	27	28	29	30		

December 2017

S	M	T	W	T	F	S
					1	2
3	4	5	6	7	8	9
10	11	12	13	14	15	16
17	18	19	20	21	22	23
24	25	26	27	28	29	30
31						

January 2018

S	M	T	W	T	F	S
	1	2	3	4	5	6
7	8	9	10	11	12	13
14	15	16	17	18	19	20
21	22	23	24	25	26	27
28	29	30	31			

18 Monday

4th ♐

New Moon	**1:30 am**	
☽ V/C	**8:10 am**	5:10 am
☽ enters ♑	**8:33 am**	5:33 am

19 Tuesday

1st ♑

♄ enters ♑	**11:49 pm**	8:49 pm

20 Wednesday

1st ♑

☽ V/C	**10:37 am**	7:37 am
☽ enters ♒	**9:29 pm**	6:29 pm

Hanukkah ends

21 Thursday

1st ♒

☉ enters ♑	**11:28 am**	8:28 am

Sun enters Capricorn • Yule • Winter Solstice • 11:28 am EST/8:28 am PST

Eastern time in bold type
Pacific time in medium type

22 Friday

1st ♒︎
☿ D **8:51 pm** 5:51 pm

23 Saturday

1st ♒︎
☽ V/C **5:13 am** 2:13 am
☽ enters ♓︎ **9:42 am** 6:42 am

24 Sunday

1st ♓︎
☽ V/C **9:48 pm** 6:48 pm
♀ enters ♑︎ 9:26 pm

Christmas Eve

November 2017

S	M	T	W	T	F	S
			1	2	3	4
5	6	7	8	9	10	11
12	13	14	15	16	17	18
19	20	21	22	23	24	25
26	27	28	29	30		

December 2017

S	M	T	W	T	F	S
					1	2
3	4	5	6	7	8	9
10	11	12	13	14	15	16
17	18	19	20	21	22	23
24	25	26	27	28	29	30
31						

January 2018

S	M	T	W	T	F	S
	1	2	3	4	5	6
7	8	9	10	11	12	13
14	15	16	17	18	19	20
21	22	23	24	25	26	27
28	29	30	31			

25 Monday

1st ♓
♀ enters ♑ **12:26 am**
☽ enters ♈ **7:27 pm** 4:27 pm

Christmas Day

26 Tuesday

1st ♈
2nd quarter **4:20 am** 1:20 am

Kwanzaa begins

27 Wednesday

2nd ♈
☽ V/C **3:57 pm** 12:57 pm
☽ enters ♉ 10:23 pm

28 Thursday

2nd ♈
☽ enters ♉ **1:23 am**

Eastern time in bold type
Pacific time in medium type

29 Friday

2nd ♉
☽ V/C **9:01 am** 6:01 am

30 Saturday

2nd ♉
☽ enters ♊ **3:31 am** 12:31 am

31 Sunday

2nd ♊
☽ V/C **6:38 pm** 3:38 pm

New Year's Eve

November 2017

S	M	T	W	T	F	S
			1	2	3	4
5	6	7	8	9	10	11
12	13	14	15	16	17	18
19	20	21	22	23	24	25
26	27	28	29	30		

December 2017

S	M	T	W	T	F	S
					1	2
3	4	5	6	7	8	9
10	11	12	13	14	15	16
17	18	19	20	21	22	23
24	25	26	27	28	29	30
31						

January 2018

S	M	T	W	T	F	S
	1	2	3	4	5	6
7	8	9	10	11	12	13
14	15	16	17	18	19	20
21	22	23	24	25	26	27
28	29	30	31			

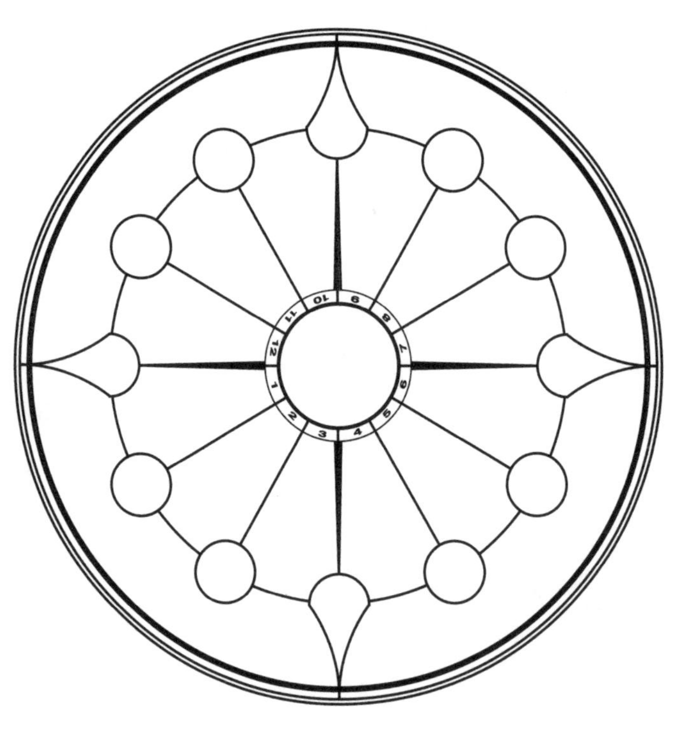

1
2
3
4
5
6
7
8
9
10
11
12

The Year 2018

January

S	M	T	W	T	F	S
	1	2	3	4	5	6
7	8	9	10	11	12	13
14	15	16	17	18	19	20
21	22	23	24	25	26	27
28	29	30	31			

February

S	M	T	W	T	F	S
				1	2	3
4	5	6	7	8	9	10
11	12	13	14	15	16	17
18	19	20	21	22	23	24
25	26	27	28			

March

S	M	T	W	T	F	S
				1	2	3
4	5	6	7	8	9	10
11	12	13	14	15	16	17
18	19	20	21	22	23	24
25	26	27	28	29	30	31

April

S	M	T	W	T	F	S
1	2	3	4	5	6	7
8	9	10	11	12	13	14
15	16	17	18	19	20	21
22	23	24	25	26	27	28
29	30					

May

S	M	T	W	T	F	S
		1	2	3	4	5
6	7	8	9	10	11	12
13	14	15	16	17	18	19
20	21	22	23	24	25	26
27	28	29	30	31		

June

S	M	T	W	T	F	S
					1	2
3	4	5	6	7	8	9
10	11	12	13	14	15	16
17	18	19	20	21	22	23
24	25	26	27	28	29	30

July

S	M	T	W	T	F	S
1	2	3	4	5	6	7
8	9	10	11	12	13	14
15	16	17	18	19	20	21
22	23	24	25	26	27	28
29	30	31				

August

S	M	T	W	T	F	S
			1	2	3	4
5	6	7	8	9	10	11
12	13	14	15	16	17	18
19	20	21	22	23	24	25
26	27	28	29	30	31	

September

S	M	T	W	T	F	S
						1
2	3	4	5	6	7	8
9	10	11	12	13	14	15
16	17	18	19	20	21	22
23	24	25	26	27	28	29
30						

October

S	M	T	W	T	F	S
	1	2	3	4	5	6
7	8	9	10	11	12	13
14	15	16	17	18	19	20
21	22	23	24	25	26	27
28	29	30	31			

November

S	M	T	W	T	F	S
				1	2	3
4	5	6	7	8	9	10
11	12	13	14	15	16	17
18	19	20	21	22	23	24
25	26	27	28	29	30	

December

S	M	T	W	T	F	S
						1
2	3	4	5	6	7	8
9	10	11	12	13	14	15
16	17	18	19	20	21	22
23	24	25	26	27	28	29
30	31					

JANUARY 2016

☽ Last Aspect day	ET / hr:mn	PT	asp	☽ Ingress sign	day	ET / hr:mn	PT
12/31		9:33 pm	△☿	♎	12/31		10:41 pm
1	**12:33 am**		△☿	♎	1	**1:41 am**	
2	**11:23 am**	8:23 am	☍♅	♏	3	**2:36 pm**	11:36 am
5	**12:47 pm**	9:47 am	⚹♃	♐	5		10:56 pm
5	**12:47 pm**	9:47 am	⚹♃	♐	6	**1:56 am**	
7	**9:44 pm**	6:44 pm	□♃	♑	8	**10:07 am**	7:07 am
10	**12:39 pm**	9:39 am	☌☿	♒	10	**3:23 pm**	12:23 pm
11	**8:09 pm**	5:09 pm	⚹♅	♓	12	**6:53 pm**	3:53 pm
14	**11:31 am**	8:31 am	⚹☉	♈	14	**9:48 pm**	6:48 pm
16	**6:26 pm**	3:26 pm	□☉	♉	16		9:48 pm
16	**6:26 pm**	3:26 pm	□☉	♉	17	**12:48 am**	
18		10:50 pm	△☉	♊	19	**4:13 am**	1:13 am
19	**1:50 am**		△☉	♊	19	**4:13 am**	1:13 am
21	**3:01 am**	12:01 am	☍♀	♋	21	**8:28 am**	5:28 am
22		10:21 pm	⚹♃	♌	23	**2:21 pm**	11:21 am
23	**1:21 am**		⚹♃	♌	26	**2:21 pm**	11:21 am
24	**9:51 pm**	6:51 pm	△♅	♍	25	**10:46 pm**	7:46 pm
27	**7:11 pm**	4:11 pm	☌♃	♎	28	**9:59 am**	6:59 am
29	**8:34 pm**	5:34 pm	☍♅	♏	30	**10:50 pm**	7:50 pm

☽ Phases & Eclipses phase	day	ET / hr:mn	PT
4th Quarter	1		9:30 pm
4th Quarter	2	**12:30 am**	
New Moon	9	**8:31 pm**	5:31 pm
2nd Quarter	16	**6:26 pm**	3:26 pm
Full Moon	23	**8:46 pm**	5:46 pm
4th Quarter	31	**10:28 pm**	7:28 pm

Planet Ingress		day	ET / hr:mn	PT
☿	♒	1	**9:20 pm**	6:20 pm
♂	♏	3	**9:32 am**	6:32 am
☿	♑	8	**2:36 pm**	11:36 am
☉	♒	20	**10:27 am**	7:27 am
♀	♒	22	**2:03 pm**	11:03 am
♀	♑	23	**3:31 pm**	12:31 pm
⚷	♓	28	**1:42 pm**	10:42 am

Planetary Motion		day	ET / hr:mn	PT
☿	℞	5	**8:06 am**	5:06 am
♃	℞	7	**11:40 pm**	8:40 pm
☿	D	25	**4:50 pm**	1:50 pm

1 FRIDAY
☽△☿ **12:33 am**
☽⚹♀ **7:05 am** 4:05 am
☽⚻♆ **5:03 pm** 2:03 pm
☽□☉ 9:30 pm
☽⚹♄ 9:35 pm
☉⚺♄ 10:35 pm

2 SATURDAY
☽□☉ **12:30 am**
☽⚹♄ **12:35 am**
☉⚺♄ **1:35 am**
☽□♇ **8:23 am** 5:23 am
☽☍♅ **11:23 am** 8:23 am
☽⚺♃ 9:50 pm

3 SUNDAY
☽⚺♃ **12:50 am**
☽☌♂ **2:51 pm** 11:51 am
☽□☿ **4:12 pm** 1:12 pm
☽⚺♀ 11:53 pm

4 MONDAY
☽⚺♀ **2:53 am**
☽△♆ **5:56 am** 2:56 am
☽⚺♄ **1:46 pm** 10:46 am
☽⚹☉ **6:43 pm** 3:43 pm
☽⚹♇ **8:59 pm** 5:59 pm
☽⚻♅ **11:47 pm** 8:47 pm

5 TUESDAY
☿□♂ **7:00 am** 4:00 am
♀□♆ **9:33 am** 6:33 am
☽⚹♃ **12:47 pm** 9:47 am
☉☌♇ **10:28 pm** 7:28 pm

6 WEDNESDAY
☽⚹☿ **3:49 am** 12:49 am
☽⚺♂ **4:54 am** 1:54 am
☽□♆ **4:39 pm** 1:39 pm
☽☌♀ **7:54 pm** 4:54 pm
☽☌♄ 9:27 pm

7 THURSDAY
☽☌♄ **12:27 am**
☽⚺♇ **6:57 am** 3:57 am
☉□♅ **7:22 am** 4:22 am
☽△♅ **9:29 am** 6:29 am
☽⚺☉ **9:39 am** 6:39 am
☽□♃ **9:44 pm** 6:44 pm

8 FRIDAY
☽⚺☿ **10:19 am** 7:19 am
☽⚹♂ **3:20 pm** 12:20 pm
♀☌♄ **11:11 pm** 8:11 pm
☽⚹♆ 9:07 pm

9 SATURDAY
☽⚹♆ **12:07 am**
☽⚺♄ **7:48 am** 4:48 am
☽⚺♀ **8:35 am** 5:35 am
☽☌♇ **1:40 pm** 10:40 am
☽□♅ **3:58 pm** 12:58 pm
☽☌☉ **8:31 pm** 5:31 pm

10 SUNDAY
☽△♃ **3:33 am** 12:33 am
☽☌☿ **12:39 pm** 9:39 am
☽□♂ **10:31 pm** 7:31 pm

11 MONDAY
☽⚺♆ **4:55 am** 1:55 am
☽⚹♄ **12:35 pm** 9:35 am
☽⚹♀ **5:59 pm** 2:59 pm
☽⚺♇ **6:00 pm** 3:00 pm
♀⚺♇ **6:18 pm** 3:18 pm
☽⚹♅ **8:09 pm** 5:09 pm

12 TUESDAY
☽⚺☉ **4:34 am** 1:34 am
☽⚻♃ **7:19 am** 4:19 am
☽⚺☿ **12:27 pm** 9:27 am
♀△♅ **7:11 pm** 4:11 pm

13 WEDNESDAY
☽△♂ **3:56 am** 12:56 am
☽☌♆ **8:17 am** 5:17 am
☽□♄ **4:06 pm** 1:06 pm
☉△♃ **5:49 pm** 2:49 pm
☽⚹♇ **9:13 pm** 6:13 pm
☽⚺♅ **11:17 pm** 8:17 pm
☽□♀ 10:54 pm

14 THURSDAY
☽□♀ **1:54 am**
☉☌☿ **9:05 am** 6:05 am
☽☍♃ **10:13 am** 7:13 am
☽⚹☿ **11:09 am** 8:09 am
☽⚹☉ **11:31 am** 8:31 am
☿△♃ **9:15 pm** 6:15 pm

15 FRIDAY
☽⚻♂ **8:50 am** 5:50 am
☽⚺♆ **11:16 am** 8:16 am
☽△♄ **7:21 pm** 4:21 pm
☽□♇ 9:15 pm
☽☌♅ 11:15 pm

16 SATURDAY
☽□♇ **12:15 am**
☽☌♅ **2:15 am**
☽△♀ **9:39 am** 6:39 am
☽□☿ **9:47 am** 6:47 am
☿⚺♀ **10:25 am** 7:25 am
☽⚻♃ **1:05 pm** 10:05 am
☽□☉ **6:26 pm** 3:26 pm

17 SUNDAY
☽☍♂ **1:53 pm** 10:53 am
☽⚹♆ **2:28 pm** 11:28 am
☽⚻♄ **10:51 pm** 7:51 pm
♀□♃ 9:10 pm

18 MONDAY
♀□♃ **12:10 am**
☽△♇ **3:33 am** 12:33 am
☽⚺♅ **5:30 am** 2:30 am
♂△♆ **6:01 am** 3:01 am
☽△☿ **9:03 am** 6:03 am
☽△♃ **4:15 pm** 1:15 pm
☽⚻♀ **5:51 pm** 2:51 pm
☽△☉ 10:50 pm

19 TUESDAY
☽△☉ **1:50 am**
☽□♆ **6:09 pm** 3:09 pm
☽⚻♂ **7:30 pm** 4:30 pm
☽☍♄ 11:54 pm

20 WEDNESDAY
☽☍♄ **2:54 am**
☽⚻♇ **7:27 am** 4:27 am
☽⚹♅ **9:24 am** 6:24 am
☽⚻☿ **9:37 am** 6:37 am
☿□♅ **1:26 pm** 10:26 am
☽□♃ **8:07 pm** 5:07 pm

21 THURSDAY
☽☍♀ **3:01 am** 12:01 am
☽⚻☉ **10:15 am** 7:15 am
☽△♆ **10:53 pm** 7:53 pm
☽△♂ 11:15 pm

22 FRIDAY
☽△♂ **2:15 am**
☿☌♇ **4:59 am** 1:59 am
☽⚻♄ **8:07 am** 5:07 am
☽☍☿ **12:17 pm** 9:17 am
☽☍♇ **12:34 pm** 9:34 am
☽□♅ **2:32 pm** 11:32 am
☽⚹♃ 10:21 pm

23 SATURDAY
☽⚹♃ **1:21 am**
☽⚻♀ **2:14 pm** 11:14 am
☽☍☉ **8:46 pm** 5:46 pm

24 SUNDAY
☽⚻♆ **5:30 am** 2:30 am
☽□♂ **11:11 am** 8:11 am
☽△♄ **3:25 pm** 12:25 pm
☽⚻☿ **6:09 pm** 3:09 pm
☽⚻♇ **7:50 pm** 4:50 pm
☽△♅ **9:51 pm** 6:51 pm

25 MONDAY
☽⚺♃ **8:52 am** 5:52 am

26 TUESDAY
☽△♀ **4:50 am** 1:50 am
☽⚻☉ **10:36 am** 7:36 am
☽☍♆ **2:52 pm** 11:52 am
☽⚹♂ **11:12 pm** 8:12 pm
☽□♄ 10:33 pm

27 WEDNESDAY
☽□♄ **1:33 am**
☽△☿ **4:10 am** 1:10 am
☽△♇ **5:56 am** 2:56 am
☽⚻♅ **8:02 am** 5:02 am
☽☌♃ **7:11 pm** 4:11 pm

28 THURSDAY
☉⚺♆ **3:45 pm** 12:45 pm
☽□♀ **11:12 pm** 8:12 pm
☽⚻♆ 11:54 pm

29 FRIDAY
☽⚻♆ **2:54 am**
☽△☉ **3:55 am** 12:55 am
☽⚺♂ **2:02 pm** 11:02 am
☽⚹♄ **2:12 pm** 11:12 am
☽□☿ **6:11 pm** 3:11 pm
☽□♇ **6:27 pm** 3:27 pm
♂⚺♄ **6:56 pm** 3:56 pm
☽☍♅ **8:34 pm** 5:34 pm
☿☌♇ 9:58 pm

30 SATURDAY
☿☌♇ **12:58 am**
☽⚺♃ **7:29 am** 4:29 am
♀⚹♆ **11:44 am** 8:44 am

31 SUNDAY
☽△♆ **3:58 pm** 12:58 pm
☽⚹♀ **7:08 pm** 4:08 pm
☽□☉ **10:28 pm** 7:28 pm
☿□♅ **10:41 pm** 7:41 pm

Eastern time in bold type
Pacific time in medium type

JANUARY 2016

DATE	SID.TIME	SUN	MOON	NODE	MERCURY	VENUS	MARS	JUPITER	SATURN	URANUS	NEPTUNE	PLUTO	CERES	PALLAS	JUNO	VESTA	CHIRON
1 F	6 40 22	9 ♑ 58 56	26 ♍ 42	24 ♍ 53	29 ♑ 17	2 ♐ 03	28 ♎ 33	23 ♍ 09	11 ♐ 09	16 ♈ 34	7 ♓ 33	15 ♑ 03	19 ♒ 36	21 ♑ 58	6 ♏ 11	5 ♈ 58	17 ♓ 28
2 Sa	6 44 18	11 00 05	8 ♎ 32	24 53 R	29 57	3 16	29 07	23 11	11 15	16 35	7 34	15 05	19 58	22 20	6 27	6 14	17 30
3 Su	6 48 15	12 01 15	20 20	24 53	0 ♒ 28	4 29	29 40	23 12	11 22	16 35	7 36	15 07	20 20	22 43	6 42	6 31	17 32
4 M	6 52 11	13 02 24	2 ♏ 11	24 51	0 49	5 42	0 ♏ 13	23 13	11 28	16 36	7 37	15 09	20 41	23 05	6 57	6 48	17 34
5 T	6 56 8	14 03 34	14 11	24 47	1 01 R	6 55	0 46	23 13	11 34	16 36	7 39	15 11	21 03	23 27	7 12	7 05	17 36
6 W	7 0 4	15 04 45	26 25	24 40	1 01	8 08	1 19	23 14	11 41	16 37	7 40	15 13	21 25	23 49	7 27	7 23	17 38
7 Th	7 4 1	16 05 55	8 ♐ 56	24 31	0 50	9 21	1 52	23 14	11 47	16 37	7 42	15 15	21 47	24 11	7 42	7 40	17 40
8 F	7 7 58	17 07 05	21 45	24 19	0 27	10 35	2 25	23 14 R	11 53	16 38	7 43	15 17	22 09	24 34	7 56	7 58	17 42
9 Sa	7 11 54	18 08 16	4 ♑ 54	24 07	29 ♑ 53	11 48	2 57	23 14	12 00	16 38	7 45	15 20	22 32	24 56	8 11	8 16	17 44
10 Su	7 15 51	19 09 26	18 22	23 56	29 07	13 01	3 30	23 14	12 06	16 39	7 47	15 22	22 54	25 18	8 25	8 34	17 47
11 M	7 19 47	20 10 36	2 ♒ 05	23 45	28 10	14 14	4 02	23 14	12 12	16 40	7 48	15 24	23 16	25 40	8 39	8 53	17 49
12 T	7 23 44	21 11 46	16 01	23 37	27 05	15 28	4 35	23 13	12 18	16 41	7 50	15 26	23 38	26 02	8 52	9 11	17 51
13 W	7 27 40	22 12 55	0 ♓ 04	23 32	25 53	16 41	5 07	23 12	12 24	16 42	7 52	15 28	24 01	26 24	9 06	9 30	17 54
14 Th	7 31 37	23 14 04	14 12	23 30 D	24 36	17 55	5 39	23 11	12 30	16 43	7 53	15 30	24 23	26 46	9 19	9 49	17 56
15 F	7 35 33	24 15 12	28 21	23 30	23 17	19 08	6 11	23 10	12 36	16 44	7 55	15 32	24 46	27 08	9 32	10 08	17 58
16 Sa	7 39 30	25 16 20	12 ♈ 29	23 31 R	21 58	20 22	6 43	23 08	12 42	16 45	7 57	15 34	25 08	27 31	9 45	10 27	18 01
17 Su	7 43 27	26 17 26	26 36	23 31	20 42	21 35	7 15	23 07	12 48	16 46	7 59	15 36	25 31	27 53	9 58	10 47	18 03
18 M	7 47 23	27 18 32	10 ♉ 39	23 30	19 31	22 49	7 47	23 05	12 53	16 47	8 00	15 38	25 53	28 15	10 11	11 06	18 06
19 T	7 51 20	28 19 37	24 39	23 27	18 26	24 02	8 18	23 03	12 59	16 48	8 02	15 40	26 16	28 37	10 23	11 26	18 09
20 W	7 55 16	29 20 41	8 ♊ 33	23 22	17 28	25 16	8 50	23 01	13 05	16 49	8 04	15 42	26 39	28 59	10 35	11 46	18 11
21 Th	7 59 13	0 ♒ 21 45	22 20	23 14	16 40	26 30	9 21	22 58	13 10	16 51	8 06	15 44	27 02	29 21	10 47	12 06	18 14
22 F	8 3 9	1 22 47	5 ♋ 57	23 05	16 01	27 43	9 52	22 56	13 16	16 52	8 08	15 46	27 24	29 43	10 59	12 27	18 17
23 Sa	8 7 6	2 23 49	19 22	22 56	15 31	28 57	10 24	22 53	13 21	16 53	8 10	15 48	27 47	0 ♒ 05	11 10	12 47	18 19
24 Su	8 11 3	3 24 50	2 ♌ 32	22 47	15 10	0 ♑ 11	10 55	22 50	13 27	16 55	8 12	15 50	28 10	0 26	11 22	13 07	18 22
25 M	8 14 59	4 25 51	15 26	22 40	14 58 D	1 24	11 25	22 47	13 32	16 56	8 14	15 52	28 33	0 48	11 33	13 28	18 25
26 T	8 18 56	5 26 50	28 03	22 35	14 55	2 38	11 56	22 44	13 37	16 58	8 16	15 54	28 56	1 10	11 43	13 49	18 28
27 W	8 22 52	6 27 49	10 ♍ 24	22 32	14 59	3 52	12 27	22 40	13 43	16 59	8 18	15 56	29 19	1 32	11 54	14 10	18 31
28 Th	8 26 49	7 28 47	22 31	22 31 D	15 11	5 06	12 57	22 37	13 48	17 01	8 20	15 58	29 42	1 54	12 04	14 31	18 34
29 F	8 30 45	8 29 44	4 ♎ 28	22 31	15 30	6 20	13 28	22 33	13 53	17 03	8 22	16 00	0 ♓ 05	2 16	12 14	14 52	18 37
30 Sa	8 34 42	9 30 41	16 18	22 33	15 55	7 34	13 58	22 29	13 58	17 04	8 24	16 02	0 28	2 37	12 24	15 14	18 40
31 Su	8 38 38	10 31 37	28 07	22 35	16 26	8 48	14 28	22 25	14 03	17 06	8 26	16 04	0 51	2 59	12 34	15 35	18 43

EPHEMERIS CALCULATED FOR 12 MIDNIGHT GREENWICH MEAN TIME. ALL OTHER DATA AND FACING ASPECTARIAN PAGE IN **EASTERN TIME (BOLD)** AND PACIFIC TIME (REGULAR).

FEBRUARY 2016

☽ Last Aspect day	ET / hr:mn / PT		asp	☽ Ingress sign	day	ET / hr:mn / PT	
1	**7:35 pm**	4:35 pm	⚹ ♃	♐	2	**10:50 am**	7:50 am
4	**5:04 am**	2:04 am	□ ♃	♑	4	**7:44 pm**	4:44 pm
6	**10:54 am**	7:54 am	△ ♃	♒	6		9:59 pm
6	**10:54 am**	7:54 am	△ ♃	♒	7	**12:59 am**	
8	**9:39 am**	6:39 am	☌ ☉	♓	9	**3:31 am**	12:31 am
10	**11:25 pm**	8:25 pm	⚹ ☿	♈	11	**4:55 am**	1:55 am
13	**5:32 am**	2:32 am	□ ☿	♉	13	**6:36 am**	3:36 am
15	**5:54 am**	2:54 am	△ ♀	♊	15	**9:35 am**	6:35 am
17	**11:37 am**	8:37 am	△ ☉	♋	17	**2:24 pm**	11:24 am
19	**9:36 am**	6:36 am	△ ♂	♌	19	**9:17 pm**	6:17 pm
21	**8:17 pm**	5:17 pm	□ ♂	♍	22	**6:24 am**	3:24 am
24	**9:22 am**	6:22 am	⚹ ♂	♎	24	**5:41 pm**	2:41 pm
26	**6:18 am**	3:18 am	☍ ♅	♏	27	**6:26 am**	3:26 am
29	**2:55 pm**	11:55 am	☌ ♂	♐	29	**6:56 pm**	3:56 pm

☽ Phases & Eclipses phase	day	ET / hr:mn / PT	
New Moon	8	**9:39 am**	6:39 am
2nd Quarter	14		11:46 pm
2nd Quarter	15	**2:46 am**	
Full Moon	22	**1:20 pm**	10:20 am

Planet Ingress	day	ET / hr:mn / PT	
☿ ♒	13	**5:43 pm**	2:43 pm
♀ ♒	16	**11:17 pm**	8:17 pm
☉ ♓	18		9:34 pm
☉ ♓	19	**12:34 am**	

Planetary Motion	day	ET / hr:mn / PT

1 MONDAY
☽ ⚺ ♄ **3:25 am** 12:25 am
☽ ☌ ♂ **5:28 am** 2:28 am
☽ ⚹ ♇ **7:20 am** 4:20 am
☽ ⚻ ♅ **9:25 am** 6:25 am
☽ ⚹ ☿ **10:01 am** 7:01 am
☽ ⚹ ♃ **7:35 pm** 4:35 pm

2 TUESDAY
No Aspects.

3 WEDNESDAY
☽ □ ♆ **3:25 am** 12:25 am
♂ ⚹ ♇ **5:53 am** 2:53 am
☽ ⚺ ♀ **12:42 pm** 9:42 am
☉ ⚹ ♄ **1:17 pm** 10:17 am
☽ ☌ ♄ **2:31 pm** 11:31 am
☽ ⚹ ☉ **2:37 pm** 11:37 am
☽ ⚺ ♇ **6:00 pm** 3:00 pm
☽ ⚺ ♂ **6:28 pm** 3:28 pm
☽ △ ♅ **7:58 pm** 4:58 pm
☽ ⚺ ☿ 9:12 pm

4 THURSDAY
☽ ⚺ ☿ **12:12 am**
☽ □ ♃ **5:04 am** 2:04 am
♀ ⚺ ♄ **8:15 am** 5:15 am

5 FRIDAY
☉ ⚺ ♇ **10:12 am** 7:12 am
☽ ⚹ ♆ **11:24 am** 8:24 am
♂ ⚻ ♅ **12:31 pm** 9:31 am
♀ ☌ ♇ **8:15 pm** 5:15 pm
☽ ⚺ ♄ **9:56 pm** 6:56 pm
☽ ☌ ♇ 10:01 pm
☽ ☌ ♀ 10:29 pm
☽ ⚺ ☉ 11:10 pm
☽ □ ♅ 11:52 pm

6 SATURDAY
☽ ☌ ♇ **1:01 am**
☽ ☌ ♀ **1:29 am**
☽ ⚺ ☉ **2:10 am**
☽ □ ♅ **2:52 am**
☽ ⚹ ♂ **3:21 am** 12:21 am
☽ ☌ ☿ **10:39 am** 7:39 am
☽ △ ♃ **10:54 am** 7:54 am
☉ ⚹ ♅ **11:39 am** 8:39 am
☿ △ ♃ **1:45 pm** 10:45 am
♀ □ ♅ **5:03 pm** 2:03 pm

7 SUNDAY
☉ □ ♂ **7:08 am** 4:08 am
♀ ⚹ ♂ **10:01 am** 7:01 am
☽ ⚺ ♆ **3:52 pm** 12:52 pm
☉ ⚺ ♀ **4:59 pm** 1:59 pm
☽ ⚹ ♄ 10:58 pm

8 MONDAY
☽ ⚹ ♄ **1:58 am**
☽ ⚺ ♇ **4:44 am** 1:44 am
☽ ⚹ ♅ **6:30 am** 3:30 am
☽ □ ♂ **8:37 am** 5:37 am
☽ ☌ ☉ **9:39 am** 6:39 am
☽ ⚺ ♀ **9:56 am** 6:56 am
☽ ⚻ ♃ **1:42 pm** 10:42 am
☽ ⚺ ☿ **5:47 pm** 2:47 pm

9 TUESDAY
☽ ☌ ♆ **6:02 pm** 3:02 pm
♀ △ ♃ 11:54 pm

10 WEDNESDAY
♀ △ ♃ **2:54 am**
☽ □ ♄ **3:59 am** 12:59 am
☽ ⚹ ♇ **6:33 am** 3:33 am
☽ ⚺ ♅ **8:18 am** 5:18 am
☽ △ ♂ **11:55 am** 8:55 am
☉ ⚻ ♃ **2:28 pm** 11:28 am
☽ ☍ ♃ **2:56 pm** 11:56 am
☽ ⚺ ☉ **2:58 pm** 11:58 am
☽ ⚹ ♀ **4:07 pm** 1:07 pm
☽ ⚹ ☿ **11:25 pm** 8:25 pm

11 THURSDAY
☽ ⚺ ♆ **7:30 pm** 4:30 pm

12 FRIDAY
☽ △ ♄ **5:35 am** 2:35 am
☽ □ ♇ **8:03 am** 5:03 am
☽ ☌ ♅ **9:50 am** 6:50 am
☽ ⚻ ♂ **3:00 pm** 12:00 pm
☽ ⚻ ♃ **4:03 pm** 1:03 pm
☽ ⚹ ☉ **8:10 pm** 5:10 pm
☽ □ ♀ **10:15 pm** 7:15 pm

13 SATURDAY
☽ □ ☿ **5:32 am** 2:32 am
♂ ⚹ ♃ **5:59 pm** 2:59 pm
☽ ⚹ ♆ **9:37 pm** 6:37 pm

14 SUNDAY
☽ ⚻ ♄ **8:03 am** 5:03 am
☽ △ ♇ **10:27 am** 7:27 am
☽ ⚺ ♅ **12:20 pm** 9:20 am
☽ △ ♃ **6:13 pm** 3:13 pm
☽ ☍ ♂ **7:13 pm** 4:13 pm
☽ □ ☉ 11:46 pm

15 MONDAY
☽ □ ☉ **2:46 am**
☽ △ ♀ **5:54 am** 2:54 am
☽ △ ☿ **1:36 pm** 10:36 am
☽ □ ♆ 10:15 pm

16 TUESDAY
☽ □ ♆ **1:15 am**
☽ ☍ ♄ **12:10 pm** 9:10 am
☽ ⚻ ♇ **2:30 pm** 11:30 am
☽ ⚹ ♅ **4:31 pm** 1:31 pm
☽ □ ♃ **10:02 pm** 7:02 pm
☽ ⚻ ♂ 10:18 pm

17 WEDNESDAY
☽ ⚻ ♂ **1:18 am**
☽ △ ☉ **11:37 am** 8:37 am
☽ ⚻ ♀ **3:56 pm** 12:56 pm
☽ ⚻ ☿ 9:26 pm

18 THURSDAY
☽ ⚻ ☿ **12:26 am**
☽ △ ♆ **6:49 am** 3:49 am
☽ ⚻ ♄ **6:15 pm** 3:15 pm
☽ ☍ ♇ **8:34 pm** 5:34 pm
☽ □ ♅ **10:42 pm** 7:42 pm

19 FRIDAY
☽ ⚹ ♃ **3:48 am** 12:48 am
☽ △ ♂ **9:36 am** 6:36 am
☽ ⚻ ☉ **11:03 pm** 8:03 pm

20 SATURDAY
☽ ☍ ♀ **4:45 am** 1:45 am
☽ ☍ ☿ **2:28 pm** 11:28 am
☽ ⚻ ♆ **2:33 pm** 11:33 am
☿ ⚺ ♆ **3:13 pm** 12:13 pm
☽ △ ♄ 11:31 pm

21 SUNDAY
☽ △ ♄ **2:31 am**
☽ ⚻ ♇ **4:48 am** 1:48 am
☽ △ ♅ **7:06 am** 4:06 am
☽ ⚺ ♃ **11:41 am** 8:41 am
☽ □ ♂ **8:17 pm** 5:17 pm

22 MONDAY
☽ ☍ ☉ **1:20 pm** 10:20 am
☽ ⚻ ♀ **8:36 pm** 5:36 pm
☽ ☍ ♆ 9:32 pm

23 TUESDAY
☽ ☍ ♆ **12:32 am**
☽ ⚻ ☿ **7:57 am** 4:57 am
☽ □ ♄ **1:02 pm** 10:02 am
☽ △ ♇ **3:17 pm** 12:17 pm
☽ ⚻ ♅ **5:46 pm** 2:46 pm
☽ ☌ ♃ **9:44 pm** 6:44 pm

24 WEDNESDAY
☽ ⚹ ♂ **9:22 am** 6:22 am
♀ ⚺ ♆ **12:32 pm** 9:32 am

25 THURSDAY
☿ ⚹ ♄ **3:05 am** 12:05 am
☽ ⚻ ☉ **6:20 am** 3:20 am
☽ ⚻ ♆ **12:35 pm** 9:35 am
☽ △ ♀ **3:17 pm** 12:17 pm
☿ ⚺ ♇ **8:53 pm** 5:53 pm
☽ ⚹ ♄ 10:29 pm

26 FRIDAY
☽ ⚹ ♄ **1:29 am**
☽ □ ♇ **3:40 am** 12:40 am
☽ △ ☿ **4:38 am** 1:38 am
☽ ☍ ♅ **6:18 am** 3:18 am
☽ ⚺ ♃ **9:30 am** 6:30 am
☿ ⚹ ♅ **6:02 pm** 3:02 pm
☽ ⚺ ♂ 9:12 pm

27 SATURDAY
☽ ⚺ ♂ **12:12 am**
☿ ⚻ ♃ **3:56 pm** 12:56 pm
☽ △ ☉ 9:51 pm
☽ △ ♆ 10:40 pm

28 SUNDAY
☽ △ ☉ **12:51 am**
☽ △ ♆ **1:40 am**
☉ ☌ ♆ **10:47 am** 7:47 am
☽ □ ♀ **11:16 am** 8:16 am
☽ ⚺ ♄ **2:35 pm** 11:35 am
☽ ⚹ ♇ **4:39 pm** 1:39 pm
☽ ⚻ ♅ **7:24 pm** 4:24 pm
☽ ⚹ ♃ **9:42 pm** 6:42 pm
☽ □ ☿ 11:30 pm

29 MONDAY
☽ □ ☿ **2:30 am**
☽ ☌ ♂ **2:55 pm** 11:55 am
♀ ⚹ ♄ **8:07 pm** 5:07 pm

Eastern time in bold type
Pacific time in medium type

FEBRUARY 2016

DATE	SID.TIME	SUN	MOON	NODE	MERCURY	VENUS	MARS	JUPITER	SATURN	URANUS	NEPTUNE	PLUTO	CERES	PALLAS	JUNO	VESTA	CHIRON
1 M	8 42 35	11 ≈ 32 32	9 ♏ 58	22 ♍ 35 ℞	17 ♑ 02	10 ♑ 02	14 ♏ 58	22 ♍ 20	14 ♐ 08	17 ♈ 08	8 ♓ 28	16 ♑ 06	1 ♓ 15	3 ≈ 21	12 ♏ 43	15 ♈ 57	18 ♓ 46
2 T	8 46 31	12 33 27	21 58	22 35	17 43	11 16	15 28	22 16 ℞	14 12	17 10	8 30	16 08	1 38	3 42	12 52	16 18	18 49
3 W	8 50 28	13 34 21	4 ♐ 12	22 33	18 28	12 30	15 57	22 11	14 17	17 12	8 32	16 10	2 01	4 04	13 01	16 40	18 52
4 Th	8 54 25	14 35 14	16 43	22 29	19 18	13 44	16 27	22 06	14 22	17 14	8 34	16 12	2 24	4 26	13 10	17 02	18 55
5 F	8 58 21	15 36 06	29 36	22 23	20 10	14 58	16 56	22 01	14 26	17 16	8 36	16 13	2 48	4 47	13 18	17 24	18 58
6 Sa	9 2 18	16 36 57	12 ♑ 52	22 17	21 06	16 12	17 25	21 56	14 31	17 18	8 38	16 15	3 11	5 09	13 26	17 46	19 02
7 Su	9 6 14	17 37 47	26 32	22 11	22 05	17 26	17 54	21 51	14 35	17 20	8 41	16 17	3 34	5 30	13 34	18 09	19 05
8 M	9 10 11	18 38 36	10 ≈ 33	22 06	23 07	18 40	18 23	21 46	14 40	17 22	8 43	16 19	3 58	5 52	13 41	18 31	19 08
9 T	9 14 7	19 39 24	24 52	22 02	24 11	19 54	18 51	21 40	14 44	17 24	8 45	16 21	4 21	6 13	13 49	18 54	19 11
10 W	9 18 4	20 40 11	9 ♓ 22	22 00 D	25 18	21 08	19 20	21 34	14 48	17 26	8 47	16 23	4 44	6 34	13 55	19 16	19 15
11 Th	9 22 0	21 40 56	23 58	21 59	26 27	22 22	19 48	21 28	14 52	17 28	8 49	16 24	5 08	6 56	14 02	19 39	19 18
12 F	9 25 57	22 41 40	8 ♈ 34	22 00	27 37	23 36	20 16	21 22	14 56	17 31	8 52	16 26	5 31	7 17	14 08	20 02	19 21
13 Sa	9 29 54	23 42 22	23 03	22 02	28 50	24 50	20 44	21 16	15 00	17 33	8 54	16 28	5 55	7 38	14 15	20 25	19 25
14 Su	9 33 50	24 43 02	7 ♉ 23	22 03	0 ≈ 04	26 04	21 11	21 10	15 04	17 35	8 56	16 30	6 18	7 59	14 20	20 48	19 28
15 M	9 37 47	25 43 41	21 31	22 04 ℞	1 20	27 18	21 39	21 04	15 08	17 38	8 58	16 31	6 42	8 20	14 26	21 11	19 32
16 T	9 41 43	26 44 18	5 ♊ 26	22 04	2 37	28 33	22 06	20 57	15 12	17 40	9 00	16 33	7 05	8 41	14 31	21 34	19 35
17 W	9 45 40	27 44 53	19 07	22 02	3 56	29 47	22 33	20 50	15 15	17 43	9 03	16 35	7 29	9 03	14 36	21 57	19 39
18 Th	9 49 36	28 45 27	2 ♋ 34	22 00	5 16	1 ≈ 01	23 00	20 44	15 19	17 45	9 05	16 36	7 52	9 23	14 40	22 21	19 42
19 F	9 53 33	29 45 59	15 47	21 57	6 38	2 15	23 26	20 37	15 22	17 48	9 07	16 38	8 16	9 44	14 45	22 44	19 45
20 Sa	9 57 29	0 ♓ 46 29	28 46	21 53	8 01	3 29	23 53	20 30	15 26	17 50	9 09	16 40	8 40	10 05	14 49	23 08	19 49
21 Su	10 1 26	1 46 57	11 ♌ 33	21 50	9 25	4 43	24 19	20 23	15 29	17 53	9 12	16 41	9 03	10 26	14 52	23 31	19 53
22 M	10 5 23	2 47 23	24 06	21 47	10 50	5 58	24 45	20 16	15 32	17 55	9 14	16 43	9 27	10 47	14 55	23 55	19 56
23 T	10 9 19	3 47 48	6 ♍ 28	21 46	12 16	7 12	25 10	20 09	15 35	17 58	9 16	16 44	9 50	11 07	14 58	24 19	20 00
24 W	10 13 16	4 48 12	18 38	21 45 D	13 44	8 26	25 36	20 01	15 38	18 01	9 19	16 46	10 14	11 28	15 01	24 43	20 03
25 Th	10 17 12	5 48 33	0 ♎ 39	21 45	15 12	9 40	26 01	19 54	15 41	18 03	9 21	16 47	10 38	11 49	15 03	25 07	20 07
26 F	10 21 9	6 48 53	12 33	21 46	16 42	10 54	26 26	19 47	15 44	18 06	9 23	16 49	11 01	12 09	15 05	25 31	20 10
27 Sa	10 25 5	7 49 12	24 22	21 47	18 13	12 09	26 51	19 39	15 47	18 09	9 25	16 50	11 25	12 30	15 07	25 55	20 14
28 Su	10 29 2	8 49 29	6 ♏ 11	21 49	19 44	13 23	27 15	19 32	15 50	18 12	9 28	16 52	11 49	12 50	15 08	26 19	20 18
29 M	10 32 58	9 49 45	18 03	21 50	21 17	14 37	27 39	19 24	15 52	18 15	9 30	16 53	12 12	13 10	15 09	26 43	20 21

EPHEMERIS CALCULATED FOR 12 MIDNIGHT GREENWICH MEAN TIME. ALL OTHER DATA AND FACING ASPECTARIAN PAGE IN **EASTERN TIME (BOLD)** AND PACIFIC TIME (REGULAR).

MARCH 2016

☽ Last Aspect day	ET / hr:mn / PT		asp	☽ Ingress sign	day	ET / hr:mn / PT	
2	**9:55 pm**	6:55 pm	✶☿	♑	3	**5:01 am**	2:01 am
5	**11:05 am**	8:05 am	✶♂	♒	5	**11:22 am**	8:22 am
7	**3:46 am**	12:46 am	☌♀	♓	7	**2:08 pm**	11:08 am
8	**8:54 pm**	5:54 pm	☌☉	♈	9	**2:40 pm**	11:40 am
11	**1:24 pm**	10:24 am	✶♀	♉	11	**2:44 pm**	11:44 am
13	**5:46 am**	2:46 am	✶☉	♊	13	**5:03 pm**	2:03 pm
15	**1:03 pm**	10:03 am	□☉	♋	15	**8:57 pm**	5:57 pm
17		9:09 pm	△☉	♌	18		12:54 am
18	**12:09 am**		△☉	♌	18	**3:54 am**	
19	**4:43 pm**	1:43 pm	△♅	♍	20	**1:39 pm**	10:39 am

☽ Last Aspect day	ET / hr:mn / PT		asp	☽ Ingress sign	day	ET / hr:mn / PT	
21	**11:55 pm**	8:55 pm	△♇	♎	22		10:23 pm
21	**11:55 pm**	8:55 pm	△♇	♎	23	**1:23 am**	
24	**4:55 pm**	1:55 pm	☍♅	♏	25	**2:09 pm**	11:09 am
27	**3:25 am**	12:25 am	△♀	♐	27		11:46 pm
27	**3:25 am**	12:25 am	△♀	♐	28	**2:46 am**	
29	**9:55 pm**	6:55 pm	□♀	♑	30	**1:45 pm**	10:45 am

☽ Phases & Eclipses phase	day	ET / hr:mn / PT	
4th Quarter	1	**6:11 pm**	3:11 pm
New Moon	8	**8:54 pm**	5:54 pm
●	8	18° ♓ 55'	
2nd Quarter	15	**1:03 pm**	10:03 am
Full Moon	23	**8:01 am**	5:01 am
●	23	3° ♎ 10'	
4th Quarter	31	**11:17 am**	8:17 am

Planet Ingress		day	ET / hr:mn / PT	
☿	♓	5	**5:23 am**	2:23 am
♂	♐	5	**9:29 pm**	6:29 pm
⚶	♉	7	**7:53 pm**	4:53 pm
♀	♓	12	**5:24 am**	2:24 am
☉	♈	19		9:30 pm
☉	♈	20	**12:30 am**	
☿	♈	21	**8:19 pm**	5:19 pm

Planetary Motion		day	ET / hr:mn / PT	
⚵	℞	2	**5:40 am**	2:40 am
♄	℞	25	**6:01 am**	3:01 am

1 TUESDAY
☽ □ ♆ **1:49 pm** 10:49 am
♀ ⚺ ♇ **3:50 pm** 12:50 pm
☽ □ ☉ **6:11 pm** 3:11 pm
☽ ☌ ♄ 11:15 pm

2 WEDNESDAY
☽ ☌ ♄ **2:15 am**
☽ ⚺ ♇ **4:09 am** 1:09 am
☽ ✶ ♀ **5:29 am** 2:29 am
☽ △ ♅ **6:54 am** 3:54 am
☽ □ ♃ **8:15 am** 5:15 am
♀ ✶ ♅ **8:13 pm** 5:13 pm
☽ ✶ ☿ **9:55 pm** 6:55 pm

3 THURSDAY
☽ ⚺ ♂ **3:04 am** 12:04 am
♀ ⚻ ♃ **7:04 am** 4:04 am
☽ ✶ ♆ **10:57 pm** 7:57 pm

4 FRIDAY
☽ ✶ ☉ **7:32 am** 4:32 am
☽ ⚺ ♄ **10:35 am** 7:35 am
☽ ☌ ♇ **12:17 pm** 9:17 am
☽ □ ♅ **2:58 pm** 11:58 am
☽ △ ♃ **3:30 pm** 12:30 pm
☽ ⚺ ♀ **7:08 pm** 4:08 pm
☿ □ ♂ 9:43 pm

5 SATURDAY
☿ □ ♂ **12:43 am**
☽ ✶ ♂ **11:05 am** 8:05 am

☽ ⚺ ☿ **12:11 pm** 9:11 am
☉ □ ♄ 10:04 pm

6 SUNDAY
☉ □ ♄ **1:04 am**
☽ ⚺ ♆ **4:12 am** 1:12 am
♃ ⚻ ♅ **6:45 am** 3:45 am
☽ ✶ ♄ **3:01 pm** 12:01 pm
☽ ⚺ ☉ **4:03 pm** 1:03 pm
☽ ⚺ ♇ **4:34 pm** 1:34 pm
☽ ⚻ ♃ **7:01 pm** 4:01 pm
☽ ✶ ♅ **7:11 pm** 4:11 pm
☉ ✶ ♇ **11:41 pm** 8:41 pm

7 MONDAY
☽ ☌ ♀ **3:46 am** 12:46 am
☽ □ ♂ **3:11 pm** 12:11 pm
☽ ☌ ☿ **9:29 pm** 6:29 pm

8 TUESDAY
☉ ☍ ♃ **5:57 am** 2:57 am
☽ ☌ ♆ **6:11 am** 3:11 am
☉ ⚺ ♅ **2:58 pm** 11:58 am
☽ □ ♄ **4:29 pm** 1:29 pm
☽ ✶ ♇ **5:56 pm** 2:56 pm
☽ ☍ ♃ **7:47 pm** 4:47 pm
☽ ⚺ ♅ **8:32 pm** 5:32 pm
☽ ☌ ☉ **8:54 pm** 5:54 pm

9 WEDNESDAY
☽ ⚺ ♀ **9:01 am** 6:01 am
☽ △ ♂ **4:51 pm** 1:51 pm

10 THURSDAY
☽ ⚺ ☿ **4:05 am** 1:05 am
☽ ⚺ ♆ **6:29 am** 3:29 am
☽ △ ♄ **4:36 pm** 1:36 pm
☽ □ ♇ **6:02 pm** 3:02 pm
☽ ⚻ ♃ **7:24 pm** 4:24 pm
☽ ☌ ♅ **8:43 pm** 5:43 pm
☽ ⚺ ☉ 9:22 pm
☿ ☌ ♆ 10:01 pm

11 FRIDAY
☽ ⚺ ☉ **12:22 am**
☿ ☌ ♆ **1:01 am**
☽ ✶ ♀ **1:24 pm** 10:24 am
☽ ⚻ ♂ **6:04 pm** 3:04 pm

12 SATURDAY
☽ ✶ ♆ **6:54 am** 3:54 am
☽ ✶ ☿ **10:56 am** 7:56 am
☽ ⚻ ♄ **5:14 pm** 2:14 pm
☽ △ ♇ **6:41 pm** 3:41 pm
☽ △ ♃ **7:36 pm** 4:36 pm
☽ ⚺ ♅ **9:34 pm** 6:34 pm

13 SUNDAY
☽ ✶ ☉ **5:46 am** 2:46 am
☽ □ ♀ **8:21 pm** 5:21 pm
☽ ☍ ♂ **9:42 pm** 6:42 pm

14 MONDAY
☽ □ ♆ **10:06 am** 7:06 am
☿ □ ♄ **3:26 pm** 12:26 pm

♀ □ ♂ **4:48 pm** 1:48 pm
☽ ☍ ♄ **8:54 pm** 5:54 pm
☽ □ ☿ **9:44 pm** 6:44 pm
☽ ⚻ ♇ **10:25 pm** 7:25 pm
☽ □ ♃ **10:51 pm** 7:51 pm
☽ ✶ ♅ 10:36 pm
☿ ✶ ♇ 11:58 pm

15 TUESDAY
☽ ✶ ♅ **1:36 am**
☿ ✶ ♇ **2:58 am**
☿ ☍ ♃ **5:42 am** 2:42 am
☽ □ ☉ **1:03 pm** 10:03 am

16 WEDNESDAY
☽ ⚻ ♂ **3:07 am** 12:07 am
☿ ⚺ ♅ **3:22 am** 12:22 am
☽ △ ♀ **5:44 am** 2:44 am
☽ △ ♆ **3:09 pm** 12:09 pm
♃ △ ♇ **4:06 pm** 1:06 pm
☽ ⚻ ♄ 11:31 pm

17 THURSDAY
☽ ⚻ ♄ **2:31 am**
☽ ✶ ♃ **4:00 am** 1:00 am
☽ ☍ ♇ **4:08 am** 1:08 am
☽ □ ♅ **7:39 am** 4:39 am
☽ △ ☿ **12:17 pm** 9:17 am
☽ △ ☉ 9:09 pm

18 FRIDAY
☽ △ ☉ **12:09 am**
☽ △ ♂ **11:46 am** 8:46 am
☽ ⚻ ♀ **7:13 pm** 4:13 pm
☽ ⚻ ♆ **11:17 pm** 8:17 pm

19 SATURDAY
☽ △ ♄ **11:08 am** 8:08 am
☽ ⚺ ♃ **12:04 pm** 9:04 am
☽ ⚻ ♇ **12:51 pm** 9:51 am
☽ △ ♅ **4:43 pm** 1:43 pm

20 SUNDAY
☽ ⚻ ☿ **7:50 am** 4:50 am
♀ ☌ ♆ **1:45 pm** 10:45 am
☽ ⚻ ☉ **2:49 pm** 11:49 am
☽ □ ♂ **11:13 pm** 8:13 pm

21 MONDAY
☽ ☍ ♆ **9:59 am** 6:59 am
☽ ☍ ♀ **12:14 pm** 9:14 am
☽ □ ♄ **10:07 pm** 7:07 pm
☽ ☌ ♃ **10:27 pm** 7:27 pm
☽ △ ♇ **11:55 pm** 8:55 pm

22 TUESDAY
☽ ⚻ ♅ **4:07 am** 1:07 am

23 WEDNESDAY
♃ □ ♄ **6:15 am** 3:15 am
☽ ☍ ☿ **7:11 am** 4:11 am
☽ ☍ ☉ **8:01 am** 5:01 am
☽ ✶ ♂ **12:33 pm** 9:33 am
☉ ☌ ☿ **4:11 pm** 1:11 pm
☽ ⚻ ♆ **10:22 pm** 7:22 pm

24 THURSDAY
☽ ⚻ ♀ **7:30 am** 4:30 am
☽ ⚺ ♃ **10:16 am** 7:16 am
☽ ✶ ♄ **10:33 am** 7:33 am
☽ □ ♇ **12:26 pm** 9:26 am

☽ ☍ ♅ **4:55 pm** 1:55 pm
☿ △ ♂ **6:45 pm** 3:45 pm

25 FRIDAY
♀ ☍ ♃ **7:58 am** 4:58 am
♀ □ ♄ **12:48 pm** 9:48 am
☽ ⚻ ☉ 11:23 pm
☽ ⚺ ♂ 11:39 pm

26 SATURDAY
☽ ⚻ ☉ **2:23 am**
☽ ⚺ ♂ **2:39 am**
☉ △ ♂ **6:33 am** 3:33 am
♀ ✶ ♇ **7:12 am** 4:12 am
☽ ⚻ ☿ **8:28 am** 5:28 am
☽ △ ♆ **11:25 am** 8:25 am
☽ ✶ ♃ **10:31 pm** 7:31 pm
☽ ⚺ ♄ **11:24 pm** 8:24 pm
☽ ✶ ♇ 10:20 pm
☿ ⚺ ♆ 10:55 pm

27 SUNDAY
☽ ✶ ♇ **1:20 am**
☿ ⚺ ♆ **1:55 am**
☽ △ ♀ **3:25 am** 12:25 am
☽ ⚻ ♅ **6:02 am** 3:02 am

28 MONDAY
♀ ⚺ ♅ **5:34 am** 2:34 am
☽ ☌ ♂ **4:12 pm** 1:12 pm
☽ △ ☉ **8:11 pm** 5:11 pm
☽ □ ♆ **11:49 pm** 8:49 pm

29 TUESDAY
☽ △ ☿ **8:56 am** 5:56 am
☽ □ ♃ **9:55 am** 6:55 am
☽ ☌ ♄ **11:18 am** 8:18 am
☽ ⚺ ♇ **1:15 pm** 10:15 am
☿ ⚻ ♃ **2:36 pm** 11:36 am
☽ △ ♅ **6:02 pm** 3:02 pm
☽ □ ♀ **9:55 pm** 6:55 pm
☿ △ ♄ **11:02 pm** 8:02 pm

30 WEDNESDAY
☿ □ ♇ **10:53 am** 7:53 am
☉ ⚺ ♆ **6:08 pm** 3:08 pm

31 THURSDAY
☽ ⚺ ♂ **3:31 am** 12:31 am
☽ ✶ ♆ **10:00 am** 7:00 am
☽ □ ☉ **11:17 am** 8:17 am
☿ ☌ ♅ **4:49 pm** 1:49 pm
☽ △ ♃ **6:57 pm** 3:57 pm
☽ ⚺ ♄ **8:41 pm** 5:41 pm
☽ ☌ ♇ **10:37 pm** 7:37 pm

Eastern time in bold type
Pacific time in medium type

MARCH 2016

DATE	SID.TIME	SUN	MOON	NODE	MERCURY	VENUS	MARS	JUPITER	SATURN	URANUS	NEPTUNE	PLUTO	CERES	PALLAS	JUNO	VESTA	CHIRON
1 T	10 36 55	10 ♓ 49 59	0 ♐ 02	21 ♍ 50	22 ♒ 51	15 ♒ 51	28 ♏ 03	19 ♍ 16 ℞	15 ♐ 55	18 ♈ 17	9 ♓ 32	16 ♑ 54	12 ♓ 36	13 ♒ 31	15 ♏ 10	27 ♈ 07	20 ♓ 25
2 W	10 40 52	11 50 11	12 13	21 51 ℞	24 26	17 05	28 26	19 09	15 57	18 20	9 34	16 56	13 00	13 51	15 10 ℞	27 32	20 28
3 Th	10 44 48	12 50 22	24 42	21 50	26 02	18 20	28 50	19 01	15 59	18 23	9 37	16 57	13 23	14 11	15 10	27 56	20 32
4 F	10 48 45	13 50 32	7 ♑ 31	21 50	27 39	19 34	29 13	18 53	16 01	18 26	9 39	16 59	13 47	14 31	15 10	28 21	20 36
5 Sa	10 52 41	14 50 40	20 44	21 49	29 17	20 48	29 35	18 45	16 03	18 29	9 41	17 00	14 11	14 51	15 09	28 45	20 39
6 Su	10 56 38	15 50 47	4 ♒ 23	21 48	0 ♓ 56	22 02	29 58	18 38	16 05	18 32	9 44	17 01	14 34	15 11	15 08	29 10	20 43
7 M	11 0 34	16 50 51	18 29	21 48	2 37	23 17	0 ♐ 20	18 30	16 07	18 35	9 46	17 02	14 58	15 31	15 07	29 34	20 47
8 T	11 4 31	17 50 54	2 ♓ 58	21 47	4 18	24 31	0 41	18 22	16 09	18 38	9 48	17 04	15 21	15 51	15 05	29 59	20 50
9 W	11 8 27	18 50 55	17 45	21 47 D	6 01	25 45	1 03	18 14	16 11	18 41	9 50	17 05	15 45	16 10	15 03	0 ♉ 24	20 54
10 Th	11 12 24	19 50 55	2 ♈ 43	21 47	7 44	26 59	1 24	18 06	16 12	18 44	9 53	17 06	16 09	16 30	15 01	0 49	20 58
11 F	11 16 21	20 50 52	17 43	21 47 ℞	9 29	28 14	1 44	17 58	16 14	18 48	9 55	17 07	16 32	16 49	14 58	1 14	21 01
12 Sa	11 20 17	21 50 47	2 ♉ 39	21 47	11 15	29 28	2 05	17 51	16 15	18 51	9 57	17 08	16 56	17 09	14 55	1 38	21 05
13 Su	11 24 14	22 50 40	17 21	21 47	13 02	0 ♓ 42	2 25	17 43	16 17	18 54	9 59	17 09	17 20	17 28	14 51	2 03	21 09
14 M	11 28 10	23 50 31	1 ♊ 45	21 47	14 50	1 56	2 44	17 35	16 18	18 57	10 02	17 10	17 43	17 48	14 47	2 28	21 12
15 T	11 32 7	24 50 20	15 48	21 47 D	16 40	3 11	3 03	17 27	16 19	19 00	10 04	17 11	18 07	18 07	14 43	2 54	21 16
16 W	11 36 3	25 50 06	29 28	21 47	18 30	4 25	3 22	17 20	16 20	19 03	10 06	17 12	18 30	18 26	14 38	3 19	21 20
17 Th	11 40 0	26 49 50	12 ♋ 47	21 47	20 22	5 39	3 40	17 12	16 21	19 07	10 08	17 13	18 54	18 45	14 33	3 44	21 23
18 F	11 43 56	27 49 32	25 47	21 48	22 15	6 53	3 58	17 04	16 22	19 10	10 10	17 14	19 18	19 04	14 28	4 09	21 27
19 Sa	11 47 53	28 49 12	8 ♌ 30	21 48	24 09	8 07	4 16	16 57	16 22	19 13	10 13	17 15	19 41	19 23	14 23	4 34	21 31
20 Su	11 51 49	29 48 49	20 58	21 49	26 04	9 22	4 33	16 49	16 23	19 16	10 15	17 16	20 05	19 41	14 17	5 00	21 34
21 M	11 55 46	0 ♈ 48 24	3 ♍ 14	21 50	28 01	10 36	4 49	16 42	16 23	19 20	10 17	17 17	20 28	20 00	14 10	5 25	21 38
22 T	11 59 43	1 47 57	15 20	21 50 ℞	29 58	11 50	5 06	16 34	16 24	19 23	10 19	17 18	20 52	20 19	14 04	5 50	21 41
23 W	12 3 39	2 47 28	27 19	21 50	1 ♈ 57	13 04	5 21	16 27	16 24	19 26	10 21	17 19	21 15	20 37	13 57	6 16	21 45
24 Th	12 7 36	3 46 57	9 ♎ 13	21 50	3 57	14 18	5 37	16 20	16 24	19 30	10 23	17 19	21 39	20 55	13 50	6 41	21 49
25 F	12 11 32	4 46 23	21 04	21 48	5 57	15 32	5 51	16 13	16 24 ℞	19 33	10 26	17 20	22 02	21 14	13 42	7 07	21 52
26 Sa	12 15 29	5 45 48	2 ♏ 53	21 47	7 58	16 47	6 06	16 06	16 24	19 36	10 28	17 21	22 25	21 32	13 34	7 32	21 56
27 Su	12 19 25	6 45 11	14 43	21 44	10 00	18 01	6 20	15 59	16 24	19 40	10 30	17 22	22 49	21 50	13 26	7 58	21 59
28 M	12 23 22	7 44 32	26 37	21 42	12 02	19 15	6 33	15 52	16 24	19 43	10 32	17 22	23 12	22 08	13 18	8 23	22 03
29 T	12 27 18	8 43 52	8 ♐ 39	21 40	14 05	20 29	6 46	15 45	16 24	19 46	10 34	17 23	23 36	22 26	13 09	8 49	22 07
30 W	12 31 15	9 43 09	20 50	21 38	16 08	21 43	6 58	15 39	16 23	19 50	10 36	17 23	23 59	22 44	13 00	9 14	22 10
31 Th	12 35 12	10 42 25	3 ♑ 16	21 37 D	18 10	22 57	7 10	15 32	16 23	19 53	10 38	17 24	24 22	23 01	12 50	9 40	22 14

EPHEMERIS CALCULATED FOR 12 MIDNIGHT GREENWICH MEAN TIME. ALL OTHER DATA AND FACING ASPECTARIAN PAGE IN **EASTERN TIME (BOLD)** AND PACIFIC TIME (REGULAR).

APRIL 2016

☽ Last Aspect day	ET / hr:mn / PT	asp	☽ Ingress sign	day	ET / hr:mn / PT
1	**12:39 pm** 9:39 am	✶ ♀	♒	1	**9:37 pm** 6:37 pm
3	**7:16 pm** 4:16 pm	✶ ☿	♓	3	10:45 pm
3	**7:16 pm** 4:16 pm	✶ ☿	♓	4	**1:45 am**
5	**6:33 am** 3:33 am	✶ ♇	♈	5	11:46 pm
5	**6:33 am** 3:33 am	✶ ♇	♈	6	**2:46 am**
7	**10:56 am** 7:56 am	☌ ♅	♉	7	11:10 pm
7	**10:56 am** 7:56 am	☌ ♅	♉	8	**2:10 am**
9	**5:49 am** 2:49 am	△ ♇	♊	9	10:59 pm
9	**5:49 am** 2:49 am	△ ♇	♊	10	**1:59 am**
11	**2:57 pm** 11:57 am	✶ ☉	♋	12	**4:07 am** 1:07 am
13	**11:59 pm** 8:59 pm	□ ☉	♌	14	**9:53 am** 6:53 am
16	**1:48 pm** 10:48 am	△ ☉	♍	16	**7:23 pm** 4:23 pm
18	**8:29 am** 5:29 am	△ ☿	♎	19	**7:24 am** 4:24 am
20	11:13 am	☍ ♅	♏	21	**8:17 pm** 5:17 pm
21	**2:13 am**	☍ ♅	♏	21	**8:17 pm** 5:17 pm
23	**5:46 pm** 2:46 pm	☍ ☿	♐	24	**8:46 am** 5:46 am
26	**11:51 am** 8:51 am	△ ♀	♑	26	**7:54 pm** 4:54 pm
29	**3:07 am** 12:07 am	□ ♀	♒	29	**4:47 am** 1:47 am
30	**10:56 pm** 7:56 pm	□ ☿	♓	5/1	**10:33 am** 7:33 am

☽ Phases & Eclipses phase	day	ET / hr:mn / PT
New Moon	7	**7:24 am** 4:24 am
2nd Quarter	13	**11:59 pm** 8:59 pm
Full Moon	21	10:24 pm
Full Moon	22	**1:24 am**
4th Quarter	29	**11:29 pm** 8:29 pm

Planet Ingress		day	ET / hr:mn / PT
♀	♈	5	**12:50 pm** 9:50 am
☿	♉	5	**7:09 pm** 4:09 pm
⚳	♈	14	**10:52 am** 7:52 am
☉	♉	19	**11:29 am** 8:29 am
♀	♓	26	**3:54 am** 12:54 am
♀	♉	29	**8:36 pm** 5:36 pm

Planetary Motion	day	ET / hr:mn / PT
♂ R	17	**8:14 am** 5:14 am
♇ R	18	**3:26 am** 12:26 am
☿ R	28	**1:20 pm** 10:20 am

1 FRIDAY
☽ □ ♅ **3:20 am** 12:20 am
☽ □ ☿ **5:13 am** 2:13 am
☽ ✶ ♀ **12:39 pm** 9:39 am

2 SATURDAY
☽ ✶ ♂ **11:14 am** 8:14 am
☽ ⚺ ♆ **4:41 pm** 1:41 pm
☽ ✶ ☉ **9:58 pm** 6:58 pm
☽ ⚻ ♃ 9:30 pm
☽ ✶ ♄ 11:28 pm

3 SUNDAY
☽ ⚻ ♃ **12:30 am**
☽ ✶ ♄ **2:28 am**
☽ ⚺ ♇ **4:21 am** 1:21 am
☽ ✶ ♅ **8:56 am** 5:56 am
☽ ✶ ☿ **7:16 pm** 4:16 pm
☽ ⚺ ♀ **10:26 pm** 7:26 pm

4 MONDAY
☉ ⚻ ♃ **6:19 am** 3:19 am
☽ □ ♂ **3:01 pm** 12:01 pm
☽ ☌ ♆ **7:42 pm** 4:42 pm
☽ ☍ ♃ 11:34 pm

5 TUESDAY
☽ ☍ ♃ **2:34 am**
☽ ⚺ ☉ **4:09 am** 1:09 am
☽ □ ♄ **4:42 am** 1:42 am
☽ ✶ ♇ **6:33 am** 2:33 am

☽ ⚺ ♅ **11:02 am** 8:02 am
☉ △ ♄ **12:09 pm** 9:09 am

6 WEDNESDAY
☽ ⚺ ☿ **3:51 am** 12:51 am
☽ ☌ ♀ **4:00 am** 1:00 am
☿ ⚺ ♀ **7:14 am** 4:14 am
☽ △ ♂ **3:51 pm** 12:51 pm
☉ □ ♇ **4:13 pm** 1:13 pm
☽ ⚺ ♆ **8:01 pm** 5:01 pm
☽ ⚻ ♃ 11:14 pm

7 THURSDAY
☽ ⚻ ♃ **2:14 am**
☽ △ ♄ **4:33 am** 1:33 am
☽ □ ♇ **6:25 am** 3:25 am
☽ ☌ ☉ **7:24 am** 4:24 am
☽ ☌ ♅ **10:56 am** 7:56 am

8 FRIDAY
☽ ⚺ ♀ **7:35 am** 4:35 am
☽ ☌ ☿ **9:41 am** 6:41 am
☽ ⚻ ♂ **3:31 pm** 12:31 pm
☽ ✶ ♆ **7:26 pm** 4:26 pm
☽ △ ♃ 10:18 pm

9 SATURDAY
☽ △ ♃ **1:18 am**
☽ ⚻ ♄ **3:51 am** 12:51 am
☽ △ ♇ **5:49 am** 2:49 am
☽ ⚺ ☉ **10:07 am** 7:07 am
☽ ⚺ ♅ **10:34 am** 7:34 am
☉ ☌ ♅ **5:27 pm** 2:27 pm

10 SUNDAY
☽ ✶ ♀ **11:59 am** 8:59 am
☽ ⚺ ☿ **4:01 pm** 1:01 pm
☽ ☍ ♂ **4:06 pm** 1:06 pm
☿ ⚻ ♂ **4:46 pm** 1:46 pm
☽ □ ♆ **7:59 pm** 4:59 pm
☽ □ ♃ 10:44 pm

11 MONDAY
☽ □ ♃ **1:44 am**
☽ ☍ ♄ **4:36 am** 1:36 am
☽ ⚻ ♇ **6:47 am** 3:47 am
☽ ✶ ♅ **11:58 am** 8:58 am
☽ ✶ ☉ **2:57 pm** 11:57 am

12 TUESDAY
☿ ✶ ♆ **5:40 am** 2:40 am
♀ △ ♂ **3:16 pm** 12:16 pm
☽ ⚻ ♂ **7:26 pm** 4:26 pm
☽ □ ♀ **7:50 pm** 4:50 pm
☽ △ ♆ **11:28 pm** 8:28 pm
☽ ✶ ☿ 10:35 pm

13 WEDNESDAY
☽ ✶ ☿ **1:35 am**
☽ ✶ ♃ **5:13 am** 2:13 am
☽ ⚻ ♄ **8:29 am** 5:29 am
☽ ☍ ♇ **10:58 am** 7:58 am
☽ □ ♅ **4:45 pm** 1:45 pm
☽ □ ☉ **11:59 pm** 8:59 pm

14 THURSDAY
☿ △ ♃ **11:27 am** 8:27 am

♀ ⚺ ♆ **12:36 pm** 9:36 am
☽ △ ♂ 11:32 pm

15 FRIDAY
☽ △ ♂ **2:32 am**
☽ ⚻ ♆ **6:48 am** 3:48 am
☽ △ ♀ **8:44 am** 5:44 am
☽ ⚺ ♃ **12:31 pm** 9:31 am
☽ □ ☿ **3:30 pm** 12:30 pm
☽ △ ♄ **4:12 pm** 1:12 pm
☽ ⚻ ♇ **6:59 pm** 3:59 pm
☿ ⚻ ♄ **10:28 pm** 7:28 pm
☽ △ ♅ 10:26 pm

16 SATURDAY
☽ △ ♅ **1:26 am**
☽ △ ☉ **1:48 pm** 10:48 am
♀ ⚻ ♃ **9:26 pm** 6:26 pm

17 SUNDAY
☿ △ ♇ **5:23 am** 2:23 am
☽ □ ♂ **1:00 pm** 10:00 am
☽ ☍ ♆ **5:34 pm** 2:34 pm
☽ ☌ ♃ **11:04 pm** 8:04 pm
☽ ⚻ ♀ 11:10 pm

18 MONDAY
☽ ⚻ ♀ **2:10 am**
☽ □ ♄ **3:04 am** 12:04 am
☽ △ ♇ **6:10 am** 3:10 am
☽ △ ☿ **8:29 am** 5:29 am
♀ △ ♄ **10:37 am** 7:37 am
☽ ⚻ ♅ **1:08 pm** 10:08 am

19 TUESDAY
☽ ⚻ ☉ **7:02 am** 4:02 am
♀ □ ♇ **4:51 pm** 1:51 pm
☽ ✶ ♂ 10:21 pm

20 WEDNESDAY
☽ ✶ ♂ **1:21 am**
☽ ⚻ ♆ **6:14 am** 3:14 am
☽ ⚺ ♃ **11:23 am** 8:23 am
☽ ✶ ♄ **3:32 pm** 12:32 pm
☽ □ ♇ **6:52 pm** 3:52 pm
☽ ☍ ♀ **9:54 pm** 6:54 pm
☽ ⚻ ☿ 10:55 pm
☽ ☍ ♅ 11:13 pm

21 THURSDAY
☽ ⚻ ☿ **1:55 am**
☽ ☍ ♅ **2:13 am**
☿ ⚺ ♅ **7:27 am** 4:27 am
☽ ☍ ☉ 10:24 pm

22 FRIDAY
☽ ☍ ☉ **1:24 am**
☽ ⚺ ♂ **1:59 pm** 10:59 am
♀ ☌ ♅ **5:00 pm** 2:00 pm
☽ △ ♆ **7:14 pm** 4:14 pm
☽ ✶ ♃ **11:57 pm** 8:57 pm

23 SATURDAY
☽ ⚺ ♄ **4:08 am** 1:08 am
☽ ✶ ♇ **7:38 am** 4:38 am
☽ ⚻ ♅ **3:13 pm** 12:13 pm
☽ ⚻ ♀ **5:39 pm** 2:39 pm

☽ ☍ ☿ **5:46 pm** 2:46 pm
☿ ⚺ ♀ **7:18 pm** 4:18 pm

24 SUNDAY
☽ ⚻ ☉ **7:06 pm** 4:06 pm
☽ ☌ ♂ 10:46 pm

25 MONDAY
☽ ☌ ♂ **1:46 am**
☽ □ ♆ **7:26 am** 4:26 am
☽ □ ♃ **11:42 am** 8:42 am
☽ ☌ ♄ **3:47 pm** 12:47 pm
☽ ⚺ ♇ **7:26 pm** 4:26 pm

26 TUESDAY
☽ △ ♅ **3:06 am** 12:06 am
☽ ⚻ ☿ **6:59 am** 3:59 am
☽ △ ♀ **11:51 am** 8:51 am

27 WEDNESDAY
☽ △ ☉ **10:53 am** 7:53 am
☽ ⚺ ♂ **11:50 am** 8:50 am
☽ ✶ ♆ **5:56 pm** 2:56 pm
☉ ⚻ ♂ **9:42 pm** 6:42 pm
☽ △ ♃ **9:45 pm** 6:45 pm
☽ ⚺ ♄ 10:38 pm

28 THURSDAY
☽ ⚺ ♄ **1:38 am**
☽ ☌ ♇ **5:21 am** 2:21 am
☽ □ ♅ **12:59 pm** 9:59 am
☽ △ ☿ **4:53 pm** 1:53 pm

29 FRIDAY
☽ □ ♀ **3:07 am** 12:07 am
☽ ✶ ♂ **7:19 pm** 4:19 pm
☽ □ ☉ **11:29 pm** 8:29 pm
☽ ⚺ ♆ 10:48 pm

30 SATURDAY
☽ ⚺ ♆ **1:48 am**
☽ ⚻ ♃ **5:11 am** 2:11 am
☽ ✶ ♄ **8:46 am** 5:46 am
☽ ⚺ ♇ **12:28 pm** 9:28 am
☽ ✶ ♅ **7:55 pm** 4:55 pm
☽ □ ☿ **10:56 pm** 7:56 pm

Eastern time in bold type
Pacific time in medium type

APRIL 2016

DATE	SID.TIME	SUN	MOON	NODE	MERCURY	VENUS	MARS	JUPITER	SATURN	URANUS	NEPTUNE	PLUTO	CERES	PALLAS	JUNO	VESTA	CHIRON
1 F	12 39 8	11 ♈ 41 39	16 ♑ 00	21 ♍ 37	20 ♈ 12	24 ♓ 11	7 ♐ 21	15 ♍ 26	16 ♐ 22	19 ♈ 57	10 ♓ 40	17 ♑ 25	24 ♓ 46	23 ≈ 19	12 ♏ 41	10 ♉ 06	22 ♓ 17
2 Sa	12 43 5	12 40 51	29 06	21 37	22 14	25 26	7 31	15 19 R	16 21 R	20 00	10 42	17 25	25 09	23 36	12 31 R	10 31	22 21
3 Su	12 47 1	13 40 01	12 ≈ 37	21 39	24 14	26 40	7 41	15 13	16 21	20 03	10 44	17 26	25 32	23 53	12 20	10 57	22 24
4 M	12 50 58	14 39 10	26 35	21 40	26 12	27 54	7 51	15 07	16 20	20 07	10 46	17 26	25 55	24 11	12 10	11 23	22 27
5 T	12 54 54	15 38 16	10 ♓ 59	21 41 R	28 09	29 08	8 00	15 01	16 19	20 10	10 48	17 26	26 19	24 28	11 59	11 49	22 31
6 W	12 58 51	16 37 21	25 46	21 41	0 ♉ 04	0 ♈ 22	8 08	14 55	16 18	20 14	10 50	17 27	26 42	24 45	11 48	12 15	22 34
7 Th	13 2 47	17 36 24	10 ♈ 51	21 40	1 56	1 36	8 15	14 50	16 16	20 17	10 52	17 27	27 05	25 02	11 37	12 40	22 38
8 F	13 6 44	18 35 25	26 05	21 38	3 45	2 50	8 22	14 44	16 15	20 21	10 54	17 27	27 28	25 18	11 25	13 06	22 41
9 Sa	13 10 40	19 34 24	11 ♉ 17	21 35	5 31	4 04	8 28	14 39	16 14	20 24	10 56	17 28	27 51	25 35	11 14	13 32	22 44
10 Su	13 14 37	20 33 21	26 18	21 31	7 13	5 18	8 34	14 34	16 12	20 27	10 57	17 28	28 14	25 51	11 02	13 58	22 48
11 M	13 18 34	21 32 16	11 ♊ 00	21 27	8 51	6 33	8 39	14 29	16 11	20 31	10 59	17 28	28 37	26 08	10 50	14 24	22 51
12 T	13 22 30	22 31 08	25 17	21 23	10 25	7 47	8 43	14 24	16 09	20 34	11 01	17 28	29 00	26 24	10 37	14 50	22 54
13 W	13 26 27	23 29 58	9 ♋ 06	21 21	11 55	9 01	8 47	14 19	16 07	20 38	11 03	17 29	29 23	26 40	10 25	15 16	22 58
14 Th	13 30 23	24 28 46	22 28	21 20 D	13 19	10 15	8 50	14 14	16 06	20 41	11 05	17 29	29 46	26 56	10 12	15 42	23 01
15 F	13 34 20	25 27 32	5 ♌ 25	21 20	14 39	11 29	8 52	14 10	16 04	20 45	11 06	17 29	0 ♈ 09	27 12	9 59	16 08	23 04
16 Sa	13 38 16	26 26 15	18 00	21 22	15 54	12 43	8 53	14 06	16 02	20 48	11 08	17 29	0 32	27 27	9 47	16 34	23 07
17 Su	13 42 13	27 24 56	0 ♍ 19	21 23	17 03	13 57	8 54 R	14 01	15 59	20 51	11 10	17 29	0 54	27 43	9 33	17 00	23 11
18 M	13 46 9	28 23 35	12 25	21 25 R	18 07	15 11	8 54	13 58	15 57	20 55	11 12	17 29 R	1 17	27 58	9 20	17 26	23 14
19 T	13 50 6	29 22 11	24 22	21 25	19 06	16 25	8 53	13 54	15 55	20 58	11 13	17 29	1 40	28 13	9 07	17 52	23 17
20 W	13 54 3	0 ♉ 20 46	6 ♎ 13	21 24	19 59	17 39	8 52	13 50	15 53	21 02	11 15	17 29	2 02	28 28	8 54	18 19	23 20
21 Th	13 57 59	1 19 18	18 02	21 21	20 46	18 53	8 50	13 47	15 50	21 05	11 17	17 29	2 25	28 43	8 40	18 45	23 23
22 F	14 1 56	2 17 49	29 51	21 16	21 28	20 07	8 47	13 43	15 48	21 08	11 18	17 29	2 47	28 58	8 27	19 11	23 26
23 Sa	14 5 52	3 16 18	11 ♏ 43	21 09	22 03	21 21	8 43	13 40	15 45	21 12	11 20	17 29	3 10	29 13	8 13	19 37	23 29
24 Su	14 9 49	4 14 45	23 37	21 01	22 33	22 35	8 38	13 37	15 42	21 15	11 21	17 29	3 32	29 27	7 59	20 03	23 32
25 M	14 13 45	5 13 10	5 ♐ 38	20 53	22 57	23 49	8 33	13 35	15 40	21 19	11 23	17 28	3 55	29 41	7 46	20 29	23 35
26 T	14 17 42	6 11 33	17 46	20 45	23 15	25 02	8 27	13 32	15 37	21 22	11 24	17 28	4 17	29 55	7 32	20 55	23 38
27 W	14 21 38	7 09 55	0 ♑ 03	20 38	23 28	26 16	8 20	13 30	15 34	21 25	11 26	17 28	4 40	0 ♓ 09	7 18	21 21	23 41
28 Th	14 25 35	8 08 15	12 32	20 33	23 35 R	27 30	8 13	13 28	15 31	21 29	11 27	17 28	5 02	0 23	7 04	21 48	23 43
29 F	14 29 32	9 06 34	25 16	20 30	23 36	28 44	8 05	13 26	15 28	21 32	11 29	17 27	5 24	0 37	6 51	22 14	23 46
30 Sa	14 33 28	10 04 51	8 ≈ 18	20 29 D	23 32	29 58	7 56	13 24	15 25	21 35	11 30	17 27	5 46	0 50	6 37	22 40	23 49

EPHEMERIS CALCULATED FOR 12 MIDNIGHT GREENWICH MEAN TIME. ALL OTHER DATA AND FACING ASPECTARIAN PAGE IN **EASTERN TIME (BOLD)** AND PACIFIC TIME (REGULAR).

MAY 2016

☽ Last Aspect day	ET / hr:mn / PT		asp	☽ Ingress sign	day	ET / hr:mn / PT	
4/30	**10:56 pm**	7:56 pm	□☿	♓	1	**10:33 am**	7:33 am
2		10:08 pm	⚹☿	♈	3	**1:04 pm**	10:04 am
3	**1:08 am**		⚹☿	♈	3	**1:04 pm**	10:04 am
4		9:17 pm	☌♅	♉	5	**1:10 pm**	10:10 am
5	**12:17 am**		☌♅	♉	5	**1:10 pm**	10:10 am
6	**10:10 pm**	7:10 am	☌☿	♊	7	**12:35 pm**	9:35 am
8		9:15 pm	⚹♅	♋	9	**1:24 pm**	10:24 am
9	**12:15 am**		⚹♅	♋	9	**1:24 pm**	10:24 am
11	**3:34 am**	12:34 am	□♅	♌	11	**5:32 pm**	2:32 pm
13	**1:02 pm**	10:02 am	□☉	♍	13		10:52 pm

☽ Last Aspect day	ET / hr:mn / PT		asp	☽ Ingress sign	day	ET / hr:mn / PT	
13	**1:02 pm**	10:02 am	□☉	♍	14	**1:52 am**	
16	**5:20 am**	2:20 am	△☉	♎	16	**1:33 pm**	10:33 am
18	**11:23 am**	8:23 am	☍♅	♏	18		11:29 pm
18	**11:23 am**	8:23 am	☍♅	♏	19	**2:29 am**	
21	**7:40 am**	4:40 am	☍♀	♐	21	**2:48 pm**	11:48 am
23	**11:37 am**	8:37 am	△♅	♑	23		10:34 pm
23	**11:37 am**	8:37 am	△♅	♑	24	**1:34 am**	
25	**9:11 pm**	6:11 pm	□♅	♒	26	**10:27 am**	7:27 am
28	**4:19 pm**	1:19 pm	□♂	♓	28	**5:06 pm**	2:06 pm
30	**7:10 pm**	4:10 pm	△♂	♈	30	**9:09 pm**	6:09 pm

☽ Phases & Eclipses phase	day	ET / hr:mn / PT	
New Moon	6	**3:30 pm**	12:30 pm
2nd Quarter	13	**1:02 pm**	10:02 am
Full Moon	21	**5:14 pm**	2:14 pm
4th Quarter	29	**8:12 am**	5:12 am

Planet Ingress		day	ET / hr:mn / PT	
⚶	♊	16	**2:29 pm**	11:29 am
☉	♊	20	**10:36 am**	7:36 am
♀	♊	24	**5:45 am**	2:45 am
♂	♏	27	**9:51 am**	6:51 am

Planetary Motion		day	ET / hr:mn / PT	
♃	D	9	**8:14 am**	5:14 am
☿	D	22	**9:20 am**	6:20 am

1 SUNDAY
☉ ⚹ ♆ **8:00 am** 5:00 am
☽ ⚹ ♀ **2:16 pm** 11:16 am
☽ □ ♂ **11:35 pm** 8:35 pm

2 MONDAY
☽ ☌ ♆ **6:23 am** 3:23 am
☽ ⚹ ☉ **7:59 am** 4:59 am
☽ ☍ ♃ **9:23 am** 6:23 am
☽ □ ♄ **12:38 pm** 9:38 am
☽ ⚹ ♇ **4:17 pm** 1:17 pm
☽ ⚺ ♅ **11:29 pm** 8:29 pm
☽ ⚹ ☿ 10:08 pm

3 TUESDAY
☽ ⚹ ☿ **1:08 am**
☉ △ ♃ **3:58 am** 12:58 am
☽ ⚺ ♀ **9:09 pm** 6:09 pm
☽ △ ♂ 9:43 pm

4 WEDNESDAY
☽ △ ♂ **12:43 am**
☽ ⚺ ♆ **7:53 am** 4:53 am
☽ ⚻ ♃ **10:35 am** 7:35 am
☽ ⚺ ☉ **12:45 pm** 9:45 am
☽ △ ♄ **1:34 pm** 10:34 am
☽ □ ♇ **5:12 pm** 2:12 pm
☽ ☌ ♅ 9:17 pm
☽ ⚺ ☿ 9:22 pm
☉ ⚻ ♄ 9:39 pm
☿ ⚺ ♅ 11:31 pm

5 THURSDAY
☽ ☌ ♅ **12:17 am**
☽ ⚺ ☿ **12:22 am**
☉ ⚻ ♄ **12:39 am**
☿ ⚺ ♅ **2:31 am**
♀ ⚻ ♂ **10:11 am** 7:11 am
☽ ⚻ ♂ **11:47 pm** 8:47 pm
☽ ☌ ♀ 10:12 pm

6 FRIDAY
☽ ☌ ♀ **1:12 am**
☽ ⚹ ♆ **7:32 am** 4:32 am
☽ △ ♃ **10:06 am** 7:06 am
☽ ⚻ ♄ **12:53 pm** 9:53 am
☽ ☌ ☉ **3:30 pm** 12:30 pm
☽ △ ♇ **4:37 pm** 1:37 pm
☽ ☌ ☿ **10:10 pm** 7:10 pm
☽ ⚺ ♅ **11:51 pm** 8:51 pm

7 SATURDAY
☉ △ ♇ **9:03 am** 6:03 am
☽ ☍ ♂ **10:34 pm** 7:34 pm

8 SUNDAY
☽ ⚺ ♀ **5:03 am** 2:03 am
☽ □ ♆ **7:18 am** 4:18 am
☽ □ ♃ **9:51 am** 6:51 am
☽ ☍ ♄ **12:32 pm** 9:32 am
☽ ⚻ ♇ **4:33 pm** 1:33 pm
☽ ⚺ ☉ **6:48 pm** 3:48 pm
☽ ⚺ ☿ **8:29 pm** 5:29 pm
☽ ⚹ ♅ 9:15 pm

9 MONDAY
☽ ⚹ ♅ **12:15 am**
♀ ⚹ ♆ **8:41 am** 5:41 am
☉ ☌ ☿ **11:12 am** 8:12 am
☽ ⚻ ♂ **11:02 pm** 8:02 pm

10 TUESDAY
☽ △ ♆ **9:18 am** 6:18 am
☽ ⚹ ♀ **11:39 am** 8:39 am
☽ ⚹ ♃ **11:56 am** 8:56 am
☽ ⚻ ♄ **2:34 pm** 11:34 am
♀ △ ♃ **3:00 pm** 12:00 pm
☽ ☍ ♇ **7:04 pm** 4:04 pm
☽ ⚹ ☿ **9:10 pm** 6:10 pm
☽ ⚹ ☉ 10:23 pm

11 WEDNESDAY
☽ ⚹ ☉ **1:23 am**
☽ □ ♅ **3:34 am** 12:34 am
♀ ⚻ ♄ **7:08 pm** 4:08 pm
☽ △ ♂ 11:50 pm

12 THURSDAY
☽ △ ♂ **2:50 am**
☉ ⚺ ♅ **9:44 am** 6:44 am
☽ ⚻ ♆ **3:07 pm** 12:07 pm
☽ ⚺ ♃ **5:57 pm** 2:57 pm
☽ △ ♄ **8:29 pm** 5:29 pm
☿ △ ♇ **10:45 pm** 7:45 pm
☽ □ ♀ **11:20 pm** 8:20 pm
☽ □ ☿ 10:28 pm
☽ ⚻ ♇ 10:35 pm

13 FRIDAY
☽ □ ☿ **1:28 am**
☽ ⚻ ♇ **1:35 am**
☽ △ ♅ **11:02 am** 8:02 am
☽ □ ☉ **1:02 pm** 10:02 am
☿ ☌ ♀ **3:10 pm** 12:10 pm
♀ △ ♇ **10:20 pm** 7:20 pm

14 SATURDAY
☽ □ ♂ **10:28 am** 7:28 am
☽ ☍ ♆ 10:02 pm

15 SUNDAY
☽ ☍ ♆ **1:02 am**
☽ ☌ ♃ **4:02 am** 1:02 am
☽ □ ♄ **6:21 am** 3:21 am
☽ △ ☿ **9:31 am** 6:31 am
☽ △ ♇ **12:00 pm** 9:00 am
☽ △ ♀ **4:21 pm** 1:21 pm
☽ ⚻ ♅ **10:17 pm** 7:17 pm

16 MONDAY
☽ △ ☉ **5:20 am** 2:20 am
☽ ⚹ ♂ **8:54 pm** 5:54 pm

17 TUESDAY
☽ ⚻ ♆ **1:34 pm** 10:34 am
☽ ⚺ ♃ **4:40 pm** 1:40 pm
☽ ⚹ ♄ **6:34 pm** 3:34 pm
☽ ⚻ ☿ **8:11 pm** 5:11 pm
☽ □ ♇ 9:37 pm

18 WEDNESDAY
☽ □ ♇ **12:37 am**
♀ ⚺ ♅ **4:14 am** 1:14 am
☽ ☍ ♅ **11:23 am** 8:23 am
☽ ⚻ ♀ **12:11 pm** 9:11 am
☽ ⚻ ☉ **11:39 pm** 8:39 pm

19 THURSDAY
☽ ⚺ ♂ **8:11 am** 5:11 am
☽ △ ♆ 11:31 pm

20 FRIDAY
☽ △ ♆ **2:31 am**
☽ ⚹ ♃ **5:39 am** 2:39 am
☽ ⚺ ♄ **7:03 am** 4:03 am
☽ ☍ ☿ **7:48 am** 4:48 am
☽ ⚹ ♇ **1:18 pm** 10:18 am
☽ ⚻ ♅ 9:13 pm

21 SATURDAY
☽ ⚻ ♅ **12:13 am**
☽ ☍ ♀ **7:40 am** 4:40 am
☽ ☍ ☉ **5:14 pm** 2:14 pm
☽ ☌ ♂ **6:43 pm** 3:43 pm

22 SUNDAY
☉ ☍ ♂ **7:17 am** 4:17 am
☽ □ ♆ **2:20 pm** 11:20 am
☽ □ ♃ **5:31 pm** 2:31 pm
☽ ☌ ♄ **6:20 pm** 3:20 pm
☽ ⚻ ☿ **7:07 pm** 4:07 pm
☽ ⚺ ♇ 9:42 pm

23 MONDAY
☽ ⚺ ♇ **12:42 am**
☽ △ ♅ **11:37 am** 8:37 am
☽ ⚻ ♀ 10:06 pm

24 TUESDAY
☽ ⚻ ♀ **1:06 am**
☽ ⚺ ♂ **3:46 am** 12:46 am
☽ ⚻ ☉ **8:50 am** 5:50 am
♀ ☍ ♂ **10:38 pm** 7:38 pm
☽ ⚹ ♆ 9:26 pm

25 WEDNESDAY
☽ ⚹ ♆ **12:26 am**
☽ △ ♃ **3:39 am** 12:39 am
☽ ⚺ ♄ **3:56 am** 12:56 am
☽ △ ☿ **5:35 am** 2:35 am
☽ ☌ ♇ **10:21 am** 7:21 am
☽ □ ♅ **9:11 pm** 6:11 pm

26 THURSDAY
♃ □ ♄ **8:28 am** 5:28 am
☽ ⚹ ♂ **11:04 am** 8:04 am
☽ △ ♀ **3:59 pm** 12:59 pm
☽ △ ☉ **9:58 pm** 6:58 pm

27 FRIDAY
☽ ⚺ ♆ **8:31 am** 5:31 am
☽ ⚹ ♄ **11:32 am** 8:32 am
☽ ⚻ ♃ **11:48 am** 8:48 am
☽ □ ☿ **2:44 pm** 11:44 am
☽ ⚺ ♇ **5:56 pm** 2:56 pm

28 SATURDAY
☽ ⚹ ♅ **4:36 am** 1:36 am
☽ □ ♂ **4:19 pm** 1:19 pm

29 SUNDAY
☽ □ ♀ **3:48 am** 12:48 am
☽ □ ☉ **8:12 am** 5:12 am
☽ ☌ ♆ **2:12 pm** 11:12 am
☽ □ ♄ **4:45 pm** 1:45 pm
☽ ☍ ♃ **5:30 pm** 2:30 pm
☽ ⚹ ☿ **9:58 pm** 6:58 pm
☽ ⚹ ♇ **11:04 pm** 8:04 pm

30 MONDAY
☽ ⚺ ♅ **9:26 am** 6:26 am
☽ △ ♂ **7:10 pm** 4:10 pm
☿ △ ♇ **11:09 pm** 8:09 pm

31 TUESDAY
☽ ⚹ ♀ **12:09 pm** 9:09 am
☽ ⚹ ☉ **3:10 pm** 12:10 pm
☽ ⚺ ♆ **5:15 pm** 2:15 pm
☽ △ ♄ **7:23 pm** 4:23 pm
☽ ⚻ ♃ **8:35 pm** 5:35 pm
☽ □ ♇ 10:35 pm
☽ ⚺ ☿ 11:53 pm

Eastern time in bold type
Pacific time in medium type

MAY 2016

DATE	SID.TIME	SUN	MOON	NODE	MERCURY	VENUS	MARS	JUPITER	SATURN	URANUS	NEPTUNE	PLUTO	CERES	PALLAS	JUNO	VESTA	CHIRON
1 Su	14 37 25	11 ♉ 03 06	21 ♒ 41	20 ♍ 30	23 ♉ 22	1 ♉ 12	7 ♐ 46	13 ♍ 22	15 ♐ 21	21 ♈ 38	11 ♓ 32	17 ♑ 27	6 ♈ 08	1 ♓ 03	6 ♏ 23	23 ♉ 06	23 ♓ 52
2 M	14 41 21	12 01 20	5 ♓ 28	20 31	23 08 ℞	2 26	7 35 ℞	13 21 ℞	15 18 ℞	21 42	11 33	17 26 ℞	6 30	1 17	6 10 ℞	23 32	23 54
3 T	14 45 18	12 59 33	19 40	20 31 ℞	22 50	3 40	7 24	13 19	15 15	21 45	11 34	17 26	6 52	1 30	5 56	23 59	23 57
4 W	14 49 14	13 57 44	4 ♈ 15	20 30	22 27	4 54	7 12	13 18	15 11	21 48	11 36	17 25	7 14	1 42	5 43	24 25	24 00
5 Th	14 53 11	14 55 53	19 11	20 28	22 00	6 08	6 59	13 17	15 08	21 52	11 37	17 25	7 36	1 55	5 29	24 51	24 02
6 F	14 57 7	15 54 01	4 ♉ 20	20 22	21 30	7 22	6 46	13 16	15 04	21 55	11 38	17 25	7 58	2 07	5 16	25 17	24 05
7 Sa	15 1 4	16 52 08	19 33	20 15	20 58	8 35	6 32	13 16	15 01	21 58	11 39	17 24	8 20	2 19	5 03	25 44	24 07
8 Su	15 5 1	17 50 13	4 ♊ 39	20 07	20 24	9 49	6 17	13 16	14 57	22 01	11 40	17 23	8 42	2 31	4 50	26 10	24 10
9 M	15 8 57	18 48 16	19 29	19 58	19 48	11 03	6 01	13 15 D	14 53	22 04	11 42	17 23	9 03	2 43	4 37	26 36	24 12
10 T	15 12 54	19 46 17	3 ♋ 56	19 50	19 12	12 17	5 45	13 15	14 50	22 07	11 43	17 22	9 25	2 55	4 25	27 02	24 15
11 W	15 16 50	20 44 17	17 54	19 44	18 35	13 31	5 29	13 16	14 46	22 11	11 44	17 22	9 46	3 06	4 12	27 29	24 17
12 Th	15 20 47	21 42 14	1 ♌ 22	19 40	17 59	14 45	5 12	13 16	14 42	22 14	11 45	17 21	10 08	3 17	4 00	27 55	24 19
13 F	15 24 43	22 40 10	14 22	19 38 D	17 24	15 59	4 54	13 16	14 38	22 17	11 46	17 20	10 29	3 28	3 47	28 21	24 22
14 Sa	15 28 40	23 38 04	26 59	19 37	16 51	17 12	4 36	13 17	14 34	22 20	11 47	17 20	10 51	3 39	3 35	28 47	24 24
15 Su	15 32 36	24 35 57	9 ♍ 15	19 38 ℞	16 20	18 26	4 17	13 18	14 30	22 23	11 48	17 19	11 12	3 49	3 24	29 14	24 26
16 M	15 36 33	25 33 47	21 18	19 38	15 52	19 40	3 58	13 19	14 26	22 26	11 49	17 18	11 33	4 00	3 12	29 40	24 28
17 T	15 40 30	26 31 36	3 ♎ 11	19 37	15 27	20 54	3 39	13 20	14 22	22 29	11 50	17 17	11 54	4 10	3 01	0 ♊ 06	24 30
18 W	15 44 26	27 29 23	15 00	19 34	15 06	22 07	3 19	13 22	14 18	22 32	11 51	17 16	12 15	4 20	2 50	0 32	24 32
19 Th	15 48 23	28 27 08	26 48	19 29	14 48	23 21	2 59	13 24	14 14	22 35	11 51	17 16	12 36	4 29	2 39	0 58	24 34
20 F	15 52 19	29 24 52	8 ♏ 39	19 21	14 35	24 35	2 39	13 25	14 09	22 38	11 52	17 15	12 57	4 39	2 28	1 25	24 36
21 Sa	15 56 16	0 ♊ 22 35	20 35	19 10	14 26	25 49	2 18	13 27	14 05	22 41	11 53	17 14	13 18	4 48	2 18	1 51	24 38
22 Su	16 0 12	1 20 16	2 ♐ 37	18 58	14 21 D	27 03	1 57	13 29	14 01	22 43	11 54	17 13	13 38	4 57	2 08	2 17	24 40
23 M	16 4 9	2 17 56	14 48	18 45	14 21	28 16	1 36	13 32	13 57	22 46	11 55	17 12	13 59	5 06	1 58	2 43	24 42
24 T	16 8 5	3 15 35	27 07	18 33	14 25	29 30	1 15	13 34	13 52	22 49	11 55	17 11	14 20	5 14	1 48	3 09	24 44
25 W	16 12 2	4 13 12	9 ♑ 37	18 22	14 34	0 ♊ 44	0 54	13 37	13 48	22 52	11 56	17 10	14 40	5 22	1 39	3 36	24 46
26 Th	16 15 59	5 10 49	22 17	18 13	14 47	1 58	0 33	13 40	13 44	22 55	11 57	17 09	15 00	5 30	1 30	4 02	24 47
27 F	16 19 55	6 08 24	5 ♒ 09	18 08	15 05	3 11	0 12	13 43	13 39	22 57	11 57	17 08	15 21	5 38	1 21	4 28	24 49
28 Sa	16 23 52	7 05 59	18 15	18 04	15 27	4 25	29 ♏ 51	13 46	13 35	23 00	11 58	17 07	15 41	5 45	1 12	4 54	24 51
29 Su	16 27 48	8 03 33	1 ♓ 38	18 03 D	15 53	5 39	29 30	13 49	13 30	23 03	11 58	17 06	16 01	5 53	1 04	5 20	24 52
30 M	16 31 45	9 01 05	15 19	18 03 ℞	16 24	6 53	29 10	13 53	13 26	23 05	11 59	17 05	16 21	6 00	0 56	5 46	24 54
31 T	16 35 41	9 58 37	29 19	18 03	16 59	8 06	28 49	13 56	13 22	23 08	11 59	17 04	16 41	6 06	0 49	6 13	24 55

EPHEMERIS CALCULATED FOR 12 MIDNIGHT GREENWICH MEAN TIME. ALL OTHER DATA AND FACING ASPECTARIAN PAGE IN **EASTERN TIME (BOLD)** AND PACIFIC TIME (REGULAR).

JUNE 2016

☽ Last Aspect day	ET / hr:mn	PT	asp	☽ Ingress sign	day	ET / hr:mn	PT
1	**11:42 am**	8:42 am	☌ ♅	♉	1	**10:46 pm**	7:46 pm
3	**7:02 pm**	4:02 pm	☍ ♂	♊	3	**11:01 pm**	8:01 pm
5	**12:47 pm**	9:47 am	⚹ ♅	♋	5	**11:41 pm**	8:41 pm
7	**8:18 pm**	5:18 pm	△ ♂	♌	7		11:47 pm
7	**8:18 pm**	5:18 pm	△ ♂	♌	8	**2:47 am**	
10	**3:14 am**	12:14 am	□ ☿	♍	10	**9:46 am**	6:46 am
12	**10:47 am**	7:47 am	⚹ ♂	♎	12	**8:33 pm**	5:33 pm
15	**3:00 am**	12:00 am	△ ♀	♏	15	**9:18 am**	6:18 am
17	**9:52 am**	6:52 am	☌ ♂	♐	17	**9:34 pm**	6:34 pm
20	**7:02 am**	4:02 am	☍ ☉	♑	20	**7:55 am**	4:55 am
22	**4:57 am**	1:57 am	□ ♅	♒	22	**4:08 pm**	1:08 pm
24	**11:48 am**	8:48 am	⚹ ♅	♓	24	**10:30 pm**	7:30 pm
26	**3:55 pm**	12:55 pm	□ ☿	♈	27	**3:08 am**	12:08 am
29	**3:46 am**	12:46 am	⚹ ☿	♉	29	**6:03 am**	3:03 am
30	**8:19 pm**	5:19 pm	☍ ♂	♊	7/1	**7:44 am**	4:44 am

☽ Phases & Eclipses phase	day	ET / hr:mn	PT
New Moon	4	**11:00 pm**	8:00 pm
2nd Quarter	12	**4:10 am**	1:10 am
Full Moon	20	**7:02 am**	4:02 am
4th Quarter	27	**2:19 pm**	11:19 am

Planet Ingress		day	ET / hr:mn	PT
⚳	♎	7	**7:03 pm**	4:03 pm
☿	♊	12	**7:22 pm**	4:22 pm
♀	♋	17	**3:39 pm**	12:39 pm
☉	♋	20	**6:34 pm**	3:34 pm
☿	♋	29	**7:24 pm**	4:24 pm

Planetary Motion		day	ET / hr:mn	PT
♆	R	13	**4:43 pm**	1:43 pm
♀	R	21	**9:21 am**	6:21 am
⚳	D	22	**4:01 pm**	1:01 pm
⚷	R	27	**7:10 am**	4:10 am
♂	D	29	**7:38 pm**	4:38 pm

1 WEDNESDAY
☽ □ ♇ **1:35 am**
☽ ⚺ ☿ **2:53 am**
☽ ☌ ♅ **11:42 am** 8:42 am
☽ ⚻ ♂ **7:46 pm** 4:46 pm
☉ □ ♆ **10:42 pm** 7:42 pm

2 THURSDAY
☽ ⚺ ♀ **5:37 pm** 2:37 pm
☽ ⚹ ♆ **6:10 pm** 3:10 pm
☽ ⚺ ☉ **7:29 pm** 4:29 pm
☽ ⚻ ♄ **7:59 pm** 4:59 pm
☽ △ ♃ **9:36 pm** 6:36 pm
♀ □ ♆ 9:14 pm
☽ △ ♇ 11:11 pm
☉ ☍ ♄ 11:37 pm

3 FRIDAY
♀ □ ♆ **12:14 am**
☽ △ ♇ **2:11 am**
☉ ☍ ♄ **2:37 am**
☽ ☌ ☿ **6:07 am** 3:07 am
☽ ⚺ ♅ **12:16 pm** 9:16 am
☽ ☍ ♂ **7:02 pm** 4:02 pm
♀ ☍ ♄ **8:47 pm** 5:47 pm

4 SATURDAY
☉ □ ♃ **6:57 am** 3:57 am
☽ □ ♆ **6:21 pm** 3:21 pm
☽ ☍ ♄ **7:55 pm** 4:55 pm
♀ □ ♃ **8:49 pm** 5:49 pm
☽ □ ♃ **10:02 pm** 7:02 pm
☽ ☌ ♀ **10:08 pm** 7:08 pm
☽ ☌ ☉ **11:00 pm** 8:00 pm
☽ ⚻ ♇ 11:22 pm

5 SUNDAY
☽ ⚻ ♇ **2:22 am**
☽ ⚺ ☿ **9:33 am** 6:33 am
☽ ⚹ ♅ **12:47 pm** 9:47 am
☽ ⚻ ♂ **6:35 pm** 3:35 pm

6 MONDAY
☉ ☌ ♀ **5:39 pm** 2:39 pm
☽ △ ♆ **7:47 pm** 4:47 pm
☽ ⚻ ♄ **9:09 pm** 6:09 pm
☽ ⚹ ♃ **11:54 pm** 8:54 pm
♀ ⚻ ♇ 9:13 pm
☉ ⚻ ♇ 11:02 pm

7 TUESDAY
♀ ⚻ ♇ **12:13 am**
☉ ⚻ ♇ **2:02 am**
☽ ☍ ♇ **4:06 am** 1:06 am
☽ ⚺ ☉ **4:15 am** 1:15 am
☽ ⚺ ♀ **4:28 am** 1:28 am
☿ ⚺ ♅ **10:14 am** 7:14 am
☽ □ ♅ **3:20 pm** 12:20 pm
☽ ⚹ ☿ **3:45 pm** 12:45 pm
☽ △ ♂ **8:18 pm** 5:18 pm

8 WEDNESDAY
☽ ⚻ ♆ 9:20 pm
☽ △ ♄ 10:30 pm

9 THURSDAY
☽ ⚻ ♆ **12:20 am**
☽ △ ♄ **1:30 am**
☽ ⚺ ♃ **5:06 am** 2:06 am
☽ ⚻ ♇ **9:12 am** 6:12 am
☿ ☍ ♂ **1:01 pm** 10:01 am
☽ ⚹ ☉ **1:40 pm** 10:40 am
☽ ⚹ ♀ **3:15 pm** 12:15 pm
☽ △ ♅ **9:34 pm** 6:34 pm
☽ □ ♂ 10:37 pm

10 FRIDAY
☽ □ ♂ **1:37 am**
☽ □ ☿ **3:14 am** 12:14 am

11 SATURDAY
☽ ☍ ♆ **8:58 am** 5:58 am
☽ □ ♄ **9:52 am** 6:52 am
☽ ☌ ♃ **2:29 pm** 11:29 am
☽ △ ♇ **6:21 pm** 3:21 pm

12 SUNDAY
☽ □ ☉ **4:10 am** 1:10 am
☽ □ ♀ **7:26 am** 4:26 am
☽ ⚻ ♅ **7:49 am** 4:49 am
☽ ⚹ ♂ **10:47 am** 7:47 am
♀ ⚹ ♅ **11:13 am** 8:13 am
☽ △ ☿ **8:42 pm** 5:42 pm

13 MONDAY
♀ ⚻ ♂ **11:39 am** 8:39 am
☽ ⚻ ♆ **8:51 pm** 5:51 pm
☽ ⚹ ♄ **9:25 pm** 6:25 pm

14 TUESDAY
☽ ⚺ ♃ **3:03 am** 12:03 am
☉ ⚹ ♅ **3:53 am** 12:53 am
☽ □ ♇ **6:26 am** 3:26 am
☽ ☍ ♅ **8:32 pm** 5:32 pm
☽ △ ☉ **9:57 pm** 6:57 pm
☽ ⚺ ♂ **10:18 pm** 7:18 pm
☉ ⚻ ♂ 10:31 pm

15 WEDNESDAY
☉ ⚻ ♂ **1:31 am**
☽ △ ♀ **3:00 am** 12:00 am
☽ ⚻ ☿ **5:50 pm** 2:50 pm

16 THURSDAY
☽ △ ♆ **9:39 am** 6:39 am
☽ ⚺ ♄ **9:52 am** 6:52 am
☽ ⚹ ♃ **4:21 pm** 1:21 pm
☽ ⚹ ♇ **7:04 pm** 4:04 pm

17 FRIDAY
☽ ⚻ ♅ **9:14 am** 6:14 am
☽ ☌ ♂ **9:52 am** 6:52 am
☽ ⚻ ☉ **3:39 pm** 12:39 pm
☽ ⚻ ♀ **10:14 pm** 7:14 pm
♄ □ ♆ **11:29 pm** 8:29 pm

18 SATURDAY
☽ ☍ ☿ **2:48 pm** 11:48 am
☽ ☌ ♄ **9:07 pm** 6:07 pm
☽ □ ♆ **9:14 pm** 6:14 pm
♂ ⚻ ♅ 10:55 pm

19 SUNDAY
♂ ⚻ ♅ **1:55 am**
☽ □ ♃ **4:15 am** 1:15 am
☽ ⚺ ♇ **6:14 am** 3:14 am
☽ ⚺ ♂ **7:56 pm** 4:56 pm
☽ △ ♅ **8:11 pm** 5:11 pm

20 MONDAY
☽ ☍ ☉ **7:02 am** 4:02 am
☿ ☍ ♄ **10:55 am** 7:55 am
☿ □ ♆ **1:11 pm** 10:11 am
☽ ☍ ♀ **2:51 pm** 11:51 am

21 TUESDAY
☽ ⚺ ♄ **6:17 am** 3:17 am
☽ ⚹ ♆ **6:41 am** 3:41 am
☽ ⚻ ☿ **9:30 am** 6:30 am
☽ △ ♃ **1:59 pm** 10:59 am
☽ ☌ ♇ **3:16 pm** 12:16 pm

22 WEDNESDAY
☽ ⚹ ♂ **4:03 am** 1:03 am
☽ □ ♅ **4:57 am** 1:57 am
☿ □ ♃ **6:59 pm** 3:59 pm
☽ ⚻ ☉ **7:44 pm** 4:44 pm
☿ ⚻ ♇ 10:39 pm

23 THURSDAY
☿ ⚻ ♇ **1:39 am**
☽ ⚻ ♀ **4:38 am** 1:38 am
☽ ⚹ ♄ **1:28 pm** 10:28 am
☽ ⚺ ♆ **2:07 pm** 11:07 am
☽ ⚻ ♃ **9:41 pm** 6:41 pm
☽ ⚺ ♇ **10:21 pm** 7:21 pm
☽ △ ☿ 10:48 pm

24 FRIDAY
☽ △ ☿ **1:48 am**
☽ □ ♂ **10:26 am** 7:26 am
☽ ⚹ ♅ **11:48 am** 8:48 am

25 SATURDAY
☽ △ ☉ **6:07 am** 3:07 am
☽ △ ♀ **3:58 pm** 12:58 pm
☽ □ ♄ **6:54 pm** 3:54 pm
☽ ☌ ♆ **7:46 pm** 4:46 pm

26 SUNDAY
☽ ☍ ♃ **3:36 am** 12:36 am
☽ ⚹ ♇ **3:39 am** 12:39 am
♃ △ ♇ **8:30 am** 5:30 am
☿ ⚻ ♂ **11:16 am** 8:16 am
☽ △ ♂ **3:14 pm** 12:14 pm
☽ □ ☿ **3:55 pm** 12:55 pm
☽ ⚺ ♅ **4:52 pm** 1:52 pm
☿ ⚹ ♅ **10:31 pm** 7:31 pm
♀ ⚻ ♄ **11:00 pm** 8:00 pm

27 MONDAY
♀ △ ♆ **9:53 am** 6:53 am
☽ □ ☉ **2:19 pm** 11:19 am
☽ △ ♄ **10:37 pm** 7:37 pm
☽ ⚺ ♆ **11:40 pm** 8:40 pm
☽ □ ♀ 9:59 pm

28 TUESDAY
☽ □ ♀ **12:59 am**
☽ □ ♇ **7:14 am** 4:14 am
☽ ⚻ ♃ **7:44 am** 4:44 am
☽ ⚻ ♂ **6:25 pm** 3:25 pm
☽ ☌ ♅ **8:12 pm** 5:12 pm

29 WEDNESDAY
☽ ⚹ ☿ **3:46 am** 12:46 am
☽ ⚹ ☉ **8:29 pm** 5:29 pm
☽ ⚻ ♄ 9:46 pm
☽ ⚹ ♆ 10:59 pm

30 THURSDAY
☽ ⚻ ♄ **12:46 am**
☽ ⚹ ♆ **1:59 am**
☽ ⚹ ♀ **7:57 am** 4:57 am
☽ △ ♇ **9:18 am** 6:18 am
☽ △ ♃ **10:20 am** 7:20 am
☽ ☍ ♂ **8:19 pm** 5:19 pm
☽ ⚺ ♅ **10:09 pm** 7:09 pm
♀ ☍ ♇ **11:32 pm** 8:32 pm

Eastern time in bold type
Pacific time in medium type

JUNE 2016

DATE	SID.TIME	SUN	MOON	NODE	MERCURY	VENUS	MARS	JUPITER	SATURN	URANUS	NEPTUNE	PLUTO	CERES	PALLAS	JUNO	VESTA	CHIRON
1 W	16 39 38	10 ♊ 56 09	13 ♈ 39	18 ♍ 01	17 ♉ 38	9 ♊ 20	28 ♏ 29	14 ♍ 00	13 ♐ 17	23 ♈ 10	12 ♓ 00	17 ♑ 03	17 ♈ 01	6 ♓ 13	0 ♏ 42	6 ♊ 39	24 ♓ 56
2 Th	16 43 34	11 53 39	28 18	17 57 R	18 20	10 34	28 09 R	14 04	13 13 R	23 13	12 00	17 02 R	17 21	6 19	0 35 R	7 05	24 58
3 F	16 47 31	12 51 09	13 ♉ 09	17 51	19 07	11 47	27 49	14 08	13 08	23 15	12 00	17 01	17 40	6 25	0 28	7 31	24 59
4 Sa	16 51 28	13 48 38	28 07	17 42	19 57	13 01	27 30	14 13	13 04	23 18	12 01	16 59	18 00	6 30	0 22	7 57	25 00
5 Su	16 55 24	14 46 06	13 ♊ 02	17 31	20 51	14 15	27 12	14 17	12 59	23 20	12 01	16 58	18 19	6 36	0 16	8 23	25 02
6 M	16 59 21	15 43 33	27 46	17 19	21 48	15 29	26 53	14 22	12 55	23 23	12 01	16 57	18 39	6 41	0 10	8 49	25 03
7 T	17 3 17	16 40 59	12 ♋ 10	17 09	22 49	16 43	26 35	14 27	12 50	23 25	12 02	16 56	18 58	6 45	0 05	9 15	25 04
8 W	17 7 14	17 38 24	26 08	17 00	23 53	17 56	26 18	14 32	12 46	23 27	12 02	16 54	19 17	6 50	0 00	9 41	25 05
9 Th	17 11 10	18 35 48	9 ♌ 39	16 54	25 00	19 10	26 02	14 37	12 42	23 30	12 02	16 53	19 36	6 54	29 ♍ 55	10 07	25 06
10 F	17 15 7	19 33 11	22 42	16 51	26 11	20 24	25 46	14 42	12 37	23 32	12 02	16 52	19 55	6 58	29 51	10 33	25 07
11 Sa	17 19 3	20 30 33	5 ♍ 21	16 49 D	27 25	21 37	25 30	14 47	12 33	23 34	12 02	16 51	20 14	7 01	29 47	10 59	25 08
12 Su	17 23 0	21 27 54	17 40	16 49 R	28 42	22 51	25 16	14 53	12 28	23 36	12 02	16 49	20 33	7 04	29 43	11 25	25 09
13 M	17 26 57	22 25 14	29 43	16 49	0 ♊ 02	24 05	25 02	14 59	12 24	23 39	12 02 R	16 48	20 51	7 07	29 40	11 51	25 09
14 T	17 30 53	23 22 33	11 ♎ 37	16 48	1 25	25 19	24 48	15 05	12 20	23 41	12 02	16 47	21 10	7 10	29 37	12 17	25 10
15 W	17 34 50	24 19 51	23 27	16 45	2 52	26 32	24 36	15 11	12 15	23 43	12 02	16 45	21 28	7 12	29 34	12 43	25 11
16 Th	17 38 46	25 17 09	5 ♏ 17	16 40	4 21	27 46	24 24	15 17	12 11	23 45	12 02	16 44	21 46	7 14	29 32	13 09	25 11
17 F	17 42 43	26 14 25	17 11	16 32	5 53	29 00	24 13	15 23	12 07	23 47	12 02	16 43	22 04	7 16	29 30	13 35	25 12
18 Sa	17 46 39	27 11 41	29 13	16 21	7 28	0 ♋ 13	24 03	15 29	12 03	23 49	12 02	16 41	22 22	7 17	29 28	14 01	25 13
19 Su	17 50 36	28 08 56	11 ♐ 24	16 09	9 06	1 27	23 53	15 36	11 59	23 51	12 02	16 40	22 40	7 18	29 27	14 27	25 13
20 M	17 54 32	29 06 11	23 47	15 56	10 48	2 41	23 45	15 43	11 54	23 53	12 02	16 39	22 58	7 19	29 26	14 52	25 14
21 T	17 58 29	0 ♋ 03 25	6 ♑ 22	15 44	12 31	3 54	23 37	15 49	11 50	23 54	12 02	16 37	23 15	7 19 R	29 25	15 18	25 14
22 W	18 2 26	1 00 38	19 08	15 33	14 18	5 08	23 30	15 56	11 46	23 56	12 01	16 36	23 33	7 19	29 24 D	15 44	25 14
23 Th	18 6 22	1 57 52	2 ♒ 06	15 25	16 08	6 22	23 24	16 03	11 42	23 58	12 01	16 34	23 50	7 19	29 24	16 10	25 14
24 F	18 10 19	2 55 05	15 15	15 19	18 00	7 36	23 18	16 11	11 38	24 00	12 01	16 33	24 07	7 18	29 24	16 35	25 15
25 Sa	18 14 15	3 52 18	28 36	15 16	19 55	8 49	23 14	16 18	11 34	24 01	12 00	16 31	24 24	7 17	29 25	17 01	25 15
26 Su	18 18 12	4 49 31	12 ♓ 08	15 15 D	21 52	10 03	23 10	16 25	11 30	24 03	12 00	16 30	24 41	7 16	29 26	17 27	25 15
27 M	18 22 8	5 46 43	25 53	15 15 R	23 52	11 17	23 07	16 33	11 26	24 04	12 00	16 29	24 58	7 14	29 27	17 53	25 15 R
28 T	18 26 5	6 43 56	9 50	15 15	25 54	12 30	23 05	16 41	11 23	24 06	11 59	16 27	25 14	7 12	29 28	18 18	25 15
29 W	18 30 1	7 41 09	24 00	15 14	27 58	13 44	23 04 D	16 48	11 19	24 07	11 59	16 26	25 31	7 10	29 30	18 44	25 15
30 Th	18 33 58	8 38 22	8 ♉ 22	15 11	0 ♋ 03	14 58	23 03	16 56	11 15	24 09	11 58	16 24	25 47	7 07	29 32	19 09	25 15

EPHEMERIS CALCULATED FOR 12 MIDNIGHT GREENWICH MEAN TIME. ALL OTHER DATA AND FACING ASPECTARIAN PAGE IN **EASTERN TIME (BOLD)** AND PACIFIC TIME (REGULAR).

JULY 2016

☽ Last Aspect day	ET / hr:mn / PT	asp	☽ Ingress sign	day	ET / hr:mn / PT
6/30	**8:19 pm** 5:19 pm	☍ ♂	♊	1	**7:44 am** 4:44 am
2	**11:43 pm** 8:43 pm	⚹ ♅	♋	3	**9:20 am** 6:20 am
4	11:29 pm	□ ♅	♌	5	**12:28 pm** 9:28 am
5	**2:29 am**	□ ♅	♌	5	**12:28 pm** 9:28 am
7	**8:07 am** 5:07 am	△ ♅	♍	7	**6:41 pm** 3:41 pm
9	**11:28 pm** 8:28 pm	⚹ ♀	♎	10	**4:32 am** 1:32 am
12	**11:01 am** 8:01 am	□ ☿	♏	12	**4:52 pm** 1:52 pm
14	**6:22 pm** 3:22 pm	☌ ♂	♐	15	**5:14 am** 2:14 am
17	**4:57 am** 1:57 am	△ ♅	♑	17	**3:33 pm** 12:33 pm
19	**6:57 pm** 3:57 pm	☍ ☉	♒	19	**11:10 pm** 8:10 pm

☽ Last Aspect day	ET / hr:mn / PT	asp	☽ Ingress sign	day	ET / hr:mn / PT
21	**9:56 pm** 6:56 pm	□ ♂	♓	22	**4:35 am** 1:35 am
24	**3:06 am** 12:06 am	△ ♂	♈	24	**8:33 am** 5:33 am
25	11:19 pm	☌ ♅	♉	26	**11:37 am** 8:37 am
26	**2:19 am**	☌ ♅	♉	26	**11:37 am** 8:37 am
28	**11:13 am** 8:13 am	☍ ♂	♊	28	**2:17 pm** 11:17 am
30	**7:46 am** 4:46 am	⚹ ♅	♋	30	**5:09 pm** 2:09 pm

☽ Phases & Eclipses phase	day	ET / hr:mn / PT
New Moon	4	**7:01 am** 4:01 am
2nd Quarter	11	**8:52 pm** 5:52 pm
Full Moon	19	**6:57 pm** 3:57 pm
4th Quarter	26	**7:00 pm** 4:00 pm

Planet Ingress	day	ET / hr:mn / PT
⚵ ♏	7	**11:45 pm** 8:45 pm
♀ ♌	11	10:34 pm
♀ ♌	12	**1:34 am**
☿ ♌	13	**8:47 pm** 5:47 pm
⚳ ♉	16	9:10 pm
⚳ ♉	17	**12:10 am**
☉ ♌	22	**5:30 am** 2:30 am
⚶ ♋	25	**5:21 pm** 2:21 pm
☿ ♍	30	**2:18 pm** 11:18 am

Planetary Motion	day	ET / hr:mn / PT
♅ ℞	29	**5:06 pm** 2:06 pm

1 FRIDAY
☽ ⊻ ☿ **1:56 pm** 10:56 am
♀ ⚹ ♃ **3:18 pm** 12:18 pm
☽ ⊻ ☉ 10:28 pm
☽ ☍ ♄ 11:03 pm

2 SATURDAY
☽ ⊻ ☉ **1:28 am**
☽ ☍ ♄ **2:03 am**
☽ □ ♆ **3:25 am** 12:25 am
☉ ⊼ ♄ **9:52 am** 6:52 am
☽ ⊼ ♇ **10:40 am** 7:40 am
☽ □ ♃ **12:15 pm** 9:15 am
☽ ⊻ ♀ **1:59 pm** 10:59 am
☽ ⊼ ♂ **9:53 pm** 6:53 pm
☽ ⚹ ♅ **11:43 pm** 8:43 pm

3 SUNDAY
☉ △ ♆ **7:01 am** 4:01 am
☽ ☌ ☿ 9:29 pm

4 MONDAY
☽ ☌ ☿ **12:29 am**
☽ ⊼ ♄ **3:48 am** 12:48 am
☽ △ ♆ **5:23 am** 2:23 am
☽ ☌ ☉ **7:01 am** 4:01 am
☽ ☍ ♇ **12:48 pm** 9:48 am
☽ ⚹ ♃ **3:02 pm** 12:02 pm
☽ ☌ ♀ **9:09 pm** 6:09 pm
☿ ⊼ ♄ **9:42 pm** 6:42 pm

☽ △ ♂ 9:44 pm
☽ □ ♅ 11:29 pm

5 TUESDAY
☽ △ ♂ **12:44 am**
☽ □ ♅ **2:29 am**
☿ △ ♆ **8:19 am** 5:19 am

6 WEDNESDAY
☽ △ ♄ **7:42 am** 4:42 am
☽ ⊼ ♆ **9:33 am** 6:33 am
☽ ⊻ ☿ **2:29 pm** 11:29 am
☽ ⊻ ☉ **3:21 pm** 12:21 pm
♀ △ ♂ **4:17 pm** 1:17 pm
☽ ⊼ ♇ **5:21 pm** 2:21 pm
☽ ⊻ ♃ **8:25 pm** 5:25 pm
☉ ☌ ☿ **11:24 pm** 8:24 pm

7 THURSDAY
☽ □ ♂ **6:30 am** 3:30 am
☽ ⊻ ♀ **7:52 am** 4:52 am
☿ ☍ ♇ **7:55 am** 4:55 am
☽ △ ♅ **8:07 am** 5:07 am
♀ □ ♅ **10:25 am** 7:25 am
☉ ☍ ♇ **6:27 pm** 3:27 pm

8 FRIDAY
☿ ⚹ ♃ **5:05 am** 2:05 am
☽ □ ♄ **3:01 pm** 12:01 pm
☽ ☍ ♆ **5:10 pm** 2:10 pm
☽ △ ♇ 10:27 pm

9 SATURDAY
☽ △ ♇ **1:27 am**
☽ ⚹ ☉ **4:07 am** 1:07 am
☽ ☌ ♃ **5:32 am** 2:32 am
☽ ⚹ ☿ **10:19 am** 7:19 am
☽ ⚹ ♂ **4:09 pm** 1:09 pm
☽ ⊼ ♅ **5:23 pm** 2:23 pm
☽ ⚹ ♀ **11:28 pm** 8:28 pm
☉ ⚹ ♃ 10:41 pm

10 SUNDAY
☉ ⚹ ♃ **1:41 am**
☿ △ ♂ **10:00 pm** 7:00 pm
☽ ⚹ ♄ 10:45 pm

11 MONDAY
☽ ⚹ ♄ **1:45 am**
☿ □ ♅ **3:29 am** 12:29 am
☽ ⊼ ♆ **4:11 am** 1:11 am
☽ □ ♇ **12:47 pm** 9:47 am
☽ ⊻ ♃ **5:55 pm** 2:55 pm
☽ □ ☉ **8:52 pm** 5:52 pm

12 TUESDAY
☽ ⊻ ♂ **4:54 am** 1:54 am
☽ ☍ ♅ **5:30 am** 2:30 am
☽ □ ☿ **11:01 am** 8:01 am
☽ □ ♀ **6:39 pm** 3:39 pm

13 WEDNESDAY
☽ ⊻ ♄ **2:09 pm** 11:09 am
☽ △ ♆ **4:46 pm** 1:46 pm
♂ ⊼ ♅ 10:13 pm
☽ ⚹ ♇ 10:20 pm

14 THURSDAY
♂ ⊼ ♅ **1:13 am**
☽ ⚹ ♇ **1:20 am**
☽ ⚹ ♃ **7:23 am** 4:23 am
☽ △ ☉ **2:45 pm** 11:45 am
☽ ⊼ ♅ **6:07 pm** 3:07 pm
☽ ☌ ♂ **6:22 pm** 3:22 pm

15 FRIDAY
☽ △ ☿ **11:42 am** 8:42 am
☽ △ ♀ **1:46 pm** 10:46 am
☽ ☌ ♄ 10:45 pm

16 SATURDAY
☽ ☌ ♄ **1:45 am**
☽ □ ♆ **4:25 am** 1:25 am
☉ □ ♅ **9:32 am** 6:32 am
☽ ⊻ ♇ **12:39 pm** 9:39 am
☿ ☌ ♀ **5:59 pm** 2:59 pm
☽ □ ♃ **7:22 pm** 4:22 pm
☉ △ ♂ **11:45 pm** 8:45 pm

17 SUNDAY
☽ △ ♅ **4:57 am** 1:57 am
☽ ⊻ ♂ **6:08 am** 3:08 am
☽ ⊼ ☉ **6:32 am** 3:32 am

18 MONDAY
☽ ⊼ ♀ **5:52 am** 2:52 am
☽ ⊼ ☿ **8:12 am** 5:12 am
☽ ⊻ ♄ **10:56 am** 7:56 am
☽ ⚹ ♆ **1:36 pm** 10:36 am
☽ ☌ ♇ **9:25 pm** 6:25 pm
☿ △ ♄ 11:28 pm

19 TUESDAY
☿ △ ♄ **2:28 am**
☽ △ ♃ **4:39 am** 1:39 am
☽ □ ♅ **1:06 pm** 10:06 am
☽ ⚹ ♂ **3:12 pm** 12:12 pm
☽ ☍ ☉ **6:57 pm** 3:57 pm
☿ ⊼ ♆ **8:44 pm** 5:44 pm

20 WEDNESDAY
♀ △ ♄ **9:19 am** 6:19 am
☽ ⚹ ♄ **5:34 pm** 2:34 pm
☽ ☍ ♀ **6:26 pm** 3:26 pm
☽ ⊻ ♆ **8:12 pm** 5:12 pm
☽ ☍ ☿ **11:58 pm** 8:58 pm

21 THURSDAY
☽ ⊻ ♇ **3:40 am** 12:40 am
☽ ⊼ ♃ **11:24 am** 8:24 am
♀ ⊼ ♆ **1:33 pm** 10:33 am
☽ ⚹ ♅ **6:54 pm** 3:54 pm
☽ □ ♂ **9:56 pm** 6:56 pm

22 FRIDAY
☿ ⊼ ♇ **3:11 am** 12:11 am
☽ ⊼ ☉ **4:31 am** 1:31 am
☽ □ ♄ **10:17 pm** 7:17 pm
☽ ☌ ♆ 9:54 pm

23 SATURDAY
☽ ☌ ♆ **12:54 am**
☽ ⊼ ♀ **4:23 am** 1:23 am
☽ ⚹ ♇ **8:08 am** 5:08 am
☽ ⊼ ☿ **12:27 pm** 9:27 am

☽ ☍ ♃ **4:25 pm** 1:25 pm
☽ ⊻ ♅ **11:05 pm** 8:05 pm

24 SUNDAY
☽ △ ♂ **3:06 am** 12:06 am
☽ △ ☉ **12:17 pm** 9:17 am
♀ ⊼ ♇ **9:57 pm** 6:57 pm
☿ ⊻ ♃ **11:26 pm** 8:26 pm
☽ △ ♄ 10:46 pm

25 MONDAY
☽ △ ♄ **1:46 am**
☽ ⊻ ♆ **4:23 am** 1:23 am
☽ □ ♇ **11:29 am** 8:29 am
☽ △ ♀ **12:48 pm** 9:48 am
☽ ⊼ ♃ **8:22 pm** 5:22 pm
☽ △ ☿ **10:55 pm** 7:55 pm
☽ ☌ ♅ 11:19 pm

26 TUESDAY
☽ ☌ ♅ **2:19 am**
☽ ⊼ ♂ **7:22 am** 4:22 am
☽ □ ☉ **7:00 pm** 4:00 pm

27 WEDNESDAY
☿ △ ♅ **3:45 am** 12:45 am
☽ ⊼ ♄ **4:33 am** 1:33 am
☽ ⚹ ♆ **7:10 am** 4:10 am
☽ △ ♇ **2:12 pm** 11:12 am
☽ □ ♀ **8:23 pm** 5:23 pm
☽ △ ♃ **11:44 pm** 8:44 pm

28 THURSDAY
☽ ⊻ ♅ **5:01 am** 2:01 am
☽ □ ☿ **8:17 am** 5:17 am
☽ ☍ ♂ **11:13 am** 8:13 am
☽ ⚹ ☉ 10:17 pm

29 FRIDAY
☽ ⚹ ☉ **1:17 am**
☽ ☍ ♄ **7:06 am** 4:06 am
☽ □ ♆ **9:44 am** 6:44 am
☽ ⊼ ♇ **4:47 pm** 1:47 pm
☿ □ ♂ **4:49 pm** 1:49 pm
♀ ⊻ ♃ **5:03 pm** 2:03 pm

30 SATURDAY
☽ □ ♃ **3:06 am** 12:06 am
☽ ⚹ ♀ **3:55 am** 12:55 am
☽ ⚹ ♅ **7:46 am** 4:46 am
☽ ⊼ ♂ **3:19 pm** 12:19 pm
☽ ⚹ ☿ **5:30 pm** 2:30 pm

31 SUNDAY
☽ ⊻ ☉ **8:04 am** 5:04 am
☽ ⊼ ♄ **10:09 am** 7:09 am
☽ △ ♆ **12:51 pm** 9:51 am
☽ ☍ ♇ **8:03 pm** 5:03 pm
♀ △ ♅ 9:09 pm

Eastern time in bold type
Pacific time in medium type

DATE	SID.TIME	SUN	MOON	NODE	MERCURY	VENUS	MARS	JUPITER	SATURN	URANUS	NEPTUNE	PLUTO	CERES	PALLAS	JUNO	VESTA	CHIRON
1 F	18 37 55	9 ♋ 35 35	22 ♉ 52	15 ♍ 06	2 ♋ 10	16 ♋ 12	23 ♏ 04	17 ♍ 04	11 ♐ 12	24 ♈ 10	11 ♓ 58	16 ♑ 23	26 ♈ 03	7 ♓ 04	29 ♍ 35	19 ♊ 35	25 ♓ 15
2 Sa	18 41 51	10 32 49	7 ♊ 27	14 58 ℞	4 19	17 25	23 05	17 13	11 08 ℞	24 12	11 57 ℞	16 21 ℞	26 19	7 01 ℞	29 37	20 00	25 14 ℞
3 Su	18 45 48	11 30 02	21 59	14 49	6 28	18 39	23 07	17 21	11 04	24 13	11 57	16 20	26 35	6 57	29 40	20 26	25 14
4 M	18 49 44	12 27 16	6 ♋ 22	14 39	8 38	19 53	23 10	17 29	11 01	24 14	11 56	16 18	26 51	6 53	29 43	20 51	25 14
5 T	18 53 41	13 24 30	20 30	14 30	10 48	21 07	23 14	17 38	10 58	24 15	11 55	16 17	27 06	6 48	29 47	21 17	25 13
6 W	18 57 37	14 21 43	4 ♌ 17	14 23	12 58	22 20	23 18	17 46	10 54	24 17	11 55	16 15	27 22	6 43	29 51	21 42	25 13
7 Th	19 1 34	15 18 56	17 42	14 17	15 09	23 34	23 24	17 55	10 51	24 18	11 54	16 14	27 37	6 38	29 55	22 08	25 13
8 F	19 5 31	16 16 10	0 ♍ 42	14 14	17 18	24 48	23 30	18 04	10 48	24 19	11 53	16 12	27 52	6 33	29 59	22 33	25 12
9 Sa	19 9 27	17 13 23	13 21	14 13 D	19 27	26 02	23 37	18 13	10 45	24 20	11 52	16 11	28 06	6 27	0 ♏ 04	22 58	25 11
10 Su	19 13 24	18 10 36	25 41	14 14	21 36	27 15	23 44	18 22	10 41	24 21	11 52	16 09	28 21	6 20	0 09	23 24	25 11
11 M	19 17 20	19 07 49	7 ♎ 46	14 15	23 43	28 29	23 53	18 31	10 38	24 22	11 51	16 08	28 35	6 14	0 14	23 49	25 10
12 T	19 21 17	20 05 02	19 41	14 15 ℞	25 49	29 43	24 02	18 40	10 36	24 23	11 50	16 06	28 50	6 07	0 20	24 14	25 09
13 W	19 25 13	21 02 15	1 ♏ 33	14 15	27 53	0 ♌ 57	24 12	18 50	10 33	24 24	11 49	16 05	29 04	6 00	0 25	24 39	25 09
14 Th	19 29 10	21 59 28	13 25	14 12	29 56	2 10	24 22	18 59	10 30	24 24	11 48	16 03	29 17	5 52	0 31	25 04	25 08
15 F	19 33 6	22 56 41	25 22	14 08	1 ♌ 57	3 24	24 33	19 09	10 27	24 25	11 47	16 02	29 31	5 44	0 38	25 29	25 07
16 Sa	19 37 3	23 53 54	7 ♐ 28	14 01	3 57	4 38	24 45	19 18	10 25	24 26	11 46	16 01	29 44	5 36	0 44	25 54	25 06
17 Su	19 40 59	24 51 07	19 47	13 54	5 55	5 52	24 58	19 28	10 22	24 26	11 45	15 59	29 58	5 27	0 51	26 19	25 05
18 M	19 44 56	25 48 21	2 ♑ 21	13 45	7 52	7 05	25 11	19 38	10 20	24 27	11 44	15 58	0 ♉ 11	5 18	0 58	26 44	25 04
19 T	19 48 53	26 45 35	15 10	13 37	9 46	8 19	25 25	19 48	10 17	24 28	11 43	15 56	0 24	5 09	1 05	27 09	25 03
20 W	19 52 49	27 42 49	28 15	13 30	11 39	9 33	25 40	19 58	10 15	24 28	11 42	15 55	0 36	4 59	1 13	27 34	25 02
21 Th	19 56 46	28 40 04	11 ♒ 34	13 24	13 30	10 47	25 55	20 08	10 13	24 29	11 41	15 53	0 49	4 49	1 21	27 59	25 00
22 F	20 0 42	29 37 20	25 07	13 21	15 19	12 00	26 11	20 18	10 11	24 29	11 40	15 52	1 01	4 39	1 29	28 24	24 59
23 Sa	20 4 39	0 ♌ 34 36	8 ♓ 50	13 20 D	17 06	13 14	26 28	20 28	10 09	24 29	11 39	15 50	1 13	4 28	1 37	28 49	24 58
24 Su	20 8 35	1 31 52	22 42	13 20	18 52	14 28	26 45	20 39	10 07	24 30	11 38	15 49	1 24	4 17	1 45	29 13	24 57
25 M	20 12 32	2 29 10	6 ♈ 42	13 21	20 36	15 41	27 02	20 49	10 05	24 30	11 37	15 48	1 36	4 06	1 54	29 38	24 55
26 T	20 16 28	3 26 28	20 47	13 22 ℞	22 18	16 55	27 20	21 00	10 03	24 30	11 36	15 46	1 47	3 55	2 03	0 ♋ 03	24 54
27 W	20 20 25	4 23 48	4 ♉ 57	13 23	23 58	18 09	27 39	21 10	10 01	24 30	11 34	15 45	1 58	3 43	2 12	0 27	24 52
28 Th	20 24 22	5 21 08	19 10	13 22	25 37	19 23	27 59	21 21	10 00	24 30	11 33	15 43	2 09	3 31	2 21	0 52	24 51
29 F	20 28 18	6 18 30	3 ♊ 23	13 20	27 14	20 36	28 18	21 32	9 58	24 30 ℞	11 32	15 42	2 19	3 19	2 31	1 16	24 49
30 Sa	20 32 15	7 15 53	17 35	13 16	28 49	21 50	28 39	21 42	9 57	24 30	11 31	15 41	2 30	3 06	2 41	1 41	24 48
31 Su	20 36 11	8 13 17	1 ♋ 40	13 11	0 ♍ 22	23 04	29 00	21 53	9 55	24 30	11 29	15 39	2 40	2 54	2 51	2 05	24 46

EPHEMERIS CALCULATED FOR 12 MIDNIGHT GREENWICH MEAN TIME. ALL OTHER DATA AND FACING ASPECTARIAN PAGE IN **EASTERN TIME (BOLD)** AND PACIFIC TIME (REGULAR).

AUGUST 2016

☽ Last Aspect day	ET / hr:mn / PT		asp	☽ Ingress sign	day	ET / hr:mn / PT	
1	**8:44 pm**	5:44 pm	△♂	♌	1	**9:12 pm**	6:12 pm
3		9:13 pm	☌♀	♍	4	**3:34 am**	12:34 am
4	**12:13 am**		☌♀	♍	4	**3:34 am**	12:34 am
5	**11:20 pm**	8:20 pm	☌♃	♎	6	**12:57 pm**	9:57 am
8	**1:41 pm**	10:41 am	☍♅	♏	8		9:51 pm
8	**1:41 pm**	10:41 am	☍♅	♏	9	**12:51 am**	
10		10:22 pm	✶♃	♐	11	**1:24 pm**	10:24 am
11	**1:22 am**		✶♃	♐	11	**1:24 pm**	10:24 am
13	**1:37 pm**	10:37 am	□♃	♑	13		9:11 pm
13	**1:37 pm**	10:37 am	□♃	♑	14	**12:11 am**	
15	**10:45 pm**	7:45 pm	△♃	♒	16	**7:52 am**	4:52 am
18	**5:27 am**	2:27 am	☍☉	♓	18	**12:34 pm**	9:34 am
20	**8:21 am**	5:21 am	☍♃	♈	20	**3:18 pm**	12:18 pm
22	**7:48 am**	4:48 am	☌♅	♉	22	**5:19 pm**	2:19 pm
24	**3:38 pm**	12:38 pm	△☿	♊	24	**7:40 pm**	4:40 pm
26	**8:30 pm**	5:30 pm	□☿	♋	26	**11:06 pm**	8:06 pm
28		11:23 pm	✶☿	♌	29	**4:11 am**	1:11 am
29	**2:23 am**		✶☿	♌	29	**4:11 am**	1:11 am
30		9:20 pm	△♅	♍	31	**11:22 am**	8:22 am
31	**12:20 am**		△♅	♍	31	**11:22 am**	8:22 am

☽ Phases & Eclipses

phase	day	ET / hr:mn / PT	
New Moon	2	**4:45 pm**	1:45 pm
2nd Quarter	10	**2:21 pm**	11:21 am
Full Moon	18	**5:27 am**	2:27 am
4th Quarter	24	**11:41 pm**	8:41 pm

Planet Ingress

		day	ET / hr:mn / PT	
♂	♐	2	**1:49 pm**	10:49 am
♀	♍	5	**11:27 am**	8:27 am
⚵	♒	12	**3:03 am**	12:03 am
☉	♍	22	**12:38 pm**	9:38 am
♀	♎	29	**10:07 pm**	7:07 pm

Planetary Motion

		day	ET / hr:mn / PT	
♄	D	13	**5:50 am**	2:50 am
☿	R	30	**9:04 am**	6:04 am
⚳	R	31	**3:09 am**	12:09 am

1 MONDAY
♀△♅ **12:09 am**
☽✶♃ **7:25 am** 4:25 am
☽□♅ **11:31 am** 8:31 am
☽⚺♀ **12:39 pm** 9:39 am
☉△♄ **1:49 pm** 10:49 am
☽△♂ **8:44 pm** 5:44 pm

2 TUESDAY
☽⚺☿ **4:05 am** 1:05 am
☽△♄ **2:47 pm** 11:47 am
☽☌☉ **4:45 pm** 1:45 pm
☽⚻♆ **5:34 pm** 2:34 pm
☽⚻♇ 10:05 pm

3 WEDNESDAY
☽⚻♇ **1:05 am**
☉⚻♆ **4:02 am** 1:02 am
☽⚺♃ **1:51 pm** 10:51 am
☽△♅ **5:23 pm** 2:23 pm
☽☌♀ 9:13 pm

4 THURSDAY
☽☌♀ **12:13 am**
☽□♂ **4:43 am** 1:43 am
☽☌☿ **5:44 pm** 2:44 pm
☽□♄ **10:02 pm** 7:02 pm
☽☍♆ 9:57 pm

5 FRIDAY
☽☍♆ **12:57 am**
☽⚺☉ **4:44 am** 1:44 am

☽△♇ **8:54 am** 5:54 am
☽☌♃ **11:20 pm** 8:20 pm
☽⚻♅ 11:10 pm

6 SATURDAY
☽⚻♅ **2:10 am**
☿□♄ **9:18 am** 6:18 am
☽⚺♀ **3:48 pm** 12:48 pm
☽✶♂ **4:06 pm** 1:06 pm
♀□♂ **8:20 pm** 5:20 pm

7 SUNDAY
☽✶♄ **8:19 am** 5:19 am
☉⚻♇ **10:12 am** 7:12 am
☽⚺☿ **11:11 am** 8:11 am
☽⚻♆ **11:19 am** 8:19 am
☿☍♆ **12:24 pm** 9:24 am
☽□♇ **7:38 pm** 4:38 pm
☽✶☉ **8:29 pm** 5:29 pm

8 MONDAY
☽⚺♃ **11:45 am** 8:45 am
☽☍♅ **1:41 pm** 10:41 am

9 TUESDAY
☽⚺♂ **6:19 am** 3:19 am
☽✶♀ **10:43 am** 7:43 am
☽⚺♄ **8:40 pm** 5:40 pm
☽△♆ **11:37 pm** 8:37 pm

10 WEDNESDAY
☽✶☿ **6:47 am** 3:47 am
☽✶♇ **8:05 am** 5:05 am

☽□☉ **2:21 pm** 11:21 am
☿△♇ **7:25 pm** 4:25 pm
☽✶♃ 10:22 pm
☽⚻♅ 11:15 pm

11 THURSDAY
☽✶♃ **1:22 am**
☽⚻♅ **2:15 am**
☽☌♂ **9:04 pm** 6:04 pm

12 FRIDAY
☽□♀ **5:58 am** 2:58 am
☽☌♄ **8:51 am** 5:51 am
☽□♆ **11:38 am** 8:38 am
☽⚺♇ **7:53 pm** 4:53 pm
☽□☿ 9:59 pm

13 SATURDAY
☽□☿ **12:59 am**
♃⚻♅ **5:02 am** 2:02 am
☽△☉ **7:05 am** 4:05 am
♀□♄ **10:31 am** 7:31 am
☽△♅ **1:28 pm** 10:28 am
☽□♃ **1:37 pm** 10:37 am

14 SUNDAY
☽⚺♂ **9:41 am** 6:41 am
♀☍♆ **1:03 pm** 10:03 am
☽⚺♄ **6:42 pm** 3:42 pm
☽✶♆ **9:14 pm** 6:14 pm
☽△♀ **10:07 pm** 7:07 pm

15 MONDAY
☽☌♇ **5:04 am** 2:04 am
☽△☿ **2:59 pm** 11:59 am

☽⚻☉ **8:13 pm** 5:13 pm
☽□♅ **9:42 pm** 6:42 pm
☽△♃ **10:45 pm** 7:45 pm

16 TUESDAY
☉△♅ **4:23 pm** 1:23 pm
☽✶♂ **6:50 pm** 3:50 pm
☽✶♄ 10:21 pm

17 WEDNESDAY
☽✶♄ **1:21 am**
☽⚺♆ **3:37 am** 12:37 am
☽⚻♀ **9:57 am** 6:57 am
☽⚺♇ **11:04 am** 8:04 am
☉⚺♃ **3:26 pm** 12:26 pm
♀△♇ **10:17 pm** 7:17 pm
☽⚻☿ 9:27 pm
☽✶♅ 11:50 pm

18 THURSDAY
☽⚻☿ **12:27 am**
☽✶♅ **2:50 am**
☽⚻♃ **4:40 am** 1:40 am
☽☍☉ **5:27 am** 2:27 am
☽□♂ 9:53 pm

19 FRIDAY
☽□♂ **12:53 am**
☽□♄ **5:19 am** 2:19 am
☽☌♆ **7:21 am** 4:21 am
☽✶♇ **2:33 pm** 11:33 am
☿⚻♅ **2:55 pm** 11:55 am
☽☍♀ **6:24 pm** 3:24 pm

20 SATURDAY
☽⚺♅ **5:48 am** 2:48 am
☽☍☿ **6:41 am** 3:41 am
☽☍♃ **8:21 am** 5:21 am
☽⚻☉ **12:03 pm** 9:03 am

21 SUNDAY
☽△♂ **5:09 am** 2:09 am
☽△♄ **7:43 am** 4:43 am
☽⚺♆ **9:36 am** 6:36 am
☽□♇ **4:43 pm** 1:43 pm
☽⚻♀ 10:15 pm

22 MONDAY
☽⚻♀ **1:15 am**
☿☌♃ **5:05 am** 2:05 am
☽☌♅ **7:48 am** 4:48 am
☽⚻♃ **11:06 am** 8:06 am
☽⚻☿ **11:18 am** 8:18 am
☽△☉ **5:39 pm** 2:39 pm

23 TUESDAY
☽⚻♂ **9:00 am** 6:00 am
☽⚻♄ **9:47 am** 6:47 am
☽✶♆ **11:32 am** 8:32 am
☽△♇ **6:43 pm** 3:43 pm

24 WEDNESDAY
♂☌♄ **7:26 am** 4:26 am
☽△♀ **8:06 am** 5:06 am
☽⚺♅ **9:56 am** 6:56 am
☽△♃ **2:06 pm** 11:06 am
☽△☿ **3:38 pm** 12:38 pm
☽□☉ **11:41 pm** 8:41 pm

25 THURSDAY
♀⚻♅ **5:08 am** 2:08 am
☽☍♄ **12:29 pm** 9:29 am
☽☍♂ **1:34 pm** 10:34 am
☽□♆ **2:06 pm** 11:06 am
☽⚻♇ **9:29 pm** 6:29 pm
♂□♆ 11:56 pm

26 FRIDAY
♂□♆ **2:56 am**
☽✶♅ **1:03 pm** 10:03 am
☽□♀ **4:12 pm** 1:12 pm
☽□♃ **6:09 pm** 3:09 pm
☽□☿ **8:30 pm** 5:30 pm

27 SATURDAY
☽✶☉ **7:08 am** 4:08 am
☽⚻♄ **4:30 pm** 1:30 pm
☽△♆ **5:58 pm** 2:58 pm
♀☌♃ **6:29 pm** 3:29 pm
☽⚻♂ **7:39 pm** 4:39 pm
☽☍♇ 10:39 pm

28 SUNDAY
☽☍♇ **1:39 am**
☽□♅ **5:41 pm** 2:41 pm
☽✶♃ **11:54 pm** 8:54 pm
☽✶♀ 11:23 pm
☽✶☿ 11:23 pm
☿☌♀ 11:32 pm

29 MONDAY
☽✶♀ **2:23 am**
☽✶☿ **2:23 am**

☿☌♀ **2:32 am**
☽⚺☉ **4:43 pm** 1:43 pm
☽△♄ **10:20 pm** 7:20 pm
☽⚻♆ **11:39 pm** 8:39 pm

30 TUESDAY
☽△♂ **3:51 am** 12:51 am
☽⚻♇ **7:41 am** 4:41 am
☽△♅ 9:20 pm

31 WEDNESDAY
☽△♅ **12:20 am**
☽⚺♃ **7:49 am** 4:49 am
☽⚺☿ **9:32 am** 6:32 am
☽⚺♀ **3:20 pm** 12:20 pm

Eastern time in bold type
Pacific time in medium type

AUGUST 2016

DATE	SID.TIME	SUN	MOON	NODE	MERCURY	VENUS	MARS	JUPITER	SATURN	URANUS	NEPTUNE	PLUTO	CERES	PALLAS	JUNO	VESTA	CHIRON
1 M	20 40 8	9 ♌ 10 42	15 ♋ 36	13 ♍ 06	1 ♍ 54	24 ♌ 18	29 ♏ 21	22 ♍ 04	9 ♐ 54	24 ♈ 30	11 ♓ 28	15 ♑ 38	2 ♉ 50	2 ♓ 41	3 ♏ 01	2 ♋ 30	24 ♓ 44
2 T	20 44 4	10 08 07	29 19	13 01 ℞	3 23	25 31	29 43	22 15	9 53 ℞	24 30 ℞	11 27 ℞	15 37 ℞	2 59	2 27 ℞	3 11	2 54	24 43 ℞
3 W	20 48 1	11 05 34	12 ♌ 46	12 57	4 51	26 45	0 ♐ 06	22 26	9 52	24 30	11 25	15 35	3 08	2 14	3 22	3 18	24 41
4 Th	20 51 58	12 03 02	25 55	12 54	6 17	27 59	0 29	22 38	9 51	24 30	11 24	15 34	3 17	2 00	3 33	3 42	24 39
5 F	20 55 54	13 00 30	8 ♍ 46	12 53 D	7 42	29 13	0 52	22 49	9 50	24 30	11 23	15 33	3 26	1 46	3 44	4 06	24 37
6 Sa	20 59 51	13 57 59	21 18	12 53	9 04	0 ♍ 26	1 16	23 00	9 49	24 29	11 21	15 31	3 34	1 32	3 55	4 31	24 35
7 Su	21 3 47	14 55 29	3 ♎ 35	12 54	10 25	1 40	1 41	23 11	9 49	24 29	11 20	15 30	3 42	1 18	4 06	4 55	24 33
8 M	21 7 44	15 53 00	15 40	12 56	11 43	2 54	2 06	23 23	9 48	24 28	11 18	15 29	3 50	1 04	4 18	5 18	24 31
9 T	21 11 40	16 50 32	27 36	12 58	13 00	4 07	2 31	23 34	9 48	24 28	11 17	15 28	3 58	0 49	4 29	5 42	24 29
10 W	21 15 37	17 48 04	9 ♏ 28	12 59 ℞	14 15	5 21	2 57	23 46	9 47	24 27	11 15	15 27	4 05	0 34	4 41	6 06	24 27
11 Th	21 19 33	18 45 38	21 20	12 59	15 27	6 35	3 23	23 58	9 47	24 27	11 14	15 25	4 12	0 19	4 53	6 30	24 25
12 F	21 23 30	19 43 12	3 ♐ 18	12 58	16 38	7 49	3 49	24 09	9 47	24 26	11 12	15 24	4 19	0 04	5 06	6 54	24 23
13 Sa	21 27 26	20 40 47	15 26	12 56	17 46	9 02	4 16	24 21	9 47 D	24 26	11 11	15 23	4 25	29 ♒ 49	5 18	7 17	24 21
14 Su	21 31 23	21 38 24	27 49	12 54	18 51	10 16	4 44	24 33	9 47	24 25	11 09	15 22	4 31	29 34	5 31	7 41	24 19
15 M	21 35 20	22 36 01	10 ♑ 28	12 51	19 55	11 30	5 12	24 45	9 47	24 24	11 08	15 21	4 37	29 19	5 43	8 04	24 17
16 T	21 39 16	23 33 39	23 27	12 48	20 55	12 43	5 40	24 56	9 47	24 23	11 06	15 20	4 42	29 04	5 56	8 28	24 14
17 W	21 43 13	24 31 19	6 ♒ 46	12 46	21 53	13 57	6 08	25 08	9 47	24 23	11 05	15 19	4 48	28 48	6 10	8 51	24 12
18 Th	21 47 9	25 28 59	20 25	12 44	22 49	15 10	6 37	25 20	9 48	24 22	11 03	15 18	4 52	28 33	6 23	9 14	24 10
19 F	21 51 6	26 26 41	4 ♓ 20	12 43 D	23 41	16 24	7 06	25 32	9 48	24 21	11 02	15 17	4 57	28 18	6 36	9 38	24 07
20 Sa	21 55 2	27 24 25	18 30	12 43	24 30	17 38	7 36	25 44	9 49	24 20	11 00	15 16	5 01	28 02	6 50	10 01	24 05
21 Su	21 58 59	28 22 09	2 ♈ 48	12 43	25 16	18 51	8 06	25 57	9 50	24 19	10 58	15 15	5 05	27 47	7 04	10 24	24 03
22 M	22 2 55	29 19 56	17 12	12 44	25 58	20 05	8 36	26 09	9 50	24 18	10 57	15 14	5 08	27 31	7 17	10 47	24 00
23 T	22 6 52	0 ♍ 17 44	1 ♉ 36	12 45	26 37	21 19	9 07	26 21	9 51	24 17	10 55	15 13	5 11	27 16	7 31	11 10	23 58
24 W	22 10 49	1 15 33	15 57	12 46	27 12	22 32	9 38	26 33	9 52	24 15	10 54	15 12	5 14	27 01	7 46	11 33	23 55
25 Th	22 14 45	2 13 25	0 ♊ 12	12 46 ℞	27 42	23 46	10 09	26 45	9 53	24 14	10 52	15 11	5 17	26 45	8 00	11 56	23 53
26 F	22 18 42	3 11 18	14 18	12 46	28 08	24 59	10 41	26 58	9 54	24 13	10 50	15 10	5 19	26 30	8 14	12 18	23 50
27 Sa	22 22 38	4 09 14	28 13	12 46	28 30	26 13	11 12	27 10	9 56	24 12	10 49	15 09	5 20	26 15	8 29	12 41	23 48
28 Su	22 26 35	5 07 11	11 ♋ 56	12 45	28 46	27 26	11 45	27 23	9 57	24 10	10 47	15 08	5 22	26 00	8 44	13 03	23 45
29 M	22 30 31	6 05 09	25 27	12 44	28 58	28 40	12 17	27 35	9 58	24 09	10 45	15 07	5 23	25 45	8 59	13 26	23 42
30 T	22 34 28	7 03 10	8 ♌ 43	12 43	29 04 ℞	29 54	12 50	27 47	10 00	24 08	10 44	15 07	5 24	25 30	9 14	13 48	23 40
31 W	22 38 24	8 01 12	21 46	12 43	29 04	1 ♎ 07	13 23	28 00	10 02	24 06	10 42	15 06	5 24 ℞	25 15	9 29	14 10	23 37

EPHEMERIS CALCULATED FOR 12 MIDNIGHT GREENWICH MEAN TIME. ALL OTHER DATA AND FACING ASPECTARIAN PAGE IN **EASTERN TIME (BOLD)** AND PACIFIC TIME (REGULAR).

SEPTEMBER 2016

☽ Last Aspect day	ET / hr:mn / PT		asp	☽ Ingress sign	day	ET / hr:mn / PT	
2	**6:13 pm**	3:13 pm	☌ ♃	♎	2	**8:55 pm**	5:55 pm
4	**8:30 pm**	5:30 pm	☍ ♅	♏	5	**8:38 am**	5:38 am
7	**8:43 pm**	5:43 pm	⚹ ♃	♐	7	**9:20 pm**	6:20 pm
9	**8:51 pm**	5:51 pm	△ ♅	♑	10	**8:55 am**	5:55 am
12	**6:00 am**	3:00 am	□ ♅	♒	12	**5:28 pm**	2:28 pm
14	**11:31 am**	8:31 am	⚹ ♅	♓	14	**10:23 pm**	7:23 pm
16	**3:05 pm**	12:05 pm	☍ ☉	♈	16		9:22 pm
16	**3:05 pm**	12:05 pm	☍ ☉	♈	17	**12:22 am**	
18	**4:11 pm**	1:11 pm	△ ♂	♉	18		9:58 pm
18	**4:11 pm**	1:11 pm	△ ♂	♉	19	**12:58 am**	
20	**11:32 pm**	8:32 pm	△ ☉	♊	20		10:53 pm
20	**11:32 pm**	8:32 pm	△ ☉	♊	21	**1:53 am**	
23	**3:57 am**	12:57 am	△ ♀	♋	23	**4:33 am**	1:33 am
24	**9:42 pm**	6:42 pm	□ ♅	♌	25	**9:48 am**	6:48 am
27	**4:52 am**	1:52 am	△ ♅	♍	27	**5:43 pm**	2:43 pm
29	**6:05 am**	3:05 am	☌ ☿	♎	30	**3:52 am**	12:52 am

☽ Phases & Eclipses phase	day	ET / hr:mn / PT	
New Moon	1	**5:03 am**	2:03 am
●	1	9° ♍ 21'	
2nd Quarter	9	**7:49 am**	4:49 am
Full Moon	16	**3:05 pm**	12:05 pm
●	16	24° ♓ 20'	
4th Quarter	23	**5:56 am**	2:56 am
New Moon	30	**8:11 pm**	5:11 pm

Planet Ingress	day	ET / hr:mn / PT	
♃ ♎	9	**7:18 am**	4:18 am
☉ ♎	22	**10:21 am**	7:21 am
♀ ♏	23	**10:51 am**	7:51 am
♂ ♑	27	**4:07 am**	1:07 am

Planetary Motion	day	ET / hr:mn / PT	
☿ D	21		10:31 pm
☿ D	22	**1:31 am**	
♇ D	26	**11:01 am**	8:01 am

1 THURSDAY
☽ ☌ ☉ **5:03 am** 2:03 am
☽ □ ♄ **6:25 am** 3:25 am
☽ ☍ ♆ **7:33 am** 4:33 am
☽ □ ♂ **2:39 pm** 11:39 am
☽ △ ♇ **3:59 pm** 12:59 pm
☉ □ ♄ **11:22 pm** 8:22 pm

2 FRIDAY
☽ ⚻ ♅ **9:18 am** 6:18 am
☉ ☍ ♆ **12:38 pm** 9:38 am
☿ ☌ ♃ **1:18 pm** 10:18 am
☽ ☌ ☿ **6:00 pm** 3:00 pm
☽ ☌ ♃ **6:13 pm** 3:13 pm
♂ ⚺ ♇ **7:54 pm** 4:54 pm

3 SATURDAY
☽ ☌ ♀ **7:30 am** 4:30 am
☽ ⚹ ♄ **4:55 pm** 1:55 pm
☽ ⚻ ♆ **5:48 pm** 2:48 pm
☽ ⚺ ☉ **8:25 pm** 5:25 pm
☽ □ ♇ 11:39 pm

4 SUNDAY
☽ □ ♇ **2:39 am**
☽ ⚹ ♂ **4:13 am** 1:13 am
☽ ☍ ♅ **8:30 pm** 5:30 pm

5 MONDAY
☽ ⚺ ☿ **3:22 am** 12:22 am
☽ ⚺ ♃ **6:55 am** 3:55 am
☽ ⚺ ♀ 11:25 pm

6 TUESDAY
☽ ⚺ ♀ **2:25 am**
☽ ⚺ ♄ **5:20 am** 2:20 am
☽ △ ♆ **5:55 am** 2:55 am
☽ ⚹ ☉ **2:06 pm** 11:06 am
☽ ⚹ ♇ **3:02 pm** 12:02 pm
☽ ⚺ ♂ **7:46 pm** 4:46 pm
☉ △ ♇ 10:19 pm

7 WEDNESDAY
☉ △ ♇ **1:19 am**
♀ ⚹ ♄ **7:34 am** 4:34 am
☽ ⚻ ♅ **9:00 am** 6:00 am
♀ ⚻ ♆ **11:39 am** 8:39 am
☽ ⚹ ☿ **12:38 pm** 9:38 am
☽ ⚹ ♃ **8:43 pm** 5:43 pm

8 THURSDAY
☽ ☌ ♄ **6:06 pm** 3:06 pm
☽ □ ♆ **6:20 pm** 3:20 pm
☽ ⚹ ♀ **9:54 pm** 6:54 pm

9 FRIDAY
☽ ⚺ ♇ **3:24 am** 12:24 am
☽ □ ☉ **7:49 am** 4:49 am
☽ ☌ ♂ **11:11 am** 8:11 am
☿ ⚻ ♅ **2:58 pm** 11:58 am
☽ □ ☿ **8:26 pm** 5:26 pm
☽ △ ♅ **8:51 pm** 5:51 pm

10 SATURDAY
♄ □ ♆ **9:04 am** 6:04 am
☽ □ ♃ **9:22 am** 6:22 am

11 SUNDAY
♀ □ ♇ **3:47 am** 12:47 am
☽ ⚹ ♆ **4:54 am** 1:54 am
☽ ⚺ ♄ **5:01 am** 2:01 am
☽ ☌ ♇ **1:37 pm** 10:37 am
☽ □ ♀ **2:40 pm** 11:40 am
☽ △ ☉ **10:36 pm** 7:36 pm
☽ ⚺ ♂ **11:51 pm** 8:51 pm
☽ △ ☿ 10:37 pm

12 MONDAY
☽ △ ☿ **1:37 am**
☽ □ ♅ **6:00 am** 3:00 am
☿ □ ♂ **2:58 pm** 11:58 am
☽ △ ♃ **6:50 pm** 3:50 pm
☉ ☌ ☿ **7:40 pm** 4:40 pm

13 TUESDAY
☽ ⚺ ♆ **12:05 pm** 9:05 am
☽ ⚹ ♄ **12:30 pm** 9:30 am
☉ □ ♂ **4:39 pm** 1:39 pm
☽ ⚺ ♇ **8:18 pm** 5:18 pm
☽ △ ♀ 11:41 pm

14 WEDNESDAY
☽ △ ♀ **2:41 am**
☽ ⚻ ☿ **3:53 am** 12:53 am
☽ ⚹ ♂ **8:23 am** 5:23 am
☽ ⚻ ☉ **8:50 am** 5:50 am
☿ ⚺ ♀ **10:44 am** 7:44 am
☽ ⚹ ♅ **11:31 am** 8:31 am
☽ ⚻ ♃ 9:28 pm

15 THURSDAY
☽ ⚻ ♃ **12:28 am**
☽ ☌ ♆ **3:45 pm** 12:45 pm
☽ □ ♄ **4:25 pm** 1:25 pm
☉ ⚻ ♅ **9:51 pm** 6:51 pm
☽ ⚹ ♇ **11:35 pm** 8:35 pm

16 FRIDAY
☽ ☍ ☿ **3:46 am** 12:46 am
☽ ⚻ ♀ **10:18 am** 7:18 am
☽ □ ♂ **1:17 pm** 10:17 am
☽ ⚺ ♅ **1:54 pm** 10:54 am
☽ ☍ ☉ **3:05 pm** 12:05 pm

17 SATURDAY
♂ △ ♅ **3:04 am** 12:04 am
☽ ☍ ♃ **3:06 am** 12:06 am
☽ ⚺ ♆ **4:59 pm** 1:59 pm
☽ △ ♄ **5:54 pm** 2:54 pm
☽ □ ♇ 9:39 pm
☽ ⚻ ☿ 11:27 pm

18 SUNDAY
☽ □ ♇ **12:39 am**
☽ ⚻ ☿ **2:27 am**
♀ ☍ ♅ **4:06 am** 1:06 am
☽ ☌ ♅ **2:32 pm** 11:32 am
☽ ☍ ♀ **3:30 pm** 12:30 pm
☽ △ ♂ **4:11 pm** 1:11 pm
☽ ⚻ ☉ **7:14 pm** 4:14 pm

19 MONDAY
☽ ⚻ ♃ **4:24 am** 1:24 am
♀ ⚹ ♂ **7:53 am** 4:53 am
☽ ⚹ ♆ **5:25 pm** 2:25 pm
☽ ⚻ ♄ **6:36 pm** 3:36 pm
☽ △ ♇ 10:11 pm
☽ △ ☿ 10:32 pm

20 TUESDAY
☽ △ ♇ **1:11 am**
☽ △ ☿ **1:32 am**
☽ ⚺ ♅ **3:08 pm** 12:08 pm
☽ ⚻ ♂ **7:07 pm** 4:07 pm
☽ ⚻ ♀ **8:40 pm** 5:40 pm
☿ △ ♇ **9:26 pm** 6:26 pm
☽ △ ☉ **11:32 pm** 8:32 pm

21 WEDNESDAY
☽ △ ♃ **6:08 am** 3:08 am
☽ □ ♆ **6:42 pm** 3:42 pm
☽ ☍ ♄ **8:13 pm** 5:13 pm
☽ □ ☿ 11:38 pm
☽ ⚻ ♇ 11:49 pm

22 THURSDAY
☽ □ ☿ **2:38 am**
☽ ⚻ ♇ **2:49 am**
☽ ⚹ ♅ **5:11 pm** 2:11 pm
☽ ☍ ♂ **11:53 pm** 8:53 pm

23 FRIDAY
☽ △ ♀ **3:57 am** 12:57 am
☿ △ ♇ **4:51 am** 1:51 am
☽ □ ☉ **5:56 am** 2:56 am
☽ □ ♃ **9:49 am** 6:49 am
☽ △ ♆ **10:06 pm** 7:06 pm
☽ ⚻ ♄ 9:01 pm

24 SATURDAY
☽ ⚻ ♄ **12:01 am**
☽ ☍ ♇ **6:42 am** 3:42 am
☽ ⚹ ☿ **7:15 am** 4:15 am
☽ □ ♅ **9:42 pm** 6:42 pm

25 SUNDAY
☽ ⚻ ♂ **7:37 am** 4:37 am
☽ □ ♀ **2:36 pm** 11:36 am
☽ ⚹ ☉ **3:33 pm** 12:33 pm
☽ ⚹ ♃ **4:14 pm** 1:14 pm

26 MONDAY
☉ ☌ ♃ **3:00 am** 12:00 am
☽ ⚻ ♆ **4:09 am** 1:09 am
☽ △ ♄ **6:34 am** 3:34 am
♀ ⚺ ♃ **11:35 am** 8:35 am
☽ ⚻ ♇ **1:19 pm** 10:19 am
☽ ⚺ ☿ **4:20 pm** 1:20 pm

27 TUESDAY
☽ △ ♅ **4:52 am** 1:52 am
☉ ⚺ ♀ **3:14 pm** 12:14 pm
☽ △ ♂ **6:27 pm** 3:27 pm
☽ ⚺ ♃ 10:25 pm

28 WEDNESDAY
☽ ⚺ ♃ **1:25 am**
☽ ⚺ ☉ **4:30 am** 1:30 am
☽ ⚹ ♀ **4:46 am** 1:46 am
☽ ☍ ♆ **12:46 pm** 9:46 am
☽ □ ♄ **3:42 pm** 12:42 pm
☽ △ ♇ **10:24 pm** 7:24 pm

29 THURSDAY
☽ ☌ ☿ **6:05 am** 3:05 am
☽ ⚻ ♅ **2:24 pm** 11:24 am

30 FRIDAY
☽ □ ♂ **7:58 am** 4:58 am
☽ ☌ ♃ **12:54 pm** 9:54 am
☽ ☌ ☉ **8:11 pm** 5:11 pm
☽ ⚺ ♀ **9:51 pm** 6:51 pm
☽ ⚻ ♆ **11:26 pm** 8:26 pm
☽ ⚹ ♄ 11:55 pm

Eastern time in bold type
Pacific time in medium type

SEPTEMBER 2016

DATE	SID.TIME	SUN	MOON	NODE	MERCURY	VENUS	MARS	JUPITER	SATURN	URANUS	NEPTUNE	PLUTO	CERES	PALLAS	JUNO	VESTA	CHIRON
1 Th	22 42 21	8 ♍ 59 16	4 ♍ 35	12♍43D	28 ♍ 58	2 ♎ 21	13 ♐ 56	28 ♍ 13	10 ♐ 03	24 ♈ 05	10 ♓ 40	15 ♑ 05	5 ♉ 24	25 ♒ 01	9 ♏ 44	14 ♋ 33	23 ♓ 35
2 F	22 46 18	9 57 22	17 10	12 43	28 47 ℞	3 34	14 30	28 25	10 05	24 03 ℞	10 39 ℞	15 04 ℞	5 23 ℞	24 47 ℞	9 59	14 55	23 32 ℞
3 Sa	22 50 14	10 55 29	29 32	12 43	28 29	4 48	15 04	28 38	10 07	24 02	10 37	15 04	5 22	24 32	10 15	15 17	23 29
4 Su	22 54 11	11 53 38	11 ♎ 42	12 43 ℞	28 04	6 01	15 38	28 50	10 09	24 00	10 35	15 03	5 21	24 18	10 31	15 39	23 27
5 M	22 58 7	12 51 48	23 43	12 43	27 34	7 15	16 13	29 03	10 11	23 58	10 34	15 02	5 20	24 04	10 46	16 00	23 24
6 T	23 2 4	13 50 00	5 ♏ 38	12 43	26 57	8 28	16 47	29 16	10 14	23 57	10 32	15 02	5 18	23 51	11 02	16 22	23 21
7 W	23 6 0	14 48 14	17 29	12 42	26 15	9 42	17 22	29 28	10 16	23 55	10 31	15 01	5 15	23 37	11 18	16 44	23 18
8 Th	23 9 57	15 46 29	29 21	12 42	25 27	10 55	17 57	29 41	10 18	23 53	10 29	15 01	5 13	23 24	11 34	17 05	23 16
9 F	23 13 53	16 44 45	11 ♐ 17	12 42 D	24 34	12 08	18 33	29 54	10 21	23 51	10 27	15 00	5 10	23 11	11 51	17 26	23 13
10 Sa	23 17 50	17 43 03	23 24	12 42	23 38	13 22	19 08	0 ♎ 07	10 23	23 50	10 26	15 00	5 06	22 59	12 07	17 48	23 10
11 Su	23 21 47	18 41 23	5 ♑ 44	12 42	22 39	14 35	19 44	0 20	10 26	23 48	10 24	14 59	5 02	22 46	12 23	18 09	23 08
12 M	23 25 43	19 39 44	18 23	12 43	21 38	15 49	20 21	0 32	10 29	23 46	10 22	14 59	4 58	22 34	12 40	18 30	23 05
13 T	23 29 40	20 38 07	1 ♒ 23	12 44	20 36	17 02	20 57	0 45	10 32	23 44	10 21	14 58	4 54	22 22	12 57	18 51	23 02
14 W	23 33 36	21 36 32	14 48	12 44	19 36	18 15	21 33	0 58	10 34	23 42	10 19	14 58	4 49	22 10	13 13	19 11	22 59
15 Th	23 37 33	22 34 58	28 36	12 45	18 38	19 29	22 10	1 11	10 37	23 40	10 18	14 58	4 44	21 59	13 30	19 32	22 57
16 F	23 41 29	23 33 26	12 ♓ 48	12 45 ℞	17 45	20 42	22 47	1 24	10 41	23 38	10 16	14 57	4 38	21 48	13 47	19 53	22 54
17 Sa	23 45 26	24 31 55	27 20	12 45	16 56	21 55	23 24	1 37	10 44	23 36	10 14	14 57	4 32	21 37	14 04	20 13	22 51
18 Su	23 49 22	25 30 27	12 ♈ 04	12 44	16 14	23 09	24 02	1 50	10 47	23 34	10 13	14 57	4 26	21 27	14 21	20 33	22 48
19 M	23 53 19	26 29 00	26 56	12 43	15 40	24 22	24 39	2 03	10 50	23 32	10 11	14 56	4 19	21 17	14 39	20 54	22 45
20 T	23 57 15	27 27 36	11 ♉ 45	12 41	15 14	25 35	25 17	2 16	10 54	23 30	10 10	14 56	4 12	21 07	14 56	21 14	22 43
21 W	0 1 12	28 26 14	26 26	12 39	14 57	26 48	25 55	2 28	10 57	23 28	10 08	14 56	4 04	20 57	15 13	21 34	22 40
22 Th	0 5 9	29 24 54	10 ♊ 53	12 38	14 50 D	28 02	26 33	2 41	11 01	23 26	10 07	14 56	3 57	20 48	15 31	21 53	22 37
23 F	0 9 5	0 ♎ 23 36	25 02	12 37 D	14 52	29 15	27 12	2 54	11 05	23 23	10 05	14 56	3 48	20 39	15 49	22 13	22 35
24 Sa	0 13 2	1 22 21	8 ♋ 52	12 37	15 05	0 ♏ 28	27 50	3 07	11 08	23 21	10 03	14 56	3 40	20 31	16 06	22 32	22 32
25 Su	0 16 58	2 21 08	22 22	12 38	15 27	1 41	28 29	3 20	11 12	23 19	10 02	14 56	3 31	20 23	16 24	22 52	22 29
26 M	0 20 55	3 19 57	5 ♌ 35	12 39	15 59	2 54	29 08	3 33	11 16	23 17	10 00	14 56 D	3 22	20 15	16 42	23 11	22 26
27 T	0 24 51	4 18 49	18 30	12 41	16 40	4 07	29 47	3 46	11 20	23 14	9 59	14 56	3 13	20 07	17 00	23 30	22 24
28 W	0 28 48	5 17 42	1 ♍ 12	12 42 ℞	17 29	5 21	0 ♑ 26	3 59	11 24	23 12	9 58	14 56	3 03	20 00	17 18	23 49	22 21
29 Th	0 32 44	6 16 38	13 41	12 42	18 26	6 34	1 05	4 12	11 28	23 10	9 56	14 56	2 53	19 53	17 36	24 08	22 18
30 F	0 36 41	7 15 36	26 00	12 42	19 31	7 47	1 45	4 25	11 33	23 08	9 55	14 56	2 42	19 47	17 54	24 26	22 16

EPHEMERIS CALCULATED FOR 12 MIDNIGHT GREENWICH MEAN TIME. ALL OTHER DATA AND FACING ASPECTARIAN PAGE IN **EASTERN TIME (BOLD)** AND PACIFIC TIME (REGULAR).

OCTOBER 2016

☽ Last Aspect day	ET / hr:mn / PT		asp	☽ Ingress sign	day	ET / hr:mn / PT	
1		10:43 pm	☍ ♅	♏	2	**3:43 pm**	12:43 pm
2	**1:43 am**		☍ ♅	♏	2	**3:43 pm**	12:43 pm
4	**9:04 pm**	6:04 pm	⚹ ☿	♐	5	**4:26 am**	1:26 am
6		11:26 pm	△ ♅	♑	7	**4:40 pm**	1:40 pm
7	**2:26 am**		△ ♅	♑	7	**4:40 pm**	1:40 pm
9	**12:51 pm**	9:51 am	□ ♅	♒	9		11:33 pm
9	**12:51 pm**	9:51 am	□ ♅	♒	10	**2:33 am**	
11	**7:49 pm**	4:49 pm	⚹ ♅	♓	12	**8:43 am**	5:43 am
14	**3:13 am**	12:13 am	△ ♀	♈	14	**11:08 am**	8:08 am
15		9:23 pm	☍ ☉	♉	16	**11:04 am**	8:04 am
16	**12:23 am**		☍ ☉	♉	16	**11:04 am**	8:04 am
17	**10:47 am**	7:47 am	△ ♇	♊	18	**10:30 am**	7:30 am
20	**7:17 am**	4:17 am	△ ☉	♋	20	**11:28 am**	8:28 am
22	**3:14 pm**	12:14 pm	□ ☉	♌	22	**3:34 pm**	12:34 pm
24	**8:21 am**	5:21 am	△ ♅	♍	24	**11:16 pm**	8:16 pm
26	**2:33 pm**	11:33 am	△ ♂	♎	27	**9:51 am**	6:51 am
29	**6:09 am**	3:09 am	□ ♂	♏	29	**10:01 pm**	7:01 pm
31	**10:44 pm**	7:44 pm	⚹ ♂	♐	11/1	**10:43 am**	7:43 am

☽ Phases & Eclipses phase	day	ET / hr:mn / PT	
2nd Quarter	8		9:33 pm
2nd Quarter	9	**12:33 am**	
Full Moon	15		9:23 pm
Full Moon	16	**12:23 am**	
4th Quarter	22	**3:14 pm**	12:14 pm
New Moon	30	**1:38 pm**	10:38 am

Planet Ingress		day	ET / hr:mn / PT	
☿	♎	7	**3:56 am**	12:56 am
⚳	♈	13	**6:41 am**	3:41 am
♀	♐	18	**3:01 am**	12:01 am
⚵	♌	19	**9:06 pm**	6:06 pm
☉	♏	22	**7:46 pm**	4:46 pm
☿	♏	24	**4:46 pm**	1:46 pm

Planetary Motion		day	ET / hr:mn / PT	
⚴	D	17	**3:31 pm**	12:31 pm

1 SATURDAY
☽ ⚹ ♄ **2:55 am**
☽ □ ♇ **9:29 am** 6:29 am
♀ △ ♆ **1:13 pm** 10:13 am
☽ ⚺ ☿ 9:02 pm
☽ ☍ ♅ 10:43 pm

2 SUNDAY
☽ ⚺ ☿ **12:02 am**
☽ ☍ ♅ **1:43 am**
☉ ⚻ ♆ **11:11 am** 8:11 am
☿ ⚻ ♅ **2:19 pm** 11:19 am
☽ ⚹ ♂ **11:27 pm** 8:27 pm
☽ ⚺ ♃ 11:03 pm
♀ ⚺ ♄ 11:59 pm

3 MONDAY
☽ ⚺ ♃ **2:03 am**
♀ ⚺ ♄ **2:59 am**
☽ △ ♆ **11:33 am** 8:33 am
☽ ⚺ ☉ **1:49 pm** 10:49 am
☽ ⚺ ♄ **3:36 pm** 12:36 pm
☽ ☌ ♀ **4:57 pm** 1:57 pm
☽ ⚹ ♇ **9:55 pm** 6:55 pm

4 TUESDAY
☉ ⚹ ♄ **12:59 pm** 9:59 am
☽ ⚻ ♅ **2:08 pm** 11:08 am
☽ ⚹ ☿ **9:04 pm** 6:04 pm

5 WEDNESDAY
☽ ⚺ ♂ **3:51 pm** 12:51 pm
☽ ⚹ ♃ **3:56 pm** 12:56 pm
♀ ⚹ ♇ **5:22 pm** 2:22 pm
♂ □ ♃ **5:45 pm** 2:45 pm
☽ □ ♆ 9:12 pm

6 THURSDAY
☽ □ ♆ **12:12 am**
☽ ☌ ♄ **4:44 am** 1:44 am
☽ ⚹ ☉ **8:02 am** 5:02 am
☽ ⚺ ♇ **10:38 am** 7:38 am
☽ ⚺ ♀ **12:35 pm** 9:35 am
☽ △ ♅ 11:26 pm

7 FRIDAY
☽ △ ♅ **2:26 am**
☉ □ ♇ **3:33 pm** 12:33 pm
☽ □ ☿ **6:40 pm** 3:40 pm

8 SATURDAY
☽ □ ♃ **4:56 am** 1:56 am
☽ ☌ ♂ **7:18 am** 4:18 am
☽ ⚹ ♆ **11:46 am** 8:46 am
☽ ⚺ ♄ **4:38 pm** 1:38 pm
☽ ☌ ♇ **9:57 pm** 6:57 pm
☽ □ ☉ 9:33 pm

9 SUNDAY
☽ □ ☉ **12:33 am**
☽ ⚹ ♀ **6:10 am** 3:10 am
☽ □ ♅ **12:51 pm** 9:51 am

10 MONDAY
☽ △ ☿ **1:07 pm** 10:07 am
☽ △ ♃ **3:05 pm** 12:05 pm
☽ ⚺ ♂ **7:30 pm** 4:30 pm
☽ ⚺ ♆ **8:27 pm** 5:27 pm
☽ ⚹ ♄ 10:28 pm

11 TUESDAY
☽ ⚹ ♄ **1:28 am**
☿ ☌ ♃ **5:45 am** 2:45 am
☽ ⚺ ♇ **6:06 am** 3:06 am
☽ △ ☉ **12:58 pm** 9:58 am
♂ ⚹ ♆ **1:03 pm** 10:03 am
☽ □ ♀ **7:15 pm** 4:15 pm
☽ ⚹ ♅ **7:49 pm** 4:49 pm
♀ ⚻ ♅ 10:16 pm

12 WEDNESDAY
♀ ⚻ ♅ **1:16 am**
☿ ⚻ ♆ **7:59 pm** 4:59 pm
☽ ⚻ ♃ **9:11 pm** 6:11 pm
☽ ☌ ♆ 10:16 pm
☽ ⚻ ☿ 11:01 pm

13 THURSDAY
☽ ☌ ♆ **1:16 am**
☽ ⚻ ☿ **2:01 am**
☽ ⚹ ♂ **3:10 am** 12:10 am
☽ □ ♄ **6:19 am** 3:19 am
☽ ⚹ ♇ **10:20 am** 7:20 am
☿ □ ♂ **5:00 pm** 2:00 pm
☽ ⚻ ☉ **8:30 pm** 5:30 pm
☽ ⚺ ♅ **10:56 pm** 7:56 pm

14 FRIDAY
☽ △ ♀ **3:13 am** 12:13 am
☿ ⚹ ♄ **2:47 pm** 11:47 am
☽ ☍ ♃ **11:34 pm** 8:34 pm
☽ ⚺ ♆ 11:38 pm

15 SATURDAY
☽ ⚺ ♆ **2:38 am**
☉ ☍ ♅ **6:43 am** 3:43 am
☽ □ ♂ **6:54 am** 3:54 am
☽ △ ♄ **7:46 am** 4:46 am
☽ ☍ ☿ **9:53 am** 6:53 am
☽ □ ♇ **11:20 am** 8:20 am
☿ □ ♇ **10:29 pm** 7:29 pm
☽ ☌ ♅ **11:11 pm** 8:11 pm
☽ ☍ ☉ 9:23 pm

16 SUNDAY
☽ ☍ ☉ **12:23 am**
♂ ⚺ ♄ **4:14 am** 1:14 am
☽ ⚻ ♀ **7:37 am** 4:37 am
☽ ⚻ ♃ **11:51 pm** 8:51 pm
☽ ⚹ ♆ 11:08 pm

17 MONDAY
☽ ⚹ ♆ **2:08 am**
☽ ⚻ ♄ **7:31 am** 4:31 am
☽ △ ♂ **8:39 am** 5:39 am
☽ △ ♇ **10:47 am** 7:47 am
☽ ⚻ ☿ **3:25 pm** 12:25 pm
☽ ⚺ ♅ **10:25 pm** 7:25 pm

18 TUESDAY
☽ ⚻ ☉ **3:04 am** 12:04 am
☽ ☍ ♀ **11:09 am** 8:09 am
☽ △ ♃ 9:11 pm
☽ □ ♆ 10:47 pm

19 WEDNESDAY
☽ △ ♃ **12:11 am**
☽ □ ♆ **1:47 am**
♂ ☌ ♇ **7:22 am** 4:22 am
☽ ☍ ♄ **7:40 am** 4:40 am
☽ ⚻ ♇ **10:46 am** 7:46 am
☽ ⚻ ♂ **10:56 am** 7:56 am
☽ △ ☿ **9:59 pm** 6:59 pm
☽ ⚹ ♅ **10:41 pm** 7:41 pm

20 THURSDAY
☿ ☍ ♅ **3:48 am** 12:48 am
☽ △ ☉ **7:17 am** 4:17 am
☽ ⚻ ♀ **4:43 pm** 1:43 pm
☽ □ ♃ 11:41 pm

21 FRIDAY
☽ □ ♃ **2:41 am**
☽ △ ♆ **3:33 am** 12:33 am
☽ ⚻ ♄ **10:13 am** 7:13 am
☽ ☍ ♇ **1:13 pm** 10:13 am
☽ ☍ ♂ **4:04 pm** 1:04 pm
☽ □ ♅ 10:44 pm

22 SATURDAY
☽ □ ♅ **1:44 am**
☽ □ ☿ **8:30 am** 5:30 am
☽ □ ☉ **3:14 pm** 12:14 pm
☽ △ ♀ 11:28 pm

23 SUNDAY
☽ △ ♀ **2:28 am**
☽ ⚹ ♃ **8:44 am** 5:44 am
☽ ⚻ ♆ **8:44 am** 5:44 am
♃ ⚻ ♆ **9:33 am** 6:33 am
☽ △ ♄ **4:20 pm** 1:20 pm
☽ ⚻ ♇ **7:12 pm** 4:12 pm
☽ ⚻ ♂ 10:22 pm

24 MONDAY
☽ ⚻ ♂ **1:22 am**
☽ △ ♅ **8:21 am** 5:21 am
☽ ⚹ ☿ 9:16 pm

25 TUESDAY
☽ ⚹ ☿ **12:16 am**
☽ ⚹ ☉ **3:43 am** 12:43 am
☽ □ ♀ **4:55 pm** 1:55 pm
☽ ☍ ♆ **5:24 pm** 2:24 pm
☽ ⚺ ♃ **6:26 pm** 3:26 pm
♀ □ ♆ **9:54 pm** 6:54 pm
☽ □ ♄ 10:56 pm

26 WEDNESDAY
☽ □ ♄ **1:56 am**
☽ △ ♇ **4:34 am** 1:34 am
♀ ⚹ ♃ **11:19 am** 8:19 am
☽ △ ♂ **2:33 pm** 11:33 am
☽ ⚻ ♅ **6:06 pm** 3:06 pm

27 THURSDAY
☉ ☌ ☿ **12:16 pm** 9:16 am
☽ ⚺ ☉ **7:46 pm** 4:46 pm
☽ ⚺ ☿ **8:14 pm** 5:14 pm

28 FRIDAY
☽ ⚻ ♆ **4:33 am** 1:33 am
☽ ☌ ♃ **6:43 am** 3:43 am
☽ ⚹ ♀ **10:44 am** 7:44 am
☽ ⚹ ♄ **1:54 pm** 10:54 am
☽ □ ♇ **4:11 pm** 1:11 pm
♂ □ ♅ 9:06 pm

29 SATURDAY
♂ □ ♅ **12:06 am**
☽ ☍ ♅ **5:46 am** 2:46 am
☽ □ ♂ **6:09 am** 3:09 am
♀ ☌ ♄ **8:45 pm** 5:45 pm

30 SUNDAY
☿ △ ♆ **8:57 am** 5:57 am
☽ ☌ ☉ **1:38 pm** 10:38 am
☽ △ ♆ **4:56 pm** 1:56 pm
♀ ⚺ ♇ **5:27 pm** 2:27 pm
☽ ☌ ☿ **6:12 pm** 3:12 pm
☽ ⚺ ♃ **8:14 pm** 5:14 pm
☽ ⚺ ♄ 11:57 pm

31 MONDAY
☽ ⚺ ♄ **2:57 am**
☽ ⚹ ♇ **4:49 am** 1:49 am
☽ ⚺ ♀ **6:05 am** 3:05 am
☿ ⚺ ♃ **10:54 am** 7:54 am
☽ ⚻ ♅ **6:13 pm** 3:13 pm
☽ ⚹ ♂ **10:44 pm** 7:44 pm

Eastern time in bold type
Pacific time in medium type

OCTOBER 2016

DATE	SID.TIME	SUN	MOON	NODE	MERCURY	VENUS	MARS	JUPITER	SATURN	URANUS	NEPTUNE	PLUTO	CERES	PALLAS	JUNO	VESTA	CHIRON
1 Sa	0 40 38	8 ♎ 14 36	8 ♎ 09	12 ♍ 40	20 ♍ 42	9 ♏ 00	2 ♑ 25	4 ♎ 38	11 ♐ 37	23 ♈ 05	9 ♓ 53	14 ♑ 56	2 ♉ 32	19 ♒ 41	18 ♏ 13	24 ♋ 45	22 ♓ 13
2 Su	0 44 34	9 13 38	20 11	12 36 ℞	21 59	10 13	3 05	4 51	11 41	23 03 ℞	9 52 ℞	14 56	2 21 ℞	19 35 ℞	18 31	25 03	22 10 ℞
3 M	0 48 31	10 12 42	2 ♏ 08	12 32	23 21	11 26	3 45	5 04	11 46	23 01	9 50	14 56	2 10	19 30	18 49	25 21	22 08
4 T	0 52 27	11 11 48	14 00	12 27	24 47	12 39	4 25	5 17	11 50	22 58	9 49	14 56	1 58	19 25	19 08	25 39	22 05
5 W	0 56 24	12 10 55	25 50	12 22	26 18	13 52	5 05	5 30	11 55	22 56	9 48	14 57	1 47	19 20	19 26	25 57	22 03
6 Th	1 0 20	13 10 05	7 ♐ 42	12 17	27 51	15 05	5 46	5 43	12 00	22 53	9 46	14 57	1 35	19 16	19 45	26 14	22 00
7 F	1 4 17	14 09 17	19 37	12 13	29 28	16 18	6 26	5 56	12 04	22 51	9 45	14 57	1 23	19 12	20 04	26 32	21 58
8 Sa	1 8 13	15 08 30	1 ♑ 41	12 10	1 ♎ 06	17 31	7 07	6 09	12 09	22 49	9 44	14 58	1 10	19 08	20 23	26 49	21 55
9 Su	1 12 10	16 07 45	13 58	12 10 D	2 46	18 44	7 48	6 22	12 14	22 46	9 43	14 58	0 58	19 05	20 42	27 06	21 53
10 M	1 16 7	17 07 02	26 31	12 10	4 28	19 57	8 29	6 35	12 19	22 44	9 41	14 58	0 45	19 02	21 00	27 23	21 50
11 T	1 20 3	18 06 21	9 ♒ 26	12 11	6 11	21 10	9 10	6 47	12 24	22 41	9 40	14 59	0 32	18 59	21 19	27 39	21 48
12 W	1 24 0	19 05 41	22 45	12 13	7 54	22 22	9 51	7 00	12 29	22 39	9 39	14 59	0 19	18 57	21 39	27 56	21 46
13 Th	1 27 56	20 05 03	6 ♓ 32	12 14 ℞	9 38	23 35	10 33	7 13	12 34	22 36	9 38	15 00	0 06	18 55	21 58	28 12	21 43
14 F	1 31 53	21 04 27	20 47	12 14	11 22	24 48	11 14	7 26	12 40	22 34	9 37	15 00	29 ♈ 53	18 54	22 17	28 28	21 41
15 Sa	1 35 49	22 03 53	5 ♈ 28	12 12	13 06	26 01	11 56	7 39	12 45	22 32	9 36	15 01	29 39	18 53	22 36	28 44	21 39
16 Su	1 39 46	23 03 21	20 28	12 08	14 51	27 13	12 38	7 51	12 50	22 29	9 34	15 01	29 26	18 52	22 55	28 59	21 36
17 M	1 43 42	24 02 51	5 ♉ 40	12 02	16 35	28 26	13 20	8 04	12 56	22 27	9 33	15 02	29 12	18 52 D	23 15	29 15	21 34
18 T	1 47 39	25 02 23	20 53	11 56	18 19	29 39	14 01	8 17	13 01	22 24	9 32	15 03	28 58	18 52	23 34	29 30	21 32
19 W	1 51 35	26 01 57	5 ♊ 56	11 49	20 02	0 ♐ 51	14 44	8 30	13 07	22 22	9 31	15 03	28 45	18 52	23 54	29 45	21 30
20 Th	1 55 32	27 01 33	20 42	11 44	21 45	2 04	15 26	8 42	13 12	22 19	9 30	15 04	28 31	18 52	24 13	29 59	21 28
21 F	1 59 29	28 01 12	5 ♋ 03	11 40	23 28	3 17	16 08	8 55	13 18	22 17	9 29	15 05	28 17	18 53	24 33	0 ♌ 14	21 26
22 Sa	2 3 25	29 00 53	18 58	11 37 D	25 10	4 29	16 50	9 07	13 23	22 14	9 28	15 05	28 03	18 54	24 52	0 28	21 24
23 Su	2 7 22	0 ♏ 00 36	2 ♌ 28	11 37	26 52	5 42	17 33	9 20	13 29	22 12	9 28	15 06	27 50	18 56	25 12	0 42	21 22
24 M	2 11 18	1 00 21	15 33	11 38	28 33	6 54	18 16	9 32	13 35	22 10	9 27	15 07	27 36	18 58	25 32	0 56	21 20
25 T	2 15 15	2 00 09	28 17	11 39	0 ♏ 14	8 07	18 58	9 45	13 41	22 07	9 26	15 08	27 22	19 00	25 51	1 09	21 18
26 W	2 19 11	2 59 59	10 ♍ 45	11 39 ℞	1 54	9 19	19 41	9 57	13 47	22 05	9 25	15 09	27 09	19 03	26 11	1 22	21 16
27 Th	2 23 8	3 59 51	23 00	11 39	3 33	10 32	20 24	10 10	13 53	22 02	9 24	15 10	26 55	19 05	26 31	1 35	21 14
28 F	2 27 4	4 59 45	5 ♎ 06	11 36	5 12	11 44	21 07	10 22	13 59	22 00	9 23	15 10	26 41	19 09	26 51	1 48	21 12
29 Sa	2 31 1	5 59 41	17 05	11 30	6 51	12 56	21 50	10 35	14 05	21 58	9 23	15 11	26 28	19 12	27 11	2 00	21 10
30 Su	2 34 58	6 59 40	29 00	11 22	8 29	14 09	22 33	10 47	14 11	21 55	9 22	15 12	26 15	19 16	27 31	2 12	21 09
31 M	2 38 54	7 59 40	10 ♏ 52	11 12	10 06	15 21	23 16	10 59	14 17	21 53	9 21	15 13	26 02	19 20	27 51	2 24	21 07

EPHEMERIS CALCULATED FOR 12 MIDNIGHT GREENWICH MEAN TIME. ALL OTHER DATA AND FACING ASPECTARIAN PAGE IN **EASTERN TIME (BOLD)** AND PACIFIC TIME (REGULAR).

NOVEMBER 2016

☽ Last Aspect				☽ Ingress			
day	ET / hr:mn / PT		asp	sign	day	ET / hr:mn / PT	
31	**10:44 pm**	7:44 pm	⚹♂	♐	1	**10:43 am**	7:43 am
3	**6:35 am**	3:35 am	△♅	♑	3	**11:05 pm**	8:05 pm
6	**4:56 am**	1:56 am	☌♂	♒	6	**8:55 am**	5:55 am
8	**8:54 am**	5:54 am	⚹♀	♓	8	**4:45 pm**	1:45 pm
10	**6:16 pm**	3:16 pm	□♀	♈	10	**8:45 pm**	5:45 pm
12	**7:45 am**	4:45 am	☌♅	♉	12	**9:24 pm**	6:24 pm
14	**8:52 am**	5:52 am	☍☉	♊	14	**8:23 pm**	5:23 pm
16	**5:58 am**	2:58 am	⚹♅	♋	16	**7:57 pm**	4:57 pm
18	**5:02 pm**	2:02 pm	△☉	♌	18	**10:14 pm**	7:14 pm
21	**3:33 am**	12:33 am	□☉	♍	21	**4:34 am**	1:34 am
22	**12:41 pm**	9:41 am	□♄	♎	23	**2:42 pm**	11:42 am
25	**8:52 am**	5:52 am	☍♅	♏	26	**3:01 am**	12:01 am
27	**4:48 pm**	1:48 pm	⚹♀	♐	28	**3:46 pm**	12:46 pm
30	**11:08 pm**	8:08 pm	☌☿	♑	12/1	**3:52 am**	12:52 am

☽ Phases & Eclipses			
phase	day	ET / hr:mn / PT	
2nd Quarter	7	**2:51 pm**	11:51 am
Full Moon	14	**8:52 am**	5:52 am
4th Quarter	21	**3:33 am**	12:33 am
New Moon	29	**7:18 am**	4:18 am

Planet Ingress				
		day	ET / hr:mn / PT	
⚵	♐	6	**4:40 am**	1:40 am
♂	♒	8		9:51 pm
♂	♒	9	**12:51 am**	
♀	♑	11	**11:54 pm**	8:54 pm
☿	♐	12	**9:40 am**	6:40 am
☉	♐	21	**4:22 pm**	1:22 pm

Planetary Motion				
		day	ET / hr:mn / PT	
♆	D	19	**11:38 pm**	8:38 pm

1 TUESDAY
☉△♆ **4:17 am** 1:17 am

2 WEDNESDAY
☽□♆ **5:34 am** 2:34 am
☽⚺☉ **7:55 am** 4:55 am
☽⚹♃ **9:58 am** 6:58 am
☿⚺♄ **2:29 pm** 11:29 am
☽☌♄ **4:09 pm** 1:09 pm
☽⚺☿ **4:24 pm** 1:24 pm
☽⚺♇ **5:34 pm** 2:34 pm
☿⚹♇ 10:10 pm
☽☌♀ 10:32 pm

3 THURSDAY
☿⚹♇ **1:10 am**
☽☌♀ **1:32 am**
☽△♅ **6:35 am** 3:35 am
☉⚺♃ **1:54 pm** 10:54 am
☽⚺♂ **3:09 pm** 12:09 pm

4 FRIDAY
☽⚹♆ **5:34 pm** 2:34 pm
☽□♃ **10:56 pm** 7:56 pm
☽⚹☉ 10:18 pm
♀△♅ 11:23 pm

5 SATURDAY
☽⚹☉ **1:18 am**
♀△♅ **2:23 am**
☽⚺♄ **4:29 am** 1:29 am
☽☌♇ **5:25 am** 2:25 am

☽⚹☿ **1:06 pm** 10:06 am
☽□♅ **5:48 pm** 2:48 pm
☽⚺♀ **7:31 pm** 4:31 pm

6 SUNDAY
☽☌♂ **4:56 am** 1:56 am
☉⚺♄ **7:15 pm** 4:15 pm
☿⚻♅ 9:11 pm
☽⚺♆ 11:35 pm

7 MONDAY
☿⚻♅ **12:11 am**
☽⚺♆ **2:35 am**
☉⚹♇ **3:25 am** 12:25 am
☽△♃ **8:38 am** 5:38 am
☽⚹♄ **1:29 pm** 10:29 am
☽⚺♇ **1:59 pm** 10:59 am
☽□☉ **2:51 pm** 11:51 am
☽⚹♅ 10:27 pm

8 TUESDAY
☽⚹♅ **1:27 am**
☽□☿ **4:57 am** 1:57 am
☽⚹♀ **8:54 am** 5:54 am
☽⚺♂ **4:17 pm** 1:17 pm

9 WEDNESDAY
☽☌♆ **9:14 am** 6:14 am
☽⚻♃ **3:41 pm** 12:41 pm
☽□♄ **7:50 pm** 4:50 pm
☽⚹♇ **7:57 pm** 4:57 pm
☽△☉ 9:52 pm

10 THURSDAY
☽△☉ **12:52 am**
☽⚺♅ **6:24 am** 3:24 am
♄⚺♇ **2:39 pm** 11:39 am
☽△☿ **4:17 pm** 1:17 pm
☽□♀ **6:16 pm** 3:16 pm
☽⚹♂ **11:06 pm** 8:06 pm

11 FRIDAY
☽⚺♆ **12:03 pm** 9:03 am
☽☍♃ **6:46 pm** 3:46 pm
☽□♇ **10:09 pm** 7:09 pm
☽△♄ **10:20 pm** 7:20 pm

12 SATURDAY
☽⚻☉ **6:16 am** 3:16 am
☽☌♅ **7:45 am** 4:45 am
☽⚻☿ **10:43 pm** 7:43 pm
☽△♀ **11:14 pm** 8:14 pm
☽□♂ 11:06 pm

13 SUNDAY
☽□♂ **2:06 am**
☉⚻♅ **3:38 am** 12:38 am
☽⚹♆ **11:58 am** 8:58 am
☽⚻♃ **7:01 pm** 4:01 pm
☿⚺♀ **7:43 pm** 4:43 pm
☽△♇ **9:45 pm** 6:45 pm
☽⚻♄ **10:13 pm** 7:13 pm

14 MONDAY
☽⚺♅ **6:54 am** 3:54 am
☽☍☉ **8:52 am** 5:52 am

☽⚻♀ 11:10 pm
☽☍☿ 11:54 pm

15 TUESDAY
☽⚻♀ **2:10 am**
☽☍☿ **2:54 am**
☽△♂ **3:25 am** 12:25 am
☽□♆ **10:53 am** 7:53 am
☿⚹♂ **12:22 pm** 9:22 am
☽△♃ **6:35 pm** 3:35 pm
☽⚻♇ **8:49 pm** 5:49 pm
☽☍♄ **9:34 pm** 6:34 pm

16 WEDNESDAY
☽⚹♅ **5:58 am** 2:58 am
☽⚻☉ **11:29 am** 8:29 am
♀⚺♂ **6:38 pm** 3:38 pm

17 THURSDAY
☽⚻♂ **5:49 am** 2:49 am
☽☍♀ **6:11 am** 3:11 am
☽⚻☿ **8:17 am** 5:17 am
☽△♆ **11:04 am** 8:04 am
☽□♃ **7:50 pm** 4:50 pm
☽☍♇ **9:39 pm** 6:39 pm
☽⚻♄ **10:45 pm** 7:45 pm

18 FRIDAY
☽□♅ **7:10 am** 4:10 am
☿□♆ **11:04 am** 8:04 am
☽△☉ **5:02 pm** 2:02 pm

19 SATURDAY
☽☍♂ **11:48 am** 8:48 am
☽⚻♀ **2:11 pm** 11:11 am
☽⚻♆ **2:31 pm** 11:31 am
☽△☿ **6:00 pm** 3:00 pm
♀⚹♆ **6:03 pm** 3:03 pm
☽⚹♃ 9:44 pm
☽⚻♇ 11:04 pm

20 SUNDAY
☽⚹♃ **12:44 am**
☽⚻♇ **2:04 am**
☽△♄ **3:36 am** 12:36 am
☽△♅ **12:08 pm** 9:08 am

21 MONDAY
☽□☉ **3:33 am** 12:33 am
♂⚺♆ **1:06 pm** 10:06 am
☽☍♆ **10:08 pm** 7:08 pm
☽⚻♂ **10:42 pm** 7:42 pm

22 TUESDAY
☽△♀ **3:36 am** 12:36 am
☽□☿ **9:32 am** 6:32 am
☽⚺♃ **9:56 am** 6:56 am
☽△♇ **10:38 am** 7:38 am
☽□♄ **12:41 pm** 9:41 am
☿⚹♃ **1:19 pm** 10:19 am
☿⚺♇ **6:48 pm** 3:48 pm
☽⚻♅ **9:08 pm** 6:08 pm

23 WEDNESDAY
☿☌♄ **1:44 pm** 10:44 am
☽⚹☉ **6:56 pm** 3:56 pm

24 THURSDAY
☽⚻♆ **9:09 am** 6:09 am
☽△♂ **1:40 pm** 10:40 am
♃□♇ **6:00 pm** 3:00 pm
☽□♀ **9:22 pm** 6:22 pm
☽□♇ **10:17 pm** 7:17 pm
☽☌♃ **10:21 pm** 7:21 pm
☽⚹♄ 9:52 pm

25 FRIDAY
☽⚹♄ **12:52 am**
☽⚹☿ **5:28 am** 2:28 am
♀☌♇ **6:50 am** 3:50 am
♀□♃ **8:45 am** 5:45 am
☽☍♅ **8:52 am** 5:52 am

26 SATURDAY
☿△♅ **8:38 am** 5:38 am
♀⚺♄ **12:13 pm** 9:13 am
☽⚺☉ **12:59 pm** 9:59 am
☽△♆ **9:47 pm** 6:47 pm

27 SUNDAY
☽□♂ **6:24 am** 3:24 am
☽⚹♇ **11:09 am** 8:09 am
☽⚺♃ **11:59 am** 8:59 am
☽⚺♄ **2:13 pm** 11:13 am
☽⚹♀ **4:48 pm** 1:48 pm
☽⚻♅ **9:30 pm** 6:30 pm
☽⚺☿ 11:44 pm

28 MONDAY
☽⚺☿ **2:44 am**

29 TUESDAY
☽☌☉ **7:18 am** 4:18 am
☽□♆ **10:26 am** 7:26 am
♀□♅ **3:20 pm** 12:20 pm
☽⚹♂ **10:59 pm** 7:59 pm
☽⚺♇ **11:47 pm** 8:47 pm
☽⚹♃ 10:20 pm

30 WEDNESDAY
☽⚹♃ **1:20 am**
☽☌♄ **3:16 am** 12:16 am
☽△♅ **9:45 am** 6:45 am
☽⚺♀ **11:47 am** 8:47 am
♂⚺♇ **12:15 pm** 9:15 am
☉□♆ **8:17 pm** 5:17 pm
☽☌☿ **11:08 pm** 8:08 pm

Eastern time in bold type
Pacific time in medium type

NOVEMBER 2016

DATE	SID.TIME	SUN	MOON	NODE	MERCURY	VENUS	MARS	JUPITER	SATURN	URANUS	NEPTUNE	PLUTO	CERES	PALLAS	JUNO	VESTA	CHIRON
1 T	2 42 51	8 ♏ 59 42	22 ♏ 44	11 ♍ 01	11 ♏ 43	16 ♐ 33	24 ♑ 00	11 ♎ 11	14 ♐ 23	21 ♈ 51	9 ♓ 21	15 ♑ 14	25 ♈ 49	19 ♒ 24	28 ♏ 11	2 ♌ 36	21 ♓ 05
2 W	2 46 47	9 59 46	4 ♐ 35	10 49 ℞	13 20	17 45	24 43	11 24	14 29	21 48 ℞	9 20 ℞	15 16	25 36 ℞	19 29	28 31	2 47	21 04 ℞
3 Th	2 50 44	10 59 52	16 29	10 38	14 56	18 58	25 27	11 36	14 36	21 46	9 19	15 17	25 23	19 34	28 51	2 58	21 02
4 F	2 54 40	11 59 59	28 27	10 28	16 32	20 10	26 10	11 48	14 42	21 44	9 19	15 18	25 11	19 39	29 11	3 09	21 01
5 Sa	2 58 37	13 00 08	10 ♑ 32	10 21	18 07	21 22	26 54	12 00	14 48	21 42	9 18	15 19	24 58	19 45	29 32	3 19	20 59
6 Su	3 2 33	14 00 19	22 47	10 16	19 42	22 34	27 38	12 12	14 55	21 39	9 18	15 20	24 46	19 51	29 52	3 29	20 58
7 M	3 6 30	15 00 31	5 ♒ 17	10 14 D	21 16	23 46	28 21	12 24	15 01	21 37	9 17	15 21	24 35	19 57	0 ♐ 12	3 39	20 57
8 T	3 10 27	16 00 45	18 05	10 13	22 51	24 58	29 05	12 36	15 08	21 35	9 17	15 22	24 23	20 03	0 32	3 48	20 55
9 W	3 14 23	17 01 00	1 ♓ 15	10 14 ℞	24 24	26 10	29 49	12 47	15 14	21 33	9 17	15 24	24 12	20 10	0 53	3 57	20 54
10 Th	3 18 20	18 01 16	14 52	10 14	25 58	27 22	0 ♒ 33	12 59	15 21	21 31	9 16	15 25	24 01	20 17	1 13	4 06	20 53
11 F	3 22 16	19 01 34	28 57	10 12	27 31	28 34	1 17	13 11	15 27	21 29	9 16	15 26	23 50	20 24	1 34	4 14	20 52
12 Sa	3 26 13	20 01 53	13 ♈ 31	10 09	29 04	29 45	2 01	13 22	15 34	21 27	9 16	15 28	23 39	20 31	1 54	4 22	20 51
13 Su	3 30 9	21 02 14	28 29	10 02	0 ♐ 36	0 ♑ 57	2 46	13 34	15 40	21 25	9 15	15 29	23 29	20 39	2 14	4 30	20 50
14 M	3 34 6	22 02 37	13 ♉ 45	9 53	2 08	2 09	3 30	13 45	15 47	21 23	9 15	15 30	23 19	20 47	2 35	4 37	20 49
15 T	3 38 2	23 03 01	29 07	9 43	3 40	3 20	4 14	13 57	15 54	21 21	9 15	15 32	23 10	20 55	2 55	4 44	20 48
16 W	3 41 59	24 03 27	14 ♊ 24	9 32	5 11	4 32	4 58	14 08	16 01	21 19	9 15	15 33	23 00	21 04	3 16	4 51	20 47
17 Th	3 45 56	25 03 54	29 25	9 22	6 43	5 43	5 43	14 19	16 07	21 17	9 15	15 34	22 51	21 12	3 36	4 57	20 46
18 F	3 49 52	26 04 23	14 ♋ 01	9 14	8 14	6 55	6 27	14 31	16 14	21 15	9 15	15 36	22 43	21 21	3 57	5 03	20 45
19 Sa	3 53 49	27 04 55	28 08	9 09	9 44	8 06	7 12	14 42	16 21	21 13	9 14	15 37	22 35	21 30	4 18	5 08	20 45
20 Su	3 57 45	28 05 27	11 ♌ 45	9 06	11 15	9 17	7 56	14 53	16 28	21 11	9 14 D	15 39	22 27	21 40	4 38	5 13	20 44
21 M	4 1 42	29 06 02	24 53	9 05 D	12 45	10 28	8 41	15 04	16 35	21 09	9 14	15 40	22 19	21 49	4 59	5 18	20 43
22 T	4 5 38	0 ♐ 06 38	7 ♍ 37	9 05 ℞	14 15	11 40	9 25	15 15	16 42	21 08	9 15	15 42	22 12	21 59	5 19	5 22	20 43
23 W	4 9 35	1 07 16	20 01	9 04	15 44	12 51	10 10	15 26	16 48	21 06	9 15	15 44	22 05	22 09	5 40	5 26	20 42
24 Th	4 13 31	2 07 56	2 ♎ 10	9 03	17 13	14 02	10 55	15 36	16 55	21 04	9 15	15 45	21 59	22 20	6 01	5 30	20 42
25 F	4 17 28	3 08 37	14 09	8 58	18 42	15 13	11 40	15 47	17 02	21 03	9 15	15 47	21 52	22 30	6 21	5 33	20 41
26 Sa	4 21 25	4 09 20	26 02	8 51	20 10	16 23	12 24	15 58	17 09	21 01	9 15	15 48	21 47	22 41	6 42	5 36	20 41
27 Su	4 25 21	5 10 04	7 ♏ 53	8 41	21 38	17 34	13 09	16 08	17 16	21 00	9 15	15 50	21 41	22 52	7 03	5 38	20 41
28 M	4 29 18	6 10 50	19 44	8 28	23 05	18 45	13 54	16 19	17 23	20 58	9 16	15 52	21 36	23 03	7 24	5 40	20 41
29 T	4 33 14	7 11 37	1 ♐ 36	8 13	24 32	19 56	14 39	16 29	17 30	20 57	9 16	15 53	21 32	23 14	7 44	5 41	20 40
30 W	4 37 11	8 12 26	13 32	7 58	25 58	21 06	15 24	16 39	17 37	20 55	9 16	15 55	21 28	23 26	8 05	5 42	20 40

EPHEMERIS CALCULATED FOR 12 MIDNIGHT GREENWICH MEAN TIME. ALL OTHER DATA AND FACING ASPECTARIAN PAGE IN **EASTERN TIME (BOLD)** AND PACIFIC TIME (REGULAR).

DECEMBER 2016

☽ Last Aspect day	ET / hr:mn / PT	asp	☽ Ingress sign	day	ET / hr:mn / PT
11/30	**11:08 pm** 8:08 pm	☌ ☿	♑	1	**3:52 am** 12:52 am
3	**5:16 pm** 2:16 pm	☌ ♀	♒	3	**2:44 pm** 11:44 am
5	**6:23 am** 3:23 am	⚹ ♅	♓	5	**11:31 pm** 8:31 pm
7	**9:05 am** 6:05 am	□ ♄	♈	8	**5:15 am** 2:15 am
9	**8:06 pm** 5:06 pm	⚹ ♂	♉	10	**7:41 am** 4:41 am
11	**11:04 pm** 8:04 pm	□ ♂	♊	12	**7:41 am** 4:41 am
13	9:58 pm	△ ♂	♋	14	**7:09 am** 4:09 am
14	**12:58 am**	△ ♂	♋	14	**7:09 am** 4:09 am
15	**4:37 pm** 1:37 pm	□ ♅	♌	16	**8:15 am** 5:15 am
18	**11:55 am** 8:55 am	☍ ♂	♍	18	**12:52 pm** 9:52 am

☽ Last Aspect day	ET / hr:mn / PT	asp	☽ Ingress sign	day	ET / hr:mn / PT
20	**8:56 pm** 5:56 pm	□ ☉	♎	20	**9:40 pm** 6:40 pm
22	**2:31 pm** 11:31 am	☍ ♅	♏	23	**9:32 am** 6:32 am
24	11:22 pm	□ ♀	♐	25	**10:19 pm** 7:19 pm
25	**2:22 am**	□ ♀	♐	25	**10:19 pm** 7:19 pm
27	**8:45 pm** 5:45 pm	⚹ ♀	♑	28	**10:12 am** 7:12 am
30	**3:07 am** 12:07 am	□ ♃	♒	30	**8:29 pm** 5:29 pm

☽ Phases & Eclipses phase	day	ET / hr:mn / PT
2nd Quarter	7	**4:03 am** 1:03 am
Full Moon	13	**7:06 pm** 4:06 pm
4th Quarter	20	**8:56 pm** 5:56 pm
New Moon	28	10:53 pm
New Moon	29	**1:53 am**

Planet Ingress	day	ET / hr:mn / PT
☿ ♑	2	**4:18 pm** 1:18 pm
♀ ♒	7	**9:51 am** 6:51 am
♂ ♓	19	**4:23 am** 1:23 am
☉ ♑	21	**5:44 am** 2:44 am
♀ ♓	27	**7:23 pm** 4:23 pm

Planetary Motion	day	ET / hr:mn / PT
⚷ D	1	**4:53 am** 1:53 am
⚵ R	1	**10:38 am** 7:38 am
⚳ D	9	**7:26 pm** 4:26 pm
☿ R	19	**5:55 am** 2:55 am
♅ D	29	**4:29 am** 1:29 am

1 THURSDAY
☽ ⚹ ♆ **10:15 pm** 7:15 pm
♂ △ ♃ **10:46 pm** 7:46 pm
☽ ⚺ ☉ 9:36 pm

2 FRIDAY
☽ ⚺ ☉ **12:36 am**
☽ ☌ ♇ **11:27 am** 8:27 am
☽ □ ♃ **1:40 pm** 10:40 am
☽ ⚺ ♂ **2:25 pm** 11:25 am
☽ ⚺ ♄ **3:18 pm** 12:18 pm
☽ □ ♅ **8:57 pm** 5:57 pm

3 SATURDAY
☽ ☌ ♀ **5:16 am** 2:16 am
♂ ⚹ ♄ **7:15 am** 4:15 am
☽ ⚺ ☿ **5:30 pm** 2:30 pm

4 SUNDAY
☽ ⚺ ♆ **8:36 am** 5:36 am
☽ ⚹ ☉ **3:56 pm** 12:56 pm
☽ ⚺ ♇ **9:28 pm** 6:28 pm
☽ △ ♃ 9:13 pm
☽ ⚹ ♄ 10:34 pm

5 MONDAY
☽ △ ♃ **12:13 am**
☽ ⚹ ♄ **1:34 am**
☽ ☌ ♂ **3:49 am** 12:49 am
☽ ⚹ ♅ **6:23 am** 3:23 am
☽ ⚺ ♀ **8:08 pm** 5:08 pm

6 TUESDAY
☽ ⚹ ☿ **8:28 am** 5:28 am
☽ ☌ ♆ **4:34 pm** 1:34 pm
♂ ⚹ ♅ **10:30 pm** 7:30 pm

7 WEDNESDAY
☽ □ ☉ **4:03 am** 1:03 am
☽ ⚹ ♇ **4:51 am** 1:51 am
☽ ⚻ ♃ **7:58 am** 4:58 am
☽ □ ♄ **9:05 am** 6:05 am
☽ ⚺ ♅ **1:04 pm** 10:04 am
☽ ⚺ ♂ **1:56 pm** 10:56 am
☉ ⚺ ♇ **2:51 pm** 11:51 am

8 THURSDAY
☽ ⚹ ♀ **7:02 am** 4:02 am
☽ □ ☿ **6:43 pm** 3:43 pm
☽ ⚺ ♆ **9:18 pm** 6:18 pm

9 FRIDAY
☽ □ ♇ **8:52 am** 5:52 am
☽ △ ☉ **11:59 am** 8:59 am
☽ ☍ ♃ **12:16 pm** 9:16 am
☽ △ ♄ **1:10 pm** 10:10 am
☽ ☌ ♅ **4:24 pm** 1:24 pm
☉ ⚹ ♃ **4:39 pm** 1:39 pm
☽ ⚹ ♂ **8:06 pm** 5:06 pm

10 SATURDAY
☿ ⚹ ♆ **3:25 am** 12:25 am
☉ ☌ ♄ **6:51 am** 3:51 am
☽ □ ♀ **1:38 pm** 10:38 am
☽ ⚹ ♆ **10:51 pm** 7:51 pm
☽ △ ☿ 9:19 pm

11 SUNDAY
☽ △ ☿ **12:19 am**
☽ △ ♇ **9:54 am** 6:54 am
☽ ⚻ ♃ **1:32 pm** 10:32 am
☽ ⚻ ♄ **2:17 pm** 11:17 am
☽ ⚻ ☉ **4:17 pm** 1:17 pm
☽ ⚺ ♅ **4:57 pm** 1:57 pm
☽ □ ♂ **11:04 pm** 8:04 pm
☉ △ ♅ 10:56 pm

12 MONDAY
☉ △ ♅ **1:56 am**
☽ △ ♀ **5:22 pm** 2:22 pm
☽ □ ♆ **10:30 pm** 7:30 pm

13 TUESDAY
☽ ⚻ ☿ **3:02 am** 12:02 am
☽ ⚻ ♇ **9:27 am** 6:27 am
☽ △ ♃ **1:24 pm** 10:24 am
☽ ☍ ♄ **2:04 pm** 11:04 am
☽ ⚹ ♅ **4:18 pm** 1:18 pm
☽ ☍ ☉ **7:06 pm** 4:06 pm
☽ △ ♂ 9:58 pm

14 WEDNESDAY
☽ △ ♂ **12:58 am**
☽ ⚻ ♀ **8:57 pm** 5:57 pm
☽ △ ♆ **10:17 pm** 7:17 pm

15 THURSDAY
☽ ☍ ☿ **5:25 am** 2:25 am
☽ ☍ ♇ **9:38 am** 6:38 am
☽ □ ♃ **2:08 pm** 11:08 am
♀ ⚺ ♆ **2:24 pm** 11:24 am
☽ ⚻ ♄ **2:43 pm** 11:43 am
☽ □ ♅ **4:37 pm** 1:37 pm
☽ ⚻ ☉ **11:15 pm** 8:15 pm

16 FRIDAY
☽ ⚻ ♂ **4:26 am** 1:26 am
☽ ⚻ ♆ 9:23 pm

17 SATURDAY
☽ ⚻ ♆ **12:23 am**
☽ ☍ ♀ **3:23 am** 12:23 am
☽ ⚻ ☿ **9:45 am** 6:45 am
☽ ⚻ ♇ **12:36 pm** 9:36 am
☽ ⚹ ♃ **5:51 pm** 2:51 pm
☽ △ ♄ **6:24 pm** 3:24 pm
☽ △ ♅ **7:57 pm** 4:57 pm

18 SUNDAY
☽ △ ☉ **7:27 am** 4:27 am
☽ ☍ ♂ **11:55 am** 8:55 am

19 MONDAY
☽ ☍ ♆ **6:23 am** 3:23 am
☽ ⚻ ♀ **2:52 pm** 11:52 am
☽ △ ☿ **4:59 pm** 1:59 pm
☽ △ ♇ **7:41 pm** 4:41 pm
☽ ⚺ ♃ 10:48 pm
☽ □ ♄ 11:19 pm

20 TUESDAY
☽ ⚺ ♃ **1:48 am**
☽ □ ♄ **2:19 am**
☽ ⚻ ♅ **3:26 am** 12:26 am
☿ ⚺ ♀ **11:58 am** 8:58 am
☽ □ ☉ **8:56 pm** 5:56 pm
☽ ⚻ ♂ 9:22 pm

21 WEDNESDAY
☽ ⚻ ♂ **12:22 am**
☽ ⚻ ♆ **4:26 pm** 1:26 pm
♀ ⚺ ♇ **10:36 pm** 7:36 pm
☽ □ ☿ 11:05 pm

22 THURSDAY
☽ □ ☿ **2:05 am**
☽ □ ♇ **6:35 am** 3:35 am
☽ △ ♀ **7:23 am** 4:23 am
☽ ☌ ♃ **1:30 pm** 10:30 am
☽ ⚹ ♄ **1:59 pm** 10:59 am
☽ ☍ ♅ **2:31 pm** 11:31 am

23 FRIDAY
☽ ⚹ ☉ **2:25 pm** 11:25 am
☽ △ ♂ **4:25 pm** 1:25 pm

24 SATURDAY
☽ △ ♆ **4:57 am** 1:57 am
☽ ⚹ ☿ **10:58 am** 7:58 am
♄ △ ♅ **7:21 pm** 4:21 pm
☽ ⚹ ♇ **7:25 pm** 4:25 pm
☽ □ ♀ 11:22 pm
☽ ⚺ ♃ 11:52 pm

25 SUNDAY
☽ □ ♀ **2:22 am**
☽ ⚺ ♃ **2:52 am**
☽ ⚻ ♅ **3:14 am** 12:14 am
☽ ⚺ ♄ **3:19 am** 12:19 am
♀ △ ♃ **8:23 am** 5:23 am
♀ ⚹ ♅ **11:35 am** 8:35 am
♀ ⚹ ♄ **1:33 pm** 10:33 am

26 MONDAY
☽ ⚺ ☉ **8:50 am** 5:50 am
☽ □ ♂ **9:16 am** 6:16 am
♃ ☍ ♅ **1:35 pm** 10:35 am
☽ □ ♆ **5:41 pm** 2:41 pm
☽ ⚺ ☿ **6:14 pm** 3:14 pm
☿ ⚹ ♆ **11:19 pm** 8:19 pm

27 TUESDAY
☉ ⚹ ♂ **3:07 am** 12:07 am
☽ ⚺ ♇ **8:00 am** 5:00 am
☽ △ ♅ **3:30 pm** 12:30 pm
☽ ⚹ ♃ **3:46 pm** 12:46 pm
☽ ☌ ♄ **4:11 pm** 1:11 pm
☽ ⚹ ♀ **8:45 pm** 5:45 pm

28 WEDNESDAY
☉ ☌ ☿ **1:47 pm** 10:47 am
☿ ⚹ ♂ **6:06 pm** 3:06 pm
☽ ☌ ☿ **11:46 pm** 8:46 pm
☽ ⚹ ♂ 9:49 pm
☽ ☌ ☉ 10:53 pm

29 THURSDAY
☽ ⚹ ♂ **12:49 am**
☽ ☌ ☉ **1:53 am**
☽ ⚹ ♆ **5:11 am** 2:11 am
☽ ☌ ♇ **7:12 pm** 4:12 pm
☽ □ ♅ 11:19 pm

30 FRIDAY
☽ □ ♅ **2:19 am**
☽ □ ♃ **3:07 am** 12:07 am
☽ ⚺ ♄ **3:32 am** 12:32 am
☽ ⚺ ♀ **1:04 pm** 10:04 am
☉ ⚹ ♆ **6:25 pm** 3:25 pm

31 SATURDAY
☽ ⚺ ☿ **4:10 am** 1:10 am
☽ ⚺ ♂ **2:20 pm** 11:20 am
☽ ⚺ ♆ **3:00 pm** 12:00 pm
☽ ⚺ ☉ **4:46 pm** 1:46 pm
♂ ☌ ♆ 10:53 pm

Eastern time in bold type
Pacific time in medium type

DECEMBER 2016

DATE	SID.TIME	SUN	MOON	NODE	MERCURY	VENUS	MARS	JUPITER	SATURN	URANUS	NEPTUNE	PLUTO	CERES	PALLAS	JUNO	VESTA	CHIRON
1 Th	4 41 7	9 ♐ 13 15	25 ♐ 32	7 ♍ 43	27 ♐ 22	22 ♑ 16	16 ♒ 09	16 ♎ 49	17 ♐ 44	20 ♈ 54	9 ♓ 16	15 ♑ 57	21 ♈ 24	23 ♒ 38	8 ♐ 26	5 ♌ 42 Rx	20 ♓ 40 D
2 F	4 45 4	10 14 06	7 ♑ 38	7 30 Rx	28 46	23 27	16 54	16 59	17 51	20 52 Rx	9 17	15 59	21 21 Rx	23 50	8 46	5 43	20 40
3 Sa	4 49 0	11 14 58	19 51	7 20	0 ♑ 09	24 37	17 39	17 09	17 58	20 51	9 17	16 00	21 18	24 02	9 07	5 42	20 40
4 Su	4 52 57	12 15 51	2 ♒ 13	7 13	1 31	25 47	18 24	17 19	18 05	20 50	9 18	16 02	21 15	24 14	9 28	5 41	20 40
5 M	4 56 54	13 16 45	14 46	7 09	2 51	26 57	19 09	17 29	18 13	20 49	9 18	16 04	21 13	24 27	9 49	5 40	20 41
6 T	5 0 50	14 17 39	27 34	7 08 D	4 09	28 07	19 54	17 39	18 20	20 47	9 19	16 06	21 11	24 39	10 09	5 38	20 41
7 W	5 4 47	15 18 34	10 ♓ 40	7 08 Rx	5 25	29 17	20 39	17 48	18 27	20 46	9 19	16 07	21 10	24 52	10 30	5 36	20 41
8 Th	5 8 43	16 19 30	24 07	7 07	6 39	0 ♒ 27	21 25	17 58	18 34	20 45	9 20	16 09	21 09	25 05	10 51	5 34	20 41
9 F	5 12 40	17 20 26	8 ♈ 00	7 06	7 50	1 36	22 10	18 07	18 41	20 44	9 21	16 11	21 08	25 19	11 12	5 30	20 42
10 Sa	5 16 36	18 21 23	22 17	7 02	8 58	2 45	22 55	18 16	18 48	20 43	9 21	16 13	21 08 D	25 32	11 32	5 27	20 42
11 Su	5 20 33	19 22 21	6 ♉ 58	6 56	10 03	3 55	23 40	18 25	18 55	20 42	9 22	16 15	21 08	25 46	11 53	5 23	20 43
12 M	5 24 29	20 23 20	21 59	6 47	11 03	5 04	24 25	18 34	19 02	20 41	9 23	16 17	21 09	25 59	12 14	5 18	20 43
13 T	5 28 26	21 24 19	7 ♊ 10	6 37	11 58	6 13	25 11	18 43	19 09	20 40	9 23	16 19	21 10	26 13	12 35	5 14	20 44
14 W	5 32 23	22 25 19	22 22	6 25	12 48	7 22	25 56	18 52	19 16	20 40	9 24	16 21	21 11	26 27	12 55	5 08	20 45
15 Th	5 36 19	23 26 19	7 ♋ 23	6 15	13 32	8 30	26 41	19 01	19 23	20 39	9 25	16 23	21 13	26 42	13 16	5 02	20 45
16 F	5 40 16	24 27 21	22 05	6 06	14 08	9 39	27 26	19 09	19 31	20 38	9 26	16 24	21 15	26 56	13 37	4 56	20 46
17 Sa	5 44 12	25 28 23	6 ♌ 19	6 00	14 37	10 47	28 12	19 18	19 38	20 37	9 27	16 26	21 17	27 11	13 58	4 50	20 47
18 Su	5 48 9	26 29 26	20 05	5 57	14 57	11 55	28 57	19 26	19 45	20 37	9 28	16 28	21 20	27 25	14 18	4 42	20 48
19 M	5 52 5	27 30 30	3 ♍ 21	5 56 D	15 07 Rx	13 03	29 42	19 34	19 52	20 36	9 29	16 30	21 23	27 40	14 39	4 35	20 49
20 T	5 56 2	28 31 35	16 11	5 56	15 06	14 11	0 ♓ 28	19 42	19 59	20 36	9 30	16 32	21 27	27 55	15 00	4 27	20 50
21 W	5 59 58	29 32 40	28 38	5 56 Rx	14 55	15 19	1 13	19 50	20 06	20 35	9 31	16 34	21 31	28 10	15 20	4 18	20 51
22 Th	6 3 55	0 ♑ 33 46	10 ♎ 49	5 56	14 31	16 26	1 58	19 58	20 13	20 35	9 32	16 36	21 35	28 25	15 41	4 09	20 52
23 F	6 7 52	1 34 53	22 48	5 53	13 56	17 34	2 44	20 06	20 20	20 35	9 33	16 38	21 40	28 41	16 01	4 00	20 53
24 Sa	6 11 48	2 36 01	4 ♏ 40	5 48	13 10	18 41	3 29	20 13	20 27	20 34	9 34	16 40	21 45	28 56	16 22	3 50	20 54
25 Su	6 15 45	3 37 09	16 30	5 41	12 12	19 48	4 14	20 21	20 34	20 34	9 35	16 42	21 50	29 12	16 43	3 40	20 56
26 M	6 19 41	4 38 18	28 22	5 31	11 06	20 54	4 59	20 28	20 41	20 34	9 36	16 44	21 56	29 28	17 03	3 30	20 57
27 T	6 23 38	5 39 28	10 ♐ 17	5 19	9 52	22 01	5 45	20 35	20 48	20 34	9 38	16 46	22 02	29 44	17 24	3 19	20 58
28 W	6 27 34	6 40 38	22 19	5 07	8 32	23 07	6 30	20 42	20 55	20 33	9 39	16 48	22 08	0 ♓ 00	17 44	3 08	21 00
29 Th	6 31 31	7 41 48	4 ♑ 28	4 56	7 11	24 13	7 15	20 49	21 02	20 33 D	9 40	16 50	22 15	0 16	18 05	2 56	21 01
30 F	6 35 28	8 42 58	16 47	4 46	5 49	25 19	8 01	20 56	21 08	20 33	9 41	16 52	22 22	0 32	18 25	2 44	21 03
31 Sa	6 39 24	9 44 09	29 14	4 38	4 30	26 24	8 46	21 02	21 15	20 34	9 43	16 54	22 30	0 49	18 46	2 31	21 05

EPHEMERIS CALCULATED FOR 12 MIDNIGHT GREENWICH MEAN TIME. ALL OTHER DATA AND FACING ASPECTARIAN PAGE IN **EASTERN TIME (BOLD)** AND PACIFIC TIME (REGULAR).

JANUARY 2017

☽ Last Aspect day	ET / hr:mn / PT	asp	☽ Ingress sign day	ET / hr:mn / PT
1	11:59 pm	☌ ♀	♓ 2	**4:57 am** 1:57 am
2	**2:59 am**	☌ ♀	♓ 2	**4:57 am** 1:57 am
4	**11:14 am** 8:14 am	□ ☿	♈ 4	**11:20 am** 8:20 am
6	**1:41 pm** 10:41 am	△ ☿	♉ 6	**3:18 pm** 12:18 pm
7	**9:23 pm** 6:23 pm	△ ☉	♊ 8	**5:06 pm** 2:06 pm
10	**4:38 pm** 1:38 pm	☍ ☿	♋ 10	**5:49 pm** 2:49 pm
12	**6:34 am** 3:34 am	☍ ☉	♌ 12	**7:08 pm** 4:08 pm
14	**10:17 am** 7:17 am	△ ♄	♍ 14	**10:52 pm** 7:52 pm
16	10:09 pm	△ ☉	♎ 17	**6:16 am** 3:16 am
17	**1:09 am**	△ ☉	♎ 17	**6:16 am** 3:16 am
19	**3:55 am** 12:55 am	⚹ ♄	♏ 19	**5:09 pm** 2:09 pm
21	**8:24 pm** 5:24 pm	△ ♂	♐ 22	**5:45 am** 2:45 am
24	**12:33 pm** 9:33 am	□ ♂	♑ 24	**5:43 pm** 2:43 pm
26	11:18 pm	⚹ ♂	♒ 27	**3:37 am** 12:37 am
27	**2:18 am**	⚹ ♂	♒ 27	**3:37 am** 12:37 am
28	9:52 pm	⚹ ♄	♓ 29	**11:10 am** 8:10 am
29	**12:52 am**	⚹ ♄	♓ 29	**11:10 am** 8:10 am
31	**12:36 pm** 9:36 am	☌ ♂	♈ 31	**4:46 pm** 1:46 pm

☽ Phases & Eclipses phase	day	ET / hr:mn / PT
2nd Quarter	5	**2:47 pm** 11:47 am
Full Moon	12	**6:34 am** 3:34 am
4th Quarter	19	**5:13 pm** 2:13 pm
New Moon	27	**7:07 pm** 4:07 pm

Planet Ingress	day	ET / hr:mn / PT
♀ ♓	2	11:47 pm
♀ ♓	3	**2:47 am**
☿ ♐	4	**9:17 am** 6:17 am
⚶ ♋	10	**1:11 pm** 10:11 am
☿ ♑	12	**9:03 am** 6:03 am
☉ ♒	19	**4:24 pm** 1:24 pm
♂ ♈	27	9:39 pm
♂ ♈	28	**12:39 am**

Planetary Motion	day	ET / hr:mn / PT
☿ D	8	**4:43 am** 1:43 am

1 SUNDAY
♂ ☌ ♆ **1:53 am**
☽ ⚺ ♇ **4:38 am** 1:38 am
☽ ⚹ ♅ **11:24 am** 8:24 am
☽ △ ♃ **12:38 pm** 9:38 am
☽ ⚹ ♄ **1:04 pm** 10:04 am
☽ ☌ ♀ 11:59 pm

2 MONDAY
☽ ☌ ♀ **2:59 am**
☽ ⚹ ☿ **7:58 am** 4:58 am
☽ ☌ ♆ **10:56 pm** 7:56 pm
☽ ☌ ♂ 10:36 pm

3 TUESDAY
☽ ☌ ♂ **1:36 am**
☽ ⚹ ☉ **5:13 am** 2:13 am
☽ ⚹ ♇ **12:07 pm** 9:07 am
☿ ⚹ ♀ **2:41 pm** 11:41 am
☽ ⚺ ♅ **6:29 pm** 3:29 pm
☽ ⚻ ♃ **8:05 pm** 5:05 pm
☽ □ ♄ **8:33 pm** 5:33 pm

4 WEDNESDAY
☽ □ ☿ **11:14 am** 8:14 am
☽ ⚺ ♀ **2:07 pm** 11:07 am

5 THURSDAY
☽ ⚺ ♆ **4:38 am** 1:38 am
☽ ⚺ ♂ **10:11 am** 7:11 am
☽ □ ☉ **2:47 pm** 11:47 am
☽ □ ♇ **5:16 pm** 2:16 pm
☽ ☌ ♅ **11:15 pm** 8:15 pm
☽ ☍ ♃ 10:06 pm
☽ △ ♄ 10:37 pm

6 FRIDAY
☽ ☍ ♃ **1:06 am**
☽ △ ♄ **1:37 am**
☽ △ ☿ **1:41 pm** 10:41 am
☽ ⚹ ♀ **10:08 pm** 7:08 pm
☉ ☌ ♇ 10:45 pm

7 SATURDAY
☉ ☌ ♇ **1:45 am**
☽ ⚹ ♆ **7:56 am** 4:56 am
☽ ⚹ ♂ **3:57 pm** 12:57 pm
☽ △ ♇ **8:03 pm** 5:03 pm
☽ △ ☉ **9:23 pm** 6:23 pm
☽ ⚺ ♅ 10:41 pm

8 SUNDAY
☽ ⚺ ♅ **1:41 am**
☽ ⚻ ♃ **3:45 am** 12:45 am
☽ ⚻ ♄ **4:19 am** 1:19 am
☽ ⚻ ☿ **3:15 pm** 12:15 pm

9 MONDAY
☽ □ ♀ **3:30 am** 12:30 am
☽ □ ♆ **9:18 am** 6:18 am
☽ □ ♂ **7:40 pm** 4:40 pm
☽ ⚻ ♇ **9:09 pm** 6:09 pm
☽ ⚻ ☉ 10:58 pm
☽ ⚹ ♅ 11:36 pm

10 TUESDAY
☽ ⚻ ☉ **1:58 am**
☽ ⚹ ♅ **2:36 am**
☽ △ ♃ **4:53 am** 1:53 am
☽ ☍ ♄ **5:32 am** 2:32 am
☉ □ ♅ **11:22 am** 8:22 am
☽ ☍ ☿ **4:38 pm** 1:38 pm
♂ ⚹ ♇ 11:15 pm

11 WEDNESDAY
♂ ⚹ ♇ **2:15 am**
☽ △ ♀ **7:51 am** 4:51 am
☽ △ ♆ **10:06 am** 7:06 am
☽ ☍ ♇ **10:06 pm** 7:06 pm
☽ △ ♂ **11:08 pm** 8:08 pm
☉ □ ♃ **11:43 pm** 8:43 pm

12 THURSDAY
☽ □ ♅ **3:34 am** 12:34 am
☽ □ ♃ **6:07 am** 3:07 am
☽ ☍ ☉ **6:34 am** 3:34 am
☽ ⚻ ♄ **6:53 am** 3:53 am
☉ ⚺ ♄ **11:32 am** 8:32 am
♀ ☌ ♆ **4:54 pm** 1:54 pm
☽ ⚻ ☿ **7:31 pm** 4:31 pm

13 FRIDAY
☽ ⚻ ♆ **12:08 pm** 9:08 am
☽ ⚻ ♀ **1:35 pm** 10:35 am
☽ ⚻ ♇ 9:44 pm

14 SATURDAY
☽ ⚻ ♇ **12:44 am**
☽ ⚻ ♂ **4:37 am** 1:37 am
☽ △ ♅ **6:26 am** 3:26 am
☽ ⚹ ♃ **9:21 am** 6:21 am
☽ △ ♄ **10:17 am** 7:17 am
☽ ⚻ ☉ **1:39 pm** 10:39 am
☽ △ ☿ 10:59 pm

15 SUNDAY
☽ △ ☿ **1:59 am**
♂ ⚺ ♅ **2:29 pm** 11:29 am
☽ ☍ ♆ **5:08 pm** 2:08 pm
☽ ☍ ♀ **10:58 pm** 7:58 pm

16 MONDAY
☽ △ ♇ **6:40 am** 3:40 am
☽ ⚻ ♅ **12:41 pm** 9:41 am
☽ ☍ ♂ **2:02 pm** 11:02 am
☽ ⚺ ♃ **4:02 pm** 1:02 pm
☽ □ ♄ **5:13 pm** 2:13 pm
☽ △ ☉ 10:09 pm

17 TUESDAY
☽ △ ☉ **1:09 am**
☽ □ ☿ **1:37 pm** 10:37 am
☽ ⚻ ♆ 10:57 pm
♂ ⚻ ♃ 11:51 pm

18 WEDNESDAY
☽ ⚻ ♆ **1:57 am**
♂ ⚻ ♃ **2:51 am**
☽ ⚻ ♀ **1:01 pm** 10:01 am
☽ □ ♇ **4:23 pm** 1:23 pm
☽ ☍ ♅ **10:42 pm** 7:42 pm
☽ ☌ ♃ 11:27 pm

19 THURSDAY
☽ ☌ ♃ **2:27 am**
☽ ⚻ ♂ **3:54 am** 12:54 am
☽ ⚹ ♄ **3:55 am** 12:55 am
♂ □ ♄ **4:16 am** 1:16 am
☽ □ ☉ **5:13 pm** 2:13 pm

20 FRIDAY
☽ ⚹ ☿ **6:14 am** 3:14 am
♀ ⚹ ♇ **8:57 am** 5:57 am
☽ △ ♆ **1:50 pm** 10:50 am

21 SATURDAY
☽ ⚹ ♇ **4:44 am** 1:44 am
☽ △ ♀ **6:24 am** 3:24 am
☽ ⚻ ♅ **11:07 am** 8:07 am
☽ ⚺ ♃ **3:07 pm** 12:07 pm
☽ ⚺ ♄ **4:52 pm** 1:52 pm
☽ △ ♂ **8:24 pm** 5:24 pm

22 SUNDAY
☽ ⚹ ☉ **11:30 am** 8:30 am
☽ ⚺ ☿ 10:08 pm
☽ □ ♆ 11:37 pm

23 MONDAY
☽ ⚺ ☿ **1:08 am**
☽ □ ♆ **2:37 am**
☿ ⚹ ♆ **4:29 pm** 1:29 pm
☽ ⚺ ♇ **5:23 pm** 2:23 pm
♀ ⚺ ♅ **7:24 pm** 4:24 pm
☽ △ ♅ **11:36 pm** 8:36 pm
☽ □ ♀ **11:56 pm** 8:56 pm

24 TUESDAY
☽ ⚹ ♃ **3:38 am** 12:38 am
☽ ☌ ♄ **5:38 am** 2:38 am
☽ □ ♂ **12:33 pm** 9:33 am

25 WEDNESDAY
☽ ⚺ ☉ **4:44 am** 1:44 am
☽ ⚹ ♆ **2:07 pm** 11:07 am
☽ ☌ ☿ **6:58 pm** 3:58 pm

26 THURSDAY
♀ ⚻ ♃ **3:02 am** 12:02 am
☽ ☌ ♇ **4:22 am** 1:22 am
☽ □ ♅ **10:18 am** 7:18 am
☽ □ ♃ **2:15 pm** 11:15 am
☽ ⚹ ♀ **3:05 pm** 12:05 pm
☽ ⚺ ♄ **4:28 pm** 1:28 pm
☽ ⚹ ♂ 11:18 pm

27 FRIDAY
☽ ⚹ ♂ **2:18 am**
♀ □ ♄ **12:50 pm** 9:50 am
☽ ☌ ☉ **7:07 pm** 4:07 pm
☽ ⚺ ♆ **11:19 pm** 8:19 pm

28 SATURDAY
☽ ⚺ ☿ **10:04 am** 7:04 am
☽ ⚺ ♇ **12:59 pm** 9:59 am
☽ ⚹ ♅ **6:39 pm** 3:39 pm
☽ △ ♃ **10:28 pm** 7:28 pm
☽ ⚹ ♄ 9:52 pm

29 SUNDAY
☽ ⚹ ♄ **12:52 am**
☽ ⚺ ♀ **3:09 am** 12:09 am
☽ ⚺ ♂ **1:14 pm** 10:14 am
☿ ☌ ♇ **3:21 pm** 12:21 pm
☉ ⚺ ♆ 11:03 pm

30 MONDAY
☉ ⚺ ♆ **2:03 am**
☽ ☌ ♆ **6:17 am** 3:17 am
☽ ⚺ ☉ **6:37 am** 3:37 am
☽ ⚹ ♇ **7:28 pm** 4:28 pm
☽ ⚹ ☿ **10:31 pm** 7:31 pm
☽ ⚺ ♅ 9:54 pm

31 TUESDAY
☽ ⚺ ♅ **12:54 am**
☽ ⚻ ♃ **4:34 am** 1:34 am
☽ □ ♄ **7:11 am** 4:11 am
☽ ☌ ♀ **12:36 pm** 9:36 am
☽ ☌ ♂ **9:52 pm** 6:52 pm
☿ □ ♅ **10:32 pm** 7:32 pm

Eastern time in bold type
Pacific time in medium type

JANUARY 2017

DATE	SID.TIME	SUN	MOON	NODE	MERCURY	VENUS	MARS	JUPITER	SATURN	URANUS	NEPTUNE	PLUTO	CERES	PALLAS	JUNO	VESTA	CHIRON
1 Su	6 43 21	10 ♑ 45 19	11 ♒ 51	4 ♍ 32 ℞	3 ♑ 17	27 ♒ 29	9 ♓ 31	21 ♎ 09	21 ♐ 22	20 ♈ 34	9 ♓ 44	16 ♑ 57	22 ♈ 37	1 ♓ 05	19 ♐ 06	2 ♌ 19	21 ♓ 06
2 M	6 47 17	11 46 29	24 38	4 30 D	2 10 ℞	28 34	10 17	21 15	21 29	20 34	9 45	16 59	22 46	1 22	19 26	2 06 ℞	21 08
3 T	6 51 14	12 47 40	7 ♓ 38	4 29	1 12	29 39	11 02	21 21	21 36	20 34	9 47	17 01	22 54	1 39	19 47	1 52	21 10
4 W	6 55 10	13 48 50	20 51	4 30	0 24	0 ♓ 43	11 47	21 27	21 43	20 34	9 48	17 03	23 03	1 56	20 07	1 39	21 11
5 Th	6 59 7	14 49 59	4 ♈ 20	4 31 ℞	29 ♐ 46	1 48	12 33	21 33	21 49	20 35	9 50	17 05	23 12	2 13	20 27	1 25	21 13
6 F	7 3 3	15 51 09	18 07	4 32	29 18	2 51	13 18	21 39	21 56	20 35	9 51	17 07	23 21	2 30	20 48	1 11	21 15
7 Sa	7 7 0	16 52 17	2 ♉ 11	4 31	29 00	3 55	14 03	21 44	22 03	20 35	9 53	17 09	23 30	2 47	21 08	0 56	21 17
8 Su	7 10 56	17 53 26	16 33	4 27	28 52 D	4 58	14 48	21 49	22 09	20 36	9 54	17 11	23 40	3 04	21 28	0 41	21 19
9 M	7 14 53	18 54 34	1 ♊ 10	4 22	28 52	6 01	15 34	21 54	22 16	20 36	9 56	17 13	23 50	3 22	21 48	0 27	21 21
10 T	7 18 50	19 55 42	15 56	4 16	29 02	7 03	16 19	21 59	22 23	20 37	9 57	17 15	24 01	3 39	22 08	0 12	21 23
11 W	7 22 46	20 56 49	0 ♋ 44	4 09	29 19	8 05	17 04	22 04	22 29	20 38	9 59	17 17	24 12	3 57	22 28	29 ♋ 56	21 25
12 Th	7 26 43	21 57 56	15 26	4 02	29 43	9 06	17 49	22 09	22 36	20 38	10 01	17 19	24 23	4 14	22 48	29 41	21 27
13 F	7 30 39	22 59 02	29 55	3 56	0 ♑ 13	10 08	18 34	22 14	22 42	20 39	10 02	17 21	24 34	4 32	23 08	29 25	21 30
14 Sa	7 34 36	24 00 08	14 ♌ 04	3 53	0 50	11 08	19 20	22 18	22 48	20 40	10 04	17 23	24 46	4 50	23 28	29 10	21 32
15 Su	7 38 32	25 01 14	27 49	3 51 D	1 31	12 09	20 05	22 22	22 55	20 41	10 06	17 25	24 57	5 08	23 48	28 54	21 34
16 M	7 42 29	26 02 19	11 ♍ 09	3 51	2 18	13 09	20 50	22 26	23 01	20 42	10 08	17 27	25 09	5 26	24 08	28 38	21 37
17 T	7 46 26	27 03 24	24 04	3 52	3 08	14 08	21 35	22 30	23 08	20 42	10 09	17 29	25 22	5 44	24 27	28 22	21 39
18 W	7 50 22	28 04 29	6 ♎ 37	3 54	4 02	15 07	22 20	22 34	23 14	20 43	10 11	17 31	25 34	6 03	24 47	28 06	21 41
19 Th	7 54 19	29 05 34	18 53	3 56 ℞	5 00	16 05	23 05	22 37	23 20	20 44	10 13	17 34	25 47	6 21	25 07	27 50	21 44
20 F	7 58 15	0 ♒ 06 38	0 ♏ 55	3 56	6 01	17 03	23 50	22 40	23 26	20 46	10 15	17 36	26 00	6 39	25 26	27 35	21 46
21 Sa	8 2 12	1 07 42	12 50	3 55	7 05	18 01	24 35	22 43	23 32	20 47	10 17	17 38	26 14	6 58	25 46	27 19	21 49
22 Su	8 6 8	2 08 45	24 41	3 53	8 11	18 58	25 20	22 46	23 38	20 48	10 19	17 40	26 27	7 16	26 06	27 03	21 51
23 M	8 10 5	3 09 48	6 ♐ 34	3 49	9 19	19 54	26 05	22 49	23 44	20 49	10 20	17 42	26 41	7 35	26 25	26 47	21 54
24 T	8 14 1	4 10 51	18 32	3 44	10 30	20 50	26 50	22 52	23 50	20 50	10 22	17 44	26 55	7 54	26 44	26 31	21 57
25 W	8 17 58	5 11 53	0 ♑ 39	3 39	11 42	21 45	27 35	22 54	23 56	20 52	10 24	17 46	27 09	8 13	27 04	26 16	21 59
26 Th	8 21 55	6 12 55	12 57	3 34	12 56	22 39	28 20	22 56	24 02	20 53	10 26	17 48	27 24	8 32	27 23	26 00	22 02
27 F	8 25 51	7 13 55	25 28	3 30	14 12	23 33	29 05	22 58	24 08	20 55	10 28	17 50	27 38	8 50	27 42	25 45	22 05
28 Sa	8 29 48	8 14 55	8 ♒ 11	3 26	15 29	24 26	29 49	23 00	24 14	20 56	10 30	17 51	27 53	9 10	28 01	25 30	22 08
29 Su	8 33 44	9 15 54	21 09	3 25 D	16 47	25 18	0 ♈ 34	23 02	24 20	20 58	10 32	17 53	28 08	9 29	28 20	25 15	22 10
30 M	8 37 41	10 16 52	4 ♓ 19	3 24	18 07	26 10	1 19	23 03	24 25	20 59	10 34	17 55	28 24	9 48	28 39	25 00	22 13
31 T	8 41 37	11 17 49	17 42	3 25	19 28	27 01	2 04	23 05	24 31	21 01	10 36	17 57	28 39	10 07	28 58	24 45	22 16

EPHEMERIS CALCULATED FOR 12 MIDNIGHT GREENWICH MEAN TIME. ALL OTHER DATA AND FACING ASPECTARIAN PAGE IN **EASTERN TIME (BOLD)** AND PACIFIC TIME (REGULAR).

FEBRUARY 2017

☽ Last Aspect			☽ Ingress			
day	ET / hr:mn / PT	asp	sign	day	ET / hr:mn / PT	
2	**11:50 am** 8:50 am	△♄	♉	2	**8:50 pm**	5:50 pm
4	**5:42 pm** 2:42 pm	△☿	♊	4	**11:44 pm**	8:44 pm
6	**5:53 pm** 2:53 pm	☍♄	♋	6		11:03 pm
6	**5:53 pm** 2:53 pm	☍♄	♋	7	**2:03 am**	
8	**5:00 pm** 2:00 pm	□♃	♌	9	**4:41 am**	1:41 am
10	9:52 pm	△♄	♍	11	**8:52 am**	5:52 am
11	**12:52 am**	△♄	♍	11	**8:52 am**	5:52 am
13	**7:36 am** 4:36 am	□♄	♎	13	**3:43 pm**	12:43 pm
15	**8:54 pm** 5:54 pm	△☉	♏	15		10:41 pm
15	**8:54 pm** 5:54 pm	△☉	♏	16	**1:41 am**	

☽ Last Aspect			☽ Ingress			
day	ET / hr:mn / PT	asp	sign	day	ET / hr:mn / PT	
17	**2:38 pm** 11:38 am	✱♇	♐	18	**1:52 pm**	10:52 am
20	**6:37 pm** 3:37 pm	☌♄	♑	20		11:08 pm
20	**6:37 pm** 3:37 pm	☌♄	♑	21	**2:08 am**	
22	**10:24 pm** 7:24 pm	□♃	♒	23	**12:17 pm**	9:17 am
25	**1:11 pm** 10:11 am	✱♄	♓	25	**7:24 pm**	4:24 pm
27	**6:08 pm** 3:08 pm	□♄	♈	27	**11:52 pm**	8:52 pm

☽ Phases & Eclipses			
phase	day	ET / hr:mn / PT	
2nd Quarter	3	**11:19 pm**	8:19 pm
Full Moon	10	**7:33 pm**	4:43 pm
☍	10	22° ♌ 28'	
4th Quarter	18	**2:33 pm**	11:33 am
New Moon	26	**9:58 am**	6:58 am
☌		8° ♓ 12'	

Planet Ingress			
	day	ET / hr:mn / PT	
⚵ ♑	2		10:47 pm
⚵ ♑	3	**1:47 am**	
♀ ♈	3	**10:51 am**	7:51 am
⚳ ♉	4	**7:17 pm**	4:17 pm
☿ ♒	7	**4:35 am**	1:35 am
☉ ♓	18	**6:31 am**	3:31 am
☿ ♓	26	**6:07 pm**	3:07 pm

Planetary Motion			
	day	ET / hr:mn / PT	
♃ ℞	5		10:52 pm
♃ ℞	6	**1:52 am**	

1 WEDNESDAY
☽⚺♆ **11:26 am** 8:26 am
☽✱☉ **3:50 pm** 12:50 pm
☽□♇ 9:13 pm

2 THURSDAY
☽□♇ **12:13 am**
☽☌♅ **5:30 am** 2:30 am
☽□☿ **8:52 am** 5:52 am
☽☍♃ **9:01 am** 6:01 am
☿□♃ **10:15 am** 7:15 am
☽△♄ **11:50 am** 8:50 am
☽⚺♀ **8:00 pm** 5:00 pm

3 FRIDAY
☽⚺♂ **4:42 am** 1:42 am
☽✱♆ **3:10 pm** 12:10 pm
☿⚺♄ **3:50 pm** 12:50 pm
☽□☉ **11:19 pm** 8:19 pm

4 SATURDAY
☽△♇ **3:38 am** 12:38 am
☽⚺♅ **8:48 am** 5:48 am
☽⚻♃ **12:10 pm** 9:10 am
☽⚻♄ **3:14 pm** 12:14 pm
☽△☿ **5:42 pm** 2:42 pm
☽✱♀ 10:51 pm

5 SUNDAY
☽✱♀ **1:51 am**
☽✱♂ **10:15 am** 7:15 am
☽□♆ **5:53 pm** 2:53 pm

6 MONDAY
☽△☉ **5:40 am** 2:40 am
☽⚻♇ **6:12 am** 3:12 am
☽✱♅ **11:19 am** 8:19 am
☉⚺♇ **1:34 pm** 10:34 am
☽△♃ **2:33 pm** 11:33 am
☽☍♄ **5:53 pm** 2:53 pm
☽⚻☿ 10:45 pm

7 TUESDAY
☽⚻☿ **1:45 am**
☽□♀ **6:55 am** 3:55 am
☽□♂ **3:18 pm** 12:18 pm
☽△♆ **8:19 pm** 5:19 pm

8 WEDNESDAY
☽☍♇ **8:41 am** 5:41 am
☽⚻☉ **11:54 am** 8:54 am
☽□♅ **1:52 pm** 10:52 am
☽□♃ **5:00 pm** 2:00 pm
☽⚻♄ **8:42 pm** 5:42 pm

9 THURSDAY
☽☍☿ **10:25 am** 7:25 am
☽△♀ **12:20 pm** 9:20 am
☉✱♅ **4:16 pm** 1:16 pm
☽△♂ **9:05 pm** 6:05 pm
☽⚻♆ **11:30 pm** 8:30 pm

10 FRIDAY
☽⚻♇ **12:14 pm** 9:14 am
☿✱♀ **4:19 pm** 1:19 pm

☽△♅ **5:36 pm** 2:36 pm
☽☍☉ **7:33 pm** 4:33 pm
☽✱♃ **8:40 pm** 5:40 pm
☽△♄ 9:52 pm

11 SATURDAY
☽△♄ **12:52 am**
☉△♃ **10:25 am** 7:25 am
☽⚻♀ **7:34 pm** 4:34 pm
♂⚺♆ **8:49 pm** 5:49 pm
☽⚻☿ **9:38 pm** 6:38 pm

12 SUNDAY
☽☍♆ **4:42 am** 1:42 am
☽⚻♂ **5:08 am** 2:08 am
☽△♇ **6:03 pm** 3:03 pm
☽⚻♅ **11:44 pm** 8:44 pm
☽⚺♃ 11:45 pm

13 MONDAY
☽⚺♃ **2:45 am**
☽⚻☉ **6:15 am** 3:15 am
☽□♄ **7:36 am** 4:36 am
☉✱♄ 9:58 pm

14 TUESDAY
☉✱♄ **12:58 am**
☽☍♀ **5:51 am** 2:51 am
☿⚺♆ **10:50 am** 7:50 am
☽⚻♆ **12:52 pm** 9:52 am
☽△☿ **1:09 pm** 10:09 am
☽☍♂ **4:42 pm** 1:42 pm
☽□♇ 11:58 pm

15 WEDNESDAY
☽□♇ **2:58 am**
☽☍♅ **9:01 am** 6:01 am
☽☌♃ **11:54 am** 8:54 am
☽✱♄ **5:30 pm** 2:30 pm
☽△☉ **8:54 pm** 5:54 pm

16 THURSDAY
☿✱♂ **1:15 pm** 10:15 am
☽⚻♀ **7:19 pm** 4:19 pm
☽△♆ 9:02 pm

17 FRIDAY
☽△♆ **12:02 am**
☽⚻♂ **7:43 am** 4:43 am
☽□☿ **9:18 am** 6:18 am
☽✱♇ **2:38 pm** 11:38 am
☽⚻♅ **8:57 pm** 5:57 pm
☽⚺♃ **11:34 pm** 8:34 pm

18 SATURDAY
☽⚺♄ **5:52 am** 2:52 am
☽□☉ **2:33 pm** 11:33 am
☿⚺♇ 9:38 pm

19 SUNDAY
☿⚺♇ **12:38 am**
☽△♀ **10:20 am** 7:20 am
☽□♆ **12:43 pm** 9:43 am
☽△♂ 9:13 pm

20 MONDAY
☽△♂ **12:13 am**
☽⚺♇ **3:18 am** 12:18 am

☽✱☿ **7:31 am** 4:31 am
☽△♅ **9:39 am** 6:39 am
☽✱♃ **11:49 am** 8:49 am
☽☌♄ **6:37 pm** 3:37 pm
☿✱♅ **11:01 pm** 8:01 pm

21 TUESDAY
☽✱☉ **8:16 am** 5:16 am
☿△♃ **1:27 pm** 10:27 am
☽□♀ 9:08 pm
☽✱♆ 9:35 pm

22 WEDNESDAY
☽□♀ **12:08 am**
☽✱♆ **12:35 am**
♂□♇ **4:03 am** 1:03 am
☽☌♇ **2:34 pm** 11:34 am
☽□♂ **3:13 pm** 12:13 pm
♀⚺♆ **4:58 pm** 1:58 pm
☽□♅ **8:44 pm** 5:44 pm
☽□♃ **10:24 pm** 7:24 pm

23 THURSDAY
☽⚺☿ **3:43 am** 12:43 am
☽⚺♄ **5:26 am** 2:26 am
☿✱♄ **4:45 pm** 1:45 pm
☽⚺☉ **11:04 pm** 8:04 pm

24 FRIDAY
☽⚺♆ **9:47 am** 6:47 am
☽✱♀ **10:41 am** 7:41 am
☽⚺♇ **10:58 pm** 7:58 pm
☽✱♂ 11:46 pm

25 SATURDAY
☽✱♂ **2:46 am**
☽✱♅ **4:53 am** 1:53 am
☽△♃ **6:02 am** 3:02 am
☽✱♄ **1:11 pm** 10:11 am
☽☌☿ **7:36 pm** 4:36 pm

26 SUNDAY
☽☌☉ **9:58 am** 6:58 am
☽☌♆ **3:56 pm** 12:56 pm
☽⚺♀ **5:39 pm** 2:39 pm
♂☌♅ **7:19 pm** 4:19 pm

27 MONDAY
☽✱♇ **4:25 am** 1:25 am
♂☍♃ **9:24 am** 6:24 am
☽⚺♅ **10:08 am** 7:08 am
☽⚻♃ **10:49 am** 7:49 am
☽⚺♂ **10:54 am** 7:54 am
☽□♄ **6:08 pm** 3:08 pm

28 TUESDAY
☽⚺☿ **7:41 am** 4:41 am
☽⚺☉ **5:51 pm** 2:51 pm
☽⚺♆ **7:46 pm** 4:46 pm
☽☌♀ **9:55 pm** 6:55 pm

Eastern time in bold type
Pacific time in medium type

FEBRUARY 2017

DATE	SID.TIME	SUN	MOON	NODE	MERCURY	VENUS	MARS	JUPITER	SATURN	URANUS	NEPTUNE	PLUTO	CERES	PALLAS	JUNO	VESTA	CHIRON
1 W	8 45 34	12 ♒ 18 44	1 ♈ 16	3 ♍ 26	20 ♑ 50	27 ♓ 51	2 ♈ 49	23 ♎ 06	24 ♐ 36	21 ♈ 02	10 ♓ 38	17 ♑ 59	28 ♈ 55	10 ♓ 26	29 ♐ 17	24 ♋ 31	22 ♓ 19
2 Th	8 49 30	13 19 38	15 01	3 27	22 14	28 40	3 33	23 07	24 42	21 04	10 40	18 01	29 11	10 46	29 36	24 17 ℞	22 22
3 F	8 53 27	14 20 31	28 56	3 29	23 38	29 29	4 18	23 07	24 47	21 06	10 42	18 03	29 27	11 05	29 55	24 03	22 25
4 Sa	8 57 24	15 21 23	13 ♉ 00	3 29 ℞	25 03	0 ♈ 16	5 03	23 08	24 53	21 08	10 44	18 05	29 43	11 25	0 ♑ 13	23 49	22 28
5 Su	9 1 20	16 22 13	27 11	3 29	26 29	1 03	5 47	23 08	24 58	21 09	10 47	18 07	0 ♉ 00	11 44	0 32	23 36	22 31
6 M	9 5 17	17 23 02	11 ♊ 28	3 28	27 57	1 48	6 32	23 08 ℞	25 03	21 11	10 49	18 09	0 16	12 04	0 50	23 23	22 34
7 T	9 9 13	18 23 49	25 48	3 26	29 25	2 33	7 16	23 08	25 08	21 13	10 51	18 10	0 33	12 23	1 09	23 11	22 37
8 W	9 13 10	19 24 35	10 ♋ 06	3 24	0 ♒ 54	3 16	8 01	23 08	25 13	21 15	10 53	18 12	0 50	12 43	1 27	22 58	22 41
9 Th	9 17 6	20 25 19	24 19	3 22	2 23	3 58	8 45	23 08	25 18	21 17	10 55	18 14	1 08	13 03	1 45	22 47	22 44
10 F	9 21 3	21 26 02	8 ♌ 21	3 21	3 54	4 40	9 30	23 07	25 23	21 19	10 57	18 16	1 25	13 23	2 03	22 35	22 47
11 Sa	9 24 59	22 26 43	22 09	3 20 D	5 25	5 20	10 14	23 06	25 28	21 21	11 00	18 18	1 43	13 43	2 21	22 24	22 50
12 Su	9 28 56	23 27 23	5 ♍ 40	3 20	6 58	5 58	10 58	23 05	25 33	21 24	11 02	18 19	2 00	14 03	2 39	22 13	22 53
13 M	9 32 53	24 28 02	18 52	3 20	8 31	6 36	11 43	23 04	25 38	21 26	11 04	18 21	2 18	14 23	2 57	22 03	22 57
14 T	9 36 49	25 28 39	1 ♎ 45	3 21	10 05	7 12	12 27	23 03	25 43	21 28	11 06	18 23	2 36	14 43	3 15	21 53	23 00
15 W	9 40 46	26 29 16	14 19	3 22	11 40	7 47	13 11	23 01	25 47	21 30	11 08	18 25	2 54	15 03	3 33	21 43	23 03
16 Th	9 44 42	27 29 50	26 37	3 23	13 16	8 20	13 56	22 59	25 52	21 33	11 11	18 26	3 13	15 23	3 50	21 34	23 07
17 F	9 48 39	28 30 24	8 ♏ 42	3 23	14 52	8 52	14 40	22 58	25 56	21 35	11 13	18 28	3 31	15 43	4 08	21 26	23 10
18 Sa	9 52 35	29 30 57	20 39	3 23 ℞	16 30	9 22	15 24	22 55	26 01	21 37	11 15	18 30	3 50	16 03	4 25	21 17	23 13
19 Su	9 56 32	0 ♓ 31 28	2 ♐ 32	3 23	18 08	9 51	16 08	22 53	26 05	21 40	11 17	18 31	4 09	16 23	4 42	21 10	23 17
20 M	10 0 28	1 31 58	14 26	3 23	19 48	10 18	16 52	22 51	26 09	21 42	11 19	18 33	4 28	16 44	5 00	21 02	23 20
21 T	10 4 25	2 32 26	26 25	3 23 D	21 28	10 43	17 36	22 48	26 13	21 45	11 22	18 35	4 47	17 04	5 17	20 55	23 24
22 W	10 8 21	3 32 54	8 ♑ 33	3 23	23 09	11 06	18 20	22 45	26 17	21 47	11 24	18 36	5 06	17 24	5 34	20 49	23 27
23 Th	10 12 18	4 33 20	20 55	3 23	24 51	11 28	19 04	22 42	26 21	21 50	11 26	18 38	5 25	17 45	5 50	20 43	23 30
24 F	10 16 15	5 33 44	3 ♒ 34	3 24	26 35	11 48	19 48	22 39	26 25	21 52	11 29	18 39	5 45	18 05	6 07	20 37	23 34
25 Sa	10 20 11	6 34 07	16 31	3 24	28 19	12 05	20 32	22 36	26 29	21 55	11 31	18 41	6 05	18 26	6 24	20 32	23 37
26 Su	10 24 8	7 34 28	29 46	3 24 ℞	0 ♓ 04	12 21	21 16	22 32	26 33	21 58	11 33	18 42	6 24	18 46	6 40	20 28	23 41
27 M	10 28 4	8 34 48	13 ♓ 20	3 24	1 50	12 34	22 00	22 28	26 37	22 00	11 35	18 44	6 44	19 07	6 57	20 23	23 44
28 T	10 32 1	9 35 06	27 10	3 23	3 37	12 46	22 43	22 24	26 40	22 03	11 38	18 45	7 04	19 27	7 13	20 20	23 48

EPHEMERIS CALCULATED FOR 12 MIDNIGHT GREENWICH MEAN TIME. ALL OTHER DATA AND FACING ASPECTARIAN PAGE IN **EASTERN TIME (BOLD)** AND PACIFIC TIME (REGULAR).

MARCH 2017

☽ Last Aspect day	ET / hr:mn / PT		asp	☽ Ingress sign	day	ET / hr:mn / PT	
1	**9:18 pm**	6:18 pm	△♄	♉	1		11:43 pm
1	**9:18 pm**	6:18 pm	△♄	♉	2	**2:43 am**	
3	**10:20 am**	7:20 am	△♇	♊	4	**5:05 am**	2:05 am
6	**3:22 am**	12:22 am	✶♂	♋	6	**7:54 am**	4:54 am
8	**9:59 am**	6:59 am	□♂	♌	8	**11:45 am**	8:45 am
10	**12:06 pm**	9:06 am	△♄	♍	10	**5:07 pm**	2:07 pm
12	**10:36 pm**	7:36 pm	☍☿	♎	12		10:28 pm
12	**10:36 pm**	7:36 pm	☍☿	♎	13	**1:28 am**	
15	**6:05 am**	3:05 am	✶♄	♏	15	**11:11 am**	8:11 am
17	**5:56 pm**	2:56 pm	△☉	♐	17	**11:00 pm**	8:00 pm
20	**6:37 am**	3:37 am	☌♄	♑	20	**11:31 am**	8:31 am
22	**9:20 am**	6:20 am	□♅	♒	22	**10:28 pm**	7:28 pm
24		10:56 pm	✶♄	♓	25	**6:06 am**	3:06 am
25	**1:56 am**		✶♄	♓	25	**6:06 am**	3:06 am
27	**6:19 am**	3:19 am	□♄	♈	27	**10:11 am**	7:11 am
29	**8:07 am**	5:07 am	△♄	♉	29	**11:48 am**	8:48 am
30	**7:12 pm**	4:12 pm	△♇	♊	31	**12:40 pm**	9:40 am

☽ Phases & Eclipses phase	day	ET / hr:mn / PT	
2nd Quarter	5	**6:32 am**	3:32 am
Full Moon	12	**10:54 am**	7:54 am
4th Quarter	20	**11:58 am**	8:58 am
New Moon	27	**10:57 pm**	7:57 pm

Planet Ingress		day	ET / hr:mn / PT	
♂	♉	9	**7:34 pm**	4:34 pm
☿	♈	13	**5:07 pm**	2:07 pm
☉	♈	20	**6:29 am**	3:29 am
♀	♈	29		9:47 pm
♀	♈	30	**12:47 am**	
☿	♉	31	**1:31 pm**	10:31 am

Planetary Motion		day	ET / hr:mn / PT	
♀	℞	4	**4:09 am**	1:09 am
⚵	D	7	**4:32 am**	1:32 am

1 WEDNESDAY
☽ □ ♇ **7:49 am** 4:49 am
☽ ☌ ♅ **1:27 pm** 10:27 am
☽ ☍ ♃ **1:43 pm** 10:43 am
☽ ☌ ♂ **4:48 pm** 1:48 pm
☽ △ ♄ **9:18 pm** 6:18 pm
☉ ☌ ♆ **9:44 pm** 6:44 pm

2 THURSDAY
☽ ✶ ☿ **5:48 pm** 2:48 pm
♃ ☍ ♅ **8:15 pm** 5:15 pm
☽ ✶ ♆ **10:26 pm** 7:26 pm
☽ ✶ ☉ 9:14 pm
☽ ⚺ ♀ 9:44 pm

3 FRIDAY
☽ ✶ ☉ **12:14 am**
☽ ⚺ ♀ **12:44 am**
☉ ⚺ ♀ **7:49 am** 4:49 am
☽ △ ♇ **10:20 am** 7:20 am
☽ ⚻ ♃ **3:52 pm** 12:52 pm
☽ ⚺ ♅ **4:02 pm** 1:02 pm
☽ ⚺ ♂ **9:54 pm** 6:54 pm
☽ ⚻ ♄ **11:53 pm** 8:53 pm

4 SATURDAY
☿ ☌ ♆ **6:10 am** 3:10 am
☿ ⚺ ♀ **11:17 pm** 8:17 pm
☽ □ ♆ 10:02 pm

5 SUNDAY
☽ □ ♆ **1:02 am**
☽ ✶ ♀ **3:14 am** 12:14 am
☽ □ ☿ **3:51 am** 12:51 am
☽ □ ☉ **6:32 am** 3:32 am
☽ ⚻ ♇ **12:59 pm** 9:59 am
♂ △ ♄ **3:46 pm** 12:46 pm
☽ △ ♃ **6:12 pm** 3:12 pm
☽ ✶ ♅ **6:50 pm** 3:50 pm
☽ ☍ ♄ 11:48 pm

6 MONDAY
☽ ☍ ♄ **2:48 am**
☽ ✶ ♂ **3:22 am** 12:22 am
☉ ☌ ☿ **7:29 pm** 4:29 pm

7 TUESDAY
☽ △ ♆ **4:20 am** 1:20 am
☽ □ ♀ **6:08 am** 3:08 am
☽ △ ☉ **1:48 pm** 10:48 am
☽ △ ☿ **3:12 pm** 12:12 pm
☽ ☍ ♇ **4:28 pm** 1:28 pm
☽ □ ♃ **9:25 pm** 6:25 pm
☽ □ ♅ **10:33 pm** 7:33 pm
☿ ✶ ♇ 9:25 pm

8 WEDNESDAY
☿ ✶ ♇ **12:25 am**
☽ ⚻ ♄ **6:43 am** 3:43 am
☽ □ ♂ **9:59 am** 6:59 am

9 THURSDAY
☉ ✶ ♇ **3:33 am** 12:33 am
☽ ⚻ ♆ **8:53 am** 5:53 am
☽ △ ♀ **9:55 am** 6:55 am
☿ ⚻ ♃ **9:57 am** 6:57 am
☿ ⚺ ♅ **8:55 pm** 5:55 pm
☽ ⚻ ♇ **9:18 pm** 6:18 pm
☽ ⚻ ☉ **10:42 pm** 7:42 pm
☽ ✶ ♃ 10:58 pm

10 FRIDAY
☽ ✶ ♃ **1:58 am**
☽ △ ♅ **3:42 am** 12:42 am
☽ ⚻ ☿ **4:49 am** 1:49 am
☽ △ ♄ **12:06 pm** 9:06 am
☽ △ ♂ **6:22 pm** 3:22 pm

11 SATURDAY
♀ ⚺ ♆ **8:53 am** 5:53 am
☽ ⚻ ♀ **2:58 pm** 11:58 am
☉ ⚻ ♃ **3:00 pm** 12:00 pm
☽ ☍ ♆ **3:08 pm** 12:08 pm

12 SUNDAY
☽ △ ♇ **4:57 am** 12:57 am
☿ □ ♄ **8:10 am** 5:10 am
☽ ⚺ ♃ **9:18 am** 6:18 am
☽ ☍ ☉ **10:54 am** 7:54 am
☽ ⚻ ♅ **11:43 am** 8:43 am
☽ □ ♄ **8:25 pm** 5:25 pm
☉ ⚺ ♅ **10:04 pm** 7:04 pm
☽ ☍ ☿ **10:36 pm** 7:36 pm

13 MONDAY
☽ ⚻ ♂ **6:05 am** 3:05 am
☽ ☍ ♀ **10:41 pm** 7:41 pm
☽ ⚻ ♆ 9:35 pm

14 TUESDAY
☽ ⚻ ♆ **12:35 am**
☽ □ ♇ **1:52 pm** 10:52 am
☽ ☌ ♃ **5:52 pm** 2:52 pm
☽ ☍ ♅ **9:05 pm** 6:05 pm
☽ ⚻ ☉ 10:00 pm

15 WEDNESDAY
☽ ⚻ ☉ **1:00 am**
☽ ✶ ♄ **6:05 am** 3:05 am
☽ ⚻ ☿ **7:18 pm** 4:18 pm
☽ ☍ ♂ **7:38 pm** 4:38 pm
☿ ⚺ ♂ **10:21 pm** 7:21 pm

16 THURSDAY
☽ ⚻ ♀ **7:13 am** 4:13 am
☽ △ ♆ **11:25 am** 8:25 am
☽ ✶ ♇ 10:05 pm

17 FRIDAY
☽ ✶ ♇ **1:05 am**
☽ ⚺ ♃ **4:38 am** 1:38 am
☽ ⚻ ♅ **8:44 am** 5:44 am
☉ □ ♄ **5:48 pm** 2:48 pm
☽ ⚺ ♄ **5:56 pm** 2:56 pm
☽ △ ☉ **5:56 pm** 2:56 pm

18 SATURDAY
☿ ☌ ♀ **8:27 am** 5:27 am
☽ ⚻ ♂ **11:31 am** 8:31 am
☽ △ ♀ **4:59 pm** 1:59 pm
☽ △ ☿ **7:06 pm** 4:06 pm
☽ □ ♆ **11:57 pm** 8:57 pm

19 SUNDAY
☽ ⚺ ♇ **1:41 pm** 10:41 am
☽ ✶ ♃ **4:36 pm** 1:36 pm
☽ △ ♅ **9:33 pm** 6:33 pm
☿ ⚺ ♆ 10:51 pm

20 MONDAY
☿ ⚺ ♆ **1:51 am**
☽ ☌ ♄ **6:37 am** 3:37 am
☽ □ ☉ **11:58 am** 8:58 am
♀ ⚺ ♂ **4:22 pm** 1:22 pm
☽ □ ♀ 11:32 pm

21 TUESDAY
☽ □ ♀ **2:32 am**
☽ △ ♂ **3:43 am** 12:43 am
☽ ✶ ♆ **12:17 pm** 9:17 am
☽ □ ☿ **6:20 pm** 3:20 pm
☽ ☌ ♇ 10:32 pm

22 WEDNESDAY
☽ ☌ ♇ **1:32 am**
☽ □ ♃ **3:44 am** 12:44 am
☽ □ ♅ **9:20 am** 6:20 am
☽ ⚺ ♄ **5:55 pm** 2:55 pm

23 THURSDAY
☽ ✶ ☉ **3:58 am** 12:58 am
☽ ✶ ♀ **10:06 am** 7:06 am
☽ □ ♂ **5:20 pm** 2:20 pm
☿ □ ♇ **8:45 pm** 5:45 pm
☽ ⚺ ♆ **10:10 pm** 7:10 pm

24 FRIDAY
☿ ☍ ♃ **8:45 am** 5:45 am
☽ ⚺ ♇ **10:33 am** 7:33 am
☽ △ ♃ **12:03 pm** 9:03 am
☽ ✶ ☿ **12:34 pm** 9:34 am
☽ ✶ ♅ **6:02 pm** 3:02 pm
☽ ✶ ♄ 10:56 pm

25 SATURDAY
☽ ✶ ♄ **1:56 am**
☉ ☌ ♀ **6:17 am** 3:17 am
☽ ⚺ ♀ **2:33 pm** 11:33 am
☽ ⚺ ☉ **3:37 pm** 12:37 pm
☽ ✶ ♂ 11:42 pm

26 SUNDAY
☽ ✶ ♂ **2:42 am**
☽ ☌ ♆ **4:23 am** 1:23 am
☿ ☌ ♅ **11:06 am** 8:06 am
☽ ✶ ♇ **3:52 pm** 12:52 pm
☽ ⚻ ♃ **4:47 pm** 1:47 pm
☽ ⚺ ♅ **11:03 pm** 8:03 pm
☽ ⚺ ☿ 9:25 pm

27 MONDAY
☽ ⚺ ☿ **12:25 am**
☽ □ ♄ **6:19 am** 3:19 am
♂ ✶ ♆ **12:44 pm** 9:44 am
☽ ☌ ♀ **3:59 pm** 12:59 pm
☽ ☌ ☉ **10:57 pm** 7:57 pm

28 TUESDAY
☽ ⚺ ♆ **7:22 am** 4:22 am
☽ ⚺ ♂ **8:16 am** 5:16 am
☽ □ ♇ **6:14 pm** 3:14 pm
☽ ☍ ♃ **6:38 pm** 3:38 pm
☽ ☌ ♅ 10:15 pm

29 WEDNESDAY
☽ ☌ ♅ **1:15 am**
☽ ☌ ☿ **7:33 am** 4:33 am
☽ △ ♄ **8:07 am** 5:07 am
☿ △ ♄ **2:16 pm** 11:16 am
☽ ⚺ ♀ **3:29 pm** 12:29 pm

30 THURSDAY
☽ ⚺ ☉ **3:45 am** 12:45 am
☽ ✶ ♆ **8:34 am** 5:34 am
☽ ☌ ♂ **11:49 am** 8:49 am
♃ □ ♇ **2:19 pm** 11:19 am
☽ ⚻ ♃ **7:09 pm** 4:09 pm
☽ △ ♇ **7:12 pm** 4:12 pm
☽ ⚺ ♅ 11:20 pm

31 FRIDAY
☽ ⚺ ♅ **2:20 am**
☽ ⚻ ♄ **9:01 am** 6:01 am
☽ ⚺ ☿ **12:36 pm** 9:36 am
☽ ✶ ♀ **2:33 pm** 11:33 am

Eastern time in bold type
Pacific time in medium type

MARCH 2017

DATE	SID.TIME	SUN	MOON	NODE	MERCURY	VENUS	MARS	JUPITER	SATURN	URANUS	NEPTUNE	PLUTO	CERES	PALLAS	JUNO	VESTA	CHIRON
1 W	10 35 57	10 ♓ 35 22	11 ♈ 13	3 ♍ 23	5 ♓ 25	12 ♈ 55	23 ♈ 27	22 ♎ 20	26 ♐ 44	22 ♈ 06	11 ♓ 40	18 ♑ 47	7 ♉ 24	19 ♓ 48	7 ♑ 29	20 ♋ 17	23 ♓ 51
2 Th	10 39 54	11 35 36	25 25	3 22 ℞	7 14	13 02	24 11	22 16 ℞	26 47	22 08	11 42	18 48	7 45	20 09	7 45	20 14 ℞	23 55
3 F	10 43 50	12 35 48	9 ♉ 42	3 21	9 05	13 07	24 55	22 12	26 50	22 11	11 44	18 49	8 05	20 29	8 01	20 12	23 59
4 Sa	10 47 47	13 35 58	24 00	3 20	10 56	13 09 ℞	25 38	22 07	26 54	22 14	11 47	18 51	8 25	20 50	8 17	20 10	24 02
5 Su	10 51 44	14 36 06	8 ♊ 15	3 19 D	12 48	13 08	26 22	22 02	26 57	22 17	11 49	18 52	8 46	21 11	8 32	20 08	24 06
6 M	10 55 40	15 36 11	22 26	3 19	14 41	13 06	27 05	21 57	27 00	22 20	11 51	18 53	9 07	21 32	8 48	20 08	24 09
7 T	10 59 37	16 36 15	6 ♋ 29	3 20	16 35	13 00	27 49	21 52	27 03	22 23	11 54	18 55	9 28	21 52	9 03	20 07 D	24 13
8 W	11 3 33	17 36 17	20 23	3 21	18 30	12 53	28 32	21 47	27 06	22 26	11 56	18 56	9 49	22 13	9 18	20 07	24 16
9 Th	11 7 30	18 36 16	4 ♌ 08	3 22	20 26	12 42	29 16	21 42	27 08	22 29	11 58	18 57	10 10	22 34	9 33	20 08	24 20
10 F	11 11 26	19 36 13	17 41	3 23	22 23	12 29	29 59	21 36	27 11	22 32	12 00	18 58	10 31	22 55	9 48	20 09	24 24
11 Sa	11 15 23	20 36 08	1 ♍ 02	3 24 ℞	24 20	12 14	0 ♉ 42	21 31	27 14	22 35	12 03	19 00	10 52	23 16	10 03	20 10	24 27
12 Su	11 19 19	21 36 01	14 11	3 23	26 18	11 56	1 26	21 25	27 16	22 38	12 05	19 01	11 13	23 37	10 17	20 12	24 31
13 M	11 23 16	22 35 52	27 05	3 22	28 16	11 36	2 09	21 19	27 19	22 41	12 07	19 02	11 35	23 58	10 32	20 14	24 35
14 T	11 27 13	23 35 42	9 ♎ 46	3 20	0 ♈ 14	11 13	2 52	21 13	27 21	22 44	12 09	19 03	11 56	24 19	10 46	20 17	24 38
15 W	11 31 9	24 35 29	22 14	3 17	2 13	10 49	3 35	21 07	27 23	22 47	12 12	19 04	12 18	24 40	11 00	20 20	24 42
16 Th	11 35 6	25 35 14	4 ♏ 29	3 13	4 11	10 22	4 18	21 01	27 25	22 50	12 14	19 05	12 40	25 00	11 14	20 24	24 45
17 F	11 39 2	26 34 58	16 34	3 09	6 09	9 53	5 01	20 54	27 27	22 53	12 16	19 06	13 01	25 21	11 28	20 28	24 49
18 Sa	11 42 59	27 34 40	28 31	3 06	8 06	9 22	5 44	20 48	27 29	22 56	12 18	19 07	13 23	25 43	11 41	20 32	24 53
19 Su	11 46 55	28 34 20	10 ♐ 24	3 03	10 01	8 50	6 27	20 41	27 31	23 00	12 21	19 08	13 45	26 04	11 55	20 37	24 56
20 M	11 50 52	29 33 58	22 17	3 02 D	11 56	8 16	7 10	20 35	27 33	23 03	12 23	19 09	14 07	26 25	12 08	20 42	25 00
21 T	11 54 48	0 ♈ 33 35	4 ♑ 15	3 02	13 48	7 41	7 53	20 28	27 35	23 06	12 25	19 10	14 29	26 46	12 21	20 48	25 03
22 W	11 58 45	1 33 10	16 22	3 03	15 38	7 05	8 36	20 21	27 36	23 09	12 27	19 11	14 52	27 07	12 34	20 54	25 07
23 Th	12 2 42	2 32 43	28 43	3 04	17 25	6 28	9 19	20 14	27 38	23 13	12 29	19 12	15 14	27 28	12 47	21 00	25 11
24 F	12 6 38	3 32 15	11 ♒ 22	3 06	19 09	5 51	10 02	20 07	27 39	23 16	12 31	19 13	15 36	27 49	13 00	21 07	25 14
25 Sa	12 10 35	4 31 44	24 24	3 07 ℞	20 50	5 13	10 44	20 00	27 40	23 19	12 34	19 13	15 59	28 10	13 12	21 14	25 18
26 Su	12 14 31	5 31 12	7 ♓ 49	3 07	22 26	4 36	11 27	19 53	27 41	23 22	12 36	19 14	16 21	28 31	13 24	21 21	25 21
27 M	12 18 28	6 30 38	21 39	3 06	23 58	3 58	12 10	19 45	27 43	23 26	12 38	19 15	16 44	28 52	13 36	21 29	25 25
28 T	12 22 24	7 30 02	5 ♈ 51	3 03	25 25	3 21	12 52	19 38	27 43	23 29	12 40	19 16	17 07	29 13	13 48	21 38	25 28
29 W	12 26 21	8 29 23	20 21	2 59	26 47	2 45	13 35	19 31	27 44	23 32	12 42	19 16	17 30	29 35	13 59	21 46	25 32
30 Th	12 30 17	9 28 43	5 ♉ 02	2 53	28 03	2 09	14 17	19 23	27 45	23 36	12 44	19 17	17 52	29 56	14 11	21 55	25 36
31 F	12 34 14	10 28 01	19 47	2 48	29 13	1 35	15 00	19 16	27 46	23 39	12 46	19 18	18 15	0 ♈ 17	14 22	22 05	25 39

EPHEMERIS CALCULATED FOR 12 MIDNIGHT GREENWICH MEAN TIME. ALL OTHER DATA AND FACING ASPECTARIAN PAGE IN **EASTERN TIME (BOLD)** AND PACIFIC TIME (REGULAR).

APRIL 2017

☽ Last Aspect day	ET / hr:mn	PT	asp	☽ Ingress sign	day	ET / hr:mn	PT
2	**10:43 am**	7:43 am	☍ ♄	♋	2	**2:27 pm**	11:27 am
4	**4:45 pm**	1:45 pm	△ ♀	♌	4	**6:13 pm**	3:13 pm
6	**8:16 pm**	5:16 pm	△ ♄	♍	6		9:20 pm
6	**8:16 pm**	5:16 pm	△ ♄	♍	7	**12:20 am**	
9	**4:21 am**	1:21 am	□ ♄	♎	9	**8:34 am**	5:34 am
11	**2:19 pm**	11:19 am	⚹ ♄	♏	11	**6:42 pm**	3:42 pm
13		9:18 pm	△ ♀	♐	14	**6:27 am**	3:27 am
14	**12:18 am**		△ ♀	♐	14	**6:27 am**	3:27 am
16	**2:26 pm**	11:26 am	☌ ♄	♑	16	**7:05 pm**	4:05 pm
19	**5:57 am**	2:57 am	□ ☉	♒	19	**6:52 am**	3:52 am
21	**2:23 pm**	11:23 am	⚹ ☿	♓	21	**3:43 pm**	12:43 pm
23	**5:34 pm**	2:34 pm	☌ ♀	♈	23	**8:32 pm**	5:32 pm
25	**5:53 pm**	2:53 pm	△ ♄	♉	25	**9:56 pm**	6:56 pm
27	**9:18 pm**	6:18 pm	⚹ ♀	♊	27	**9:39 pm**	6:39 pm
29	**5:28 pm**	2:28 pm	☍ ♄	♋	29	**9:48 pm**	6:48 pm

☽ Phases & Eclipses phase	day	ET / hr:mn	PT
2nd Quarter	3	**2:39 pm**	11:39 am
Full Moon	10		11:08 pm
Full Moon	11	**2:08 am**	
4th Quarter	19	**5:57 am**	2:57 am
New Moon	26	**8:16 am**	5:16 am

Planet Ingress		day	ET / hr:mn	PT
♀	♓	2	**8:25 pm**	5:25 pm
☉	♉	19	**5:27 pm**	2:27 pm
☿	♈	20	**1:37 pm**	10:37 am
♂	♊	21	**6:32 am**	3:32 am
♀	♈	28	**9:13 am**	6:13 am
⚳	♊	29	**11:42 am**	8:42 am

Planetary Motion		day	ET / hr:mn	PT
♄	R	5		10:06 pm
♄	R	6	**1:06 am**	
☿	R	9	**7:14 pm**	4:14 pm
♀	D	15	**6:18 am**	3:18 am
♇	R	20	**8:49 am**	5:49 am

1 SATURDAY
☿ ⚺ ♀ **7:53 am** 4:53 am
☽ ⚹ ☉ **8:20 am** 5:20 am
☽ □ ♆ **9:46 am** 6:46 am
☽ ⚺ ♂ **3:29 pm** 12:29 pm
☽ △ ♃ **8:01 pm** 5:01 pm
☽ ⚻ ♇ **8:32 pm** 5:32 pm

2 SUNDAY
☽ ⚹ ♅ **4:00 am** 1:00 am
☉ ⚺ ♆ **6:02 am** 3:02 am
☽ ☍ ♄ **10:43 am** 7:43 am
☽ □ ♀ **2:39 pm** 11:39 am
☽ ⚹ ☿ **5:52 pm** 2:52 pm

3 MONDAY
☽ △ ♆ **12:25 pm** 9:25 am
☽ □ ☉ **2:39 pm** 11:39 am
☽ ⚹ ♂ **8:59 pm** 5:59 pm
☽ □ ♃ **10:31 pm** 7:31 pm
☽ ☍ ♇ **11:33 pm** 8:33 pm

4 TUESDAY
☽ □ ♅ **7:31 am** 4:31 am
☽ ⚻ ♄ **2:20 pm** 11:20 am
☽ △ ♀ **4:45 pm** 1:45 pm
♂ ⚻ ♃ **10:53 pm** 7:53 pm
☽ □ ☿ 9:31 pm

5 WEDNESDAY
☽ □ ☿ **12:31 am**
☽ ⚻ ♆ **5:20 pm** 2:20 pm
☽ △ ☉ **11:46 pm** 8:46 pm
♂ △ ♇ 9:01 pm

6 THURSDAY
♂ △ ♇ **12:01 am**
☽ ⚹ ♃ **3:15 am** 12:15 am
☽ ⚻ ♇ **4:51 am** 1:51 am
☽ □ ♂ **5:08 am** 2:08 am
☽ △ ♅ **1:23 pm** 10:23 am
☽ △ ♄ **8:16 pm** 5:16 pm
☽ ⚻ ♀ **9:16 pm** 6:16 pm

7 FRIDAY
☽ △ ☿ **8:40 am** 5:40 am
☉ ☍ ♃ **5:39 pm** 2:39 pm
☽ ☍ ♆ 9:32 pm

8 SATURDAY
☽ ☍ ♆ **12:32 am**
☽ ⚺ ♃ **10:09 am** 7:09 am
☽ ⚻ ☉ **11:42 am** 8:42 am
☽ △ ♇ **12:24 pm** 9:24 am
☽ △ ♂ **3:54 pm** 12:54 pm
♀ □ ♄ **4:28 pm** 1:28 pm
☉ □ ♇ **8:49 pm** 5:49 pm
☽ ⚻ ♅ **9:29 pm** 6:29 pm

9 SUNDAY
☽ ☍ ♀ **4:07 am** 1:07 am
☽ □ ♄ **4:21 am** 1:21 am
☽ ⚻ ☿ **5:50 pm** 2:50 pm

10 MONDAY
☽ ⚻ ♆ **9:46 am** 6:46 am
☽ ☌ ♃ **6:58 pm** 3:58 pm
☽ □ ♇ **9:54 pm** 6:54 pm
☽ ☍ ☉ 11:08 pm

11 TUESDAY
☽ ☍ ☉ **2:08 am**
☽ ⚻ ♂ **4:58 am** 1:58 am
☽ ☍ ♅ **7:31 am** 4:31 am
☽ ⚻ ♀ **1:10 pm** 10:10 am
☽ ⚹ ♄ **2:19 pm** 11:19 am

12 WEDNESDAY
☽ ☍ ☿ **3:40 am** 12:40 am
☽ △ ♆ **8:48 pm** 5:48 pm

13 THURSDAY
☽ ⚺ ♃ **5:29 am** 2:29 am
♂ ⚺ ♅ **5:37 am** 2:37 am
☽ ⚹ ♇ **9:09 am** 6:09 am
☽ ⚻ ☉ **6:46 pm** 3:46 pm
☽ ⚻ ♅ **7:17 pm** 4:17 pm
☽ ☍ ♂ **8:04 pm** 5:04 pm
☽ △ ♀ 9:18 pm
☉ ☌ ♅ 10:30 pm
☽ ⚺ ♄ 10:54 pm

14 FRIDAY
☽ △ ♀ **12:18 am**
☉ ☌ ♅ **1:30 am**
☽ ⚺ ♄ **1:54 am**
☽ ⚻ ☿ **1:54 pm** 10:54 am

15 SATURDAY
☽ □ ♆ **9:15 am** 6:15 am
☽ ⚹ ♃ **5:16 pm** 2:16 pm
☽ ⚺ ♇ **9:38 pm** 6:38 pm
☉ ⚺ ♂ **10:38 pm** 7:38 pm

16 SUNDAY
☽ △ ♅ **8:09 am** 5:09 am
☽ ⚻ ♂ **12:25 pm** 9:25 am
☽ △ ☉ **12:46 pm** 9:46 am
☽ □ ♀ **12:54 pm** 9:54 am
☉ ⚺ ♀ **2:26 pm** 11:26 am
☽ ☌ ♄ **2:26 pm** 11:26 am
♀ ⚹ ♂ **9:26 pm** 6:26 pm
☽ △ ☿ **11:55 pm** 8:55 pm

17 MONDAY
☉ △ ♄ **8:43 am** 5:43 am
☽ ⚹ ♆ **9:55 pm** 6:55 pm
♂ ⚻ ♄ **10:14 pm** 7:14 pm

18 TUESDAY
☽ □ ♃ **5:03 am** 2:03 am
☽ ☌ ♇ **9:58 am** 6:58 am
☽ □ ♅ **8:32 pm** 5:32 pm
☽ ⚹ ♀ 10:21 pm
☽ ⚺ ♄ 11:16 pm

19 WEDNESDAY
☽ ⚹ ♀ **1:21 am**
☽ ⚺ ♄ **2:16 am**
☽ △ ♂ **4:00 am** 1:00 am
☽ □ ☉ **5:57 am** 2:57 am
☽ □ ☿ **8:31 am** 5:31 am
☉ ☌ ☿ 10:54 pm

20 THURSDAY
☉ ☌ ☿ **1:54 am**
☽ ⚺ ♆ **8:45 am** 5:45 am
☽ △ ♃ **2:50 pm** 11:50 am
☽ ⚺ ♇ **8:04 pm** 5:04 pm
☿ ⚺ ♂ **10:00 pm** 7:00 pm

21 FRIDAY
☽ ⚹ ♅ **6:16 am** 3:16 am
♀ □ ♄ **7:09 am** 4:09 am
☽ ⚹ ♄ **11:19 am** 8:19 am
☽ ⚺ ♀ **11:23 am** 8:23 am
☽ ⚹ ☿ **2:23 pm** 11:23 am
☽ □ ♂ **4:13 pm** 1:13 pm

22 SATURDAY
☽ ☌ ♆ **3:57 pm** 12:57 pm
☽ ⚻ ♃ **9:01 pm** 6:01 pm
☽ ⚹ ♇ 11:19 pm

23 SUNDAY
☽ ⚹ ♇ **2:19 am**
☿ ⚺ ♀ **6:39 am** 3:39 am
☽ ⚺ ♅ **12:00 pm** 9:00 am
☽ □ ♄ **4:22 pm** 1:22 pm
☽ ⚺ ☿ **4:52 pm** 1:52 pm
☽ ☌ ♀ **5:34 pm** 2:34 pm
☽ ⚹ ♂ **11:43 pm** 8:43 pm

24 MONDAY
☽ ⚺ ☉ **3:50 am** 12:50 am
☿ △ ♄ **4:15 am** 1:15 am
☽ ⚺ ♆ **7:10 pm** 4:10 pm
☽ ☍ ♃ **11:24 pm** 8:24 pm

25 TUESDAY
☽ □ ♇ **4:46 am** 1:46 am
☽ ☌ ♅ **2:04 pm** 11:04 am
☽ ☌ ☿ **4:29 pm** 1:29 pm
☽ △ ♄ **5:53 pm** 2:53 pm
☽ ⚺ ♀ **8:17 pm** 5:17 pm

26 WEDNESDAY
☽ ⚺ ♂ **3:20 am** 12:20 am
☽ ☌ ☉ **8:16 am** 5:16 am
☽ ⚹ ♆ **7:38 pm** 4:38 pm
☽ ⚻ ♃ **11:16 pm** 8:16 pm

27 THURSDAY
☽ △ ♇ **4:50 am** 1:50 am
☽ ⚺ ♅ **2:05 pm** 11:05 am
☽ ⚺ ☿ **2:44 pm** 11:44 am
☽ ⚻ ♄ **5:33 pm** 2:33 pm
☽ ⚹ ♀ **9:18 pm** 6:18 pm

28 FRIDAY
☽ ☌ ♂ **5:16 am** 2:16 am
☿ ☌ ♅ **10:49 am** 7:49 am
☽ ⚺ ☉ **11:11 am** 8:11 am
☽ □ ♆ **7:22 pm** 4:22 pm
☽ △ ♃ **10:36 pm** 7:36 pm

29 SATURDAY
☽ ⚻ ♇ **4:35 am** 1:35 am
☽ ⚹ ☿ **1:29 pm** 10:29 am
☽ ⚹ ♅ **2:13 pm** 11:13 am
☽ ☍ ♄ **5:28 pm** 2:28 pm
☽ □ ♀ **10:59 pm** 7:59 pm

30 SUNDAY
☽ ⚺ ♂ **8:04 am** 5:04 am
☽ ⚹ ☉ **3:20 pm** 12:20 pm
☽ △ ♆ **8:26 pm** 5:26 pm
☽ □ ♃ **11:23 pm** 8:23 pm

Eastern time in bold type
Pacific time in medium type

APRIL 2017

DATE	SID.TIME	SUN	MOON	NODE	MERCURY	VENUS	MARS	JUPITER	SATURN	URANUS	NEPTUNE	PLUTO	CERES	PALLAS	JUNO	VESTA	CHIRON
1 Sa	12 38 10	11 ♈ 27 16	4 ♊ 28	2 ♍ 42	0 ♉ 17	1 ♈ 02	15 ♉ 42	19 ♎ 08	27 ♐ 46	23 ♈ 42	12 ♓ 48	19 ♑ 18	18 ♉ 38	0 ♈ 38	14 ♑ 33	22 ♋ 15	25 ♓ 43
2 Su	12 42 7	12 26 29	19 00	2 39 ℞	1 14	0 30 ℞	16 25	19 01 ℞	27 47	23 46	12 50	19 19	19 01	0 59	14 44	22 25	25 46
3 M	12 46 4	13 25 40	3 ♋ 17	2 37 D	2 05	0 01	17 07	18 53	27 47	23 49	12 52	19 19	19 24	1 20	14 54	22 35	25 50
4 T	12 50 0	14 24 49	17 17	2 36	2 50	29 ♓ 33	17 49	18 45	27 47	23 53	12 54	19 20	19 48	1 42	15 04	22 46	25 53
5 W	12 53 57	15 23 55	1 ♌ 00	2 37	3 27	29 07	18 32	18 38	27 48	23 56	12 56	19 20	20 11	2 03	15 15	22 57	25 57
6 Th	12 57 53	16 22 58	14 27	2 38	3 58	28 43	19 14	18 30	27 48 ℞	23 59	12 58	19 21	20 34	2 24	15 24	23 08	26 00
7 F	13 1 50	17 22 00	27 39	2 39 ℞	4 21	28 21	19 56	18 22	27 48	24 03	13 00	19 21	20 58	2 45	15 34	23 20	26 03
8 Sa	13 5 46	18 20 59	10 ♍ 37	2 39	4 38	28 02	20 38	18 14	27 48	24 06	13 02	19 22	21 21	3 06	15 43	23 32	26 07
9 Su	13 9 43	19 19 56	23 23	2 37	4 48 ℞	27 45	21 20	18 07	27 47	24 10	13 04	19 22	21 44	3 27	15 53	23 44	26 10
10 M	13 13 39	20 18 50	5 ♎ 58	2 33	4 51	27 30	22 02	17 59	27 47	24 13	13 06	19 22	22 08	3 49	16 01	23 57	26 14
11 T	13 17 36	21 17 43	18 24	2 26	4 47	27 18	22 44	17 51	27 47	24 17	13 08	19 23	22 31	4 10	16 10	24 10	26 17
12 W	13 21 33	22 16 34	0 ♏ 40	2 18	4 38	27 09	23 26	17 44	27 46	24 20	13 10	19 23	22 55	4 31	16 19	24 23	26 20
13 Th	13 25 29	23 15 22	12 48	2 08	4 22	27 02	24 08	17 36	27 45	24 23	13 12	19 23	23 19	4 52	16 27	24 37	26 24
14 F	13 29 26	24 14 09	24 48	1 58	4 01	26 57	24 50	17 28	27 45	24 27	13 14	19 23	23 43	5 13	16 35	24 50	26 27
15 Sa	13 33 22	25 12 54	6 ♐ 43	1 49	3 35	26 55 D	25 32	17 21	27 44	24 30	13 15	19 23	24 06	5 34	16 42	25 04	26 30
16 Su	13 37 19	26 11 38	18 35	1 41	3 04	26 55	26 13	17 13	27 43	24 34	13 17	19 24	24 30	5 55	16 50	25 19	26 33
17 M	13 41 15	27 10 19	0 ♑ 27	1 35	2 30	26 57	26 55	17 06	27 42	24 37	13 19	19 24	24 54	6 17	16 57	25 33	26 37
18 T	13 45 12	28 08 59	12 24	1 32	1 52	27 02	27 37	16 58	27 41	24 41	13 21	19 24	25 18	6 38	17 04	25 48	26 40
19 W	13 49 8	29 07 37	24 28	1 30 D	1 12	27 09	28 19	16 51	27 40	24 44	13 23	19 24	25 42	6 59	17 10	26 03	26 43
20 Th	13 53 5	0 ♉ 06 14	6 ♒ 46	1 30	0 31	27 19	29 00	16 43	27 38	24 47	13 24	19 24 ℞	26 06	7 20	17 17	26 19	26 46
21 F	13 57 2	1 04 48	19 22	1 31 ℞	29 ♈ 49	27 30	29 42	16 36	27 37	24 51	13 26	19 24	26 30	7 41	17 23	26 34	26 49
22 Sa	14 0 58	2 03 21	2 ♓ 21	1 31	29 07	27 44	0 ♊ 23	16 29	27 36	24 54	13 28	19 24	26 54	8 02	17 29	26 50	26 52
23 Su	14 4 55	3 01 53	15 47	1 31	28 25	28 00	1 05	16 22	27 34	24 58	13 29	19 24	27 18	8 23	17 34	27 06	26 55
24 M	14 8 51	4 00 23	29 41	1 28	27 45	28 17	1 46	16 15	27 32	25 01	13 31	19 24	27 42	8 44	17 39	27 23	26 58
25 T	14 12 48	4 58 51	14 ♈ 03	1 22	27 07	28 37	2 28	16 08	27 31	25 05	13 32	19 24	28 07	9 05	17 44	27 39	27 02
26 W	14 16 44	5 57 17	28 48	1 14	26 32	28 58	3 09	16 01	27 29	25 08	13 34	19 23	28 31	9 26	17 49	27 56	27 04
27 Th	14 20 41	6 55 41	13 ♉ 49	1 05	26 00	29 21	3 50	15 54	27 27	25 11	13 36	19 23	28 55	9 47	17 53	28 13	27 07
28 F	14 24 37	7 54 04	28 58	0 55	25 32	29 46	4 32	15 47	27 25	25 15	13 37	19 23	29 20	10 08	17 57	28 30	27 10
29 Sa	14 28 34	8 52 25	14 ♊ 02	0 46	25 08	0 ♈ 12	5 13	15 41	27 23	25 18	13 39	19 23	29 44	10 29	18 01	28 48	27 13
30 Su	14 32 30	9 50 44	28 54	0 38	24 48	0 40	5 54	15 34	27 20	25 21	13 40	19 23	0 ♊ 08	10 50	18 04	29 06	27 16

EPHEMERIS CALCULATED FOR 12 MIDNIGHT GREENWICH MEAN TIME. ALL OTHER DATA AND FACING ASPECTARIAN PAGE IN **EASTERN TIME (BOLD)** AND PACIFIC TIME (REGULAR).

MAY 2017

☽ Last Aspect day	ET / hr:mn	PT	asp	☽ Ingress sign day	ET / hr:mn	PT
1	**4:23 pm**	1:23 pm	□ ♅	♌ 1		9:12 pm
1	**4:23 pm**	1:23 pm	□ ♅	♌ 2	**12:12 am**	
3		9:35 pm	△ ♄	♍ 4	**5:47 am**	2:47 am
4	**12:35 am**		△ ♄	♍ 4	**5:47 am**	2:47 am
6	**8:42 am**	5:42 am	□ ♄	♎ 6	**2:20 pm**	11:20 am
8	**6:59 pm**	3:59 pm	⚹ ♄	♏ 8		10:01 pm
8	**6:59 pm**	3:59 pm	⚹ ♄	♏ 9	**1:01 am**	
10	**5:42 pm**	2:42 pm	☍ ☉	♐ 11	**12:59 pm**	9:59 am
13	**10:14 pm**	7:14 pm	△ ☿	♑ 13		10:37 pm
13	**10:14 pm**	7:14 pm	△ ☿	♑ 14	**1:37 am**	

☽ Last Aspect day	ET / hr:mn	PT	asp	☽ Ingress sign day	ET / hr:mn	PT
16	**6:22 am**	3:22 am	□ ♅	♒ 16	**1:50 pm**	10:50 am
18	**8:33 pm**	5:33 pm	□ ☉	♓ 18	**11:52 pm**	8:52 pm
20	**11:39 pm**	8:39 pm	□ ♄	♈ 21	**6:10 am**	3:10 am
22		11:59 pm	☌ ♅	♉ 23	**8:33 am**	5:33 am
23	**2:59 am**		☌ ♅	♉ 23	**8:33 am**	5:33 am
24	**3:08 pm**	12:08 pm	△ ♇	♊ 25	**8:15 am**	5:15 am
26		11:18 pm	⚹ ♅	♋ 27	**7:25 am**	4:25 am
27	**2:18 am**		⚹ ♅	♋ 27	**7:25 am**	4:25 am
29	**2:59 am**	(11:59 pm)	□ ♅	♌ 29	**8:12 am**	5:12 am
31	**7:14 am**	4:14 am	⚹ ♂	♍ 31	**12:16 pm**	9:16 am

☽ Phases & Eclipses phase	day	ET / hr:mn	PT
2nd Quarter	2	**10:47 pm**	7:47 pm
Full Moon	10	**5:42 pm**	2:42 pm
4th Quarter	18	**8:33 pm**	5:33 pm
New Moon	25	**3:44 pm**	12:44 pm

Planet Ingress	day	ET / hr:mn	PT
⚶ ♌	2	**7:57 pm**	4:57 pm
☿ ♉	15		9:07 pm
☿ ♉	16	**12:07 am**	
☉ ♊	20	**4:31 pm**	1:31 pm

Planetary Motion	day	ET / hr:mn	PT
☿ D	2	**12:33 pm**	9:33 am
⚵ R	9	**7:06 pm**	4:06 pm

1 MONDAY
☽ ☍ ♇ **6:00 am** 3:00 am
☽ □ ☿ **2:35 pm** 11:35 am
☽ □ ♅ **4:23 pm** 1:23 pm
☽ ⚻ ♄ **7:29 pm** 4:29 pm

2 TUESDAY
☽ △ ♀ **3:23 am** 12:23 am
☽ ⚹ ♂ **1:47 pm** 10:47 am
☽ □ ☉ **10:47 pm** 7:47 pm
☽ ⚻ ♆ 9:20 pm
☽ ⚹ ♃ 11:58 pm

3 WEDNESDAY
☽ ⚻ ♆ **12:20 am**
☽ ⚹ ♃ **2:58 am**
☽ ⚻ ♇ **10:24 am** 7:24 am
☽ △ ☿ **7:17 pm** 4:17 pm
☉ ⚹ ♆ **8:51 pm** 5:51 pm
☽ △ ♅ **9:41 pm** 6:41 pm
☽ △ ♄ 9:35 pm

4 THURSDAY
☽ △ ♄ **12:35 am**
☽ ⚻ ♀ **11:35 am** 8:35 am
☽ □ ♂ **11:15 pm** 8:15 pm

5 FRIDAY
☉ ⚻ ♃ **3:59 am** 12:59 am
☽ ☍ ♆ **7:27 am** 4:27 am
☽ ⚺ ♃ **9:43 am** 6:43 am
☽ △ ☉ **10:15 am** 7:15 am
☽ △ ♇ **5:57 pm** 2:57 pm

6 SATURDAY
☽ ⚻ ☿ **3:51 am** 12:51 am
☽ ⚻ ♅ **6:06 am** 3:06 am
☽ □ ♄ **8:42 am** 5:42 am
☽ ☍ ♀ **11:22 pm** 8:22 pm

7 SUNDAY
☽ △ ♂ **11:56 am** 8:56 am
☽ ⚻ ♆ **5:12 pm** 2:12 pm
☽ ☌ ♃ **7:01 pm** 4:01 pm
☽ ⚻ ☉ 9:57 pm

8 MONDAY
☽ ⚻ ☉ **12:57 am**
☽ □ ♇ **3:56 am** 12:56 am
☽ ☍ ☿ **3:42 pm** 12:42 pm
☽ ☍ ♅ **4:47 pm** 1:47 pm
☽ ⚹ ♄ **6:59 pm** 3:59 pm

9 TUESDAY
☽ ⚻ ♀ **1:42 pm** 10:42 am
☉ △ ♇ **2:24 pm** 11:24 am
☿ ☌ ♅ 10:20 pm
☽ ⚻ ♂ 11:44 pm

10 WEDNESDAY
☿ ☌ ♅ **1:20 am**
☽ ⚻ ♂ **2:44 am**
☽ △ ♆ **4:40 am** 1:40 am
☽ ⚺ ♃ **5:59 am** 2:59 am
☽ ⚹ ♇ **3:29 pm** 12:29 pm
☽ ☍ ☉ **5:42 pm** 2:42 pm

11 THURSDAY
☽ ⚻ ♅ **4:54 am** 1:54 am
☽ ⚻ ☿ **6:04 am** 3:04 am
☽ ⚺ ♄ **6:36 am** 3:36 am
♂ □ ♆ **1:52 pm** 10:52 am
☿ △ ♄ **4:14 pm** 1:14 pm

12 FRIDAY
☽ △ ♀ **5:41 am** 2:41 am
♂ △ ♃ **6:19 am** 3:19 am
☽ □ ♆ **5:08 pm** 2:08 pm
☽ ⚹ ♃ **5:57 pm** 2:57 pm
☽ ☍ ♂ **6:45 pm** 3:45 pm

13 SATURDAY
☽ ⚺ ♇ **3:55 am** 12:55 am
☽ ⚻ ☉ **11:35 am** 8:35 am
☽ △ ♅ **5:46 pm** 2:46 pm
☽ ☌ ♄ **6:56 pm** 3:56 pm
☽ △ ☿ **10:14 pm** 7:14 pm

14 SUNDAY
☽ □ ♀ **10:24 pm** 7:24 pm

15 MONDAY
☽ ⚹ ♆ **5:51 am** 2:51 am
☽ □ ♃ **6:11 am** 3:11 am
☽ ⚻ ♂ **11:00 am** 8:00 am
☽ ☌ ♇ **4:24 pm** 1:24 pm

16 TUESDAY
☽ △ ☉ **5:17 am** 2:17 am
☽ □ ♅ **6:22 am** 3:22 am
☽ ⚺ ♄ **6:59 am** 3:59 am
☽ □ ☿ **2:55 pm** 11:55 am
☉ ⚺ ♅ **7:35 pm** 4:35 pm
☉ ⚻ ♄ 10:29 pm

17 WEDNESDAY
☉ ⚻ ♄ **1:29 am**
♃ ⚻ ♆ **4:37 am** 1:37 am
☽ ⚹ ♀ **2:09 pm** 11:09 am
☽ △ ♃ **5:16 pm** 2:16 pm
☽ ⚺ ♆ **5:21 pm** 2:21 pm
☽ △ ♂ 10:38 pm

18 THURSDAY
☽ △ ♂ **1:38 am**
☽ ⚺ ♇ **3:22 am** 12:22 am
☽ ⚹ ♅ **5:01 pm** 2:01 pm
☽ ⚹ ♄ **5:06 pm** 2:06 pm
☽ □ ☉ **8:33 pm** 5:33 pm
♄ △ ♅ 11:14 pm

19 FRIDAY
♄ △ ♅ **2:14 am**
☽ ⚹ ☿ **5:38 am** 2:38 am
♂ ⚻ ♇ **9:06 am** 6:06 am
♀ ☍ ♃ **10:12 am** 7:12 am
♀ ⚺ ♆ **3:30 pm** 12:30 pm
☽ ⚻ ♃ 10:26 pm
☽ ☌ ♆ 10:50 pm
☽ ⚺ ♀ 11:31 pm

20 SATURDAY
☽ ⚻ ♃ **1:26 am**
☽ ☌ ♆ **1:50 am**
☽ ⚺ ♀ **2:31 am**
☽ ⚹ ♇ **11:04 am** 8:04 am
☽ □ ♂ **12:28 pm** 9:28 am
☽ □ ♄ **11:39 pm** 8:39 pm
☽ ⚺ ♅ 9:01 pm

21 SUNDAY
☽ ⚺ ♅ **12:01 am**
☽ ⚹ ☉ **7:12 am** 4:12 am
☽ ⚺ ☿ **4:07 pm** 1:07 pm

22 MONDAY
☽ ☍ ♃ **5:38 am** 2:38 am
☽ ⚺ ♆ **6:17 am** 3:17 am
☽ ☌ ♀ **10:09 am** 7:09 am
☽ □ ♇ **2:44 pm** 11:44 am
☽ ⚹ ♂ **6:36 pm** 3:36 pm
☽ △ ♄ 11:15 pm
☽ ☌ ♅ 11:59 pm

23 TUESDAY
☽ △ ♄ **2:15 am**
☽ ☌ ♅ **2:59 am**
☽ ⚺ ☉ **12:59 pm** 9:59 am
☽ ☌ ☿ **10:13 pm** 7:13 pm

24 WEDNESDAY
☽ ⚻ ♃ **6:24 am** 3:24 am
☽ ⚹ ♆ **7:13 am** 4:13 am
☽ ⚺ ♀ **1:48 pm** 10:48 am
☽ △ ♇ **3:08 pm** 12:08 pm
☽ ⚺ ♂ **9:06 pm** 6:06 pm
☽ ⚻ ♄ 10:59 pm

25 THURSDAY
☽ ⚻ ♄ **1:59 am**
☽ ⚺ ♅ **3:03 am** 12:03 am
♀ □ ♇ **12:22 pm** 9:22 am
☽ ☌ ☉ **3:44 pm** 12:44 pm
☽ ⚺ ☿ 10:58 pm

26 FRIDAY
☽ ⚺ ☿ **1:58 am**
☽ △ ♃ **5:26 am** 2:26 am
☽ □ ♆ **6:25 am** 3:25 am
☽ ⚻ ♇ **2:11 pm** 11:11 am
☽ ⚹ ♀ **3:49 pm** 12:49 pm
☽ ☌ ♂ **10:21 pm** 7:21 pm
☽ ☍ ♄ 9:53 pm
☽ ⚹ ♅ 11:18 pm

27 SATURDAY
☽ ☍ ♄ **12:53 am**
☽ ⚹ ♅ **2:18 am**
☿ ⚻ ♃ **3:17 pm** 12:17 pm
☽ ⚺ ☉ **6:15 pm** 3:15 pm

28 SUNDAY
☿ ⚹ ♆ **3:04 am** 12:04 am
☽ □ ♃ **4:57 am** 1:57 am
☽ △ ♆ **6:07 am** 3:07 am
☽ ⚹ ☿ **6:27 am** 3:27 am
☽ ☍ ♇ **2:06 pm** 11:06 am
☽ □ ♀ **7:02 pm** 4:02 pm
☽ ⚺ ♂ 10:01 pm
☽ ⚻ ♄ 10:07 pm
♂ ☍ ♄ 11:55 pm
☽ □ ♅ 11:59 pm

29 MONDAY
☽ ⚺ ♂ **1:01 am**
☽ ⚻ ♄ **1:07 am**
♂ ☍ ♄ **2:55 am**
☽ □ ♅ **2:59 am**
☽ ⚹ ☉ **11:17 pm** 8:17 pm

30 TUESDAY
☽ ⚹ ♃ **6:56 am** 3:56 am
☽ ⚻ ♆ **8:21 am** 5:21 am
☽ □ ☿ **2:47 pm** 11:47 am
☽ ⚻ ♇ **4:46 pm** 1:46 pm
♂ ⚹ ♅ **10:39 pm** 7:39 pm
☽ △ ♀ 10:53 pm

31 WEDNESDAY
☽ △ ♀ **1:53 am**
☽ △ ♄ **4:23 am** 1:23 am
☽ △ ♅ **6:50 am** 3:50 am
☽ ⚹ ♂ **7:14 am** 4:14 am
☿ △ ♇ **8:03 am** 5:03 am

Eastern time in bold type
Pacific time in medium type

MAY 2017

DATE	SID.TIME	SUN	MOON	NODE	MERCURY	VENUS	MARS	JUPITER	SATURN	URANUS	NEPTUNE	PLUTO	CERES	PALLAS	JUNO	VESTA	CHIRON
1 M	14 36 27	10 ♉ 49 01	13 ♋ 26	0 ♍ 33 ℞	24 ♈ 33	1 ♈ 09	6 ♊ 35	15 ♎ 28	27 ♐ 18	25 ♈ 25	13 ♓ 41	19 ♑ 22	0 ♊ 33	11 ♈ 11	18 ♑ 07	29 ♋ 24	27 ♓ 19
2 T	14 40 24	11 47 16	27 34	0 31	24 23 ℞	1 40	7 17	15 21 ℞	27 16 ℞	25 28	13 43	19 22 ℞	0 57	11 32	18 10	29 42	27 22
3 W	14 44 20	12 45 28	11 ♌ 18	0 30 D	24 17 D	2 13	7 58	15 15	27 13	25 31	13 44	19 22	1 22	11 53	18 12	0 ♌ 00	27 25
4 Th	14 48 17	13 43 39	24 40	0 30 ℞	24 16	2 46	8 39	15 09	27 11	25 35	13 46	19 21	1 46	12 14	18 15	0 19	27 27
5 F	14 52 13	14 41 48	7 ♍ 41	0 30	24 20	3 21	9 20	15 03	27 08	25 38	13 47	19 21	2 11	12 35	18 16	0 37	27 30
6 Sa	14 56 10	15 39 54	20 25	0 29	24 29	3 58	10 01	14 57	27 06	25 41	13 48	19 20	2 36	12 55	18 18	0 56	27 33
7 Su	15 0 6	16 37 59	2 ♎ 56	0 25	24 42	4 35	10 42	14 52	27 03	25 45	13 50	19 20	3 00	13 16	18 19	1 15	27 35
8 M	15 4 3	17 36 02	15 16	0 18	25 00	5 14	11 22	14 46	27 00	25 48	13 51	19 19	3 25	13 37	18 20	1 35	27 38
9 T	15 7 59	18 34 03	27 28	0 09	25 22	5 53	12 03	14 41	26 57	25 51	13 52	19 19	3 50	13 58	18 20 ℞	1 54	27 40
10 W	15 11 56	19 32 02	9 ♏ 33	29 ♌ 57	25 49	6 34	12 44	14 35	26 54	25 54	13 53	19 18	4 14	14 18	18 20	2 14	27 43
11 Th	15 15 53	20 30 00	21 33	29 44	26 19	7 16	13 25	14 30	26 51	25 57	13 54	19 18	4 39	14 39	18 20	2 34	27 45
12 F	15 19 49	21 27 56	3 ♐ 29	29 30	26 54	7 59	14 06	14 25	26 48	26 01	13 56	19 17	5 04	15 00	18 20	2 54	27 48
13 Sa	15 23 46	22 25 51	15 21	29 17	27 33	8 43	14 46	14 20	26 45	26 04	13 57	19 17	5 29	15 20	18 19	3 14	27 50
14 Su	15 27 42	23 23 45	27 13	29 05	28 15	9 27	15 27	14 16	26 41	26 07	13 58	19 16	5 54	15 41	18 18	3 34	27 53
15 M	15 31 39	24 21 37	9 ♑ 06	28 56	29 01	10 13	16 08	14 11	26 38	26 10	13 59	19 15	6 18	16 01	18 16	3 55	27 55
16 T	15 35 35	25 19 27	21 03	28 50	29 51	10 59	16 48	14 07	26 35	26 13	14 00	19 15	6 43	16 22	18 14	4 15	27 57
17 W	15 39 32	26 17 17	3 ♒ 07	28 46	0 ♉ 44	11 46	17 29	14 03	26 31	26 16	14 01	19 14	7 08	16 42	18 12	4 36	27 59
18 Th	15 43 28	27 15 05	15 24	28 45	1 40	12 34	18 09	13 59	26 28	26 19	14 02	19 13	7 33	17 03	18 09	4 57	28 02
19 F	15 47 25	28 12 52	27 57	28 45	2 40	13 23	18 50	13 55	26 24	26 22	14 03	19 12	7 58	17 23	18 07	5 18	28 04
20 Sa	15 51 22	29 10 38	10 ♓ 51	28 44	3 43	14 13	19 30	13 51	26 21	26 25	14 04	19 12	8 23	17 44	18 03	5 40	28 06
21 Su	15 55 18	0 ♊ 08 23	24 12	28 43	4 48	15 03	20 11	13 47	26 17	26 28	14 04	19 11	8 48	18 04	18 00	6 01	28 08
22 M	15 59 15	1 06 07	8 ♈ 01	28 40	5 56	15 54	20 51	13 44	26 13	26 31	14 05	19 10	9 13	18 24	17 56	6 23	28 10
23 T	16 3 11	2 03 49	22 20	28 34	7 08	16 45	21 31	13 41	26 09	26 34	14 06	19 09	9 38	18 45	17 51	6 45	28 12
24 W	16 7 8	3 01 31	7 ♉ 06	28 26	8 22	17 38	22 12	13 38	26 05	26 37	14 07	19 08	10 03	19 05	17 47	7 07	28 14
25 Th	16 11 4	3 59 12	22 12	28 15	9 39	18 30	22 52	13 35	26 02	26 40	14 08	19 07	10 28	19 25	17 42	7 29	28 16
26 F	16 15 1	4 56 51	7 ♊ 30	28 04	10 58	19 24	23 32	13 32	25 58	26 43	14 08	19 06	10 53	19 45	17 36	7 51	28 18
27 Sa	16 18 57	5 54 29	22 47	27 54	12 20	20 17	24 12	13 30	25 54	26 46	14 09	19 05	11 18	20 05	17 30	8 13	28 20
28 Su	16 22 54	6 52 06	7 ♋ 53	27 46	13 44	21 12	24 53	13 27	25 50	26 49	14 10	19 04	11 43	20 25	17 24	8 36	28 21
29 M	16 26 51	7 49 42	22 39	27 40	15 12	22 07	25 33	13 25	25 46	26 52	14 10	19 03	12 09	20 45	17 18	8 58	28 23
30 T	16 30 47	8 47 16	6 ♌ 59	27 36	16 41	23 02	26 13	13 23	25 41	26 54	14 11	19 02	12 34	21 05	17 11	9 21	28 25
31 W	16 34 44	9 44 49	20 52	27 35 D	18 13	23 58	26 53	13 21	25 37	26 57	14 11	19 01	12 59	21 25	17 04	9 44	28 26

EPHEMERIS CALCULATED FOR 12 MIDNIGHT GREENWICH MEAN TIME. ALL OTHER DATA AND FACING ASPECTARIAN PAGE IN **EASTERN TIME (BOLD)** AND PACIFIC TIME (REGULAR).

JUNE 2017

☽ Last Aspect day	ET / hr:mn / PT		asp	☽ Ingress sign	day	ET / hr:mn / PT	
2	**5:48 pm**	2:48 pm	□♂	♎	2	**8:04 pm**	5:04 pm
5	**4:57 am**	1:57 am	☍♀	♏	5	**6:46 am**	3:46 am
6	**8:35 pm**	5:35 pm	⚹♇	♐	7	**6:59 pm**	3:59 pm
9		11:20 pm	△♅	♑	10	**7:36 am**	4:36 am
10	**2:20 am**		△♅	♑	10	**7:36 am**	4:36 am
12	**2:45 pm**	11:45 am	□♅	♒	12	**7:45 pm**	4:45 pm
14		10:40 pm	⚹♅	♓	15	**6:17 am**	3:17 am
15	**1:40 am**		⚹♅	♓	15	**6:17 am**	3:17 am
17	**7:33 am**	4:33 am	□☉	♈	17	**1:55 pm**	10:55 am
19	**3:42 pm**	12:42 pm	⚹☉	♉	19	**5:53 pm**	2:53 pm
20		9:26 pm	△♇	♊	21	**6:44 pm**	3:44 pm
21	**12:26 am**		△♇	♊	21	**6:44 pm**	3:44 pm
23	**2:45 pm**	11:45 am	⚹♅	♋	23	**6:07 pm**	3:07 pm
25	**2:44 pm**	11:44 am	□♅	♌	25	**6:06 pm**	3:06 pm
27	**5:12 pm**	2:12 pm	△♅	♍	27	**8:41 pm**	5:41 pm
29	**4:35 pm**	1:35 pm	△♀	♎	30	**3:02 am**	12:02 am

☽ Phases & Eclipses phase	day	ET / hr:mn / PT	
2nd Quarter	1	**8:42 am**	5:42 am
Full Moon	9	**9:10 am**	6:10 am
4th Quarter	17	**7:33 am**	4:33 am
New Moon	23	**10:31 pm**	7:31 pm
2nd Quarter	30	**8:51 pm**	5:51 pm

Planet Ingress	day	ET / hr:mn / PT	
♂ ♋	4	**12:16 pm**	9:16 am
♀ ♉	6	**3:27 am**	12:27 am
☿ ♊	6	**6:15 pm**	3:15 pm
☉ ♋	20		9:24 pm
☉ ♋	21	**12:24 am**	
☿ ♋	21	**5:57 am**	2:57 am
♀ ♉	26	**10:34 pm**	7:34 pm

Planetary Motion	day	ET / hr:mn / PT	
♃ D	9	**10:03 am**	7:03 am
♆ ℞	16	**7:09 am**	4:09 am

1 THURSDAY
☽ □ ☉ **8:42 am** 5:42 am
♀ △ ♄ **11:23 am** 8:23 am
☽ ⊻ ♃ **12:35 pm** 9:35 am
☽ ☍ ♆ **2:15 pm** 11:15 am
☽ △ ♇ **11:10 pm** 8:10 pm

2 FRIDAY
☽ △ ☿ **4:54 am** 1:54 am
☽ □ ♄ **11:21 am** 8:21 am
☽ ⊼ ♀ **1:27 pm** 10:27 am
☽ ⊼ ♅ **2:28 pm** 11:28 am
☽ □ ♂ **5:48 pm** 2:48 pm

3 SATURDAY
♀ ☌ ♅ **3:32 am** 12:32 am
☉ △ ♃ **12:12 pm** 9:12 am
☽ ☌ ♃ **9:44 pm** 6:44 pm
☽ △ ☉ **10:33 pm** 7:33 pm
☽ ⊼ ♆ **11:37 pm** 8:37 pm

4 SUNDAY
☿ ⊼ ♄ **3:24 am** 12:24 am
☽ □ ♇ **8:52 am** 5:52 am
☉ □ ♆ **12:13 pm** 9:13 am
☽ ⚹ ♄ **9:22 pm** 6:22 pm
☽ ⊼ ☿ 9:32 pm
☽ ☍ ♅ 10:10 pm

5 MONDAY
☽ ⊼ ☿ **12:32 am**
☽ ☍ ♅ **1:10 am**
☽ ☍ ♀ **4:57 am** 1:57 am
☿ ⊻ ♅ **4:58 am** 1:58 am
☽ △ ♂ **7:51 am** 4:51 am

6 TUESDAY
☽ ⊻ ♃ **9:13 am** 6:13 am
☽ △ ♆ **11:14 am** 8:14 am
☽ ⊼ ☉ **3:18 pm** 12:18 pm
☽ ⚹ ♇ **8:35 pm** 5:35 pm

7 WEDNESDAY
☽ ⊻ ♄ **9:04 am** 6:04 am
☿ ⊻ ♀ **10:54 am** 7:54 am
☽ ⊼ ♅ **1:31 pm** 10:31 am
☽ ⊼ ♀ **10:33 pm** 7:33 pm
☽ ☍ ☿ **11:36 pm** 8:36 pm
☽ ⊼ ♂ **11:39 pm** 8:39 pm
☿ ⊻ ♂ 9:05 pm

8 THURSDAY
☿ ⊻ ♂ **12:05 am**
☽ ⚹ ♃ **9:42 pm** 6:42 pm
☽ □ ♆ **11:47 pm** 8:47 pm

9 FRIDAY
☉ ⊼ ♇ **7:57 am** 4:57 am
☽ ⊻ ♇ **9:04 am** 6:04 am
☽ ☍ ☉ **9:10 am** 6:10 am
♀ ⚹ ♂ **11:41 am** 8:41 am
☽ ☌ ♄ **9:19 pm** 6:19 pm
☽ △ ♅ 11:20 pm

10 SATURDAY
☽ △ ♅ **2:20 am**
☽ ☍ ♂ **3:50 pm** 12:50 pm
☽ △ ♀ **4:42 pm** 1:42 pm
☽ ⊼ ☿ 9:03 pm

11 SUNDAY
☽ ⊼ ☿ **12:03 am**
☽ □ ♃ **10:14 am** 7:14 am
☽ ⚹ ♆ **12:18 pm** 9:18 am
☽ ☌ ♇ **9:23 pm** 6:23 pm
☽ ⊼ ☉ 11:49 pm

12 MONDAY
☽ ⊼ ☉ **2:49 am**
☽ ⊻ ♄ **9:14 am** 6:14 am
☽ □ ♅ **2:45 pm** 11:45 am

13 TUESDAY
☽ ⊼ ♂ **7:17 am** 4:17 am
☽ □ ♀ **10:08 am** 7:08 am
☿ △ ♃ **11:45 am** 8:45 am
☽ △ ♃ **9:52 pm** 6:52 pm
☿ □ ♆ **11:29 pm** 8:29 pm
☽ ⊻ ♆ **11:52 pm** 8:52 pm
☽ △ ☿ **11:56 pm** 8:56 pm

14 WEDNESDAY
☽ ⊻ ♇ **8:35 am** 5:35 am
☽ △ ☉ **6:52 pm** 3:52 pm
☽ ⚹ ♄ **7:49 pm** 4:49 pm
☽ ⚹ ♅ 10:40 pm

15 THURSDAY
☽ ⚹ ♅ **1:40 am**
☉ ☍ ♄ **6:18 am** 3:18 am
☽ △ ♂ **8:32 pm** 5:32 pm
☽ ⚹ ♀ 10:08 pm
☿ ⊼ ♇ 10:35 pm

16 FRIDAY
☽ ⚹ ♀ **1:08 am**
☿ ⊼ ♇ **1:35 am**
☽ ⊼ ♃ **7:21 am** 4:21 am
☽ ☌ ♆ **9:10 am** 6:10 am
☽ ⚹ ♇ **5:20 pm** 2:20 pm
☽ □ ☿ **8:29 pm** 5:29 pm

17 SATURDAY
☽ □ ♄ **3:44 am** 12:44 am
☽ □ ☉ **7:33 am** 4:33 am
☽ ⊻ ♅ **9:43 am** 6:43 am

18 SUNDAY
☽ □ ♂ **6:03 am** 3:03 am
☽ ⊻ ♀ **12:01 pm** 9:01 am
☽ ☍ ♃ **1:28 pm** 10:28 am
☉ ⚹ ♅ **2:47 pm** 11:47 am
☽ ⊻ ♆ **3:04 pm** 12:04 pm
☿ ☍ ♄ **3:07 pm** 12:07 pm
☽ □ ♇ **10:37 pm** 7:37 pm

19 MONDAY
♀ ⊼ ♃ **7:49 am** 4:49 am
☽ △ ♄ **8:07 am** 5:07 am
☽ ⚹ ☿ **11:20 am** 8:20 am
☽ ☌ ♅ **2:05 pm** 11:05 am
☽ ⚹ ☉ **3:42 pm** 12:42 pm

20 TUESDAY
♀ ⚹ ♆ **4:25 am** 1:25 am
☿ ⚹ ♅ **5:30 am** 2:30 am
☽ ⚹ ♂ **11:21 am** 8:21 am
☽ ⊼ ♃ **4:01 pm** 1:01 pm
☽ ⚹ ♆ **5:25 pm** 2:25 pm
☽ ☌ ♀ **6:24 pm** 3:24 pm
☽ △ ♇ 9:26 pm

21 WEDNESDAY
☽ △ ♇ **12:26 am**
☽ ⊼ ♄ **9:14 am** 6:14 am
☉ ☌ ☿ **10:14 am** 7:14 am
☽ ⊻ ♅ **3:15 pm** 12:15 pm
☽ ⊻ ☉ **7:59 pm** 4:59 pm
☽ ⊻ ☿ **8:55 pm** 5:55 pm

22 THURSDAY
☽ ⊻ ♂ **1:38 pm** 10:38 am
☽ △ ♃ **4:05 pm** 1:05 pm
☽ □ ♆ **5:18 pm** 2:18 pm
☽ ⊻ ♀ **9:51 pm** 6:51 pm
☽ ⊼ ♇ 9:03 pm

23 FRIDAY
☽ ⊼ ♇ **12:03 am**
☽ ☍ ♄ **8:31 am** 5:31 am
☽ ⚹ ♅ **2:45 pm** 11:45 am
☽ ☌ ☉ **10:31 pm** 7:31 pm

24 SATURDAY
☽ ☌ ☿ **4:13 am** 1:13 am
♀ △ ♇ **4:59 am** 1:59 am
☽ ☌ ♂ **3:09 pm** 12:09 pm
☽ □ ♃ **3:36 pm** 12:36 pm
☽ △ ♆ **4:42 pm** 1:42 pm
☽ ☍ ♇ **11:29 pm** 8:29 pm
☽ ⚹ ♀ 9:56 pm
♂ □ ♃ 11:07 pm

25 SUNDAY
☽ ⚹ ♀ **12:56 am**
♂ □ ♃ **2:07 am**
☽ ⊼ ♄ **7:59 am** 4:59 am
☽ □ ♅ **2:44 pm** 11:44 am
☽ ⊻ ☉ 11:03 pm
♂ △ ♆ 11:18 pm

26 MONDAY
☽ ⊻ ☉ **2:03 am**
♂ △ ♆ **2:18 am**
☽ ⊻ ☿ **1:04 pm** 10:04 am
☽ ⚹ ♃ **4:43 pm** 1:43 pm
☽ ⊼ ♆ **5:41 pm** 2:41 pm
☽ ⊻ ♂ **6:26 pm** 3:26 pm
☽ ⊼ ♇ 9:48 pm

27 TUESDAY
☽ ⊼ ♇ **12:48 am**
☽ □ ♀ **6:29 am** 3:29 am
☽ △ ♄ **9:38 am** 6:38 am
☿ □ ♃ **2:21 pm** 11:21 am
☽ △ ♅ **5:12 pm** 2:12 pm
☿ △ ♆ **8:22 pm** 5:22 pm

28 WEDNESDAY
☽ ⚹ ☉ **9:03 am** 6:03 am
☿ ☌ ♂ **3:50 pm** 12:50 pm
♀ ⊼ ♄ **9:07 pm** 6:07 pm
☽ ⊻ ♃ **9:09 pm** 6:09 pm
☽ ☍ ♆ **9:57 pm** 6:57 pm
☽ ⚹ ♂ 10:30 pm
☽ ⚹ ☿ 11:44 pm

29 THURSDAY
☽ ⚹ ♂ **1:30 am**
☽ ⚹ ☿ **2:44 am**
☽ △ ♇ **5:32 am** 2:32 am
☽ □ ♄ **2:52 pm** 11:52 am
☽ △ ♀ **4:35 pm** 1:35 pm
☿ ☍ ♇ **8:36 pm** 5:36 pm
☽ ⊼ ♅ **11:24 pm** 8:24 pm

30 FRIDAY
☽ □ ☉ **8:51 pm** 5:51 pm

Eastern time in bold type
Pacific time in medium type

JUNE 2017

DATE	SID.TIME	SUN	MOON	NODE	MERCURY	VENUS	MARS	JUPITER	SATURN	URANUS	NEPTUNE	PLUTO	CERES	PALLAS	JUNO	VESTA	CHIRON
1 Th	16 38 40	10 ♊ 42 21	4 ♍ 17	27 ♌ 35	19 ♉ 48	24 ♈ 54	27 ♊ 33	13 ♎ 20	25 ♐ 33	27 ♈ 00	14 ♓ 12	19 ♑ 00	13 ♊ 24	21 ♈ 45	16 ♑ 57	10 ♌ 07	28 ♓ 28
2 F	16 42 37	11 39 51	17 18	27 35 ℞	21 25	25 51	28 13	13 18 ℞	25 29 ℞	27 03	14 12	18 59 ℞	13 49	22 05	16 49 ℞	10 30	28 29
3 Sa	16 46 33	12 37 20	29 58	27 34	23 05	26 48	28 53	13 17	25 25	27 05	14 13	18 58	14 14	22 24	16 41	10 53	28 31
4 Su	16 50 30	13 34 47	12 ♎ 22	27 31	24 47	27 46	29 33	13 16	25 20	27 08	14 13	18 57	14 40	22 44	16 33	11 17	28 32
5 M	16 54 26	14 32 13	24 35	27 25	26 32	28 43	0 ♋ 13	13 15	25 16	27 10	14 14	18 56	15 05	23 04	16 24	11 40	28 34
6 T	16 58 23	15 29 38	6 ♏ 38	27 17	28 19	29 42	0 53	13 14	25 12	27 13	14 14	18 55	15 30	23 23	16 15	12 04	28 35
7 W	17 2 20	16 27 03	18 36	27 06	0 ♊ 08	0 ♉ 41	1 33	13 14	25 07	27 15	14 14	18 53	15 55	23 43	16 06	12 27	28 36
8 Th	17 6 16	17 24 26	0 ♐ 30	26 54	2 00	1 40	2 12	13 13	25 03	27 18	14 15	18 52	16 20	24 02	15 56	12 51	28 38
9 F	17 10 13	18 21 48	12 23	26 41	3 54	2 39	2 52	13 13 D	24 59	27 20	14 15	18 51	16 46	24 22	15 46	13 15	28 39
10 Sa	17 14 9	19 19 09	24 15	26 29	5 51	3 39	3 32	13 13	24 54	27 23	14 15	18 50	17 11	24 41	15 36	13 39	28 40
11 Su	17 18 6	20 16 30	6 ♑ 09	26 19	7 49	4 39	4 12	13 13	24 50	27 25	14 15	18 48	17 36	25 00	15 25	14 03	28 41
12 M	17 22 2	21 13 50	18 06	26 11	9 50	5 39	4 51	13 13	24 46	27 28	14 16	18 47	18 01	25 19	15 15	14 28	28 42
13 T	17 25 59	22 11 09	0 ♒ 08	26 05	11 53	6 40	5 31	13 14	24 41	27 30	14 16	18 46	18 27	25 38	15 04	14 52	28 43
14 W	17 29 56	23 08 28	12 17	26 02	13 58	7 41	6 11	13 15	24 37	27 32	14 16	18 45	18 52	25 57	14 53	15 16	28 44
15 Th	17 33 52	24 05 47	24 38	26 01 D	16 04	8 43	6 50	13 16	24 32	27 34	14 16	18 43	19 17	26 16	14 41	15 41	28 45
16 F	17 37 49	25 03 05	7 ♓ 14	26 01	18 12	9 44	7 30	13 17	24 28	27 37	14 16 ℞	18 42	19 42	26 35	14 29	16 06	28 46
17 Sa	17 41 45	26 00 22	20 08	26 02 ℞	20 21	10 46	8 09	13 18	24 23	27 39	14 16	18 41	20 08	26 54	14 17	16 30	28 46
18 Su	17 45 42	26 57 39	3 ♈ 24	26 02	22 31	11 48	8 49	13 19	24 19	27 41	14 16	18 39	20 33	27 13	14 05	16 55	28 47
19 M	17 49 38	27 54 56	17 07	26 00	24 42	12 51	9 28	13 21	24 15	27 43	14 16	18 38	20 58	27 32	13 53	17 20	28 48
20 T	17 53 35	28 52 13	1 ♉ 16	25 57	26 54	13 54	10 08	13 23	24 10	27 45	14 16	18 37	21 23	27 50	13 40	17 45	28 49
21 W	17 57 31	29 49 30	15 51	25 51	29 05	14 57	10 47	13 25	24 06	27 47	14 16	18 35	21 49	28 09	13 28	18 10	28 49
22 Th	18 1 28	0 ♋ 46 46	0 ♊ 48	25 44	1 ♋ 17	16 00	11 27	13 27	24 01	27 49	14 15	18 34	22 14	28 27	13 15	18 36	28 50
23 F	18 5 25	1 44 02	15 58	25 36	3 28	17 03	12 06	13 29	23 57	27 51	14 15	18 33	22 39	28 46	13 01	19 01	28 50
24 Sa	18 9 21	2 41 18	1 ♋ 12	25 28	5 39	18 07	12 45	13 31	23 53	27 53	14 15	18 31	23 04	29 04	12 48	19 26	28 50
25 Su	18 13 18	3 38 34	16 19	25 22	7 49	19 11	13 25	13 34	23 48	27 55	14 15	18 30	23 30	29 22	12 35	19 52	28 51
26 M	18 17 14	4 35 49	1 ♌ 09	25 18	9 58	20 15	14 04	13 37	23 44	27 56	14 14	18 28	23 55	29 40	12 21	20 18	28 51
27 T	18 21 11	5 33 04	15 37	25 15 D	12 06	21 19	14 43	13 40	23 40	27 58	14 14	18 27	24 20	29 58	12 08	20 43	28 51
28 W	18 25 7	6 30 18	29 36	25 15	14 12	22 23	15 23	13 43	23 35	28 00	14 14	18 25	24 45	0 ♉ 16	11 54	21 09	28 52
29 Th	18 29 4	7 27 32	13 ♍ 08	25 16	16 16	23 28	16 02	13 46	23 31	28 02	14 13	18 24	25 11	0 34	11 40	21 35	28 52
30 F	18 33 0	8 24 45	26 14	25 17	18 20	24 33	16 41	13 50	23 27	28 03	14 13	18 23	25 36	0 51	11 26	22 01	28 52

EPHEMERIS CALCULATED FOR 12 MIDNIGHT GREENWICH MEAN TIME. ALL OTHER DATA AND FACING ASPECTARIAN PAGE IN **EASTERN TIME (BOLD)** AND PACIFIC TIME (REGULAR).

JULY 2017

☽ Last Aspect day	ET / hr:mn / PT		asp	☽ Ingress sign	day	ET / hr:mn / PT	
2	**9:16 am**	6:16 am	☍ ♅	♏	2	**12:59 pm**	9:59 am
4	**9:34 pm**	6:34 pm	△ ☿	♐	4		10:08 pm
4	**9:34 pm**	6:34 pm	△ ☿	♐	5	**1:08 am**	
7	**10:12 am**	7:12 am	△ ♅	♑	7	**1:45 pm**	10:45 am
9	**10:12 pm**	7:12 pm	□ ♅	♒	9		10:35 pm
9	**10:12 pm**	7:12 pm	□ ♅	♒	10	**1:35 am**	
12	**8:40 am**	5:40 am	⚹ ♅	♓	12	**11:51 am**	8:51 am
14	**1:00 pm**	10:00 am	△ ♂	♈	14	**7:52 pm**	4:52 pm
16	**10:19 pm**	7:19 pm	☌ ♅	♉	16		10:04 pm
16	**10:19 pm**	7:19 pm	☌ ♅	♉	17	**1:04 am**	
18		11:11 pm	⚹ ♂	♊	19	**3:31 am**	12:31 am
19	**2:11 am**		⚹ ♂	♊	19	**3:31 am**	12:31 am
20		10:41 pm	⚹ ♅	♋	21	**4:09 am**	1:09 am
21	**1:41 am**		⚹ ♅	♋	21	**4:09 am**	1:09 am
22		11:05 pm	□ ♅	♌	23	**4:34 am**	1:34 am
23	**2:05 am**		□ ♅	♌	23	**4:34 am**	1:34 am
25	**5:22 am**	2:22 am	☌ ☿	♍	25	**6:32 am**	3:32 am
27	**2:31 am**	(11:31 pm)	□ ♀	♎	27	**11:37 am**	8:37 am
29	**5:30 pm**	2:30 pm	☍ ♅	♏	29	**8:23 pm**	5:23 pm
31	**7:10 am**	4:10 am	⚹ ♇	♐	8/1	**8:01 am**	5:01 am

☽ Phases & Eclipses phase	day	ET / hr:mn / PT	
Full Moon	8		9:07 pm
Full Moon	9	**12:07 am**	
4th Quarter	16	**3:26 pm**	12:26 pm
New Moon	23	**5:46 am**	2:46 am
2nd Quarter	30	**11:23 am**	8:23 am

Planet Ingress		day	ET / hr:mn / PT	
♀	♊	4	**8:11 pm**	5:11 pm
☿	♌	5	**8:20 pm**	5:20 pm
⚵	♋	10	**7:47 am**	4:47 am
⚶	♍	17	**7:15 pm**	4:15 pm
♂	♌	20	**8:19 am**	5:19 am
☉	♌	22	**11:15 am**	8:15 am
☿	♍	25	**7:41 pm**	4:41 pm
♀	♋	31	**10:54 am**	7:54 am

Planetary Motion	day	ET / hr:mn / PT	
⚷ ℞	1	**3:09 am**	12:09 am

1 SATURDAY
☽ ☌ ♃ **5:32 am** 2:32 am
☽ ⚻ ♆ **6:05 am** 3:05 am
☽ □ ♂ **1:03 pm** 10:03 am
☽ □ ♇ **2:06 pm** 11:06 am
☽ □ ☿ **10:16 pm** 7:16 pm
☽ ⚹ ♄ **11:47 pm** 8:47 pm

2 SUNDAY
☿ ⚻ ♄ **7:29 am** 4:29 am
☽ ⚻ ♀ **7:32 am** 4:32 am
♂ ☍ ♇ **8:02 am** 5:02 am
☽ ☍ ♅ **9:16 am** 6:16 am

3 MONDAY
♀ ⚺ ♅ **3:23 am** 12:23 am
☽ △ ☉ **12:46 pm** 9:46 am
☽ ⚺ ♃ **5:03 pm** 2:03 pm
☽ △ ♆ **5:16 pm** 2:16 pm
☽ ⚹ ♇ 10:29 pm

4 TUESDAY
☽ ⚹ ♇ **1:29 am**
☽ △ ♂ **3:58 am** 12:58 am
☽ ⚺ ♄ **11:16 am** 8:16 am
☿ □ ♅ **8:51 pm** 5:51 pm
☽ ⚻ ♅ **9:27 pm** 6:27 pm
☽ △ ☿ **9:34 pm** 6:34 pm
♃ ⚻ ♆ 9:19 pm
☽ ☍ ♀ 10:38 pm

5 WEDNESDAY
♃ ⚻ ♆ **12:19 am**
☽ ☍ ♀ **1:38 am**
☉ △ ♆ **8:46 pm** 5:46 pm
☉ □ ♃ **10:44 pm** 7:44 pm

6 THURSDAY
☽ □ ♆ **5:46 am** 2:46 am
☽ ⚹ ♃ **5:59 am** 2:59 am
☽ ⚻ ☉ **6:34 am** 3:34 am
☽ ⚺ ♇ **1:58 pm** 10:58 am
☽ ⚻ ♂ **8:06 pm** 5:06 pm
☽ ☌ ♄ **11:34 pm** 8:34 pm

7 FRIDAY
☿ ⚹ ♀ **9:19 am** 6:19 am
☽ △ ♅ **10:12 am** 7:12 am
☽ ⚻ ♀ **8:24 pm** 5:24 pm
☽ ⚻ ☿ **9:08 pm** 6:08 pm

8 SATURDAY
☽ ⚹ ♆ **6:05 pm** 3:05 pm
☽ □ ♃ **6:45 pm** 3:45 pm
☽ ☍ ☉ 9:07 pm
☽ ☌ ♇ 11:06 pm

9 SUNDAY
☽ ☍ ☉ **12:07 am**
☽ ☌ ♇ **2:06 am**
♂ ⚻ ♄ **6:09 am** 3:09 am
☽ ⚺ ♄ **11:21 am** 8:21 am
☽ ☍ ♂ **11:40 am** 8:40 am
☽ □ ♅ **10:12 pm** 7:12 pm
☉ ☍ ♇ 9:35 pm

10 MONDAY
☉ ☍ ♇ **12:35 am**
☽ △ ♀ **2:03 pm** 11:03 am
☽ ☍ ☿ **6:38 pm** 3:38 pm

11 TUESDAY
☽ ⚺ ♆ **5:13 am** 2:13 am
☽ △ ♃ **6:20 am** 3:20 am
☽ ⚺ ♇ **12:57 pm** 9:57 am
☽ ⚻ ☉ **4:03 pm** 1:03 pm
☽ ⚹ ♄ **9:46 pm** 6:46 pm
☽ ⚻ ♂ 10:36 pm

12 WEDNESDAY
☽ ⚻ ♂ **1:36 am**
☽ ⚹ ♅ **8:40 am** 5:40 am

13 THURSDAY
☽ □ ♀ **5:28 am** 2:28 am
☽ ⚻ ☿ **12:46 pm** 9:46 am
☽ ☌ ♆ **2:27 pm** 11:27 am
☽ ⚻ ♃ **4:00 pm** 1:00 pm
☽ ⚹ ♇ **9:50 pm** 6:50 pm
☿ ⚻ ♆ 11:19 pm

14 FRIDAY
☿ ⚻ ♆ **2:19 am**
☽ △ ☉ **5:26 am** 2:26 am
☽ □ ♄ **6:08 am** 3:08 am
☽ △ ♂ **1:00 pm** 10:00 am
☉ ⚻ ♄ **2:29 pm** 11:29 am
☿ ⚹ ♃ **4:46 pm** 1:46 pm
☽ ⚺ ♅ **4:54 pm** 1:54 pm

15 SATURDAY
☽ ⚹ ♀ **5:40 pm** 2:40 pm
☽ ⚺ ♆ **9:08 pm** 6:08 pm
☽ ☍ ♃ **11:03 pm** 8:03 pm
☽ △ ☿ 11:38 pm

16 SUNDAY
☽ △ ☿ **2:38 am**
☽ □ ♇ **4:06 am** 1:06 am
☽ △ ♄ **11:50 am** 8:50 am
☽ □ ☉ **3:26 pm** 12:26 pm
☿ ⚻ ♇ **3:50 pm** 12:50 pm
☽ □ ♂ **9:12 pm** 6:12 pm
☽ ☌ ♅ **10:19 pm** 7:19 pm

17 MONDAY
♀ □ ♆ **10:33 am** 7:33 am
♂ □ ♅ **9:37 pm** 6:37 pm
☽ ⚹ ♆ 9:55 pm
☽ ⚺ ♀ 11:10 pm

18 TUESDAY
☽ ⚹ ♆ **12:55 am**
☽ ⚺ ♀ **2:10 am**
☽ ⚻ ♃ **3:11 am** 12:11 am
☽ △ ♇ **7:30 am** 4:30 am
☽ □ ☿ **12:01 pm** 9:01 am
☽ ⚻ ♄ **2:44 pm** 11:44 am
♀ △ ♃ **4:09 pm** 1:09 pm
☽ ⚹ ☉ **9:56 pm** 6:56 pm
☽ ⚺ ♅ 9:57 pm
☽ ⚹ ♂ 11:11 pm

19 WEDNESDAY
☽ ⚺ ♅ **12:57 am**
☽ ⚹ ♂ **2:11 am**
☿ △ ♄ **3:16 pm** 12:16 pm
☽ □ ♆ 11:19 pm

20 THURSDAY
☽ □ ♆ **2:19 am**
☽ △ ♃ **4:54 am** 1:54 am
☽ ☌ ♀ **7:39 am** 4:39 am
☽ ⚻ ♇ **8:38 am** 5:38 am
☽ ☍ ♄ **3:32 pm** 12:32 pm
☽ ⚹ ☿ **6:04 pm** 3:04 pm
♀ ⚻ ♇ **8:17 pm** 5:17 pm
☉ □ ♅ **8:26 pm** 5:26 pm
☽ ⚹ ♅ 10:41 pm
☽ ⚺ ☉ 11:02 pm

21 FRIDAY
☽ ⚹ ♅ **1:41 am**
☽ ⚺ ☉ **2:02 am**
☽ ⚺ ♂ **5:03 am** 2:03 am
☽ △ ♆ 11:34 pm

22 SATURDAY
☽ △ ♆ **2:34 am**
☽ □ ♃ **5:34 am** 2:34 am
☽ ☍ ♇ **8:50 am** 5:50 am
☽ ⚺ ♀ **11:55 am** 8:55 am
☽ ⚻ ♄ **3:40 pm** 12:40 pm
☽ ⚺ ☿ **10:59 pm** 7:59 pm
☽ □ ♅ 11:05 pm

23 SUNDAY
☽ □ ♅ **2:05 am**
☽ ☌ ☉ **5:46 am** 2:46 am
☽ ☌ ♂ **7:41 am** 4:41 am

24 MONDAY
☽ ⚻ ♆ **3:25 am** 12:25 am
☽ ⚹ ♃ **6:59 am** 3:59 am
☽ ⚻ ♇ **9:53 am** 6:53 am
♀ ☍ ♄ **10:54 am** 7:54 am
☿ △ ♅ **12:33 pm** 9:33 am
☽ △ ♄ **4:53 pm** 1:53 pm
☽ ⚹ ♀ **5:26 pm** 2:26 pm

25 TUESDAY
☽ △ ♅ **3:58 am** 12:58 am
☽ ☌ ☿ **5:22 am** 2:22 am
☽ ⚺ ☉ **11:28 am** 8:28 am
☽ ⚺ ♂ **12:16 pm** 9:16 am

26 WEDNESDAY
☽ ☍ ♆ **6:37 am** 3:37 am
☽ ⚺ ♃ **10:56 am** 7:56 am
☽ △ ♇ **1:28 pm** 10:28 am
☽ □ ♄ **8:51 pm** 5:51 pm
☉ ☌ ♂ **8:57 pm** 5:57 pm
☽ □ ♀ 11:31 pm

27 THURSDAY
☽ □ ♀ **2:31 am**
☽ ⚻ ♅ **8:53 am** 5:53 am
☽ ⚺ ☿ **3:17 pm** 12:17 pm
☽ ⚹ ♂ **8:32 pm** 5:32 pm
☽ ⚹ ☉ **9:09 pm** 6:09 pm

28 FRIDAY
☽ ⚻ ♆ **1:19 pm** 10:19 am
☽ ☌ ♃ **6:35 pm** 3:35 pm
☽ □ ♇ **8:38 pm** 5:38 pm

29 SATURDAY
☽ ⚹ ♄ **4:27 am** 1:27 am
☽ △ ♀ **4:25 pm** 1:25 pm
☽ ☍ ♅ **5:30 pm** 2:30 pm

30 SUNDAY
♀ ⚹ ♅ **4:04 am** 1:04 am
☽ ⚹ ☿ **5:21 am** 2:21 am
☽ □ ♂ **9:02 am** 6:02 am
☽ □ ☉ **11:23 am** 8:23 am
☽ △ ♆ **11:29 pm** 8:29 pm

31 MONDAY
☽ ⚺ ♃ **5:46 am** 2:46 am
☽ ⚹ ♇ **7:10 am** 4:10 am
☽ ⚺ ♄ **3:16 pm** 12:16 pm

Eastern time in bold type
Pacific time in medium type

JULY 2017

DATE	SID.TIME	SUN	MOON	NODE	MERCURY	VENUS	MARS	JUPITER	SATURN	URANUS	NEPTUNE	PLUTO	CERES	PALLAS	JUNO	VESTA	CHIRON
1 Sa	18 36 57	9 ♋ 21 58	8 ♎ 57	25 ♌ 18	20 ♋ 21	25 ♉ 38	17 ♋ 20	13 ♎ 53	23 ♐ 23	28 ♈ 05	14 ♓ 12	18 ♑ 21	26 ♊ 01	1 ♉ 09	11 ♑ 12	22 ♌ 27	28 ♓ 52 ℞
2 Su	18 40 54	10 19 10	21 22	25 17 ℞	22 20	26 43	17 59	13 57	23 19 ℞	28 06	14 12 ℞	18 20 ℞	26 26	1 27	10 58 ℞	22 53	28 52
3 M	18 44 50	11 16 22	3 ♏ 32	25 15	24 18	27 48	18 38	14 01	23 15	28 08	14 12	18 18	26 52	1 44	10 44	23 19	28 52
4 T	18 48 47	12 13 34	15 33	25 10	26 13	28 54	19 18	14 05	23 10	28 09	14 11	18 17	27 17	2 01	10 30	23 46	28 52
5 W	18 52 43	13 10 46	27 28	25 04	28 07	29 59	19 57	14 10	23 06	28 11	14 10	18 15	27 42	2 18	10 16	24 12	28 52
6 Th	18 56 40	14 07 57	9 ♐ 20	24 57	29 58	1 ♊ 05	20 36	14 14	23 02	28 12	14 10	18 14	28 07	2 35	10 02	24 38	28 51
7 F	19 0 36	15 05 08	21 12	24 50	1 ♌ 48	2 11	21 15	14 19	22 59	28 14	14 09	18 12	28 32	2 52	9 48	25 05	28 51
8 Sa	19 4 33	16 02 19	3 ♑ 07	24 43	3 36	3 18	21 54	14 23	22 55	28 15	14 09	18 11	28 57	3 09	9 34	25 31	28 51
9 Su	19 8 29	16 59 31	15 06	24 37	5 21	4 24	22 33	14 28	22 51	28 16	14 08	18 09	29 23	3 26	9 20	25 58	28 50
10 M	19 12 26	17 56 42	27 10	24 33	7 05	5 30	23 12	14 33	22 47	28 17	14 07	18 08	29 48	3 42	9 07	26 25	28 50
11 T	19 16 23	18 53 54	9 ♒ 23	24 30	8 46	6 37	23 51	14 38	22 43	28 18	14 06	18 06	0 ♋ 13	3 59	8 53	26 51	28 49
12 W	19 20 19	19 51 05	21 44	24 29 D	10 26	7 44	24 29	14 44	22 40	28 19	14 06	18 05	0 38	4 15	8 39	27 18	28 49
13 Th	19 24 16	20 48 18	4 ♓ 17	24 29	12 03	8 51	25 08	14 49	22 36	28 21	14 05	18 03	1 03	4 31	8 26	27 45	28 48
14 F	19 28 12	21 45 30	17 03	24 30	13 39	9 58	25 47	14 55	22 32	28 22	14 04	18 02	1 28	4 48	8 12	28 12	28 48
15 Sa	19 32 9	22 42 43	0 ♈ 04	24 32	15 12	11 05	26 26	15 01	22 29	28 23	14 03	18 01	1 53	5 03	7 59	28 39	28 47
16 Su	19 36 5	23 39 57	13 24	24 33 ℞	16 44	12 12	27 05	15 07	22 25	28 23	14 02	17 59	2 18	5 19	7 46	29 06	28 46
17 M	19 40 2	24 37 11	27 04	24 33	18 13	13 20	27 44	15 13	22 22	28 24	14 01	17 58	2 43	5 35	7 33	29 34	28 45
18 T	19 43 58	25 34 26	11 ♉ 05	24 33	19 41	14 27	28 23	15 19	22 19	28 25	14 00	17 56	3 08	5 50	7 20	0 ♍ 01	28 45
19 W	19 47 55	26 31 42	25 26	24 31	21 06	15 35	29 01	15 25	22 15	28 26	13 59	17 55	3 33	6 06	7 07	0 28	28 44
20 Th	19 51 52	27 28 59	10 ♊ 05	24 28	22 29	16 43	29 40	15 32	22 12	28 27	13 58	17 53	3 58	6 21	6 55	0 56	28 43
21 F	19 55 48	28 26 16	24 56	24 24	23 50	17 51	0 ♌ 19	15 38	22 09	28 27	13 57	17 52	4 23	6 36	6 43	1 23	28 42
22 Sa	19 59 45	29 23 34	9 ♋ 52	24 21	25 09	18 59	0 58	15 45	22 06	28 28	13 56	17 50	4 48	6 51	6 30	1 51	28 41
23 Su	20 3 41	0 ♌ 20 53	24 44	24 18	26 25	20 07	1 36	15 52	22 03	28 28	13 55	17 49	5 13	7 06	6 19	2 18	28 40
24 M	20 7 38	1 18 12	9 ♌ 25	24 16	27 40	21 16	2 15	15 59	22 00	28 29	13 54	17 47	5 38	7 20	6 07	2 46	28 39
25 T	20 11 34	2 15 32	23 48	24 16 D	28 51	22 24	2 54	16 06	21 57	28 29	13 53	17 46	6 03	7 35	5 56	3 13	28 37
26 W	20 15 31	3 12 52	7 ♍ 48	24 16	0 ♍ 01	23 33	3 32	16 14	21 54	28 30	13 52	17 45	6 28	7 49	5 45	3 41	28 36
27 Th	20 19 27	4 10 13	21 23	24 17	1 08	24 41	4 11	16 21	21 52	28 30	13 51	17 43	6 52	8 03	5 34	4 09	28 35
28 F	20 23 24	5 07 34	4 ♎ 33	24 19	2 12	25 50	4 50	16 29	21 49	28 31	13 50	17 42	7 17	8 17	5 23	4 37	28 34
29 Sa	20 27 21	6 04 56	17 21	24 20	3 14	26 59	5 28	16 36	21 46	28 31	13 48	17 40	7 42	8 30	5 13	5 05	28 32
30 Su	20 31 17	7 02 18	29 48	24 21 ℞	4 13	28 08	6 07	16 44	21 44	28 31	13 47	17 39	8 07	8 44	5 03	5 33	28 31
31 M	20 35 14	7 59 41	12 ♏ 00	24 21	5 09	29 17	6 45	16 52	21 42	28 31	13 46	17 38	8 31	8 57	4 53	6 01	28 29

EPHEMERIS CALCULATED FOR 12 MIDNIGHT GREENWICH MEAN TIME. ALL OTHER DATA AND FACING ASPECTARIAN PAGE IN **EASTERN TIME (BOLD)** AND PACIFIC TIME (REGULAR).

AUGUST 2017

☽ Last Aspect day	ET / hr:mn / PT		asp	☽ Ingress sign	day	ET / hr:mn / PT	
7/31	**7:10 am**	4:10 am	✶♇	♐	1	**8:01 am**	5:01 am
3	**5:38 pm**	2:38 pm	△♅	♑	3	**8:37 pm**	5:37 pm
6	**5:22 am**	2:22 am	□♅	♒	6	**8:15 am**	5:15 am
8	**3:07 pm**	12:07 pm	✶♅	♓	8	**5:56 pm**	2:56 pm
10	**9:38 am**	6:38 am	□♄	♈	10		10:22 pm
10	**9:38 am**	6:38 am	□♄	♈	11	**1:22 am**	
13	**4:01 am**	1:01 am	☌♅	♉	13	**6:40 am**	3:40 am
14	**9:15 pm**	6:15 pm	□☉	♊	15	**10:06 am**	7:06 am
17	**9:38 am**	6:38 am	✶♅	♋	17	**12:13 pm**	9:13 pm
19	**11:17 am**	8:17 am	□♅	♌	19	**1:55 pm**	10:55 am
21	**2:30 pm**	11:30 am	☌☉	♍	21	**4:25 pm**	1:25 pm
23	**4:02 pm**	1:02 pm	✶♀	♎	23	**9:05 pm**	6:05 pm
25		10:39 pm	☍♅	♏	26	**4:53 am**	1:53 am
26	**1:39 am**		☍♅	♏	26	**4:53 am**	1:53 am
28	**5:38 am**	2:38 am	□♂	♐	28	**3:48 pm**	12:48 pm
30		9:42 pm	△♅	♑	31	**4:18 am**	1:18 am
31	**12:42 am**		△♅	♑	31	**4:18 am**	1:18 am

☽ Phases & Eclipses phase	day	ET / hr:mn / PT	
Full Moon	7	**2:11 pm**	11:11 am
	7	15° ♒ 25'	
4th Quarter	14	**9:15 pm**	6:15 pm
New Moon	21	**2:30 pm**	11:30 am
	21	28° ♌ 53'	
2nd Quarter	29	**4:13 am**	1:13 am

Planet Ingress	day	ET / hr:mn / PT	
☉ ♍	22	**6:20 pm**	3:20 pm
♀ ♌	25		9:30 pm
♀ ♌	26	**12:30 am**	
☿ ♌	31	**11:28 am**	8:28 am

Planetary Motion	day	ET / hr:mn / PT	
♅ ℞	2		10:31 pm
♅ ℞	3	**1:31 am**	
☿ ℞	12	**9:00 pm**	6:00 pm
♄ D	25	**8:08 am**	5:08 am
⚵ D	26	**1:14 pm**	10:14 am

1 TUESDAY
☽⚻♅ **5:03 am** 2:03 am
☽⚻♀ **10:17 am** 7:17 am
☽□☿ **10:00 pm** 7:00 pm
☽△♂ 9:30 pm

2 WEDNESDAY
☽△♂ **12:30 am**
☽△☉ **4:44 am** 1:44 am
☽□♆ **11:43 am** 8:43 am
☽✶♃ **6:55 pm** 3:55 pm
☽⚺♇ **7:31 pm** 4:31 pm

3 THURSDAY
☽☌♄ **3:37 am** 12:37 am
☽△♅ **5:38 pm** 2:38 pm

4 FRIDAY
☽☍♀ **5:22 am** 2:22 am
☽△☿ **2:22 pm** 11:22 am
♃□♇ **2:48 pm** 11:48 am
☽⚻♂ **4:24 pm** 1:24 pm
☽⚻☉ **10:24 pm** 7:24 pm
☽✶♆ **11:58 pm** 8:58 pm

5 SATURDAY
☽☌♇ **7:37 am** 4:37 am
☽□♃ **7:51 am** 4:51 am
☽⚺♄ **3:31 pm** 12:31 pm
☉⚻♆ **5:31 pm** 2:31 pm

6 SUNDAY
☽□♅ **5:22 am** 2:22 am
☽⚻♀ **10:57 pm** 7:57 pm

7 MONDAY
☽⚻☿ **4:15 am** 1:15 am
☽☍♂ **6:41 am** 3:41 am
☽⚺♆ **10:40 am** 7:40 am
☽☍☉ **2:11 pm** 11:11 am
☽⚺♇ **6:05 pm** 3:05 pm
☽△♃ **7:06 pm** 4:06 pm
☽✶♄ 10:40 pm

8 TUESDAY
☽✶♄ **1:40 am**
☽✶♅ **3:07 pm** 12:07 pm

9 WEDNESDAY
☽△♀ **1:45 pm** 10:45 am
☽☍☿ **2:51 pm** 11:51 am
☉⚻♇ **4:10 pm** 1:10 pm
☽⚻♂ **6:28 pm** 3:28 pm
☽☌♆ **7:14 pm** 4:14 pm
☽✶♇ 11:22 pm

10 THURSDAY
☽✶♇ **2:22 am**
☽⚻☉ **3:12 am** 12:12 am
☽⚻♃ **4:05 am** 1:05 am
☿✶♀ **5:03 am** 2:03 am
♂⚻♆ **9:31 am** 6:31 am
☽□♄ **9:38 am** 6:38 am
☉✶♃ **5:24 pm** 2:24 pm
☽⚺♅ **10:39 pm** 7:39 pm

11 FRIDAY
☽⚻☿ **10:13 pm** 7:13 pm
♀△♆ 10:17 pm
☽⚺♆ 10:35 pm
☽□♀ 10:36 pm

12 SATURDAY
♀△♆ **1:17 am**
☽⚺♆ **1:35 am**
☽□♀ **1:36 am**
☽△♂ **3:39 am** 12:39 am
☽□♇ **8:27 am** 5:27 am
☽☍♃ **10:48 am** 7:48 am
☽△☉ **1:27 pm** 10:27 am
☽△♄ **3:26 pm** 12:26 pm

13 SUNDAY
☽☌♅ **4:01 am** 1:01 am
☉△♄ **5:06 pm** 2:06 pm
☽△☿ 11:42 pm
♀⚺♂ 11:43 pm

14 MONDAY
☽△☿ **2:42 am**
♀⚺♂ **2:43 am**
☽✶♆ **5:54 am** 2:54 am
☽□♂ **10:30 am** 7:30 am
☽✶♀ **10:49 am** 7:49 am
☽△♇ **12:34 pm** 9:34 am
☽⚻♃ **3:29 pm** 12:29 pm
☽⚻♄ **7:18 pm** 4:18 pm
☽□☉ **9:15 pm** 6:15 pm

15 TUESDAY
♀☍♇ **7:17 am** 4:17 am
☽⚺♅ **7:30 am** 4:30 am

16 WEDNESDAY
☽□☿ **4:49 am** 1:49 am
♂⚻♇ **6:37 am** 3:37 am
☽□♆ **8:34 am** 5:34 am
☽⚻♇ **3:05 pm** 12:05 pm
☽✶♂ **3:29 pm** 12:29 pm
☽⚺♀ **5:57 pm** 2:57 pm
☽△♃ **6:35 pm** 3:35 pm
☽☍♄ **9:40 pm** 6:40 pm
♀□♃ 11:40 pm

17 THURSDAY
♀□♃ **2:40 am**
☽✶☉ **3:13 am** 12:13 am
☽✶♅ **9:38 am** 6:38 am

18 FRIDAY
☽✶☿ **5:19 am** 2:19 am
☽△♆ **10:17 am** 7:17 am
♀⚻♄ **2:55 pm** 11:55 am
☽☍♇ **4:45 pm** 1:45 pm
☽⚺♂ **7:31 pm** 4:31 pm
☽□♃ **8:52 pm** 5:52 pm
☽⚻♄ **11:20 pm** 8:20 pm
☽☌♀ 9:05 pm

19 SATURDAY
☽☌♀ **12:05 am**
☽⚺☉ **8:27 am** 5:27 am
☽□♅ **11:17 am** 8:17 am

20 SUNDAY
☽⚺☿ **5:12 am** 2:12 am
☽⚻♆ **12:04 pm** 9:04 am
♂✶♃ **12:42 pm** 9:42 am
☽⚻♇ **6:41 pm** 3:41 pm
☽✶♃ **11:32 pm** 8:32 pm
☽☌♂ **11:55 pm** 8:55 pm
☽△♄ 10:26 pm
☉△♅ 11:22 pm

21 MONDAY
☽△♄ **1:26 am**
☉△♅ **2:22 am**
☽⚺♀ **6:49 am** 3:49 am
☽△♅ **1:40 pm** 10:40 am
☽☌☉ **2:30 pm** 11:30 am

22 TUESDAY
☽☌☿ **5:41 am** 2:41 am
♂△♄ **9:21 am** 6:21 am
☽☍♆ **3:17 pm** 12:17 pm
☽△♇ **10:13 pm** 7:13 pm

23 WEDNESDAY
☽⚺♃ **4:01 am** 1:01 am
☽□♄ **5:19 am** 2:19 am
☽⚺♂ **6:18 am** 3:18 am
☽✶♀ **4:02 pm** 1:02 pm
☽⚻♅ **6:07 pm** 3:07 pm
☽⚺☉ **11:10 pm** 8:10 pm

24 THURSDAY
☽⚺☿ **7:50 am** 4:50 am
♀□♅ **3:01 pm** 12:01 pm
☽⚻♆ **9:08 pm** 6:08 pm

25 FRIDAY
☽□♇ **4:32 am** 1:32 am
☽☌♃ **11:31 am** 8:31 am
☽✶♄ **12:08 pm** 9:08 am
☽✶♂ **4:05 pm** 1:05 pm
☽☍♅ 10:39 pm

26 SATURDAY
☽☍♅ **1:39 am**
☽□♀ **5:21 am** 2:21 am
☽✶☉ **11:48 am** 8:48 am
☽✶☿ **12:29 pm** 9:29 am
☉☌☿ **4:42 pm** 1:42 pm

27 SUNDAY
☽△♆ **6:16 am** 3:16 am
♃✶♄ **8:15 am** 5:15 am
☽✶♇ **2:08 pm** 11:08 am
☽⚺♄ **10:14 pm** 7:14 pm
☽⚺♃ **10:26 pm** 7:26 pm

28 MONDAY
☿⚺♀ **3:14 am** 12:14 am
☽□♂ **5:38 am** 2:38 am
☽⚻♅ **12:20 pm** 9:20 am
☽□☿ **7:41 pm** 4:41 pm
☽△♀ **10:48 pm** 7:48 pm

29 TUESDAY
☽□☉ **4:13 am** 1:13 am
☽□♆ **6:00 pm** 3:00 pm
☽⚺♇ 11:10 pm

30 WEDNESDAY
☽⚺♇ **2:10 am**
☽☌♄ **10:32 am** 7:32 am
☽✶♃ **11:38 am** 8:38 am
☽△♂ **9:27 pm** 6:27 pm
☽△♅ 9:42 pm

31 THURSDAY
☽△♅ **12:42 am**
☽△☿ **4:40 am** 1:40 am
☽⚻♀ **6:07 pm** 3:07 pm
☽△☉ **10:06 pm** 7:06 pm

Eastern time in bold type
Pacific time in medium type

AUGUST 2017

DATE	SID.TIME	SUN	MOON	NODE	MERCURY	VENUS	MARS	JUPITER	SATURN	URANUS	NEPTUNE	PLUTO	CERES	PALLAS	JUNO	VESTA	CHIRON
1 T	20 39 10	8 ♌ 57 04	24 ♏ 02	24 ♌ 20	6 ♍ 02	0 ♋ 26	7 ♌ 24	17 ♎ 00	21 ♐ 39	28 ♈ 31	13 ♓ 45	17 ♑ 36	8 ♋ 56	9 ♉ 10	4 ♑ 44	6 ♍ 29	28 ♓ 28
2 W	20 43 7	9 54 28	5 ♐ 56	24 19 ℞	6 51	1 36	8 02	17 08	21 37 ℞	28 32	13 43 ℞	17 35 ℞	9 21	9 23	4 35 ℞	6 57	28 26 ℞
3 Th	20 47 3	10 51 52	17 48	24 17	7 38	2 45	8 41	17 16	21 35	28 32 ℞	13 42	17 34	9 45	9 36	4 26	7 25	28 25
4 F	20 51 0	11 49 18	29 42	24 15	8 21	3 54	9 19	17 25	21 33	28 32	13 41	17 32	10 10	9 48	4 18	7 54	28 23
5 Sa	20 54 56	12 46 44	11 ♑ 40	24 14	9 00	5 04	9 58	17 33	21 31	28 31	13 39	17 31	10 34	10 01	4 10	8 22	28 21
6 Su	20 58 53	13 44 11	23 46	24 12	9 35	6 14	10 36	17 42	21 29	28 31	13 38	17 30	10 59	10 13	4 02	8 50	28 20
7 M	21 2 50	14 41 38	6 ♒ 01	24 11	10 07	7 23	11 15	17 51	21 27	28 31	13 37	17 29	11 23	10 24	3 55	9 19	28 18
8 T	21 6 46	15 39 07	18 27	24 11 D	10 34	8 33	11 53	17 59	21 26	28 31	13 35	17 27	11 48	10 36	3 48	9 47	28 16
9 W	21 10 43	16 36 37	1 ♓ 06	24 11	10 56	9 43	12 32	18 08	21 24	28 31	13 34	17 26	12 12	10 47	3 41	10 16	28 14
10 Th	21 14 39	17 34 08	13 58	24 11	11 14	10 53	13 10	18 17	21 22	28 30	13 32	17 25	12 37	10 59	3 35	10 44	28 12
11 F	21 18 36	18 31 40	27 03	24 12	11 27	12 04	13 48	18 26	21 21	28 30	13 31	17 24	13 01	11 09	3 29	11 13	28 10
12 Sa	21 22 32	19 29 13	10 ♈ 22	24 12	11 36	13 14	14 27	18 36	21 20	28 30	13 30	17 22	13 25	11 20	3 23	11 41	28 08
13 Su	21 26 29	20 26 48	23 54	24 13	11 38 ℞	14 24	15 05	18 45	21 18	28 29	13 28	17 21	13 49	11 31	3 18	12 10	28 06
14 M	21 30 25	21 24 24	7 ♉ 41	24 13	11 36	15 35	15 44	18 54	21 17	28 29	13 27	17 20	14 14	11 41	3 13	12 39	28 04
15 T	21 34 22	22 22 02	21 41	24 13 ℞	11 28	16 45	16 22	19 04	21 16	28 28	13 25	17 19	14 38	11 51	3 09	13 08	28 02
16 W	21 38 19	23 19 41	5 ♊ 53	24 13 D	11 14	17 56	17 00	19 14	21 15	28 28	13 24	17 18	15 02	12 00	3 04	13 36	28 00
17 Th	21 42 15	24 17 22	20 14	24 13	10 55	19 06	17 39	19 23	21 14	28 27	13 22	17 17	15 26	12 10	3 01	14 05	27 58
18 F	21 46 12	25 15 05	4 ♋ 42	24 13	10 31	20 17	18 17	19 33	21 14	28 26	13 21	17 15	15 50	12 19	2 57	14 34	27 56
19 Sa	21 50 8	26 12 49	19 12	24 13	10 01	21 28	18 55	19 43	21 13	28 26	13 19	17 14	16 14	12 27	2 54	15 03	27 54
20 Su	21 54 5	27 10 35	3 ♌ 40	24 13	9 25	22 39	19 34	19 53	21 12	28 25	13 17	17 13	16 38	12 36	2 51	15 32	27 51
21 M	21 58 1	28 08 22	17 59	24 13 ℞	8 45	23 50	20 12	20 03	21 12	28 24	13 16	17 12	17 02	12 44	2 49	16 01	27 49
22 T	22 1 58	29 06 11	2 ♍ 05	24 13	8 01	25 01	20 50	20 13	21 12	28 23	13 14	17 11	17 26	12 52	2 47	16 30	27 47
23 W	22 5 54	0 ♍ 04 01	15 55	24 13	7 13	26 13	21 28	20 24	21 11	28 22	13 13	17 10	17 50	12 59	2 46	17 00	27 45
24 Th	22 9 51	1 01 52	29 24	24 13	6 22	27 24	22 07	20 34	21 11	28 21	13 11	17 09	18 13	13 07	2 44	17 29	27 42
25 F	22 13 48	1 59 44	12 ♎ 33	24 12	5 29	28 35	22 45	20 45	21 11 D	28 20	13 09	17 08	18 37	13 14	2 44	17 58	27 40
26 Sa	22 17 44	2 57 38	25 21	24 11	4 34	29 47	23 23	20 55	21 11	28 19	13 08	17 07	19 01	13 20	2 43 D	18 27	27 37
27 Su	22 21 41	3 55 33	7 ♏ 50	24 10	3 40	0 ♌ 58	24 01	21 06	21 11	28 18	13 06	17 07	19 24	13 26	2 43	18 57	27 35
28 M	22 25 37	4 53 30	20 04	24 09	2 47	2 10	24 39	21 16	21 11	28 17	13 05	17 06	19 48	13 32	2 43	19 26	27 33
29 T	22 29 34	5 51 28	2 ♐ 06	24 08 D	1 56	3 21	25 18	21 27	21 12	28 16	13 03	17 05	20 11	13 38	2 44	19 55	27 30
30 W	22 33 30	6 49 27	14 01	24 08	1 08	4 33	25 56	21 38	21 12	28 14	13 01	17 04	20 34	13 43	2 45	20 25	27 28
31 Th	22 37 27	7 47 27	25 53	24 09	0 25	5 45	26 34	21 49	21 12	28 13	13 00	17 03	20 58	13 48	2 46	20 54	27 25

EPHEMERIS CALCULATED FOR 12 MIDNIGHT GREENWICH MEAN TIME. ALL OTHER DATA AND FACING ASPECTARIAN PAGE IN **EASTERN TIME (BOLD)** AND PACIFIC TIME (REGULAR).

SEPTEMBER 2017

☽ Last Aspect day	ET / hr:mn / PT		asp	☽ Ingress sign	day	ET / hr:mn / PT	
2	**12:30 pm**	9:30 am	□ ♅	♒	2	**4:06 pm**	1:06 pm
4		10:15 pm	☍ ♂	♓	4		10:28 pm
5	**1:15 am**		☍ ♂	♓	5	**1:28 am**	
6	**4:29 pm**	1:29 pm	□ ♄	♈	7	**8:01 am**	5:01 am
9	**11:52 am**	8:52 am	△ ☿	♉	9	**12:23 pm**	9:23 am
10	**8:54 pm**	5:54 pm	□ ♀	♊	11	**3:29 pm**	12:29 pm
13	**2:35 pm**	11:35 am	⚹ ♅	♋	13	**6:12 pm**	3:12 pm
15	**5:23 pm**	2:23 pm	□ ♅	♌	15	**9:09 pm**	6:09 pm
17	**8:55 pm**	5:55 pm	△ ♅	♍	17		9:52 pm
17	**8:55 pm**	5:55 pm	△ ♅	♍	18	**12:52 am**	
19		10:30 pm	☌ ☉	♎	20	**6:06 am**	3:06 am
20	**1:30 am**		☌ ☉	♎	20	**6:06 am**	3:06 am
22	**9:04 am**	6:04 am	☍ ♅	♏	22	**1:40 pm**	10:40 am
24	**3:33 am**	12:33 am	⚹ ☿	♐	24		9:01 pm
24	**3:33 am**	12:33 am	⚹ ☿	♐	25	**12:01 am**	
27	**7:08 am**	4:08 am	△ ♅	♑	27	**12:24 pm**	9:24 am
29	**8:14 pm**	5:14 pm	□ ♃	♒	29		9:40 pm
29	**8:14 pm**	5:14 pm	□ ♃	♒	30	**12:40 am**	

☽ Phases & Eclipses phase	day	ET / hr:mn / PT	
Full Moon	6	**3:03 am**	12:03 am
4th Quarter	12		11:25 pm
4th Quarter	13	**2:25 am**	
New Moon	19		10:30 pm
New Moon	20	**1:30 am**	
2nd Quarter	27	**10:54 pm**	7:54 pm

Planet Ingress	day	ET / hr:mn / PT	
♂ ♍	5	**5:35 am**	2:35 am
☿ ♍	9	**10:52 pm**	7:52 pm
⚵ ♎	18	**3:50 am**	12:50 am
♀ ♍	19	**9:15 pm**	6:15 pm
☉ ♎	22	**4:02 pm**	1:02 pm
⚳ ♌	23		10:45 pm
⚳ ♌	24	**1:45 am**	
☿ ♎	29	**8:42 pm**	5:42 pm

Planetary Motion	day	ET / hr:mn / PT	
☿ D	5	**7:29 am**	4:29 am
♀ ℞	11	**1:46 pm**	10:46 am
♇ D	28	**3:36 pm**	12:36 pm

1 FRIDAY
☽ ⚹ ♆ **6:21 am** 3:21 am
☽ ☌ ♇ **2:29 pm** 11:29 am
☽ ⚺ ♄ **10:49 pm** 7:49 pm
☽ □ ♃ 9:47 pm

2 SATURDAY
☽ □ ♃ **12:47 am**
♂ △ ♅ **8:13 am** 5:13 am
☽ □ ♅ **12:30 pm** 9:30 am
☽ ⚻ ♂ **12:44 pm** 9:44 am
☽ ⚻ ☿ **2:02 pm** 11:02 am

3 SUNDAY
☿ ☌ ♂ **5:38 am** 2:38 am
☽ ☍ ♀ **11:49 am** 8:49 am
☽ ⚻ ☉ **2:18 pm** 11:18 am
☽ ⚺ ♆ **5:06 pm** 2:06 pm
☽ ⚺ ♇ 9:58 pm

4 MONDAY
☽ ⚺ ♇ **12:58 am**
☽ ⚹ ♄ **9:04 am** 6:04 am
☽ △ ♃ **11:44 am** 8:44 am
☽ ⚹ ♅ **9:56 pm** 6:56 pm
☽ ☍ ☿ **10:33 pm** 7:33 pm
☽ ☍ ♂ 10:15 pm
☉ ☍ ♆ 10:28 pm

5 TUESDAY
☽ ☍ ♂ **1:15 am**
☉ ☍ ♆ **1:28 am**
♀ ⚻ ♆ **5:33 pm** 2:33 pm
☽ ☌ ♆ 10:07 pm
☽ ⚻ ♀ 10:54 pm

6 WEDNESDAY
☽ ☌ ♆ **1:07 am**
☽ ⚻ ♀ **1:54 am**
☽ ☍ ☉ **3:03 am** 12:03 am
☽ ⚹ ♇ **8:40 am** 5:40 am
☽ □ ♄ **4:29 pm** 1:29 pm
☽ ⚻ ♃ **7:44 pm** 4:44 pm

7 THURSDAY
☽ ⚺ ♅ **4:32 am** 1:32 am
☽ ⚻ ☿ **5:42 am** 2:42 am
☽ ⚻ ♂ **10:30 am** 7:30 am

8 FRIDAY
☽ ⚺ ♆ **6:31 am** 3:31 am
☽ △ ♀ **12:30 pm** 9:30 am
☽ ⚻ ☉ **12:31 pm** 9:31 am
☉ ⚺ ♀ **1:26 pm** 10:26 am
☽ □ ♇ **1:49 pm** 10:49 am
☽ △ ♄ **9:27 pm** 6:27 pm
☽ ☍ ♃ 10:15 pm

9 SATURDAY
☽ ☍ ♃ **1:15 am**
♀ ⚻ ♇ **3:23 am** 12:23 am
☉ △ ♇ **6:45 am** 3:45 am
☽ ☌ ♅ **8:54 am** 5:54 am
☽ △ ☿ **11:52 am** 8:52 am
☽ △ ♂ **5:16 pm** 2:16 pm

10 SUNDAY
☽ ⚹ ♆ **10:07 am** 7:07 am
☽ △ ♇ **5:19 pm** 2:19 pm
☽ △ ☉ **7:54 pm** 4:54 pm
☽ □ ♀ **8:54 pm** 5:54 pm
☽ ⚻ ♄ 9:55 pm

11 MONDAY
☽ ⚻ ♄ **12:55 am**
☽ ⚻ ♃ **5:16 am** 2:16 am
☽ ⚺ ♅ **11:58 am** 8:58 am
☽ □ ☿ **5:54 pm** 2:54 pm
☽ □ ♂ **10:42 pm** 7:42 pm

12 TUESDAY
☽ □ ♆ **12:53 pm** 9:53 am
☽ ⚻ ♇ **8:05 pm** 5:05 pm
♀ △ ♄ **8:50 pm** 5:50 pm
☽ □ ☉ 11:25 pm

13 WEDNESDAY
☽ □ ☉ **2:25 am**
☽ ☍ ♄ **3:47 am** 12:47 am
☽ ⚹ ♀ **4:25 am** 1:25 am
☽ △ ♃ **8:43 am** 5:43 am
☽ ⚹ ♅ **2:35 pm** 11:35 am
☉ □ ♄ **10:58 pm** 7:58 pm
☽ ⚹ ☿ 9:41 pm

14 THURSDAY
☽ ⚹ ☿ **12:41 am**
☽ ⚹ ♂ **3:48 am** 12:48 am
☽ △ ♆ **3:31 pm** 12:31 pm
☽ ☍ ♇ **10:51 pm** 7:51 pm

15 FRIDAY
☽ ⚻ ♄ **6:43 am** 3:43 am
☽ ⚹ ☉ **9:00 am** 6:00 am
☽ ⚺ ♀ **12:02 pm** 9:02 am
☽ □ ♃ **12:18 pm** 9:18 am
♀ ⚹ ♃ **3:44 pm** 12:44 pm
☽ □ ♅ **5:23 pm** 2:23 pm

16 SATURDAY
☽ ⚺ ☿ **8:54 am** 5:54 am
☽ ⚺ ♂ **9:16 am** 6:16 am
☿ ☌ ♂ **3:01 pm** 12:01 pm
☽ ⚻ ♆ **6:37 pm** 3:37 pm
☽ ⚻ ♇ 11:08 pm

17 SUNDAY
☽ ⚻ ♇ **2:08 am**
☽ △ ♄ **10:18 am** 7:18 am
☽ ⚺ ☉ **4:23 pm** 1:23 pm
☽ ⚹ ♃ **4:37 pm** 1:37 pm
☉ ⚺ ♃ **8:17 pm** 5:17 pm
☽ ☌ ♀ **8:34 pm** 5:34 pm
☽ △ ♅ **8:55 pm** 5:55 pm
♀ △ ♅ 9:27 pm

18 MONDAY
♀ △ ♅ **12:27 am**
☽ ☌ ♂ **3:48 pm** 12:48 pm
☽ ☌ ☿ **7:20 pm** 4:20 pm
☽ ☍ ♆ **10:46 pm** 7:46 pm

19 TUESDAY
☽ △ ♇ **6:35 am** 3:35 am
☽ □ ♄ **3:10 pm** 12:10 pm
☽ ⚺ ♃ **10:22 pm** 7:22 pm
☿ ☍ ♆ **11:50 pm** 8:50 pm
☽ ☌ ☉ 10:30 pm
☽ ⚻ ♅ 10:52 pm

20 WEDNESDAY
☽ ☌ ☉ **1:30 am**
☽ ⚻ ♅ **1:52 am**
☉ ⚻ ♅ **6:21 am** 3:21 am
☽ ⚺ ♀ **7:00 am** 4:00 am
☽ ⚺ ♂ 9:21 pm

21 THURSDAY
☽ ⚺ ♂ **12:21 am**
☽ ⚻ ♆ **4:46 am** 1:46 am
☽ ⚺ ☿ **9:08 am** 6:08 am
☽ □ ♇ **1:00 pm** 10:00 am
☽ ⚹ ♄ **10:12 pm** 7:12 pm

22 FRIDAY
☽ ☌ ♃ **6:27 am** 3:27 am
☽ ☍ ♅ **9:04 am** 6:04 am
☽ ⚺ ☉ **1:28 pm** 10:28 am
☿ △ ♇ **2:01 pm** 11:01 am
☽ ⚹ ♀ **8:35 pm** 5:35 pm

23 SATURDAY
☽ ⚹ ♂ **11:53 am** 8:53 am
☽ △ ♆ **1:22 pm** 10:22 am
☽ ⚹ ♇ **10:08 pm** 7:08 pm

24 SUNDAY
☽ ⚹ ☿ **3:33 am** 12:33 am
☽ ⚺ ♄ **8:01 am** 5:01 am
♂ ☍ ♆ **3:49 pm** 12:49 pm
☽ ⚺ ♃ **5:27 pm** 2:27 pm
☽ ⚻ ♅ **7:02 pm** 4:02 pm

25 MONDAY
☽ ⚹ ☉ **4:58 am** 1:58 am
☿ □ ♄ **10:36 am** 7:36 am
☽ □ ♀ **1:55 pm** 10:55 am
☽ □ ♆ 9:36 pm
☽ □ ♂ 11:31 pm

26 TUESDAY
☽ □ ♆ **12:36 am**
☽ □ ♂ **2:31 am**
☽ ⚺ ♇ **9:48 am** 6:48 am
☽ ☌ ♄ **8:15 pm** 5:15 pm
☽ □ ☿ 11:10 pm

27 WEDNESDAY
☽ □ ☿ **2:10 am**
☽ ⚹ ♃ **6:46 am** 3:46 am
☽ △ ♅ **7:08 am** 4:08 am
☽ □ ☉ **10:54 pm** 7:54 pm
♃ ☍ ♅ 9:25 pm

28 THURSDAY
♃ ☍ ♅ **12:25 am**
☽ △ ♀ **9:29 am** 6:29 am
☿ ⚻ ♅ **9:55 am** 6:55 am
☿ ⚺ ♃ **11:22 am** 8:22 am
☽ ⚹ ♆ **1:08 pm** 10:08 am
☽ △ ♂ **6:35 pm** 3:35 pm
☽ ☌ ♇ **10:27 pm** 7:27 pm

29 FRIDAY
☽ ⚺ ♄ **9:05 am** 6:05 am
☽ □ ♅ **7:20 pm** 4:20 pm
♀ ☍ ♆ **8:12 pm** 5:12 pm
☽ □ ♃ **8:14 pm** 5:14 pm
☽ △ ☿ 10:22 pm

30 SATURDAY
☽ △ ☿ **1:22 am**
☽ △ ☉ **4:06 pm** 1:06 pm
☽ ⚺ ♆ 9:30 pm

Eastern time in bold type
Pacific time in medium type

SEPTEMBER 2017

DATE	SID.TIME	SUN	MOON	NODE	MERCURY	VENUS	MARS	JUPITER	SATURN	URANUS	NEPTUNE	PLUTO	CERES	PALLAS	JUNO	VESTA	CHIRON
1 F	22 41 23	8 ♍ 45 29	7 ♑ 48	24 ♌ 10	29 ♌ 47	6 ♌ 57	27 ♌ 12	22 ♎ 00	21 ♐ 13	28 ♈ 12	12 ♓ 58	17 ♑ 02	21 ♋ 21	13 ♉ 53	2 ♑ 48	21 ♍ 24	27 ♓ 22
2 Sa	22 45 20	9 43 32	19 48	24 11	29 16 R	8 09	27 50	22 11	21 14	28 11 R	12 56 R	17 02 R	21 44	13 57	2 50	21 53	27 20 R
3 Su	22 49 16	10 41 37	1 ♒ 59	24 13	28 51	9 21	28 29	22 22	21 14	28 09	12 55	17 01	22 07	14 00	2 53	22 23	27 17
4 M	22 53 13	11 39 43	14 24	24 14 R	28 35	10 33	29 07	22 33	21 15	28 08	12 53	17 00	22 30	14 04	2 56	22 52	27 15
5 T	22 57 10	12 37 51	27 04	24 14	28 26 D	11 45	29 45	22 45	21 16	28 06	12 51	17 00	22 53	14 07	2 59	23 22	27 12
6 W	23 1 6	13 36 00	10 ♓ 02	24 13	28 27	12 57	0 ♍ 23	22 56	21 17	28 05	12 50	16 59	23 16	14 09	3 02	23 52	27 09
7 Th	23 5 3	14 34 11	23 16	24 12	28 36	14 10	1 01	23 07	21 19	28 03	12 48	16 58	23 39	14 12	3 06	24 21	27 07
8 F	23 8 59	15 32 24	6 ♈ 46	24 09	28 53	15 22	1 39	23 19	21 20	28 02	12 46	16 58	24 02	14 13	3 10	24 51	27 04
9 Sa	23 12 56	16 30 39	20 31	24 06	29 20	16 35	2 17	23 30	21 21	28 00	12 45	16 57	24 25	14 15	3 15	25 21	27 01
10 Su	23 16 52	17 28 55	4 ♉ 27	24 03	29 55	17 47	2 55	23 42	21 23	27 58	12 43	16 56	24 47	14 16	3 20	25 51	26 59
11 M	23 20 49	18 27 14	18 31	24 00	0 ♍ 39	19 00	3 33	23 54	21 24	27 57	12 42	16 56	25 10	14 16 R	3 25	26 20	26 56
12 T	23 24 45	19 25 35	2 ♊ 40	23 58	1 30	20 12	4 11	24 05	21 26	27 55	12 40	16 55	25 32	14 16	3 30	26 50	26 53
13 W	23 28 42	20 23 58	16 52	23 57 D	2 30	21 25	4 50	24 17	21 28	27 53	12 38	16 55	25 55	14 16	3 36	27 20	26 51
14 Th	23 32 39	21 22 23	1 ♋ 04	23 57	3 36	22 38	5 28	24 29	21 29	27 51	12 37	16 55	26 17	14 15	3 42	27 50	26 48
15 F	23 36 35	22 20 50	15 14	23 58	4 49	23 51	6 06	24 41	21 31	27 49	12 35	16 54	26 39	14 14	3 49	28 20	26 45
16 Sa	23 40 32	23 19 20	29 20	24 00	6 08	25 04	6 44	24 53	21 33	27 48	12 33	16 54	27 01	14 12	3 55	28 50	26 42
17 Su	23 44 28	24 17 52	13 ♌ 20	24 01 R	7 32	26 17	7 22	25 05	21 35	27 46	12 32	16 53	27 23	14 10	4 03	29 20	26 40
18 M	23 48 25	25 16 25	27 12	24 01	9 01	27 30	8 00	25 17	21 38	27 44	12 30	16 53	27 45	14 08	4 10	29 50	26 37
19 T	23 52 21	26 15 01	10 ♍ 54	24 00	10 34	28 43	8 38	25 29	21 40	27 42	12 29	16 53	28 07	14 05	4 18	0 ♎ 20	26 34
20 W	23 56 18	27 13 39	24 24	23 57	12 11	29 56	9 16	25 41	21 42	27 40	12 27	16 52	28 29	14 01	4 26	0 50	26 32
21 Th	0 0 14	28 12 18	7 ♎ 38	23 53	13 51	1 ♍ 09	9 54	25 53	21 45	27 38	12 25	16 52	28 51	13 57	4 34	1 21	26 29
22 F	0 4 11	29 11 00	20 37	23 47	15 33	2 23	10 32	26 06	21 47	27 36	12 24	16 52	29 12	13 52	4 43	1 51	26 26
23 Sa	0 8 8	0 ♎ 09 43	3 ♏ 20	23 41	17 18	3 36	11 10	26 18	21 50	27 34	12 22	16 52	29 34	13 47	4 52	2 21	26 23
24 Su	0 12 4	1 08 28	15 46	23 35	19 04	4 50	11 48	26 30	21 53	27 32	12 21	16 52	29 55	13 42	5 01	2 51	26 21
25 M	0 16 1	2 07 15	27 59	23 29	20 52	6 03	12 26	26 43	21 56	27 29	12 19	16 51	0 ♌ 16	13 36	5 10	3 21	26 18
26 T	0 19 57	3 06 04	10 ♐ 00	23 25	22 40	7 17	13 04	26 55	21 59	27 27	12 18	16 51	0 37	13 29	5 20	3 52	26 15
27 W	0 23 54	4 04 55	21 54	23 22	24 29	8 30	13 42	27 08	22 02	27 25	12 16	16 51	0 58	13 22	5 30	4 22	26 12
28 Th	0 27 50	5 03 47	3 ♑ 45	23 21 D	26 18	9 44	14 20	27 20	22 05	27 23	12 15	16 51 D	1 19	13 15	5 40	4 52	26 10
29 F	0 31 47	6 02 41	15 38	23 22	28 08	10 57	14 58	27 33	22 08	27 21	12 13	16 51	1 40	13 07	5 51	5 22	26 07
30 Sa	0 35 43	7 01 37	27 39	23 23	29 57	12 11	15 36	27 45	22 11	27 18	12 12	16 51	2 01	12 58	6 02	5 53	26 04

EPHEMERIS CALCULATED FOR 12 MIDNIGHT GREENWICH MEAN TIME. ALL OTHER DATA AND FACING ASPECTARIAN PAGE IN **EASTERN TIME (BOLD)** AND PACIFIC TIME (REGULAR).

OCTOBER 2017

☽ Last Aspect day	ET / hr:mn / PT		asp	☽ Ingress sign	day	ET / hr:mn / PT	
2	**7:13 am**	4:13 am	△ ♃	♓	2	**10:26 am**	7:26 am
4	**3:19 am**	12:19 am	□ ♄	♈	4	**4:40 pm**	1:40 pm
6	**6:38 pm**	3:38 pm	☍ ♃	♉	6	**7:56 pm**	4:56 pm
8	**9:45 am**	6:45 am	△ ♀	♊	8	**9:44 pm**	6:44 pm
10	**6:25 pm**	3:25 pm	⚹ ♅	♋	10	**11:38 pm**	8:38 pm
12		9:00 pm	⚹ ♀	♌	12		11:41 pm
13	**12:00 am**		⚹ ♀	♌	13	**2:41 am**	
14		10:28 pm	△ ♅	♍	15	**7:19 am**	4:19 am
15	**1:28 am**		△ ♅	♍	15	**7:19 am**	4:19 am
17	**7:27 am**	4:27 am	☌ ♂	♎	17	**1:35 pm**	10:35 am

☽ Last Aspect day	ET / hr:mn / PT		asp	☽ Ingress sign	day	ET / hr:mn / PT	
19	**3:12 pm**	12:12 pm	☌ ☉	♏	19	**9:41 pm**	6:41 pm
22	**7:35 am**	4:35 am	⚹ ♂	♐	22	**7:57 am**	4:57 am
24	**12:44 pm**	9:44 am	△ ♅	♑	24	**8:12 pm**	5:12 pm
26		10:22 pm	□ ♅	♒	27	**8:59 am**	5:59 am
27	**1:22 am**		□ ♅	♒	27	**8:59 am**	5:59 am
29	**12:22 pm**	9:22 am	⚹ ♅	♓	29	**7:46 pm**	4:46 pm
31	**5:08 pm**	2:08 pm	□ ♄	♈	31		11:43 pm
31	**5:08 pm**	2:08 pm	□ ♄	♈	11/1	**2:43 am**	

☽ Phases & Eclipses phase	day	ET / hr:mn / PT	
Full Moon	5	**2:40 pm**	11:40 am
4th Quarter	12	**8:25 am**	5:25 am
New Moon	19	**3:12 pm**	12:12 pm
2nd Quarter	27	**6:22 pm**	3:22 pm

Planet Ingress		day	ET / hr:mn / PT	
♃	♏	10	**9:20 am**	6:20 am
♀	♎	14	**6:11 am**	3:11 am
☿	♏	17	**3:59 am**	12:59 am
♂	♎	22	**2:29 pm**	11:29 am
☉	♏	22		10:27 pm
☉	♏	23	**1:27 am**	

Planetary Motion	day	ET / hr:mn / PT

1 SUNDAY
- ☽ ⚺ ♆ **12:30 am**
- ☽ ⚻ ♀ **3:40 am** 12:40 am
- ☽ ⚻ ♂ **9:00 am** 6:00 am
- ☽ ⚺ ♇ **9:33 am** 6:33 am
- ♂ △ ♇ **7:36 pm** 4:36 pm
- ☽ ⚹ ♄ **7:56 pm** 4:56 pm

2 MONDAY
- ☽ ⚹ ♅ **5:13 am** 2:13 am
- ☽ △ ♃ **7:13 am** 4:13 am
- ☽ ⚻ ☿ **8:30 pm** 5:30 pm

3 TUESDAY
- ☽ ⚻ ☉ **5:35 am** 2:35 am
- ☽ ☌ ♆ **8:45 am** 5:45 am
- ♀ △ ♇ **3:09 pm** 12:09 pm
- ☽ ⚹ ♇ **5:20 pm** 2:20 pm
- ☽ ☍ ♀ **5:34 pm** 2:34 pm
- ☽ ☍ ♂ **7:36 pm** 4:36 pm

4 WEDNESDAY
- ☽ □ ♄ **3:19 am** 12:19 am
- ☽ ⚺ ♅ **11:37 am** 8:37 am
- ☽ ⚻ ♃ **2:29 pm** 11:29 am
- ☉ ⚻ ♆ **11:09 pm** 8:09 pm

5 THURSDAY
- ☽ ☍ ☿ **10:00 am** 7:00 am
- ♀ ☌ ♂ **12:53 pm** 9:53 am
- ☽ ⚺ ♆ **1:33 pm** 10:33 am
- ☽ ☍ ☉ **2:40 pm** 11:40 am
- ☽ □ ♇ **9:46 pm** 6:46 pm

Eastern time in bold type
Pacific time in medium type

- ☽ ⚻ ♂ 11:21 pm
- ☽ ⚻ ♀ 11:58 pm

6 FRIDAY
- ☽ ⚻ ♂ **2:21 am**
- ☽ ⚻ ♀ **2:58 am**
- ☽ △ ♄ **7:26 am** 4:26 am
- ☿ ⚻ ♆ **1:44 pm** 10:44 am
- ☽ ☌ ♅ **2:58 pm** 11:58 am
- ☽ ☍ ♃ **6:38 pm** 3:38 pm

7 SATURDAY
- ☽ ⚹ ♆ **3:58 pm** 12:58 pm
- ☽ ⚻ ☿ **7:37 pm** 4:37 pm
- ☽ ⚻ ☉ **8:49 pm** 5:49 pm
- ☽ △ ♇ 9:01 pm

8 SUNDAY
- ☽ △ ♇ **12:01 am**
- ☽ △ ♂ **6:46 am** 3:46 am
- ♀ □ ♄ **8:54 am** 5:54 am
- ☽ ⚻ ♄ **9:41 am** 6:41 am
- ☽ △ ♀ **9:45 am** 6:45 am
- ☽ ⚺ ♅ **4:43 pm** 1:43 pm
- ☉ ☌ ☿ **4:54 pm** 1:54 pm
- ☽ ⚻ ♃ **9:12 pm** 6:12 pm

9 MONDAY
- ☿ □ ♇ **8:26 am** 5:26 am
- ☽ □ ♆ **5:34 pm** 2:34 pm
- ☉ □ ♇ **8:12 pm** 5:12 pm
- ☽ ⚻ ♇ 10:44 pm
- ☽ △ ☉ 11:08 pm

10 TUESDAY
- ☽ ⚻ ♇ **1:44 am**
- ☽ △ ☉ **2:08 am**
- ☽ △ ☿ **4:04 am** 1:04 am
- ☽ □ ♂ **10:47 am** 7:47 am
- ☽ ☍ ♄ **11:41 am** 8:41 am
- ☽ □ ♀ **4:12 pm** 1:12 pm
- ☽ ⚹ ♅ **6:25 pm** 3:25 pm
- ☽ △ ♃ **11:51 pm** 8:51 pm

11 WEDNESDAY
- ♂ □ ♄ **9:37 am** 6:37 am
- ♀ ⚻ ♅ **5:04 pm** 2:04 pm
- ☽ △ ♆ **7:45 pm** 4:45 pm

12 THURSDAY
- ☽ ☍ ♇ **4:13 am** 1:13 am
- ☽ □ ☉ **8:25 am** 5:25 am
- ☽ □ ☿ **1:33 pm** 10:33 am
- ☽ ⚻ ♄ **2:39 pm** 11:39 am
- ☽ ⚹ ♂ **3:52 pm** 12:52 pm
- ☽ □ ♅ **9:10 pm** 6:10 pm
- ☿ ⚹ ♄ **11:02 pm** 8:02 pm
- ☽ ⚹ ♀ 9:00 pm

13 FRIDAY
- ☽ ⚹ ♀ **12:00 am**
- ☽ □ ♃ **3:43 am** 12:43 am
- ☿ ⚺ ♂ **7:07 pm** 4:07 pm
- ☽ ⚻ ♆ **11:20 pm** 8:20 pm

14 SATURDAY
- ☽ ⚻ ♇ **8:10 am** 5:10 am
- ☽ ⚹ ☉ **4:34 pm** 1:34 pm

- ☽ △ ♄ **7:11 pm** 4:11 pm
- ☽ ⚺ ♂ **10:43 pm** 7:43 pm
- ☽ ⚹ ☿ 10:07 pm
- ☽ △ ♅ 10:28 pm
- ♀ ⚺ ♃ 10:45 pm

15 SUNDAY
- ☽ ⚹ ☿ **1:07 am**
- ☽ △ ♅ **1:28 am**
- ♀ ⚺ ♃ **1:45 am**
- ☿ ☍ ♅ **3:52 am** 12:52 am
- ☽ ⚹ ♃ **9:14 am** 6:14 am
- ☽ ⚺ ♀ **9:52 am** 6:52 am

16 MONDAY
- ☽ ☍ ♆ **4:32 am** 1:32 am
- ☉ ⚹ ♄ **7:13 am** 4:13 am
- ☽ △ ♇ **1:44 pm** 10:44 am
- ☽ □ ♄ 10:23 pm
- ☽ ⚺ ☉ 11:45 pm

17 TUESDAY
- ☽ □ ♄ **1:23 am**
- ☽ ⚺ ☉ **2:45 am**
- ♂ ⚻ ♅ **6:03 am** 3:03 am
- ☽ ⚻ ♅ **7:22 am** 4:22 am
- ☽ ☌ ♂ **7:27 am** 4:27 am
- ☽ ⚺ ☿ **2:57 pm** 11:57 am
- ☽ ⚺ ♃ **4:29 pm** 1:29 pm
- ☽ ☌ ♀ **9:57 pm** 6:57 pm

18 WEDNESDAY
- ☿ ☌ ♃ **4:54 am** 1:54 am
- ☽ ⚻ ♆ **11:24 am** 8:24 am
- ☽ □ ♇ **9:02 pm** 6:02 pm

19 THURSDAY
- ☽ ⚹ ♄ **9:24 am** 6:24 am
- ☉ ☍ ♅ **1:35 pm** 10:35 am
- ☽ ☍ ♅ **3:04 pm** 12:04 pm
- ☽ ☌ ☉ **3:12 pm** 12:12 pm
- ☽ ⚺ ♂ **6:16 pm** 3:16 pm
- ☽ ☌ ♃ 10:41 pm

20 FRIDAY
- ☽ ☌ ♃ **1:41 am**
- ☽ ☌ ☿ **7:23 am** 4:23 am
- ☽ ⚺ ♀ **12:35 pm** 9:35 am
- ☽ △ ♆ **8:14 pm** 5:14 pm

21 SATURDAY
- ☽ ⚹ ♇ **6:23 am** 3:23 am
- ☽ ⚺ ♄ **7:34 pm** 4:34 pm
- ☽ ⚻ ♅ 9:53 pm

22 SUNDAY
- ☽ ⚻ ♅ **12:53 am**
- ☽ ⚺ ☉ **6:23 am** 3:23 am
- ☽ ⚹ ♂ **7:35 am** 4:35 am
- ☽ ⚺ ♃ **1:10 pm** 10:10 am
- ☽ ⚺ ☿ 11:56 pm

23 MONDAY
- ☽ ⚺ ☿ **2:56 am**
- ☽ ⚹ ♀ **6:14 am** 3:14 am
- ☽ □ ♆ **7:17 am** 4:17 am
- ♀ ⚻ ♆ **4:11 pm** 1:11 pm
- ☽ ⚺ ♇ **5:56 pm** 2:56 pm
- ☉ ⚺ ♂ **8:27 pm** 5:27 pm

24 TUESDAY
- ☽ ☌ ♄ **7:55 am** 4:55 am
- ☿ △ ♆ **11:55 am** 8:55 am
- ☽ △ ♅ **12:44 pm** 9:44 am
- ☽ □ ♂ **11:14 pm** 8:14 pm
- ☽ ⚹ ☉ 9:08 pm
- ☽ ⚹ ♃ 11:42 pm

25 WEDNESDAY
- ☽ ⚹ ☉ **12:08 am**
- ☽ ⚹ ♃ **2:42 am**
- ☽ ⚹ ♆ **7:55 pm** 4:55 pm
- ☽ ⚹ ☿ 9:49 pm
- ☽ □ ♀ 11:06 pm

26 THURSDAY
- ☽ ⚹ ☿ **12:49 am**
- ☽ □ ♀ **2:06 am**
- ☽ ☌ ♇ **6:49 am** 3:49 am
- ☉ ☌ ♃ **2:09 pm** 11:09 am
- ☽ ⚺ ♄ **9:13 pm** 6:13 pm
- ☽ □ ♅ 10:22 pm

27 FRIDAY
- ☽ □ ♅ **1:22 am**
- ☽ △ ♂ **3:21 pm** 12:21 pm
- ☽ □ ♃ **4:30 pm** 1:30 pm
- ☽ □ ☉ **6:22 pm** 3:22 pm
- ♀ □ ♇ **11:21 pm** 8:21 pm
- ☿ ⚹ ♇ **11:25 pm** 8:25 pm
- ☿ ⚺ ♀ **11:42 pm** 8:42 pm

28 SATURDAY
- ☽ ⚺ ♆ **8:10 am** 5:10 am
- ☽ ⚺ ♇ **6:51 pm** 3:51 pm
- ☽ △ ♀ **9:02 pm** 6:02 pm
- ☽ □ ☿ **9:35 pm** 6:35 pm
- ♂ ⚺ ♃ 9:16 pm

29 SUNDAY
- ♂ ⚺ ♃ **12:16 am**
- ☽ ⚹ ♄ **9:01 am** 6:01 am
- ☽ ⚹ ♅ **12:22 pm** 9:22 am

30 MONDAY
- ☽ △ ♃ **3:54 am** 12:54 am
- ☽ ⚻ ♂ **4:50 am** 1:50 am
- ☽ △ ☉ **9:34 am** 6:34 am
- ☽ ☌ ♆ **5:32 pm** 2:32 pm

31 TUESDAY
- ☽ ⚹ ♇ **3:38 am** 12:38 am
- ☽ ⚻ ♀ **11:28 am** 8:28 am
- ☽ △ ☿ **1:21 pm** 10:21 am
- ☽ □ ♄ **5:08 pm** 2:08 pm
- ☽ ⚺ ♅ **7:41 pm** 4:41 pm

OCTOBER 2017

DATE	SID.TIME	SUN	MOON	NODE	MERCURY	VENUS	MARS	JUPITER	SATURN	URANUS	NEPTUNE	PLUTO	CERES	PALLAS	JUNO	VESTA	CHIRON
1 Su	0 39 40	8 ♎ 00 34	9 ♒ 51	23 ♌ 25	1 ♎ 46	13 ♍ 25	16 ♍ 14	27 ♎ 58	22 ♐ 15	27 ♈ 16	12 ♓ 10	16 ♑ 51	2 ♌ 21	12 ♉ 49	6 ♑ 13	6 ♎ 23	26 ♓ 02
2 M	0 43 36	8 59 34	22 20	23 25 ℞	3 35	14 39	16 52	28 11	22 18	27 14 ℞	12 09 ℞	16 51	2 42	12 40 ℞	6 24	6 54	25 59 ℞
3 T	0 47 33	9 58 35	5 ♓ 09	23 25	5 23	15 53	17 30	28 23	22 22	27 12	12 07	16 52	3 02	12 30	6 36	7 24	25 56
4 W	0 51 30	10 57 38	18 20	23 22	7 11	17 07	18 08	28 36	22 25	27 09	12 06	16 52	3 22	12 19	6 48	7 54	25 54
5 Th	0 55 26	11 56 43	1 ♈ 55	23 17	8 58	18 21	18 46	28 49	22 29	27 07	12 05	16 52	3 42	12 09	7 00	8 25	25 51
6 F	0 59 23	12 55 49	15 50	23 10	10 44	19 35	19 24	29 01	22 33	27 05	12 03	16 52	4 02	11 57	7 12	8 55	25 49
7 Sa	1 3 19	13 54 58	0 ♉ 02	23 02	12 30	20 49	20 02	29 14	22 36	27 02	12 02	16 52	4 22	11 45	7 25	9 26	25 46
8 Su	1 7 16	14 54 09	14 27	22 54	14 15	22 03	20 40	29 27	22 40	27 00	12 01	16 52	4 42	11 33	7 38	9 56	25 43
9 M	1 11 12	15 53 23	28 57	22 46	15 59	23 17	21 18	29 40	22 44	26 57	11 59	16 53	5 01	11 20	7 51	10 27	25 41
10 T	1 15 9	16 52 38	13 ♊ 26	22 40	17 43	24 31	21 56	29 53	22 49	26 55	11 58	16 53	5 20	11 07	8 04	10 57	25 38
11 W	1 19 5	17 51 56	27 50	22 36	19 26	25 45	22 34	0 ♏ 06	22 53	26 53	11 57	16 53	5 40	10 53	8 18	11 28	25 36
12 Th	1 23 2	18 51 17	12 ♋ 04	22 35 D	21 08	27 00	23 12	0 19	22 57	26 50	11 55	16 54	5 59	10 39	8 32	11 59	25 33
13 F	1 26 59	19 50 39	26 07	22 35	22 49	28 14	23 49	0 32	23 01	26 48	11 54	16 54	6 18	10 24	8 46	12 29	25 31
14 Sa	1 30 55	20 50 04	9 ♌ 58	22 35 ℞	24 30	29 28	24 27	0 45	23 06	26 45	11 53	16 55	6 36	10 09	9 00	13 00	25 29
15 Su	1 34 52	21 49 31	23 38	22 36	26 10	0 ♎ 43	25 05	0 58	23 10	26 43	11 52	16 55	6 55	9 54	9 15	13 30	25 26
16 M	1 38 48	22 49 01	7 ♍ 06	22 35	27 49	1 57	25 43	1 11	23 15	26 41	11 51	16 56	7 13	9 38	9 29	14 01	25 24
17 T	1 42 45	23 48 33	20 23	22 32	29 27	3 12	26 21	1 24	23 19	26 38	11 50	16 56	7 32	9 22	9 44	14 32	25 22
18 W	1 46 41	24 48 07	3 ♎ 29	22 26	1 ♏ 05	4 26	26 59	1 37	23 24	26 36	11 48	16 57	7 50	9 05	9 59	15 02	25 19
19 Th	1 50 38	25 47 43	16 24	22 17	2 43	5 41	27 37	1 50	23 29	26 33	11 47	16 57	8 08	8 48	10 15	15 33	25 17
20 F	1 54 34	26 47 21	29 07	22 06	4 19	6 56	28 15	2 03	23 34	26 31	11 46	16 58	8 26	8 31	10 30	16 04	25 15
21 Sa	1 58 31	27 47 01	11 ♏ 38	21 54	5 55	8 10	28 53	2 16	23 38	26 28	11 45	16 59	8 43	8 13	10 46	16 34	25 13
22 Su	2 2 28	28 46 43	23 57	21 41	7 30	9 25	29 31	2 29	23 43	26 26	11 44	16 59	9 01	7 56	11 02	17 05	25 10
23 M	2 6 24	29 46 27	6 ♐ 04	21 30	9 05	10 40	0 ♎ 09	2 42	23 48	26 23	11 43	17 00	9 18	7 37	11 18	17 36	25 08
24 T	2 10 21	0 ♏ 46 13	18 02	21 20	10 40	11 54	0 47	2 55	23 54	26 21	11 42	17 01	9 35	7 19	11 35	18 07	25 06
25 W	2 14 17	1 46 00	29 54	21 13	12 13	13 09	1 25	3 08	23 59	26 19	11 41	17 02	9 52	7 00	11 51	18 37	25 04
26 Th	2 18 14	2 45 49	11 ♑ 43	21 08	13 46	14 24	2 02	3 21	24 04	26 16	11 41	17 02	10 08	6 42	12 08	19 08	25 02
27 F	2 22 10	3 45 41	23 33	21 06 D	15 19	15 39	2 40	3 34	24 09	26 14	11 40	17 03	10 25	6 23	12 25	19 39	25 00
28 Sa	2 26 7	4 45 33	5 ♒ 31	21 06	16 51	16 54	3 18	3 47	24 15	26 11	11 39	17 04	10 41	6 03	12 42	20 10	24 58
29 Su	2 30 3	5 45 28	17 40	21 06 ℞	18 23	18 09	3 56	4 00	24 20	26 09	11 38	17 05	10 57	5 44	12 59	20 40	24 56
30 M	2 34 0	6 45 24	0 ♓ 07	21 06	19 54	19 23	4 34	4 14	24 25	26 06	11 37	17 06	11 13	5 25	13 17	21 11	24 54
31 T	2 37 57	7 45 21	12 57	21 04	21 24	20 38	5 12	4 27	24 31	26 04	11 36	17 07	11 28	5 05	13 34	21 42	24 53

EPHEMERIS CALCULATED FOR 12 MIDNIGHT GREENWICH MEAN TIME. ALL OTHER DATA AND FACING ASPECTARIAN PAGE IN **EASTERN TIME (BOLD)** AND PACIFIC TIME (REGULAR).

NOVEMBER 2017

☽ Last Aspect day	ET / hr:mn / PT		asp	☽ Ingress sign	day	ET / hr:mn / PT	
10/31	**5:08 pm**	2:08 pm	□ ♄	♈	1	**2:43 am**	
2	**11:03 pm**	8:03 pm	☌ ♅	♉	3	**5:46 am**	2:46 am
5	**4:29 am**	1:29 am	☍ ☿	♊	5	**5:26 am**	2:26 am
7	**5:40 am**	2:40 am	△ ♀	♋	7	**5:45 am**	2:45 am
8		9:14 pm	□ ♅	♌	9	**7:29 am**	4:29 am
9	**12:14 am**		□ ♅	♌	9	**7:29 am**	4:29 am
11	**3:55 am**	12:55 am	△ ♅	♍	11	**11:41 am**	8:41 am
13	**10:45 am**	7:45 am	□ ♄	♎	13	**6:26 pm**	3:26 pm
15	**7:50 pm**	4:50 pm	⚹ ♄	♏	16	**3:19 am**	12:19 am
18	**6:42 am**	3:42 am	☌ ☉	♐	18	**1:59 pm**	10:59 am

☽ Last Aspect day	ET / hr:mn / PT		asp	☽ Ingress sign	day	ET / hr:mn / PT	
20	**7:26 pm**	4:26 pm	☌ ♄	♑	20		11:14 pm
20	**7:26 pm**	4:26 pm	☌ ♄	♑	21	**2:14 am**	
23	**5:33 am**	2:33 am	□ ♅	♒	23	**3:14 pm**	12:14 pm
25	**9:37 pm**	6:37 pm	⚹ ♄	♓	26	**3:04 am**	12:04 am
28	**7:09 am**	4:09 am	□ ☿	♈	28	**11:30 am**	8:30 am
30	**1:37 pm**	10:37 am	△ ☿	♉	30	**3:38 pm**	12:38 pm

☽ Phases & Eclipses phase	day	ET / hr:mn / PT	
Full Moon	3		10:23 pm
Full Moon	4	**1:23 am**	
4th Quarter	10	**3:36 pm**	12:36 pm
New Moon	18	**6:42 am**	3:42 am
2nd Quarter	26	**12:03 pm**	9:03 am

Planet Ingress		day	ET / hr:mn / PT	
☿	♐	5	**2:19 pm**	11:19 am
♀	♏	7	**6:38 am**	3:38 am
⚳	♈	15	**9:53 pm**	6:53 pm
⚶	♏	15	**11:16 pm**	8:16 pm
☉	♐	21	**10:05 pm**	7:05 pm

Planetary Motion		day	ET / hr:mn / PT	
♆	D	22	**9:21 am**	6:21 am

1 WEDNESDAY
☽ ⚻ ♃ **11:07 am** 8:07 am
☽ ☍ ♂ **1:42 pm** 10:42 am
☽ ⚻ ☉ **7:40 pm** 4:40 pm
☽ ⚺ ♆ **10:49 pm** 7:49 pm
☿ ⚺ ♄ 10:16 pm

2 THURSDAY
☿ ⚺ ♄ **1:16 am**
☽ □ ♇ **8:18 am** 5:18 am
☽ ☍ ♀ **8:30 pm** 5:30 pm
☿ ⚻ ♅ **9:02 pm** 6:02 pm
☽ △ ♄ **9:09 pm** 6:09 pm
☽ ☌ ♅ **11:03 pm** 8:03 pm
☽ ⚻ ☿ **11:17 pm** 8:17 pm

3 FRIDAY
♀ ⚹ ♄ **4:31 am** 1:31 am
☽ ☍ ♃ **2:26 pm** 11:26 am
☉ △ ♆ **3:23 pm** 12:23 pm
☽ ⚻ ♂ **6:22 pm** 3:22 pm
☽ ⚹ ♆ 9:42 pm
♀ ☍ ♅ 10:02 pm
☽ ☍ ☉ 10:23 pm

4 SATURDAY
☽ ⚹ ♆ **12:42 am**
♀ ☍ ♅ **1:02 am**
☽ ☍ ☉ **1:23 am**
☽ △ ♇ **9:49 am** 6:49 am
☽ ⚻ ♄ **10:24 pm** 7:24 pm

☽ ⚺ ♅ **11:48 pm** 8:48 pm
☽ ⚻ ♀ 10:56 pm

5 SUNDAY
☽ ⚻ ♀ **1:56 am**
☽ ☍ ☿ **4:29 am** 1:29 am
☽ ⚻ ♃ **2:36 pm** 11:36 am
☽ △ ♂ **7:53 pm** 4:53 pm
☽ □ ♆ **11:57 pm** 8:57 pm

6 MONDAY
☽ ⚻ ☉ **4:08 am** 1:08 am
☽ ⚻ ♇ **9:05 am** 6:05 am
☽ ☍ ♄ **9:57 pm** 6:57 pm
☽ ⚹ ♅ **10:55 pm** 7:55 pm

7 TUESDAY
☽ △ ♀ **5:40 am** 2:40 am
☽ ⚻ ☿ **10:02 am** 7:02 am
☽ △ ♃ **3:47 pm** 12:47 pm
☽ □ ♂ **10:39 pm** 7:39 pm
☽ △ ♆ 9:36 pm

8 WEDNESDAY
☽ △ ♆ **12:36 am**
☽ △ ☉ **8:34 am** 5:34 am
☽ ☍ ♇ **10:06 am** 7:06 am
☽ ⚻ ♄ **11:43 pm** 8:43 pm
☽ □ ♅ 9:14 pm

9 THURSDAY
☽ □ ♅ **12:14 am**
☉ ⚹ ♇ **7:12 am** 4:12 am

☽ □ ♀ **12:15 pm** 9:15 am
☽ △ ☿ **5:36 pm** 2:36 pm
☽ □ ♃ **6:46 pm** 3:46 pm
♂ ⚻ ♆ **7:10 pm** 4:10 pm

10 FRIDAY
☽ ⚻ ♆ **3:12 am** 12:12 am
☽ ⚹ ♂ **3:35 am** 12:35 am
☿ ⚺ ♃ **7:07 am** 4:07 am
☽ ⚻ ♇ **1:17 pm** 10:17 am
☽ □ ☉ **3:36 pm** 12:36 pm

11 SATURDAY
☽ △ ♄ **3:55 am** 12:55 am
☽ △ ♅ **3:55 am** 12:55 am
♄ △ ♅ **4:45 am** 1:45 am
☽ ⚹ ♀ **10:07 pm** 7:07 pm
☽ ⚹ ♃ 9:26 pm

12 SUNDAY
☽ ⚹ ♃ **12:26 am**
☽ □ ☿ **4:31 am** 1:31 am
☽ ☍ ♆ **8:23 am** 5:23 am
☽ ⚺ ♂ **11:29 am** 8:29 am
☽ △ ♇ **7:05 pm** 4:05 pm
☽ ⚹ ☉ 10:55 pm

13 MONDAY
☽ ⚹ ☉ **1:55 am**
♀ ☌ ♃ **3:16 am** 12:16 am
☽ ⚻ ♅ **10:10 am** 7:10 am
☽ □ ♄ **10:45 am** 7:45 am
☿ □ ♆ **5:48 pm** 2:48 pm

14 TUESDAY
☽ ⚺ ♃ **8:40 am** 5:40 am
☽ ⚺ ♀ **11:20 am** 8:20 am
☽ ⚻ ♆ **3:59 pm** 12:59 pm
☽ ⚹ ☿ **6:37 pm** 3:37 pm
☽ ☌ ♂ **10:09 pm** 7:09 pm

15 WEDNESDAY
☽ □ ♇ **3:12 am** 12:12 am
☽ ⚺ ☉ **3:07 pm** 12:07 pm
☽ ☍ ♅ **6:36 pm** 3:36 pm
☽ ⚹ ♄ **7:50 pm** 4:50 pm

16 THURSDAY
♀ △ ♆ **10:21 am** 7:21 am
☽ ☌ ♃ **7:02 pm** 4:02 pm
☽ △ ♆ 10:33 pm

17 FRIDAY
☽ △ ♆ **1:33 am**
☽ ☌ ♀ **3:17 am** 12:17 am
☉ ⚻ ♅ **9:04 am** 6:04 am
☿ ⚹ ♂ **9:24 am** 6:24 am
☽ ⚺ ♂ **11:04 am** 8:04 am
☽ ⚺ ☿ **11:10 am** 8:10 am
☽ ⚹ ♇ **1:15 pm** 10:15 am

18 SATURDAY
☽ ⚻ ♅ **4:51 am** 1:51 am
☽ ☌ ☉ **6:42 am** 3:42 am
☽ ⚺ ♄ **6:48 am** 3:48 am
☿ ⚺ ♇ **7:50 am** 4:50 am
☉ ⚺ ♄ **8:03 am** 5:03 am

19 SUNDAY
☽ ⚺ ♃ **7:14 am** 4:14 am
♂ □ ♇ **7:15 am** 4:15 am
☽ □ ♆ **12:51 pm** 9:51 am
☽ ⚺ ♀ **9:37 pm** 6:37 pm
☽ ⚺ ♇ 10:01 pm
☽ ⚹ ♂ 10:58 pm

20 MONDAY
☽ ⚺ ♇ **1:01 am**
☽ ⚹ ♂ **1:58 am**
☽ ☌ ☿ **5:37 am** 2:37 am
☽ △ ♅ **4:43 pm** 1:43 pm
☽ ☌ ♄ **7:26 pm** 4:26 pm
☽ ⚺ ☉ 9:23 pm

21 TUESDAY
☽ ⚺ ☉ **12:23 am**
♀ ⚹ ♇ **6:29 am** 3:29 am
☽ ⚹ ♃ **8:57 pm** 5:57 pm
☽ ⚹ ♆ 10:33 pm

22 WEDNESDAY
☽ ⚹ ♆ **1:33 am**
☽ ☌ ♇ **2:00 pm** 11:00 am
☽ ⚹ ♀ **5:41 pm** 2:41 pm
☽ □ ♂ **6:16 pm** 3:16 pm
☽ ⚺ ☿ 9:58 pm

23 THURSDAY
☽ ⚺ ☿ **12:58 am**
♀ ⚺ ♂ **4:10 am** 1:10 am
☽ □ ♅ **5:33 am** 2:33 am

☽ ⚺ ♄ **9:01 am** 6:01 am
☽ ⚹ ☉ **7:05 pm** 4:05 pm

24 FRIDAY
☽ □ ♃ **10:56 am** 7:56 am
☽ ⚺ ♆ **2:23 pm** 11:23 am
☽ ⚺ ♇ 11:44 pm

25 SATURDAY
☽ ⚺ ♇ **2:44 am**
☿ △ ♅ **5:56 am** 2:56 am
☽ △ ♂ **10:05 am** 7:05 am
☽ □ ♀ **1:12 pm** 10:12 am
☽ ⚹ ♅ **5:35 pm** 2:35 pm
☽ ⚹ ☿ **6:32 pm** 3:32 pm
☽ ⚹ ♄ **9:37 pm** 6:37 pm

26 SUNDAY
☽ □ ☉ **12:03 pm** 9:03 am
☽ △ ♃ **10:52 pm** 7:52 pm
☽ ☌ ♆ 10:08 pm

27 MONDAY
☽ ☌ ♆ **1:08 am**
♀ ⚻ ♅ **6:48 am** 3:48 am
☽ ⚹ ♇ **12:54 pm** 9:54 am
☽ ⚻ ♂ **10:37 pm** 7:37 pm
☿ ☌ ♄ 10:58 pm
☽ ⚺ ♅ 11:33 pm

28 TUESDAY
☿ ☌ ♄ **1:58 am**
☽ ⚺ ♅ **2:33 am**
☽ △ ♀ **4:41 am** 1:41 am
☽ □ ♄ **6:55 am** 3:55 am

☽ □ ☿ **7:09 am** 4:09 am
☽ △ ☉ 9:22 pm

29 WEDNESDAY
☽ △ ☉ **12:22 am**
♀ ⚺ ♄ **6:11 am** 3:11 am
☽ ⚻ ♃ **6:41 am** 3:41 am
☽ ⚺ ♆ **7:57 am** 4:57 am
☽ □ ♇ **6:53 pm** 3:53 pm
☿ ⚺ ♀ 10:00 pm

30 THURSDAY
☿ ⚺ ♀ **1:00 am**
☽ ☍ ♂ **6:13 am** 3:13 am
☽ ☌ ♅ **7:16 am** 4:16 am
☽ △ ♄ **11:50 am** 8:50 am
☽ △ ☿ **1:37 pm** 10:37 am
☽ ⚻ ♀ **2:25 pm** 11:25 am

Eastern time in bold type
Pacific time in medium type

NOVEMBER 2017

DATE	SID.TIME	SUN	MOON	NODE	MERCURY	VENUS	MARS	JUPITER	SATURN	URANUS	NEPTUNE	PLUTO	CERES	PALLAS	JUNO	VESTA	CHIRON
1 W	2 41 53	8 ♏ 45 20	26 ♓ 13	21 ♌ 00	22 ♏ 54	21 ♎ 53	5 ♎ 50	4 ♏ 40	24 ♐ 37	26 ♈ 02	11 ♓ 36	17 ♑ 08	11 ♌ 44	4 ♉ 46	13 ♑ 52	22 ♎ 13	24 ♓ 51
2 Th	2 45 50	9 45 21	9 ♈ 56	20 53 ℞	24 24	23 08	6 28	4 53	24 42	25 59 ℞	11 35 ℞	17 09	11 59	4 26 ℞	14 10	22 44	24 49 ℞
3 F	2 49 46	10 45 24	24 07	20 44	25 53	24 23	7 05	5 06	24 48	25 57	11 34	17 10	12 14	4 06	14 28	23 14	24 47
4 Sa	2 53 43	11 45 28	8 ♉ 41	20 32	27 22	25 38	7 43	5 19	24 54	25 55	11 34	17 11	12 28	3 47	14 47	23 45	24 46
5 Su	2 57 39	12 45 34	23 30	20 21	28 50	26 53	8 21	5 32	24 59	25 52	11 33	17 12	12 43	3 27	15 05	24 16	24 44
6 M	3 1 36	13 45 43	8 ♊ 27	20 10	0 ♐ 17	28 08	8 59	5 45	25 05	25 50	11 33	17 13	12 57	3 08	15 24	24 47	24 42
7 T	3 5 32	14 45 53	23 22	20 00	1 44	29 24	9 37	5 58	25 11	25 48	11 32	17 14	13 11	2 48	15 43	25 17	24 41
8 W	3 9 29	15 46 05	8 ♋ 07	19 54	3 10	0 ♏ 39	10 15	6 11	25 17	25 45	11 32	17 15	13 25	2 29	16 02	25 48	24 39
9 Th	3 13 26	16 46 19	22 36	19 50	4 36	1 54	10 53	6 24	25 23	25 43	11 31	17 16	13 38	2 10	16 21	26 19	24 38
10 F	3 17 22	17 46 35	6 ♌ 45	19 49	6 01	3 09	11 30	6 37	25 29	25 41	11 31	17 18	13 51	1 51	16 40	26 50	24 37
11 Sa	3 21 19	18 46 54	20 34	19 49	7 25	4 24	12 08	6 50	25 35	25 39	11 30	17 19	14 04	1 32	16 59	27 21	24 35
12 Su	3 25 15	19 47 14	4 ♍ 05	19 49	8 49	5 39	12 46	7 03	25 42	25 37	11 30	17 20	14 17	1 14	17 19	27 51	24 34
13 M	3 29 12	20 47 36	17 19	19 47	10 12	6 55	13 24	7 16	25 48	25 34	11 30	17 21	14 29	0 55	17 39	28 22	24 33
14 T	3 33 8	21 48 00	0 ♎ 18	19 43	11 33	8 10	14 02	7 29	25 54	25 32	11 29	17 23	14 41	0 37	17 59	28 53	24 32
15 W	3 37 5	22 48 26	13 05	19 35	12 54	9 25	14 40	7 42	26 00	25 30	11 29	17 24	14 53	0 20	18 19	29 24	24 30
16 Th	3 41 1	23 48 53	25 41	19 25	14 14	10 40	15 17	7 55	26 07	25 28	11 29	17 25	15 05	0 02	18 39	29 55	24 29
17 F	3 44 58	24 49 23	8 ♏ 07	19 12	15 32	11 56	15 55	8 08	26 13	25 26	11 28	17 27	15 16	29 ♈ 45	18 59	0 ♏ 25	24 28
18 Sa	3 48 54	25 49 54	20 23	18 58	16 48	13 11	16 33	8 20	26 19	25 24	11 28	17 28	15 27	29 28	19 20	0 56	24 27
19 Su	3 52 51	26 50 27	2 ♐ 32	18 43	18 04	14 26	17 11	8 33	26 26	25 22	11 28	17 29	15 37	29 12	19 40	1 27	24 26
20 M	3 56 48	27 51 01	14 32	18 30	19 17	15 42	17 49	8 46	26 32	25 20	11 28	17 31	15 48	28 56	20 01	1 58	24 26
21 T	4 0 44	28 51 36	26 26	18 18	20 28	16 57	18 27	8 59	26 39	25 18	11 28	17 32	15 58	28 40	20 22	2 28	24 25
22 W	4 4 41	29 52 14	8 ♑ 15	18 09	21 36	18 12	19 04	9 11	26 45	25 16	11 28 D	17 34	16 07	28 25	20 43	2 59	24 24
23 Th	4 8 37	0 ♐ 52 52	20 02	18 03	22 42	19 28	19 42	9 24	26 52	25 14	11 28	17 35	16 17	28 11	21 04	3 30	24 23
24 F	4 12 34	1 53 31	1 ♒ 51	17 59	23 45	20 43	20 20	9 37	26 59	25 13	11 28	17 37	16 26	27 57	21 25	4 00	24 23
25 Sa	4 16 30	2 54 12	13 46	17 58 D	24 44	21 59	20 58	9 49	27 05	25 11	11 28	17 38	16 34	27 43	21 46	4 31	24 22
26 Su	4 20 27	3 54 54	25 53	17 58 ℞	25 39	23 14	21 35	10 02	27 12	25 09	11 28	17 40	16 43	27 30	22 08	5 02	24 21
27 M	4 24 24	4 55 37	8 ♓ 15	17 58	26 30	24 29	22 13	10 14	27 19	25 07	11 28	17 42	16 51	27 17	22 29	5 32	24 21
28 T	4 28 20	5 56 20	20 59	17 57	27 15	25 45	22 51	10 27	27 25	25 06	11 28	17 43	16 58	27 05	22 51	6 03	24 21
29 W	4 32 17	6 57 05	4 ♈ 10	17 54	27 55	27 00	23 29	10 39	27 32	25 04	11 29	17 45	17 06	26 54	23 13	6 34	24 20
30 Th	4 36 13	7 57 51	17 50	17 49	28 27	28 16	24 06	10 52	27 39	25 02	11 29	17 47	17 13	26 43	23 35	7 04	24 20

EPHEMERIS CALCULATED FOR 12 MIDNIGHT GREENWICH MEAN TIME. ALL OTHER DATA AND FACING ASPECTARIAN PAGE IN **EASTERN TIME (BOLD)** AND PACIFIC TIME (REGULAR).

DECEMBER 2017

☽ Last Aspect day	ET / hr:mn	PT	asp	☽ Ingress sign	day	ET / hr:mn	PT
1	**8:53 pm**	5:53 pm	△♇	♊	2	**4:21 pm**	1:21 pm
4	**2:13 pm**	11:13 am	☍☿	♋	4	**3:37 pm**	12:37 pm
6	**12:56 pm**	9:56 am	□♂	♌	6	**3:37 pm**	12:37 pm
8	**5:40 pm**	2:40 pm	✶♂	♍	8	**6:09 pm**	3:09 pm
10	**10:02 pm**	7:02 pm	□♄	♎	10		9:01 pm
10	**10:02 pm**	7:02 pm	□♄	♎	11	**12:01 am**	
13	**7:27 am**	4:27 am	✶♄	♏	13	**8:59 am**	5:59 am
14	**8:42 pm**	5:42 pm	✶♇	♐	15	**8:07 pm**	5:07 pm
18	**8:10 am**	5:10 am	☌♄	♑	18	**8:33 am**	5:33 am
20	**10:37 am**	7:37 am	□♅	♒	20	**9:29 pm**	6:29 pm
23	**5:13 am**	2:13 am	✶♀	♓	23	**9:42 am**	6:42 am
24	**9:48 pm**	6:48 pm	✶♇	♈	25	**7:27 pm**	4:27 pm
27	**3:57 pm**	12:57 pm	☌♅	♉	27		10:23 pm
27	**3:57 pm**	12:57 pm	☌♅	♉	28	**1:23 am**	
29	**9:01 am**	6:01 am	△♇	♊	30	**3:31 am**	12:31 am
31	**6:38 pm**	3:38 pm	✶♅	♋	1/1	**3:10 am**	12:10 am

☽ Phases & Eclipses phase	day	ET / hr:mn	PT
Full Moon	3	**10:47 am**	7:47 am
4th Quarter	9		11:51 pm
4th Quarter	10	**2:51 am**	
New Moon	17		10:30 pm
New Moon	18	**1:30 am**	
2nd Quarter	26	**4:20 am**	1:20 am

Planet Ingress	day	ET / hr:mn	PT
♀ ♐	1	**4:14 am**	1:14 am
♂ ♏	9	**3:59 am**	12:59 am
✳ ♒	16	**2:18 pm**	11:18 am
♄ ♑	19	**11:49 pm**	8:49 pm
☉ ♑	21	**11:28 am**	8:28 am
♀ ♑	24		9:26 pm
♀ ♑	25	**12:26 am**	

Planetary Motion	day	ET / hr:mn	PT
☿ ℞	2		11:34 pm
☿ ℞	3	**2:34 am**	
⚷ D	5	**4:47 am**	1:47 am
⚳ ℞	16	**5:28 pm**	2:28 pm
♀ D	17	**6:36 pm**	3:36 pm
☿ D	22	**8:51 pm**	5:51 pm

1 FRIDAY
♂☍♅ **5:05 am** 2:05 am
☽⚻☉ **7:21 am** 4:21 am
☽☍♃ **10:07 am** 7:07 am
☽✶♆ **10:36 am** 7:36 am
☽△♇ **8:53 pm** 5:53 pm

2 SATURDAY
☽⚺♅ **8:21 am** 5:21 am
☽⚻♂ **9:35 am** 6:35 am
☽⚻♄ **1:07 pm** 10:07 am
☽⚻☿ **3:13 pm** 12:13 pm
☽☍♀ **7:37 pm** 4:37 pm
♃△♆ **9:19 pm** 6:19 pm

3 SUNDAY
☉□♆ **6:44 am** 3:44 am
☉⚺♃ **9:01 am** 6:01 am
☽□♆ **10:31 am** 7:31 am
☽⚻♃ **10:41 am** 7:41 am
☽☍☉ **10:47 am** 7:47 am
☽⚻♇ **8:34 pm** 5:34 pm

4 MONDAY
☽✶♅ **7:37 am** 4:37 am
☽△♂ **10:57 am** 7:57 am
☽☍♄ **12:46 pm** 9:46 am
☽☍☿ **2:13 pm** 11:13 am
☽⚻♀ **11:08 pm** 8:08 pm

5 TUESDAY
☽△♆ **9:50 am** 6:50 am
☽△♃ **10:38 am** 7:38 am
☽⚻☉ **1:30 pm** 10:30 am
☽☍♇ **8:07 pm** 5:07 pm

6 WEDNESDAY
☿☌♄ **7:05 am** 4:05 am
☽□♅ **7:17 am** 4:17 am
☿✶♂ **10:58 am** 7:58 am
☽⚻☿ **12:46 pm** 9:46 am
☽□♂ **12:56 pm** 9:56 am
☽⚻♄ **1:03 pm** 10:03 am
♂✶♄ **4:21 pm** 1:21 pm

7 THURSDAY
☽△♀ **4:01 am** 1:01 am
☽⚻♆ **10:40 am** 7:40 am
☽□♃ **12:10 pm** 9:10 am
☽△☉ **6:15 pm** 3:15 pm
☽⚻♇ **9:34 pm** 6:34 pm

8 FRIDAY
☽△♅ **9:13 am** 6:13 am
☽△☿ **12:21 pm** 9:21 am
☽△♄ **3:50 pm** 12:50 pm
☽✶♂ **5:40 pm** 2:40 pm

9 SATURDAY
☽□♀ **12:37 pm** 9:37 am
☽☍♆ **2:29 pm** 11:29 am
☽✶♃ **4:50 pm** 1:50 pm
☉⚺♇ **5:58 pm** 2:58 pm
☽△♇ 11:12 pm
☽□☉ 11:51 pm

10 SUNDAY
☽△♇ **2:12 am**
☽□☉ **2:51 am**
☿△♅ **4:29 am** 1:29 am
♀□♆ **8:47 am** 5:47 am
☽□☿ **1:34 pm** 10:34 am
☽⚻♅ **2:25 pm** 11:25 am
☽□♄ **10:02 pm** 7:02 pm
☽⚺♂ 11:16 pm

11 MONDAY
☽⚺♂ **2:16 am**
♀⚺♃ **5:16 pm** 2:16 pm
☽⚻♆ **9:40 pm** 6:40 pm
☽⚺♃ 9:59 pm
☽✶♀ 10:42 pm

12 TUESDAY
☽⚺♃ **12:59 am**
☽✶♀ **1:42 am**
☽□♇ **10:09 am** 7:09 am
☽✶☉ **3:39 pm** 12:39 pm
☽✶☿ **4:32 pm** 1:32 pm
☉☌☿ **8:49 pm** 5:49 pm
☽☍♅ **10:49 pm** 7:49 pm

13 WEDNESDAY
☽✶♄ **7:27 am** 4:27 am
☽☌♂ **2:23 pm** 11:23 am

14 THURSDAY
☽△♆ **7:39 am** 4:39 am
☽☌♃ **11:58 am** 8:58 am
☽⚺♀ **6:29 pm** 3:29 pm
☽✶♇ **8:42 pm** 5:42 pm
☽⚺☿ **9:15 pm** 6:15 pm
☿⚺♇ 11:16 pm

15 FRIDAY
☿⚺♇ **2:16 am**
☽⚺☉ **7:37 am** 4:37 am
☿☌♀ **9:09 am** 6:09 am
☽⚻♅ **9:34 am** 6:34 am
♀⚺♇ **4:23 pm** 1:23 pm
☽⚺♄ **7:08 pm** 4:08 pm

16 SATURDAY
☽⚺♂ **4:57 am** 1:57 am
☉△♅ **6:28 am** 3:28 am
☽□♆ **7:27 pm** 4:27 pm
☽⚺♃ 9:47 pm

17 SUNDAY
☽⚺♃ **12:47 am**
☽☌☿ **3:56 am** 12:56 am
☽⚺♇ **8:53 am** 5:53 am
☽☌♀ **1:34 pm** 10:34 am
☽△♅ **9:46 pm** 6:46 pm
☽☌☉ 10:30 pm

18 MONDAY
☽☌☉ **1:30 am**
☽☌♄ **8:10 am** 5:10 am
☿⚺♃ **2:34 pm** 11:34 am
☽✶♂ **8:55 pm** 5:55 pm

19 TUESDAY
☽✶♆ **8:16 am** 5:16 am
☽⚺☿ **12:54 pm** 9:54 am
☽✶♃ **2:33 pm** 11:33 am
☽☌♇ **9:54 pm** 6:54 pm

20 WEDNESDAY
☽⚺♀ **9:42 am** 6:42 am
☽□♅ **10:37 am** 7:37 am
♀△♅ **6:13 pm** 3:13 pm
☽⚺☉ **8:10 pm** 5:10 pm
☽⚺♄ **9:42 pm** 6:42 pm

21 THURSDAY
☽□♂ **1:13 pm** 10:13 am
☉☌♄ **4:08 pm** 1:08 pm
☽⚺♆ **9:10 pm** 6:10 pm
☽✶☿ **11:54 pm** 8:54 pm

22 FRIDAY
☽□♃ **4:16 am** 1:16 am
☽⚺♇ **10:45 am** 7:45 am
☽✶♅ **11:01 pm** 8:01 pm

23 SATURDAY
☽✶♀ **5:13 am** 2:13 am
☽✶♄ **10:30 am** 7:30 am
☽✶☉ **1:55 pm** 10:55 am

24 SUNDAY
☽△♂ **4:09 am** 1:09 am
☽☌♆ **8:43 am** 5:43 am
☽□☿ **11:31 am** 8:31 am
☽△♃ **4:20 pm** 1:20 pm
☽✶♇ **9:48 pm** 6:48 pm

25 MONDAY
☽⚺♅ **9:18 am** 6:18 am
♀☌♄ **12:55 pm** 9:55 am
☽□♄ **8:44 pm** 5:44 pm
☽□♀ **9:30 pm** 6:30 pm

26 TUESDAY
☽□☉ **4:20 am** 1:20 am
☽⚻♂ **3:37 pm** 12:37 pm
☽⚺♆ **5:09 pm** 2:09 pm
☽△☿ **9:26 pm** 6:26 pm
☽⚻♃ 9:56 pm

27 WEDNESDAY
☽⚻♃ **12:56 am**
☽□♇ **5:25 am** 2:25 am
☽☌♅ **3:57 pm** 12:57 pm
♂△♆ 9:59 pm

28 THURSDAY
♂△♆ **12:59 am**
☽△♄ **3:03 am** 12:03 am
☽△♀ **8:37 am** 5:37 am
☽△☉ **1:47 pm** 10:47 am
☽✶♆ **9:35 pm** 6:35 pm
☽☍♂ **10:29 pm** 7:29 pm

29 FRIDAY
☽⚻☿ **3:59 am** 12:59 am
☽☍♃ **5:22 am** 2:22 am
☽△♇ **9:01 am** 6:01 am
☽⚺♅ **6:41 pm** 3:41 pm

30 SATURDAY
☽⚻♄ **5:28 am** 2:28 am
☿⚺♃ **10:09 am** 7:09 am
☽⚻♀ **2:52 pm** 11:52 am
☽⚻☉ **6:45 pm** 3:45 pm
☽□♆ **10:35 pm** 7:35 pm
☽⚻♂ 10:29 pm

31 SUNDAY
☽⚻♂ **1:29 am**
☽⚻♃ **6:27 am** 3:27 am
☽☍☿ **7:29 am** 4:29 am
☽⚻♇ **9:29 am** 6:29 am
☽✶♅ **6:38 pm** 3:38 pm

Eastern time in bold type
Pacific time in medium type

DECEMBER 2017

DATE	SID.TIME	SUN	MOON	NODE	MERCURY	VENUS	MARS	JUPITER	SATURN	URANUS	NEPTUNE	PLUTO	CERES	PALLAS	JUNO	VESTA	CHIRON
1 F	4 40 10	8 ♐ 58 38	2 ♉ 01	17 ♌ 41	28 ♐ 53	29 ♏ 31	24 ♎ 44	11 ♏ 04	27 ♐ 46	25 ♈ 01	11 ♓ 29	17 ♑ 48	17 ♌ 19	26 ♈ 32	23 ♑ 57	7 ♏ 35	24 ♓ 20
2 Sa	4 44 6	9 59 26	16 40	17 31 R	29 10	0 ♐ 46	25 22	11 16	27 53	24 59 R	11 29	17 50	17 25	26 22 R	24 19	8 05	24 19 R
3 Su	4 48 3	11 00 15	1 ♊ 40	17 20	29 18 R	2 02	26 00	11 29	27 59	24 58	11 30	17 52	17 31	26 13	24 42	8 36	24 19
4 M	4 51 59	12 01 05	16 54	17 10	29 16	3 17	26 37	11 41	28 06	24 56	11 30	17 53	17 37	26 04	25 04	9 06	24 19
5 T	4 55 56	13 01 56	2 ♋ 09	17 02	29 03	4 33	27 15	11 53	28 13	24 55	11 31	17 55	17 42	25 56	25 26	9 37	24 19 D
6 W	4 59 53	14 02 48	17 15	16 56	28 40	5 48	27 53	12 05	28 20	24 53	11 31	17 57	17 47	25 49	25 49	10 07	24 19
7 Th	5 3 49	15 03 42	2 ♌ 04	16 53	28 05	7 04	28 30	12 17	28 27	24 52	11 32	17 59	17 51	25 42	26 12	10 38	24 19
8 F	5 7 46	16 04 36	16 29	16 52 D	27 19	8 19	29 08	12 29	28 34	24 51	11 32	18 00	17 55	25 36	26 35	11 08	24 19
9 Sa	5 11 42	17 05 32	0 ♍ 30	16 53	26 22	9 35	29 46	12 41	28 41	24 50	11 33	18 02	17 58	25 30	26 58	11 38	24 19
10 Su	5 15 39	18 06 30	14 05	16 53 R	25 16	10 50	0 ♏ 24	12 53	28 48	24 48	11 33	18 04	18 02	25 25	27 21	12 09	24 20
11 M	5 19 35	19 07 28	27 17	16 53	24 02	12 06	1 01	13 05	28 55	24 47	11 34	18 06	18 04	25 20	27 44	12 39	24 20
12 T	5 23 32	20 08 27	10 ♎ 10	16 51	22 43	13 21	1 39	13 17	29 02	24 46	11 34	18 08	18 07	25 16	28 07	13 10	24 20
13 W	5 27 28	21 09 28	22 46	16 46	21 20	14 37	2 17	13 28	29 09	24 45	11 35	18 09	18 08	25 13	28 30	13 40	24 21
14 Th	5 31 25	22 10 30	5 ♏ 09	16 39	19 58	15 52	2 54	13 40	29 16	24 44	11 36	18 11	18 10	25 10	28 54	14 10	24 21
15 F	5 35 22	23 11 32	17 22	16 30	18 37	17 08	3 32	13 51	29 23	24 43	11 37	18 13	18 11	25 08	29 17	14 40	24 22
16 Sa	5 39 18	24 12 36	29 26	16 20	17 22	18 23	4 10	14 03	29 30	24 42	11 37	18 15	18 12 R	25 07	29 41	15 10	24 22
17 Su	5 43 15	25 13 40	11 ♐ 25	16 09	16 14	19 39	4 47	14 14	29 37	24 41	11 38	18 17	18 12	25 06 D	0 ♒ 05	15 41	24 23
18 M	5 47 11	26 14 45	23 18	15 59	15 15	20 54	5 25	14 26	29 44	24 40	11 39	18 19	18 11	25 05	0 28	16 11	24 23
19 T	5 51 8	27 15 51	5 ♑ 09	15 51	14 27	22 10	6 02	14 37	29 51	24 40	11 40	18 21	18 11	25 06	0 52	16 41	24 24
20 W	5 55 4	28 16 57	16 57	15 44	13 49	23 25	6 40	14 48	29 59	24 39	11 41	18 23	18 10	25 07	1 16	17 11	24 25
21 Th	5 59 1	29 18 04	28 46	15 40	13 22	24 41	7 18	14 59	0 ♑ 06	24 38	11 42	18 25	18 08	25 08	1 40	17 41	24 26
22 F	6 2 57	0 ♑ 19 11	10 ♒ 38	15 38 D	13 06	25 56	7 55	15 10	0 13	24 38	11 43	18 27	18 06	25 10	2 05	18 11	24 27
23 Sa	6 6 54	1 20 19	22 36	15 39	13 00 D	27 12	8 33	15 21	0 20	24 37	11 44	18 29	18 04	25 13	2 29	18 41	24 28
24 Su	6 10 51	2 21 26	4 ♓ 44	15 40	13 04	28 27	9 10	15 32	0 27	24 37	11 45	18 31	18 01	25 16	2 53	19 11	24 29
25 M	6 14 47	3 22 34	17 05	15 41	13 17	29 43	9 48	15 43	0 34	24 36	11 46	18 33	17 58	25 20	3 18	19 40	24 30
26 T	6 18 44	4 23 42	29 46	15 42 R	13 38	0 ♑ 58	10 25	15 54	0 41	24 36	11 47	18 35	17 54	25 24	3 42	20 10	24 31
27 W	6 22 40	5 24 50	12 ♈ 49	15 42	14 07	2 14	11 03	16 04	0 48	24 35	11 48	18 37	17 50	25 29	4 07	20 40	24 32
28 Th	6 26 37	6 25 57	26 20	15 40	14 42	3 29	11 40	16 15	0 55	24 35	11 49	18 39	17 45	25 35	4 31	21 10	24 33
29 F	6 30 33	7 27 05	10 ♉ 19	15 37	15 24	4 45	12 18	16 25	1 02	24 35	11 50	18 41	17 40	25 41	4 56	21 39	24 34
30 Sa	6 34 30	8 28 13	24 46	15 32	16 10	6 00	12 55	16 36	1 09	24 35	11 52	18 43	17 35	25 47	5 21	22 09	24 36
31 Su	6 38 26	9 29 21	9 ♊ 38	15 26	17 02	7 16	13 33	16 46	1 16	24 34	11 53	18 45	17 29	25 54	5 46	22 38	24 37

EPHEMERIS CALCULATED FOR 12 MIDNIGHT GREENWICH MEAN TIME. ALL OTHER DATA AND FACING ASPECTARIAN PAGE IN **EASTERN TIME (BOLD)** AND PACIFIC TIME (REGULAR).

JANUARY 2018

☽ Last Aspect day	ET / hr:mn / PT	asp	☽ Ingress sign	day	ET / hr:mn / PT
12/31	**6:38 pm** 3:38 pm	⚹ ♅	♋	1	**3:10 am** 12:10 am
2	**5:46 pm** 2:46 pm	□ ♅	♌	2	11:23 pm
2	**5:46 pm** 2:46 pm	□ ♅	♌	3	**2:23 am**
4	**6:10 pm** 3:10 pm	△ ♅	♍	5	**3:12 am** 12:12 am
6	**9:51 pm** 6:51 pm	□ ☿	♎	7	**7:15 am** 4:15 am
9	**11:13 am** 8:13 am	⚹ ☿	♏	9	**3:05 pm** 12:05 pm
11	**9:53 am** 6:53 am	⚹ ♀	♐	11	11:04 pm
11	**9:53 am** 6:53 am	⚹ ♀	♐	12	**2:04 am**
14	**3:48 am** 12:48 am	△ ♅	♑	14	**2:42 pm** 11:42 am
16	10:30 pm	☌ ♀	♒	17	**3:32 am** 12:32 am
17	**1:30 am**	☌ ♀	♒	17	**3:32 am** 12:32 am
19	**6:52 am** 3:52 am	□ ♂	♓	19	**3:26 pm** 12:26 pm
21	**8:13 pm** 5:13 pm	△ ♂	♈	21	10:27 pm
21	**8:13 pm** 5:13 pm	△ ♂	♈	22	**1:27 am**
23	**11:16 pm** 8:16 pm	☌ ♅	♉	24	**8:39 am** 5:39 am
25	**10:17 pm** 7:17 pm	△ ☿	♊	26	**12:40 pm** 9:40 am
28	**5:39 am** 2:39 am	⚹ ♅	♋	28	**1:57 pm** 10:57 am
30	**11:40 am** 8:40 am	☍ ☿	♌	30	**1:53 pm** 10:53 am

☽ Phases & Eclipses phase	day	ET / hr:mn / PT
Full Moon	1	**9:24 pm** 6:24 pm
4th Quarter	8	**5:25 pm** 2:25 pm
New Moon	16	**9:17 pm** 6:17 pm
2nd Quarter	24	**5:20 pm** 2:20 pm
Full Moon	31	**8:27 am** 5:27 am
●	31	11° ♌ 37'

Planet Ingress		day	ET / hr:mn / PT
☿	♑	10	9:09 pm
☿	♑	11	**12:09 pm**
⚶	♐	14	**11:45 pm** 8:45 pm
♀	♒	17	**8:44 pm** 5:44 pm
⚴	♉	19	**9:35 pm** 6:35 pm
☉	♒	19	**10:09 pm** 7:09 pm
♂	♐	26	**7:56 am** 4:56 am
☿	♒	31	**8:39 am** 5:39 am

Planetary Motion		day	ET / hr:mn / PT
♅	D	2	**9:13 am** 6:13 am

1 MONDAY
☽ ☍ ♄ **5:26 am** 2:26 am
☿ ⚺ ♇ **3:51 pm** 12:51 pm
☽ ☍ ♀ **6:28 pm** 3:28 pm
☽ ☍ ☉ **9:24 pm** 6:24 pm
☽ △ ♆ **9:52 pm** 6:52 pm
☽ △ ♂ 11:41 pm

2 TUESDAY
☽ △ ♂ **2:41 am**
☉ ⚹ ♆ **4:37 am** 1:37 am
☽ △ ♃ **6:07 am** 3:07 am
☽ ☍ ♇ **8:43 am** 5:43 am
☽ ⚻ ☿ **9:54 am** 6:54 am
☽ □ ♅ **5:46 pm** 2:46 pm

3 WEDNESDAY
☽ ⚻ ♄ **5:02 am** 2:02 am
♀ ⚹ ♆ **12:38 pm** 9:38 am
☽ ⚻ ♆ **9:34 pm** 6:34 pm
☽ ⚻ ♀ **10:23 pm** 7:23 pm
☽ ⚻ ☉ 9:31 pm

4 THURSDAY
☽ ⚻ ☉ **12:31 am**
☽ □ ♂ **4:34 am** 1:34 am
☽ □ ♃ **6:34 am** 3:34 am
☽ ⚻ ♇ **8:50 am** 5:50 am
☽ △ ☿ **1:52 pm** 10:52 am
☽ △ ♅ **6:10 pm** 3:10 pm

5 FRIDAY
☽ △ ♄ **6:25 am** 3:25 am
☽ ☍ ♆ **11:37 pm** 8:37 pm

6 SATURDAY
☽ △ ♀ **5:23 am** 2:23 am
☽ △ ☉ **6:40 am** 3:40 am
☽ ⚹ ♂ **9:22 am** 6:22 am
☽ ⚹ ♃ **9:43 am** 6:43 am
☽ △ ♇ **11:41 am** 8:41 am
☿ △ ♅ **6:39 pm** 3:39 pm
♂ ☌ ♃ **7:39 pm** 4:39 pm
☽ ⚻ ♅ **9:33 pm** 6:33 pm
☽ □ ☿ **9:51 pm** 6:51 pm

7 SUNDAY
☽ □ ♄ **11:09 am** 8:09 am

8 MONDAY
☽ ⚻ ♆ **5:17 am** 2:17 am
☉ ⚹ ♃ **7:07 am** 4:07 am
♀ ⚹ ♃ **11:13 am** 8:13 am
♂ ⚹ ♇ **2:59 pm** 11:59 am
☽ ⚺ ♃ **4:43 pm** 1:43 pm
☽ □ ♀ **5:15 pm** 2:15 pm
☽ □ ☉ **5:25 pm** 2:25 pm
☽ □ ♇ **6:17 pm** 3:17 pm
☽ ⚺ ♂ **6:26 pm** 3:26 pm
☉ ☌ ♀ 11:02 pm

9 TUESDAY
☉ ☌ ♀ **2:02 am**
♀ ☌ ♇ **4:03 am** 1:03 am
☉ ☌ ♇ **4:33 am** 1:33 am
☽ ☍ ♅ **4:45 am** 1:45 am
☽ ⚹ ☿ **11:13 am** 8:13 am
♀ ⚹ ♂ **4:08 pm** 1:08 pm
☽ ⚹ ♄ **7:47 pm** 4:47 pm
☉ ⚹ ♂ 9:36 pm

10 WEDNESDAY
☉ ⚹ ♂ **12:36 am**
☽ △ ♆ **2:39 pm** 11:39 am

11 THURSDAY
☽ ☌ ♃ **3:21 am** 12:21 am
☽ ⚹ ♇ **4:26 am** 1:26 am
☽ ☌ ♂ **7:34 am** 4:34 am
☽ ⚹ ☉ **8:41 am** 5:41 am
☽ ⚹ ♀ **9:53 am** 6:53 am
☽ ⚻ ♅ **3:18 pm** 12:18 pm

12 FRIDAY
☽ ⚺ ☿ **5:21 am** 2:21 am
☽ ⚺ ♄ **7:32 am** 4:32 am
☿ ☌ ♄ 11:03 pm
☽ □ ♆ 11:38 pm

13 SATURDAY
☿ ☌ ♄ **2:03 am**
☽ □ ♆ **2:38 am**
♀ □ ♅ **2:09 pm** 11:09 am
☽ ⚺ ♃ **4:19 pm** 1:19 pm
☽ ⚺ ♇ **4:49 pm** 1:49 pm
☽ ⚺ ♂ **11:12 pm** 8:12 pm
☽ ⚺ ☉ 11:41 pm

14 SUNDAY
☽ ⚺ ☉ **2:41 am**
☽ △ ♅ **3:48 am** 12:48 am
☽ ⚺ ♀ **5:25 am** 2:25 am
☉ □ ♅ **3:45 pm** 12:45 pm
☽ ☌ ♄ **8:49 pm** 5:49 pm
☽ ☌ ☿ 11:03 pm

15 MONDAY
☽ ☌ ☿ **2:03 am**
☽ ⚹ ♆ **3:39 pm** 12:39 pm
♃ ⚹ ♇ **11:13 pm** 8:13 pm

16 TUESDAY
☽ ☌ ♇ **5:54 am** 2:54 am
☽ ⚹ ♃ **5:58 am** 2:58 am
☽ ⚹ ♂ **3:27 pm** 12:27 pm
☽ □ ♅ **4:44 pm** 1:44 pm
☽ ☌ ☉ **9:17 pm** 6:17 pm
☽ ☌ ♀ 10:30 pm

17 WEDNESDAY
☽ ☌ ♀ **1:30 am**
☽ ⚺ ♄ **10:11 am** 7:11 am
♂ ⚻ ♅ **4:37 pm** 1:37 pm
☽ ⚺ ☿ **10:59 pm** 7:59 pm

18 THURSDAY
☽ ⚺ ♆ **4:22 am** 1:22 am
☽ ⚺ ♇ **6:25 pm** 3:25 pm
☽ □ ♃ **7:00 pm** 4:00 pm

19 FRIDAY
☽ ⚹ ♅ **4:57 am** 1:57 am
☽ □ ♂ **6:52 am** 3:52 am
☽ ⚺ ☉ **2:50 pm** 11:50 am
☿ ⚹ ♆ **8:08 pm** 5:08 pm
☽ ⚺ ♀ **8:21 pm** 5:21 pm
☽ ⚹ ♄ **10:28 pm** 7:28 pm

20 SATURDAY
☽ ☌ ♆ **3:45 pm** 12:45 pm
☽ ⚹ ☿ **6:20 pm** 3:20 pm
♀ ⚺ ♄ **6:45 pm** 3:45 pm

21 SUNDAY
☽ ⚹ ♇ **5:22 am** 2:22 am
☽ △ ♃ **6:25 am** 3:25 am
☽ ⚺ ♅ **3:27 pm** 12:27 pm
☽ △ ♂ **8:13 pm** 5:13 pm

22 MONDAY
☽ ⚹ ☉ **5:55 am** 2:55 am
☽ □ ♄ **8:41 am** 5:41 am
☽ ⚹ ♀ **12:28 pm** 9:28 am
☽ ⚺ ♆ 9:50 pm

23 TUESDAY
☽ ⚺ ♆ **12:50 am**
☽ □ ☿ **10:29 am** 7:29 am
☽ □ ♇ **1:47 pm** 10:47 am
☽ ⚻ ♃ **3:11 pm** 12:11 pm
☉ ⚺ ♄ **8:31 pm** 5:31 pm
☽ ☌ ♅ **11:16 pm** 8:16 pm

24 WEDNESDAY
☽ ⚻ ♂ **6:23 am** 3:23 am
☿ ☌ ♇ **3:50 pm** 12:50 pm
☽ △ ♄ **3:56 pm** 12:56 pm
☽ □ ☉ **5:20 pm** 2:20 pm
☽ □ ♀ 9:35 pm

25 THURSDAY
☽ □ ♀ **12:35 am**
☿ ⚹ ♃ **6:28 am** 3:28 am
☽ ⚹ ♆ **6:49 am** 3:49 am
☽ △ ♇ **7:02 pm** 4:02 pm
☽ ☍ ♃ **8:40 pm** 5:40 pm
☽ △ ☿ **10:17 pm** 7:17 pm

26 FRIDAY
☽ ⚺ ♅ **3:53 am** 12:53 am
☽ ☍ ♂ **12:52 pm** 9:52 am
☽ ⚻ ♄ **7:54 pm** 4:54 pm
☽ △ ☉ 9:45 pm

27 SATURDAY
☽ △ ☉ **12:45 am**
☽ △ ♀ **8:31 am** 5:31 am
☽ □ ♆ **9:41 am** 6:41 am
☽ ⚻ ♇ **9:15 pm** 6:15 pm
♀ ⚺ ♆ **10:22 pm** 7:22 pm
☽ ⚻ ♃ **11:07 pm** 8:07 pm
☿ □ ♅ 11:08 pm

28 SUNDAY
☿ □ ♅ **2:08 am**
☽ ⚹ ♅ **5:39 am** 2:39 am
☽ ⚻ ☿ **6:03 am** 3:03 am
☽ ⚻ ♂ **4:17 pm** 1:17 pm
☽ ☍ ♄ **9:15 pm** 6:15 pm

29 MONDAY
☽ ⚻ ☉ **5:07 am** 2:07 am
☽ △ ♆ **10:19 am** 7:19 am
☽ ⚻ ♀ **1:30 pm** 10:30 am
☽ ☍ ♇ **9:34 pm** 6:34 pm
☽ △ ♃ **11:38 pm** 8:38 pm

30 TUESDAY
☽ □ ♅ **5:46 am** 2:46 am
☽ ☍ ☿ **11:40 am** 8:40 am
☽ △ ♂ **6:13 pm** 3:13 pm
☽ ⚻ ♄ **9:27 pm** 6:27 pm

31 WEDNESDAY
☽ ☍ ☉ **8:27 am** 5:27 am
☽ ⚻ ♆ **10:17 am** 7:17 am
☽ ☍ ♀ **5:48 pm** 2:48 pm
☽ ⚻ ♇ **9:39 pm** 6:39 pm
☽ □ ♃ 9:00 pm

Eastern time in bold type
Pacific time in medium type

JANUARY 2018

DATE	SID.TIME	SUN	MOON	NODE	MERCURY	VENUS	MARS	JUPITER	SATURN	URANUS	NEPTUNE	PLUTO	CERES	PALLAS	JUNO	VESTA	CHIRON
1 M	6 42 23	10♑30 29	24♊48	15♌21℞	17♐57	8♑31	14♏10	16♏56	1♑23	24♈34℞	11♓54	18♑47	17♌23℞	26♈02	6♒11	23♏08	24♓39
2 T	6 46 20	11 31 37	10♋06	15 16	18 56	9 47	14 47	17 06	1 30	24 34D	11 56	18 49	17 16	26 10	6 36	23 37	24 40
3 W	6 50 16	12 32 44	25 21	15 13	19 59	11 02	15 25	17 16	1 37	24 34	11 57	18 51	17 09	26 19	7 01	24 07	24 42
4 Th	6 54 13	13 33 52	10♌23	15 12 D	21 05	12 18	16 02	17 26	1 44	24 34	11 58	18 53	17 02	26 28	7 26	24 36	24 43
5 F	6 58 9	14 35 00	25 05	15 12	22 13	13 33	16 40	17 36	1 51	24 34	12 00	18 55	16 54	26 38	7 51	25 05	24 45
6 Sa	7 2 6	15 36 08	9♍20	15 14	23 23	14 49	17 17	17 46	1 58	24 35	12 01	18 57	16 45	26 48	8 17	25 34	24 46
7 Su	7 6 2	16 37 17	23 08	15 15	24 36	16 04	17 54	17 55	2 05	24 35	12 03	18 59	16 37	26 59	8 42	26 04	24 48
8 M	7 9 59	17 38 25	6♎29	15 17℞	25 50	17 20	18 32	18 05	2 12	24 35	12 04	19 01	16 28	27 10	9 07	26 33	24 50
9 T	7 13 55	18 39 34	19 26	15 17	27 06	18 35	19 09	18 14	2 19	24 35	12 06	19 03	16 18	27 21	9 33	27 02	24 52
10 W	7 17 52	19 40 42	2♏02	15 16	28 24	19 51	19 46	18 23	2 26	24 36	12 07	19 05	16 09	27 33	9 58	27 31	24 54
11 Th	7 21 49	20 41 51	14 21	15 14	29 43	21 06	20 24	18 32	2 33	24 36	12 09	19 07	15 58	27 46	10 24	27 59	24 55
12 F	7 25 45	21 43 00	26 28	15 11	1♑03	22 22	21 01	18 41	2 40	24 37	12 10	19 09	15 48	27 59	10 50	28 28	24 57
13 Sa	7 29 42	22 44 08	8♐25	15 08	2 24	23 37	21 38	18 50	2 47	24 37	12 12	19 11	15 37	28 12	11 16	28 57	24 59
14 Su	7 33 38	23 45 17	20 18	15 04	3 47	24 53	22 15	18 59	2 53	24 38	12 14	19 13	15 26	28 26	11 41	29 26	25 02
15 M	7 37 35	24 46 25	2♑07	15 00	5 10	26 08	22 53	19 08	3 00	24 38	12 15	19 15	15 15	28 40	12 07	29 54	25 04
16 T	7 41 31	25 47 33	13 56	14 57	6 35	27 24	23 30	19 16	3 07	24 39	12 17	19 17	15 03	28 55	12 33	0♐23	25 06
17 W	7 45 28	26 48 40	25 47	14 55	8 00	28 39	24 07	19 25	3 14	24 40	12 19	19 19	14 51	29 10	12 59	0 51	25 08
18 Th	7 49 25	27 49 47	7♒41	14 54 D	9 26	29 55	24 44	19 33	3 20	24 40	12 20	19 21	14 39	29 26	13 25	1 20	25 10
19 F	7 53 21	28 50 53	19 41	14 54	10 52	1♒10	25 21	19 41	3 27	24 41	12 22	19 23	14 26	29 42	13 52	1 48	25 12
20 Sa	7 57 18	29 51 59	1♓48	14 55	12 20	2 25	25 58	19 49	3 34	24 42	12 24	19 25	14 14	29 58	14 18	2 16	25 15
21 Su	8 1 14	0♒53 04	14 06	14 56	13 48	3 41	26 35	19 57	3 40	24 43	12 26	19 27	14 01	0♉15	14 44	2 44	25 17
22 M	8 5 11	1 54 08	26 36	14 57	15 17	4 56	27 12	20 05	3 47	24 44	12 27	19 30	13 47	0 32	15 10	3 12	25 20
23 T	8 9 7	2 55 11	9♈21	14 58	16 46	6 12	27 49	20 13	3 53	24 45	12 29	19 32	13 34	0 50	15 37	3 40	25 22
24 W	8 13 4	3 56 13	22 25	14 59℞	18 16	7 27	28 26	20 20	4 00	24 46	12 31	19 34	13 21	1 08	16 03	4 08	25 24
25 Th	8 17 0	4 57 14	5♉49	14 59	19 47	8 42	29 03	20 27	4 06	24 47	12 33	19 35	13 07	1 26	16 30	4 36	25 27
26 F	8 20 57	5 58 14	19 37	14 59	21 19	9 58	29 40	20 35	4 12	24 48	12 35	19 37	12 53	1 45	16 56	5 04	25 29
27 Sa	8 24 53	6 59 13	3♊47	14 58	22 51	11 13	0♐17	20 42	4 19	24 50	12 37	19 39	12 39	2 04	17 23	5 31	25 32
28 Su	8 28 50	8 00 10	18 19	14 58	24 24	12 29	0 54	20 49	4 25	24 51	12 39	19 41	12 25	2 23	17 49	5 59	25 35
29 M	8 32 47	9 01 07	3♋08	14 57	25 57	13 44	1 31	20 56	4 31	24 52	12 41	19 43	12 11	2 43	18 16	6 26	25 37
30 T	8 36 43	10 02 03	18 09	14 56	27 31	14 59	2 08	21 02	4 38	24 54	12 43	19 45	11 57	3 03	18 43	6 53	25 40
31 W	8 40 40	11 02 57	3♌13	14 56 D	29 06	16 14	2 44	21 09	4 44	24 55	12 45	19 47	11 43	3 23	19 09	7 21	25 43

EPHEMERIS CALCULATED FOR 12 MIDNIGHT GREENWICH MEAN TIME. ALL OTHER DATA AND FACING ASPECTARIAN PAGE IN **EASTERN TIME (BOLD)** AND PACIFIC TIME (REGULAR).

FEBRUARY 2018

☽ Last Aspect day	ET / hr:mn / PT		asp	☽ Ingress sign	day	ET / hr:mn / PT	
1	**5:59 am**	2:59 am	△♅	♍	1	**2:13 pm**	11:13 am
2		11:07 pm	⚹♃	♎	3	**4:47 pm**	1:47 pm
3	**2:07 am**		⚹♃	♎	3	**4:47 pm**	1:47 pm
5	**1:46 pm**	10:46 am	☍♅	♏	5	**10:56 pm**	7:56 pm
7		11:16 pm	□♀	♐	8	**8:53 am**	5:53 am
8	**2:16 am**		□♀	♐	8	**8:53 am**	5:53 am
10	**11:38 am**	8:38 am	△♅	♑	10	**9:21 pm**	6:21 pm
12		9:43 pm	□♅	♒	13	**10:11 am**	7:11 am
13	**12:43 am**		□♅	♒	13	**10:11 am**	7:11 am
15	**4:05 pm**	1:05 pm	☌☉	♓	15	**9:42 pm**	6:42 pm

☽ Last Aspect day	ET / hr:mn / PT		asp	☽ Ingress sign	day	ET / hr:mn / PT	
17	**5:14 pm**	2:14 pm	△♃	♈	18	**7:05 am**	4:05 am
20	**6:11 am**	3:11 am	☌♅	♉	20	**2:12 pm**	11:12 am
22	**6:46 am**	3:46 am	☍♃	♊	22	**7:07 pm**	4:07 pm
24	**2:58 pm**	11:58 am	⚹♅	♋	24	**10:06 pm**	7:06 pm
26	**4:51 pm**	1:51 pm	□♅	♌	26	**11:42 pm**	8:42 pm
28	**6:13 pm**	3:13 pm	△♅	♍	28		9:57 pm
28	**6:13 pm**	3:13 pm	△♅	♍	3/1	**12:57 am**	

☽ Phases & Eclipses phase	day	ET / hr:mn / PT	
4th Quarter	7	**10:54 am**	7:54 am
New Moon	15	**4:05 pm**	1:05 pm
●	15	27° ♒ 08'	
2nd Quarter	23	**3:09 am**	12:09 am

Planet Ingress	day	ET / hr:mn / PT	
♀ ♓	10	**6:20 pm**	3:20 pm
☿ ♓	17	**11:28 pm**	8:28 pm
☉ ♓	18	**12:18 pm**	9:18 am
✱ ♓	23	**3:10 pm**	12:10 pm

Planetary Motion	day	ET / hr:mn / PT

1 THURSDAY
☽□♃ **12:00 am**
☽△♅ **5:59 am** 2:59 am
☉⚺♆ **12:30 pm** 9:30 am
☽⚻☿ **5:51 pm** 2:51 pm
☽□♂ **8:48 pm** 5:48 pm
☽△♄ **10:22 pm** 7:22 pm

2 FRIDAY
☽☍♆ **11:29 am** 8:29 am
☽⚻☉ **1:11 pm** 10:11 am
♀⚺♇ **4:36 pm** 1:36 pm
☽△♇ **11:24 pm** 8:24 pm
☽⚻♀ 9:02 pm
☽⚹♃ 11:07 pm

3 SATURDAY
☽⚻♀ **12:02 am**
☽⚹♃ **2:07 am**
☽⚻♅ **8:09 am** 5:09 am
☿⚹♂ **10:57 am** 7:57 am
☿⚺♄ **12:51 pm** 9:51 am
♂⚺♄ **4:36 pm** 1:36 pm
♀□♃ 10:07 pm
☽□♄ 10:50 pm
☽⚹♂ 11:11 pm

4 SUNDAY
♀□♃ **1:07 am**
☽□♄ **1:50 am**
☽⚹♂ **2:11 am**
☽△☿ **3:29 am** 12:29 am

☽⚻♆ **3:36 pm** 12:36 pm
☽△☉ **9:35 pm** 6:35 pm

5 MONDAY
☽□♇ **4:22 am** 1:22 am
☽⚺♃ **7:34 am** 4:34 am
☽△♀ **10:33 am** 7:33 am
☽☍♅ **1:46 pm** 10:46 am

6 TUESDAY
☽⚹♄ **9:05 am** 6:05 am
☽⚺♂ **11:50 am** 8:50 am
☽□☿ **6:45 pm** 3:45 pm
♀⚹♅ **8:37 pm** 5:37 pm
☽△♆ **11:37 pm** 8:37 pm

7 WEDNESDAY
☽□☉ **10:54 am** 7:54 am
☽⚹♇ **1:16 pm** 10:16 am
☽☌♃ **4:57 pm** 1:57 pm
☽⚻♅ **11:17 pm** 8:17 pm
☽□♀ 11:16 pm

8 THURSDAY
☽□♀ **2:16 am**
☿⚺♆ **7:37 am** 4:37 am
☉⚺♇ **4:29 pm** 1:29 pm
☽⚺♄ **8:06 pm** 5:06 pm
☽☌♂ 10:40 pm

9 FRIDAY
☽☌♂ **1:40 am**
☽□♆ **11:04 am** 8:04 am
☽⚹☿ **3:32 pm** 12:32 pm
☽⚺♇ 10:16 pm

10 SATURDAY
☽⚺♇ **1:16 am**
☽⚹☉ **4:14 am** 1:14 am
☽⚺♃ **5:21 am** 2:21 am
☽△♅ **11:38 am** 8:38 am
☉□♃ **6:21 pm** 3:21 pm
☽⚹♀ **9:43 pm** 6:43 pm

11 SUNDAY
☽☌♄ **9:17 am** 6:17 am
☽⚺♂ **5:44 pm** 2:44 pm
☽⚹♆ 9:08 pm

12 MONDAY
☽⚹♆ **12:08 am**
☿⚺♇ **11:24 am** 8:24 am
☽☌♇ **2:22 pm** 11:22 am
☽⚺☿ **2:52 pm** 11:52 am
☽⚹♃ **6:42 pm** 3:42 pm
☽⚺☉ **10:52 pm** 7:52 pm
☽□♅ 9:43 pm

13 TUESDAY
☽□♅ **12:43 am**
☿□♃ **5:39 pm** 2:39 pm
☽⚺♀ **5:40 pm** 2:40 pm
☉⚹♅ **9:23 pm** 6:23 pm
☽⚺♄ **10:26 pm** 7:26 pm

14 WEDNESDAY
☽⚹♂ **9:29 am** 6:29 am
☽⚺♆ **12:44 pm** 9:44 am
☽⚺♇ 11:35 pm

15 THURSDAY
☽⚺♇ **2:35 am**
☽□♃ **7:00 am** 4:00 am
☿⚹♅ **10:07 am** 7:07 am
☽⚹♅ **12:41 pm** 9:41 am
☽☌☿ **1:06 pm** 10:06 am
☽☌☉ **4:05 pm** 1:05 pm
♀⚹♄ **6:19 pm** 3:19 pm

16 FRIDAY
☽⚹♄ **9:58 am** 6:58 am
☽☌♀ **11:36 am** 8:36 am
☽□♂ **11:11 pm** 8:11 pm
☽☌♆ **11:31 pm** 8:31 pm

17 SATURDAY
♂□♆ **6:20 am** 3:20 am
☉☌☿ **7:27 am** 4:27 am
☽⚹♇ **12:49 pm** 9:49 am
☽△♃ **5:14 pm** 2:14 pm
☽⚺♅ **10:34 pm** 7:34 pm

18 SUNDAY
☽⚺☉ **6:38 am** 3:38 am
☽⚺☿ **8:20 am** 5:20 am
☽□♄ **7:15 pm** 4:15 pm
☽⚺♀ 11:31 pm

19 MONDAY
☽⚺♀ **2:31 am**
☽⚺♆ **8:03 am** 5:03 am
☽△♂ **10:18 am** 7:18 am
☽□♇ **8:47 pm** 5:47 pm
☽⚻♃ 10:08 pm

20 TUESDAY
☽⚻♃ **1:08 am**
☽☌♅ **6:11 am** 3:11 am
☽⚹☉ **6:16 pm** 3:16 pm
☽⚹☿ 9:12 pm
☽△♄ 11:14 pm

21 WEDNESDAY
☽⚹☿ **12:12 am**
☽△♄ **2:14 am**
♀☌♆ **1:42 pm** 10:42 am
☽⚹♆ **2:19 pm** 11:19 am
☽⚹♀ **2:23 pm** 11:23 am
☿⚹♄ **3:23 pm** 12:23 pm
☽⚻♂ **6:49 pm** 3:49 pm
☽△♇ 11:30 pm

22 THURSDAY
☽△♇ **2:30 am**
☽☍♃ **6:46 am** 3:46 am
☽⚺♅ **11:35 am** 8:35 am

23 FRIDAY
☽□☉ **3:09 am** 12:09 am
☽⚻♄ **7:00 am** 4:00 am
☽□☿ **12:51 pm** 9:51 am
☽□♆ **6:28 pm** 3:28 pm
☽□♀ **11:26 pm** 8:26 pm
☽☍♂ 9:57 pm

24 SATURDAY
☽☍♂ **12:57 am**
☽⚻♇ **6:09 am** 3:09 am
☽⚻♃ **10:19 am** 7:19 am
☽⚹♅ **2:58 pm** 11:58 am

25 SUNDAY
♀□♂ **7:01 am** 4:01 am
☿☌♆ **7:26 am** 4:26 am
☽△☉ **9:40 am** 6:40 am
☽☍♄ **9:52 am** 6:52 am
☉⚹♄ **12:46 pm** 9:46 am
☽△♆ **8:51 pm** 5:51 pm
☽△☿ **10:49 pm** 7:49 pm

26 MONDAY
☽⚻♂ **5:09 am** 2:09 am
☽△♀ **6:14 am** 3:14 am
☽☍♇ **8:11 am** 5:11 am
☽△♃ **12:17 pm** 9:17 am
☽□♅ **4:51 pm** 1:51 pm

27 TUESDAY
♀⚹♇ **5:20 am** 2:20 am
☽⚻♄ **11:32 am** 8:32 am
☽⚻☉ **2:43 pm** 11:43 am
☽⚻♆ **10:15 pm** 7:15 pm

28 WEDNESDAY
☽⚻☿ **7:25 am** 4:25 am
☽△♂ **8:29 am** 5:29 am
☽⚻♇ **9:30 am** 6:30 am
☽⚻♀ **12:04 pm** 9:04 am
☽□♃ **1:36 pm** 10:36 am
☽△♅ **6:13 pm** 3:13 pm
☿□♂ **6:56 pm** 3:56 pm
☿⚹♇ **11:42 pm** 8:42 pm

Eastern time in bold type
Pacific time in medium type

FEBRUARY 2018

DATE	SID.TIME	SUN	MOON	NODE	MERCURY	VENUS	MARS	JUPITER	SATURN	URANUS	NEPTUNE	PLUTO	CERES	PALLAS	JUNO	VESTA	CHIRON
1 Th	8 44 36	12♒03 50	18♌11	14♌56	0♒41	17♒30	3♐21	21♏15	4♑50	24♈57	12♓47	19♑49	11♌29 Rx	3♉44	19♒36	7♐48	25♓46
2 F	8 48 33	13 04 42	2♍55	14 56	2 17	18 45	3 58	21 21	4 56	24 58	12 49	19 51	11 15	4 05	20 03	8 15	25 48
3 Sa	8 52 29	14 05 34	17 18	14 56 Rx	3 54	20 00	4 35	21 27	5 02	25 00	12 51	19 53	11 01	4 26	20 30	8 42	25 51
4 Su	8 56 26	15 06 24	1♎16	14 56	5 32	21 16	5 11	21 33	5 08	25 01	12 53	19 55	10 46	4 48	20 57	9 08	25 54
5 M	9 0 22	16 07 13	14 48	14 56	7 10	22 31	5 48	21 39	5 14	25 03	12 55	19 57	10 32	5 10	21 24	9 35	25 57
6 T	9 4 19	17 08 02	27 53	14 56	8 49	23 46	6 24	21 45	5 20	25 05	12 57	19 59	10 18	5 32	21 51	10 01	26 00
7 W	9 8 16	18 08 50	10♏35	14 56 D	10 29	25 01	7 01	21 50	5 26	25 06	12 59	20 01	10 04	5 54	22 18	10 28	26 03
8 Th	9 12 12	19 09 36	22 58	14 56	12 09	26 17	7 38	21 55	5 32	25 08	13 01	20 02	9 51	6 17	22 45	10 54	26 06
9 F	9 16 9	20 10 22	5♐05	14 56	13 51	27 32	8 14	22 01	5 37	25 10	13 03	20 04	9 37	6 40	23 12	11 20	26 09
10 Sa	9 20 5	21 11 07	17 01	14 56	15 33	28 47	8 51	22 06	5 43	25 12	13 06	20 06	9 23	7 04	23 40	11 46	26 12
11 Su	9 24 2	22 11 51	28 51	14 57	17 16	0♓02	9 27	22 10	5 49	25 14	13 08	20 08	9 10	7 27	24 07	12 12	26 15
12 M	9 27 58	23 12 33	10♑39	14 58	18 59	1 17	10 03	22 15	5 54	25 16	13 10	20 10	8 57	7 51	24 34	12 38	26 18
13 T	9 31 55	24 13 15	22 28	14 59	20 44	2 32	10 40	22 19	6 00	25 18	13 12	20 11	8 44	8 16	25 01	13 04	26 21
14 W	9 35 51	25 13 55	4♒23	15 00 Rx	22 29	3 48	11 16	22 24	6 05	25 20	13 14	20 13	8 31	8 40	25 29	13 29	26 24
15 Th	9 39 48	26 14 34	16 25	15 00	24 16	5 03	11 52	22 28	6 11	25 22	13 16	20 15	8 19	9 05	25 56	13 55	26 28
16 F	9 43 45	27 15 11	28 37	14 59	26 03	6 18	12 29	22 32	6 16	25 24	13 19	20 17	8 06	9 30	26 24	14 20	26 31
17 Sa	9 47 41	28 15 47	11♓00	14 58	27 51	7 33	13 05	22 36	6 21	25 26	13 21	20 18	7 54	9 55	26 51	14 45	26 34
18 Su	9 51 38	29 16 21	23 35	14 57	29 40	8 48	13 41	22 39	6 26	25 28	13 23	20 20	7 42	10 21	27 19	15 10	26 37
19 M	9 55 34	0♓16 54	6♈23	14 54	1♓29	10 03	14 17	22 43	6 31	25 31	13 25	20 22	7 31	10 46	27 46	15 35	26 41
20 T	9 59 31	1 17 25	19 25	14 52	3 20	11 18	14 53	22 46	6 36	25 33	13 27	20 23	7 20	11 12	28 14	16 00	26 44
21 W	10 3 27	2 17 54	2♉40	14 50	5 11	12 33	15 29	22 49	6 41	25 35	13 30	20 25	7 09	11 38	28 41	16 24	26 47
22 Th	10 7 24	3 18 21	16 11	14 48	7 03	13 48	16 05	22 52	6 46	25 38	13 32	20 26	6 58	12 05	29 09	16 48	26 51
23 F	10 11 20	4 18 47	29 56	14 47 D	8 55	15 03	16 41	22 55	6 51	25 40	13 34	20 28	6 48	12 32	29 37	17 13	26 54
24 Sa	10 15 17	5 19 11	13♊55	14 47	10 48	16 18	17 17	22 57	6 56	25 42	13 36	20 30	6 38	12 58	0♓04	17 37	26 57
25 Su	10 19 14	6 19 32	28 09	14 48	12 41	17 33	17 52	22 59	7 01	25 45	13 39	20 31	6 29	13 26	0 32	18 01	27 01
26 M	10 23 10	7 19 52	12♋34	14 50	14 35	18 48	18 28	23 02	7 05	25 47	13 41	20 33	6 20	13 53	1 00	18 24	27 04
27 T	10 27 7	8 20 10	27 08	14 51	16 28	20 03	19 04	23 04	7 10	25 50	13 43	20 34	6 11	14 20	1 28	18 48	27 08
28 W	10 31 3	9 20 25	11♌47	14 52 Rx	18 22	21 18	19 40	23 05	7 14	25 53	13 46	20 36	6 03	14 48	1 56	19 11	27 11

EPHEMERIS CALCULATED FOR 12 MIDNIGHT GREENWICH MEAN TIME. ALL OTHER DATA AND FACING ASPECTARIAN PAGE IN **EASTERN TIME (BOLD)** AND PACIFIC TIME (REGULAR).

MARCH 2018

☽ Last Aspect day	ET / hr:mn / PT		asp	☽ Ingress sign	day	ET / hr:mn / PT	
2/28	**6:13 pm**	3:13 pm	△♅	♍	1	**12:57 am**	
2	**6:50 pm**	3:50 pm	☍♀	♎	3	**3:20 am**	12:20 am
4		10:19 pm	☍♅	♏	5	**8:23 am**	5:23 am
5	**1:19 am**		☍♅	♏	5	**8:23 am**	5:23 am
7	**3:55 am**	12:55 am	☌♃	♐	7	**5:03 pm**	2:03 pm
9	**9:27 pm**	6:27 pm	△♅	♑	10	**4:52 am**	1:52 am
12	**11:36 am**	8:36 am	□♅	♒	12	**6:44 pm**	3:44 pm
15	**3:32 am**	12:32 am	⚹♂	♓	15	**6:12 am**	3:12 am
17	**9:12 am**	6:12 am	☌☉	♈	17	**2:57 pm**	11:57 am
19	**3:29 pm**	12:29 pm	☌♅	♉	19	**9:07 pm**	6:07 pm

☽ Last Aspect day	ET / hr:mn / PT		asp	☽ Ingress sign	day	ET / hr:mn / PT	
21	**1:21 pm**	10:21 am	☍♃	♊	21		10:30 pm
21	**1:21 pm**	10:21 am	☍♃	♊	22	**1:30 am**	
23	**11:52 pm**	8:52 pm	⚹♅	♋	24	**4:53 am**	1:53 am
25		11:58 pm	□♅	♌	26	**7:45 am**	4:45 am
26	**2:58 am**		□♅	♌	26	**7:45 am**	4:45 am
28	**5:54 am**	2:54 am	△♅	♍	28	**10:30 am**	7:30 am
29		9:59 pm	⚹♃	♎	30	**1:52 pm**	10:52 am
30	**12:59 am**		⚹♃	♎	30	**1:52 pm**	10:52 am

☽ Phases & Eclipses phase	day	ET / hr:mn / PT	
Full Moon	1	**7:51 pm**	4:51 pm
4th Quarter	9	**6:20 am**	3:20 am
New Moon	17	**9:12 am**	6:12 am
2nd Quarter	24	**11:35 am**	8:35 am
Full Moon	31	**8:37 am**	5:37 am

Planet Ingress		day	ET / hr:mn / PT	
☿	♈	5		11:34 pm
☿	♈	6	**2:34 am**	
♀	♈	6	**6:45 pm**	3:45 pm
♂	♑	17	**12:40 pm**	9:40 am
☉	♈	20	**12:15 pm**	9:15 am
⚵	♊	29	**9:34 pm**	6:34 pm
♀	♉	30		9:54 pm
♀	♉	31	**12:54 am**	

Planetary Motion		day	ET / hr:mn / PT	
♃	℞	8	**11:45 pm**	8:45 pm
⚳	D	18		9:12 pm
⚳	D	19	**12:12 am**	
☿	℞	22	**8:19 pm**	5:19 pm

1 THURSDAY
♀△♃ **6:22 am** 3:22 am
♂⚺♇ **10:32 am** 7:32 am
☽△♄ **1:10 pm** 10:10 am
☽☍☉ **7:51 pm** 4:51 pm
☽☍♆ **11:58 pm** 8:58 pm

2 FRIDAY
☿△♃ **8:05 am** 5:05 am
☽△♇ **11:26 am** 8:26 am
☽□♂ **12:29 pm** 9:29 am
☽⚹♃ **3:40 pm** 12:40 pm
☽☍☿ **4:48 pm** 1:48 pm
☽☍♀ **6:50 pm** 3:50 pm
☽⚻♅ **8:31 pm** 5:31 pm

3 SATURDAY
♀⚺♅ **2:31 pm** 11:31 am
☽□♄ **4:20 pm** 1:20 pm
☿⚺♅ **9:49 pm** 6:49 pm

4 SUNDAY
☽⚻☉ **3:08 am** 12:08 am
☽⚻♆ **3:33 am** 12:33 am
☉☌♆ **8:54 am** 5:54 am
☿☌♀ **1:05 pm** 10:05 am
☽□♇ **3:36 pm** 12:36 pm
☽⚹♂ **7:01 pm** 4:01 pm
☽⚺♃ **8:03 pm** 5:03 pm
☽☍♅ 10:19 pm

5 MONDAY
☽☍♅ **1:19 am**
☽⚻♀ **4:48 am** 1:48 am
☽⚻☿ **5:34 am** 2:34 am
♂⚺♃ **7:07 pm** 4:07 pm
☽⚹♄ **10:31 pm** 7:31 pm

6 TUESDAY
☽△♆ **10:23 am** 7:23 am
☽△☉ **2:27 pm** 11:27 am
☽⚹♇ **11:12 pm** 8:12 pm

7 WEDNESDAY
☽☌♃ **3:55 am** 12:55 am
☽⚺♂ **5:31 am** 2:31 am
☽⚻♅ **9:42 am** 6:42 am
☽△♀ **7:33 pm** 4:33 pm
☽△☿ **11:15 pm** 8:15 pm

8 THURSDAY
☽⚺♄ **8:25 am** 5:25 am
☽□♆ **8:52 pm** 5:52 pm

9 FRIDAY
☽□☉ **6:20 am** 3:20 am
☽⚺♇ **10:19 am** 7:19 am
☽⚺♃ **3:10 pm** 12:10 pm
☽☌♂ **7:54 pm** 4:54 pm
☽△♅ **9:27 pm** 6:27 pm

10 SATURDAY
☽□♀ **2:31 pm** 11:31 am
☽□☿ **8:25 pm** 5:25 pm
☽☌♄ **9:05 pm** 6:05 pm
☿□♄ 11:00 pm

11 SUNDAY
☿□♄ **2:00 am**
♂△♅ **7:23 am** 4:23 am
☉⚹♇ **7:56 am** 4:56 am
☽⚹♆ **10:43 am** 7:43 am
☽☌♇ 9:15 pm
☽⚹☉ 10:44 pm

12 MONDAY
☽☌♇ **12:15 am**
☽⚹☉ **1:44 am**
☽⚹♃ **5:00 am** 2:00 am
☽□♅ **11:36 am** 8:36 am
☽⚺♂ **12:56 pm** 9:56 am

13 TUESDAY
♀□♄ **8:39 am** 5:39 am
☽⚺♄ **11:05 am** 8:05 am
☽⚹♀ **11:21 am** 8:21 am
☉△♃ **4:06 pm** 1:06 pm
☽⚹☿ **5:36 pm** 2:36 pm
☽⚺♆ **11:22 pm** 8:22 pm

14 WEDNESDAY
☽⚺♇ **12:27 pm** 9:27 am
☽□♃ **4:53 pm** 1:53 pm
☽⚺☉ **7:07 pm** 4:07 pm
☽⚹♅ **11:34 pm** 8:34 pm

15 THURSDAY
☽⚹♂ **3:32 am** 12:32 am
☽⚹♄ **10:07 pm** 7:07 pm

16 FRIDAY
☽⚺♀ **4:33 am** 1:33 am
☽⚺☿ **9:14 am** 6:14 am
☽☌♆ **9:46 am** 6:46 am
☿⚺♆ **5:44 pm** 2:44 pm
☽⚹♇ **10:09 pm** 7:09 pm
☽△♃ 11:11 pm

17 SATURDAY
☽△♃ **2:11 am**
☉⚺♅ **4:41 am** 1:41 am
☽⚺♅ **8:52 am** 5:52 am
☽☌☉ **9:12 am** 6:12 am
☽□♂ **3:03 pm** 12:03 pm

18 SUNDAY
☽□♄ **6:19 am** 3:19 am
♀⚺♆ **11:13 am** 8:13 am
☽⚺♆ **5:21 pm** 2:21 pm
☽☌♀ **5:58 pm** 2:58 pm
☽☌☿ **7:47 pm** 4:47 pm

19 MONDAY
☽□♇ **5:05 am** 2:05 am
☽⚻♃ **8:46 am** 5:46 am
☽☌♅ **3:29 pm** 12:29 pm
☽⚺☉ **7:55 pm** 4:55 pm
☽△♂ **11:36 pm** 8:36 pm
☿☌♀ 9:03 pm

20 TUESDAY
☿☌♀ **12:03 am**
☽△♄ **12:05 pm** 9:05 am
☽⚹♆ **10:42 pm** 7:42 pm
☽⚺☿ 11:27 pm

21 WEDNESDAY
☽⚺☿ **2:27 am**
☽⚺♀ **4:24 am** 1:24 am
☽△♇ **9:58 am** 6:58 am
☽☍♃ **1:21 pm** 10:21 am
☽⚺♅ **8:13 pm** 5:13 pm

22 THURSDAY
☽⚹☉ **4:22 am** 1:22 am
☽⚻♂ **6:09 am** 3:09 am
☽⚻♄ **4:17 pm** 1:17 pm
☽□♆ 11:39 pm

23 FRIDAY
☽□♆ **2:39 am**
☽⚹☿ **6:31 am** 3:31 am
☽⚹♀ **1:07 pm** 10:07 am
☽⚻♇ **1:39 pm** 10:39 am
☽⚻♃ **4:45 pm** 1:45 pm
♀□♇ **7:17 pm** 4:17 pm
☽⚹♅ **11:52 pm** 8:52 pm

24 SATURDAY
☽□☉ **11:35 am** 8:35 am
☽☍♂ **11:36 am** 8:36 am
☉□♂ **12:08 pm** 9:08 am
☽☍♄ **7:37 pm** 4:37 pm

25 SUNDAY
♀⚻♃ **5:08 am** 2:08 am
☽△♆ **5:52 am** 2:52 am
☽□☿ **8:54 am** 5:54 am
☽☍♇ **4:41 pm** 1:41 pm
☽△♃ **7:32 pm** 4:32 pm
☽□♀ **8:58 pm** 5:58 pm
☽□♅ 11:58 pm

26 MONDAY
☽□♅ **2:58 am**
☽⚻♂ **4:31 pm** 1:31 pm
☽△☉ **6:13 pm** 3:13 pm
☽⚻♄ **10:33 pm** 7:33 pm

27 TUESDAY
☽⚻♆ **8:45 am** 5:45 am
☽△☿ **10:09 am** 7:09 am
☽⚻♇ **7:28 pm** 4:28 pm
☽□♃ **10:05 pm** 7:05 pm

28 WEDNESDAY
☽△♀ **4:33 am** 1:33 am
☽△♅ **5:54 am** 2:54 am
☿⚺♆ **6:01 pm** 3:01 pm
♀☌♅ **8:47 pm** 5:47 pm
☽△♂ **9:24 pm** 6:24 pm
☽⚻☉ 9:52 pm
☽△♄ 10:30 pm

29 THURSDAY
☽⚻☉ **12:52 am**
☽△♄ **1:30 am**
☉□♄ **10:16 am** 7:16 am
☽⚻☿ **10:57 am** 7:57 am
☽☍♆ **11:49 am** 8:49 am
☽△♇ **10:35 pm** 7:35 pm
☽⚹♃ 9:59 pm

30 FRIDAY
☽⚹♃ **12:59 am**
☽⚻♅ **9:23 am** 6:23 am
☽⚻♀ **12:47 pm** 9:47 am

31 SATURDAY
☽□♂ **3:12 am** 12:12 am
☽□♄ **5:22 am** 2:22 am
☽☍☉ **8:37 am** 5:37 am
☽☍☿ **12:16 pm** 9:16 am
☽⚻♆ **4:01 pm** 1:01 pm

Eastern time in bold type
Pacific time in medium type

MARCH 2018

DATE	SID.TIME	SUN	MOON	NODE	MERCURY	VENUS	MARS	JUPITER	SATURN	URANUS	NEPTUNE	PLUTO	CERES	PALLAS	JUNO	VESTA	CHIRON
1 Th	10 35 0	10♓20 39	26♌23	14♌52℞	20♓15	22♓32	20♐15	23♏07	7♑19	25♈55	13♓48	20♑37	5♌55℞	15♉16	2♓23	19♐34	27♓14
2 F	10 38 56	11 20 51	10♍52	14 50	22 08	23 47	20 51	23 09	7 23	25 58	13 50	20 39	5 47	15 44	2 51	19 57	27 18
3 Sa	10 42 53	12 21 01	25 07	14 47	24 00	25 02	21 26	23 10	7 28	26 00	13 52	20 40	5 40	16 12	3 19	20 20	27 21
4 Su	10 46 49	13 21 09	9♎03	14 43	25 51	26 17	22 02	23 11	7 32	26 03	13 55	20 41	5 33	16 41	3 47	20 43	27 25
5 M	10 50 46	14 21 16	22 37	14 38	27 40	27 31	22 37	23 12	7 36	26 06	13 57	20 43	5 27	17 10	4 15	21 05	27 28
6 T	10 54 43	15 21 21	5♏47	14 33	29 27	28 46	23 12	23 12	7 40	26 09	13 59	20 44	5 21	17 38	4 43	21 27	27 32
7 W	10 58 39	16 21 25	18 34	14 29	1♈11	0♈01	23 47	23 13	7 44	26 11	14 01	20 46	5 16	18 07	5 11	21 49	27 35
8 Th	11 2 36	17 21 27	1♐00	14 26	2 53	1 15	24 23	23 13	7 48	26 14	14 04	20 47	5 11	18 37	5 39	22 11	27 39
9 F	11 6 32	18 21 27	13 10	14 25D	4 31	2 30	24 58	23 13℞	7 51	26 17	14 06	20 48	5 06	19 06	6 07	22 33	27 42
10 Sa	11 10 29	19 21 26	25 07	14 25	6 05	3 45	25 33	23 13	7 55	26 20	14 08	20 49	5 02	19 36	6 35	22 54	27 46
11 Su	11 14 25	20 21 23	6♑58	14 26	7 35	4 59	26 08	23 13	7 59	26 23	14 11	20 51	4 58	20 05	7 03	23 16	27 50
12 M	11 18 22	21 21 18	18 46	14 28	8 59	6 14	26 43	23 13	8 02	26 26	14 13	20 52	4 55	20 35	7 32	23 37	27 53
13 T	11 22 18	22 21 12	0♒37	14 29	10 18	7 28	27 18	23 12	8 06	26 29	14 15	20 53	4 52	21 05	8 00	23 57	27 57
14 W	11 26 15	23 21 04	12 36	14 30℞	11 31	8 43	27 52	23 11	8 09	26 32	14 17	20 54	4 49	21 35	8 28	24 18	28 00
15 Th	11 30 12	24 20 54	24 46	14 30	12 37	9 57	28 27	23 10	8 13	26 35	14 20	20 55	4 47	22 06	8 56	24 38	28 04
16 F	11 34 8	25 20 42	7♓09	14 27	13 36	11 12	29 02	23 09	8 16	26 38	14 22	20 56	4 45	22 36	9 24	24 58	28 07
17 Sa	11 38 5	26 20 29	19 49	14 23	14 29	12 26	29 36	23 08	8 19	26 41	14 24	20 57	4 44	23 07	9 53	25 18	28 11
18 Su	11 42 1	27 20 13	2♈45	14 17	15 13	13 41	0♑11	23 06	8 22	26 44	14 26	20 58	4 44	23 38	10 21	25 38	28 15
19 M	11 45 58	28 19 56	15 56	14 09	15 49	14 55	0 45	23 04	8 25	26 47	14 29	21 00	4 43D	24 09	10 49	25 57	28 18
20 T	11 49 54	29 19 36	29 22	14 01	16 18	16 09	1 19	23 02	8 28	26 50	14 31	21 00	4 43	24 40	11 18	26 16	28 22
21 W	11 53 51	0♈19 14	13♉01	13 54	16 38	17 24	1 53	23 00	8 30	26 53	14 33	21 01	4 44	25 11	11 46	26 35	28 25
22 Th	11 57 47	1 18 50	26 49	13 48	16 50	18 38	2 27	22 58	8 33	26 57	14 35	21 02	4 45	25 42	12 14	26 53	28 29
23 F	12 1 44	2 18 24	10♊45	13 44	16 54℞	19 52	3 01	22 55	8 36	27 00	14 37	21 03	4 46	26 14	12 43	27 12	28 32
24 Sa	12 5 40	3 17 56	24 47	13 42D	16 51	21 06	3 35	22 53	8 38	27 03	14 40	21 04	4 48	26 46	13 11	27 30	28 36
25 Su	12 9 37	4 17 25	8♋54	13 41	16 39	22 21	4 09	22 50	8 40	27 06	14 42	21 05	4 51	27 17	13 39	27 47	28 40
26 M	12 13 34	5 16 52	23 03	13 42	16 21	23 35	4 43	22 47	8 43	27 09	14 44	21 06	4 53	27 49	14 08	28 05	28 43
27 T	12 17 30	6 16 16	7♌15	13 43℞	15 55	24 49	5 16	22 44	8 45	27 13	14 46	21 07	4 56	28 21	14 36	28 22	28 47
28 W	12 21 27	7 15 39	21 26	13 43	15 24	26 03	5 50	22 40	8 47	27 16	14 48	21 07	5 00	28 53	15 05	28 39	28 50
29 Th	12 25 23	8 14 58	5♍35	13 41	14 47	27 17	6 23	22 37	8 49	27 19	14 50	21 08	5 04	29 26	15 33	28 55	28 54
30 F	12 29 20	9 14 16	19 39	13 37	14 06	28 31	6 56	22 33	8 51	27 23	14 53	21 09	5 08	29 58	16 01	29 12	28 57
31 Sa	12 33 16	10 13 32	3♎32	13 30	13 21	29 45	7 30	22 29	8 53	27 26	14 55	21 10	5 13	0♊30	16 30	29 28	29 01

EPHEMERIS CALCULATED FOR 12 MIDNIGHT GREENWICH MEAN TIME. ALL OTHER DATA AND FACING ASPECTARIAN PAGE IN **EASTERN TIME (BOLD)** AND PACIFIC TIME (REGULAR).

APRIL 2018

☽ Last Aspect day	ET / hr:mn / PT	asp	☽ Ingress sign day	ET / hr:mn / PT
1	**2:29 pm** 11:29 am	☍ ♅	♏ 1	**6:57 pm** 3:57 pm
3	**12:06 pm** 9:06 am	☌ ♃	♐ 3	11:55 pm
3	**12:06 pm** 9:06 am	☌ ♃	♐ 4	**2:55 am**
6	**9:36 am** 6:36 am	△ ♅	♑ 6	**2:01 pm** 11:01 am
8	**10:40 pm** 7:40 pm	□ ♅	♒ 8	11:50 pm
8	**10:40 pm** 7:40 pm	□ ♅	♒ 9	**2:50 am**
11	**10:55 am** 7:55 am	⚹ ♅	♓ 11	**2:40 pm** 11:40 am
13	**7:27 am** 4:27 am	△ ♃	♈ 13	**11:25 pm** 8:25 pm
15	10:59 pm	☌ ♅	♉ 16	**4:51 am** 1:51 am
16	**1:59 am**	☌ ♅	♉ 16	**4:51 am** 1:51 am

☽ Last Aspect day	ET / hr:mn / PT	asp	☽ Ingress sign day	ET / hr:mn / PT
17	**6:05 pm** 3:05 pm	☌ ♀	♊ 18	**8:02 am** 5:02 am
20	**8:05 am** 5:05 am	⚹ ♅	♋ 20	**10:26 am** 7:26 am
22	**10:58 am** 7:58 am	□ ♅	♌ 22	**1:09 pm** 10:09 am
24	**2:40 pm** 11:40 am	△ ♅	♍ 24	**4:40 pm** 1:40 pm
26	**5:49 am** 2:49 am	△ ♇	♎ 26	**9:13 pm** 6:13 pm
28	10:32 pm	☍ ♅	♏ 29	**3:11 am** 12:11 am
29	**1:32 am**	☍ ♅	♏ 29	**3:11 am** 12:11 am
30	**10:56 pm** 7:56 pm	⚹ ♂	♐ 5/1	**11:20 am** 8:20 am

☽ Phases & Eclipses phase	day	ET / hr:mn / PT
4th Quarter	8	**3:18 am** 12:18 am
New Moon	15	**9:57 pm** 6:57 pm
2nd Quarter	22	**5:46 pm** 2:46 pm
Full Moon	29	**8:58 pm** 5:58 pm

Planet Ingress	day	ET / hr:mn / PT
⚶ ♑	1	**9:54 pm** 6:54 pm
⚷ ♈	17	**4:12 am** 1:12 am
☉ ♉	19	**11:13 pm** 8:13 pm
♀ ♊	24	**12:40 pm** 9:40 am
⚵ ♈	28	**3:44 am** 12:44 am

Planetary Motion	day	ET / hr:mn / PT
☿ D	15	**5:21 am** 2:21 am
♄ R	17	**9:47 pm** 6:47 pm
♇ R	22	**11:26 am** 8:26 am

1 SUNDAY
- ☽ □ ♇ **3:05 am** 12:05 am
- ☽ ⚺ ♃ **5:16 am** 2:16 am
- ☉ ☌ ☿ **1:53 pm** 10:53 am
- ☽ ☍ ♅ **2:29 pm** 11:29 am
- ☽ ☍ ♀ **11:17 pm** 8:17 pm

2 MONDAY
- ☽ ⚹ ♂ **11:18 am** 8:18 am
- ☽ ⚹ ♄ **11:19 am** 8:19 am
- ♂ ☌ ♄ **11:44 am** 8:44 am
- ☽ ⚻ ☿ **3:14 pm** 12:14 pm
- ☽ ⚻ ☉ **7:05 pm** 4:05 pm
- ☽ △ ♆ **10:34 pm** 7:34 pm

3 TUESDAY
- ☽ ⚹ ♇ **10:09 am** 7:09 am
- ☽ ☌ ♃ **12:06 pm** 9:06 am
- ☽ ⚻ ♅ **10:26 pm** 7:26 pm

4 WEDNESDAY
- ☿ □ ♂ **3:05 am** 12:05 am
- ☽ ⚻ ♀ **1:41 pm** 10:41 am
- ☉ ⚺ ♆ **6:10 pm** 3:10 pm
- ☽ ⚺ ♄ **8:22 pm** 5:22 pm
- ☽ △ ☿ **8:51 pm** 5:51 pm
- ☽ ⚺ ♂ **10:53 pm** 7:53 pm

5 THURSDAY
- ☿ □ ♄ **4:22 am** 1:22 am
- ☽ □ ♆ **8:19 am** 5:19 am
- ☽ △ ☉ **9:31 am** 6:31 am
- ☽ ⚺ ♇ **8:27 pm** 5:27 pm
- ☽ ⚺ ♃ **10:04 pm** 7:04 pm

6 FRIDAY
- ☽ △ ♅ **9:36 am** 6:36 am
- ☿ ⚺ ♀ **1:05 pm** 10:05 am

7 SATURDAY
- ☽ □ ☿ **5:15 am** 2:15 am
- ☽ △ ♀ **8:10 am** 5:10 am
- ☽ ☌ ♄ **8:19 am** 5:19 am
- ♀ △ ♄ **9:37 am** 6:37 am
- ☽ ☌ ♂ **1:41 pm** 10:41 am
- ☽ ⚹ ♆ **8:45 pm** 5:45 pm

8 SUNDAY
- ☽ □ ☉ **3:18 am** 12:18 am
- ☽ ☌ ♇ **9:03 am** 6:03 am
- ☽ ⚹ ♃ **10:14 am** 7:14 am
- ☽ □ ♅ **10:40 pm** 7:40 pm

9 MONDAY
- ☽ ⚹ ☿ **3:16 pm** 12:16 pm
- ☽ ⚺ ♄ **9:12 pm** 6:12 pm

10 TUESDAY
- ☽ □ ♀ **3:56 am** 12:56 am
- ☽ ⚺ ♂ **5:17 am** 2:17 am
- ☽ ⚺ ♆ **9:34 am** 6:34 am
- ☽ ⚹ ☉ **9:11 pm** 6:11 pm
- ☽ ⚺ ♇ **9:29 pm** 6:29 pm
- ☽ □ ♃ **10:09 pm** 7:09 pm
- ☉ □ ♇ 9:54 pm
- ♀ △ ♂ 11:03 pm

11 WEDNESDAY
- ☉ □ ♇ **12:54 am**
- ♀ △ ♂ **2:03 am**
- ☉ ⚻ ♃ **8:15 am** 5:15 am
- ☽ ⚹ ♅ **10:55 am** 7:55 am
- ☽ ⚺ ☿ 9:48 pm

12 THURSDAY
- ☽ ⚺ ☿ **12:48 am**
- ☽ ⚹ ♄ **8:18 am** 5:18 am
- ♀ ⚹ ♆ **12:26 pm** 9:26 am
- ☽ ⚹ ♂ **6:29 pm** 3:29 pm
- ☽ ☌ ♆ **8:09 pm** 5:09 pm
- ☽ ⚹ ♀ **8:57 pm** 5:57 pm

13 FRIDAY
- ☽ ⚹ ♇ **7:16 am** 4:16 am
- ☽ △ ♃ **7:27 am** 4:27 am
- ☽ ⚺ ☉ **11:43 am** 8:43 am
- ☽ ⚺ ♅ **8:10 pm** 5:10 pm

14 SATURDAY
- ♃ ⚹ ♇ **5:58 am** 2:58 am
- ☽ ☌ ☿ **8:12 am** 5:12 am
- ♂ ⚹ ♆ **1:27 pm** 10:27 am
- ☽ □ ♄ **4:01 pm** 1:01 pm

15 SUNDAY
- ☽ ⚺ ♆ **3:15 am** 12:15 am
- ☽ □ ♂ **3:46 am** 12:46 am
- ☽ ⚺ ♀ **9:20 am** 6:20 am
- ☽ ⚻ ♃ **1:22 pm** 10:22 am
- ☽ □ ♇ **1:36 pm** 10:36 am
- ☽ ☌ ☉ **9:57 pm** 6:57 pm
- ☽ ☌ ♅ 10:59 pm

16 MONDAY
- ☽ ☌ ♅ **1:59 am**
- ☽ ⚺ ☿ **1:15 pm** 10:15 am
- ☽ △ ♄ **8:38 pm** 5:38 pm

17 TUESDAY
- ♀ ☍ ♃ **3:00 am** 12:00 am
- ☽ ⚹ ♆ **7:27 am** 4:27 am
- ♀ △ ♇ **9:04 am** 6:04 am
- ☽ △ ♂ **9:48 am** 6:48 am
- ☽ ☍ ♃ **4:40 pm** 1:40 pm
- ☽ △ ♇ **5:18 pm** 2:18 pm
- ☽ ☌ ♀ **6:05 pm** 3:05 pm

18 WEDNESDAY
- ☽ ⚺ ☉ **5:09 am** 2:09 am
- ☽ ⚺ ♅ **5:28 am** 2:28 am
- ☉ ☌ ♅ **10:00 am** 7:00 am
- ☽ ⚹ ☿ **4:57 pm** 1:57 pm
- ☽ ⚻ ♄ **11:26 pm** 8:26 pm

19 THURSDAY
- ☽ □ ♆ **10:10 am** 7:10 am
- ☽ ⚻ ♂ **2:15 pm** 11:15 am
- ☽ ⚻ ♃ **6:47 pm** 3:47 pm
- ☽ ⚻ ♇ **7:48 pm** 4:48 pm
- ☽ ⚺ ♀ 10:17 pm

20 FRIDAY
- ☽ ⚺ ♀ **1:17 am**
- ☽ ⚹ ♅ **8:05 am** 5:05 am
- ☽ ⚹ ☉ **11:16 am** 8:16 am
- ☽ □ ☿ **8:42 pm** 5:42 pm
- ☽ ☍ ♄ 10:49 pm

21 SATURDAY
- ☽ ☍ ♄ **1:49 am**
- ☽ △ ♆ **12:44 pm** 9:44 am
- ☽ ☍ ♂ **6:36 pm** 3:36 pm
- ☽ △ ♃ **8:56 pm** 5:56 pm
- ☽ ☍ ♇ **10:21 pm** 7:21 pm

22 SUNDAY
- ☽ ⚹ ♀ **8:40 am** 5:40 am
- ☽ □ ♅ **10:58 am** 7:58 am
- ☽ □ ☉ **5:46 pm** 2:46 pm
- ☽ △ ☿ 10:32 pm

23 MONDAY
- ☽ △ ☿ **1:32 am**
- ☽ ⚻ ♄ **4:44 am** 1:44 am
- ♀ ⚺ ♅ **12:34 pm** 9:34 am
- ☽ ⚻ ♆ **3:56 pm** 12:56 pm
- ☽ ⚻ ♂ **11:40 pm** 8:40 pm
- ☽ □ ♃ **11:44 pm** 8:44 pm
- ♂ ⚹ ♃ 10:13 pm
- ☽ ⚻ ♇ 10:37 pm

24 TUESDAY
- ♂ ⚹ ♃ **1:13 am**
- ☽ ⚻ ♇ **1:37 am**
- ☽ △ ♅ **2:40 pm** 11:40 am
- ☽ □ ♀ **5:03 pm** 2:03 pm
- ☽ △ ☉ 10:17 pm

25 WEDNESDAY
- ☽ △ ☉ **1:17 am**
- ☽ ⚻ ☿ **7:58 am** 4:58 am
- ☽ △ ♄ **8:30 am** 5:30 am
- ☿ □ ♄ **5:28 pm** 2:28 pm
- ☽ ☍ ♆ **8:04 pm** 5:04 pm

26 THURSDAY
- ☽ ⚹ ♃ **3:28 am** 12:28 am
- ☽ △ ♂ **5:47 am** 2:47 am
- ☽ △ ♇ **5:49 am** 2:49 am
- ♂ ☌ ♇ **7:00 am** 4:00 am
- ☽ ⚻ ♅ **7:23 pm** 4:23 pm
- ☽ △ ♀ 11:48 pm

27 FRIDAY
- ☽ △ ♀ **2:48 am**
- ☽ ⚻ ☉ **10:08 am** 7:08 am
- ☽ □ ♄ **1:21 pm** 10:21 am
- ☽ ☍ ☿ **4:17 pm** 1:17 pm
- ☽ ⚻ ♆ 10:24 pm

28 SATURDAY
- ☽ ⚻ ♆ **1:24 am**
- ☽ ⚺ ♃ **8:25 am** 5:25 am
- ☽ □ ♇ **11:19 am** 8:19 am
- ☽ □ ♂ **1:17 pm** 10:17 am
- ☽ ☍ ♅ 10:32 pm

29 SUNDAY
- ☽ ☍ ♅ **1:32 am**
- ☉ △ ♄ **6:04 am** 3:04 am
- ☽ ⚻ ♀ **2:32 pm** 11:32 am
- ☽ ⚹ ♄ **7:50 pm** 4:50 pm
- ☽ ☍ ☉ **8:58 pm** 5:58 pm

30 MONDAY
- ☽ ⚻ ☿ **3:15 am** 12:15 am
- ☽ △ ♆ **8:31 am** 5:31 am
- ☽ ☌ ♃ **3:11 pm** 12:11 pm
- ☽ ⚹ ♇ **6:43 pm** 3:43 pm
- ☽ ⚹ ♂ **10:56 pm** 7:56 pm

Eastern time in bold type
Pacific time in medium type

APRIL 2018

DATE	SID.TIME	SUN	MOON	NODE	MERCURY	VENUS	MARS	JUPITER	SATURN	URANUS	NEPTUNE	PLUTO	CERES	PALLAS	JUNO	VESTA	CHIRON
1 Su	12 37 13	11 ♈ 12 45	17 ♎ 12	13 ♌ 21 ℞	12 ♈ 33 ℞	0 ♉ 59	8 ♑ 03	22 ♏ 25 ℞	8 ♑ 55	27 ♈ 29	14 ♓ 57	21 ♑ 10	5 ♌ 18	1 ♊ 03	16 ♓ 58	29 ♐ 43	29 ♓ 04
2 M	12 41 9	12 11 56	0 ♏ 35	13 10	11 44	2 13	8 36	22 21	8 56	27 33	14 59	21 11	5 23	1 36	17 27	29 59	29 08
3 T	12 45 6	13 11 06	13 39	13 00	10 55	3 27	9 08	22 17	8 58	27 36	15 01	21 11	5 29	2 08	17 55	0 ♑ 14	29 11
4 W	12 49 3	14 10 14	26 23	12 51	10 05	4 40	9 41	22 12	8 59	27 39	15 03	21 12	5 36	2 41	18 24	0 29	29 15
5 Th	12 52 59	15 09 19	8 ♐ 49	12 43	9 17	5 54	10 14	22 07	9 00	27 43	15 05	21 13	5 42	3 14	18 53	0 43	29 18
6 F	12 56 56	16 08 23	21 00	12 37	8 31	7 08	10 46	22 03	9 02	27 46	15 07	21 13	5 49	3 47	19 21	0 57	29 22
7 Sa	13 0 52	17 07 26	2 ♑ 58	12 34	7 48	8 22	11 19	21 58	9 03	27 49	15 09	21 14	5 57	4 20	19 50	1 11	29 25
8 Su	13 4 49	18 06 26	14 49	12 33D	7 09	9 35	11 51	21 52	9 04	27 53	15 11	21 14	6 04	4 54	20 18	1 24	29 29
9 M	13 8 45	19 05 25	26 38	12 33	6 34	10 49	12 23	21 47	9 05	27 56	15 13	21 14	6 12	5 27	20 47	1 37	29 32
10 T	13 12 42	20 04 22	8 ♒ 30	12 34 ℞	6 03	12 03	12 55	21 42	9 06	28 00	15 15	21 15	6 21	6 00	21 15	1 50	29 36
11 W	13 16 38	21 03 17	20 30	12 33	5 38	13 16	13 27	21 36	9 06	28 03	15 17	21 15	6 29	6 34	21 44	2 02	29 39
12 Th	13 20 35	22 02 10	2 ♓ 45	12 31	5 17	14 30	13 58	21 31	9 07	28 06	15 19	21 16	6 39	7 07	22 13	2 14	29 42
13 F	13 24 32	23 01 02	15 16	12 27	5 02	15 43	14 30	21 25	9 08	28 10	15 21	21 16	6 48	7 41	22 41	2 25	29 46
14 Sa	13 28 28	23 59 52	28 08	12 20	4 52	16 57	15 01	21 19	9 08	28 13	15 23	21 16	6 58	8 15	23 10	2 37	29 49
15 Su	13 32 25	24 58 40	11 ♈ 21	12 11	4 47D	18 10	15 32	21 13	9 08	28 17	15 24	21 16	7 08	8 49	23 38	2 47	29 52
16 M	13 36 21	25 57 26	24 55	12 00	4 48	19 24	16 03	21 06	9 09	28 20	15 26	21 17	7 18	9 23	24 07	2 58	29 56
17 T	13 40 18	26 56 10	8 ♉ 47	11 48	4 53	20 37	16 34	21 00	9 09	28 24	15 28	21 17	7 29	9 57	24 36	3 08	29 59
18 W	13 44 14	27 54 52	22 52	11 37	5 04	21 50	17 05	20 54	9 09 ℞	28 27	15 30	21 17	7 40	10 31	25 04	3 17	0 ♈ 02
19 Th	13 48 11	28 53 32	7 ♊ 06	11 27	5 20	23 04	17 35	20 47	9 09	28 31	15 32	21 17	7 51	11 05	25 33	3 26	0 05
20 F	13 52 7	29 52 10	21 24	11 20	5 40	24 17	18 06	20 41	9 09	28 34	15 34	21 17	8 03	11 39	26 02	3 35	0 09
21 Sa	13 56 4	0 ♉ 50 46	5 ♋ 41	11 16	6 05	25 30	18 36	20 34	9 09	28 37	15 35	21 17	8 15	12 13	26 30	3 43	0 12
22 Su	14 0 1	1 49 19	19 54	11 14D	6 34	26 43	19 06	20 27	9 08	28 41	15 37	21 17 ℞	8 27	12 47	26 59	3 51	0 15
23 M	14 3 57	2 47 51	4 ♌ 01	11 14 ℞	7 08	27 56	19 36	20 20	9 08	28 44	15 39	21 17	8 40	13 22	27 28	3 58	0 18
24 T	14 7 54	3 46 20	18 02	11 14	7 45	29 09	20 05	20 13	9 07	28 48	15 40	21 17	8 53	13 56	27 56	4 05	0 21
25 W	14 11 50	4 44 47	1 ♍ 55	11 13	8 26	0 ♊ 22	20 35	20 06	9 07	28 51	15 42	21 17	9 06	14 31	28 25	4 12	0 24
26 Th	14 15 47	5 43 11	15 41	11 10	9 11	1 35	21 04	19 59	9 06	28 55	15 44	21 17	9 19	15 05	28 53	4 18	0 27
27 F	14 19 43	6 41 34	29 19	11 04	9 59	2 48	21 33	19 52	9 05	28 58	15 45	21 17	9 33	15 40	29 22	4 24	0 30
28 Sa	14 23 40	7 39 55	12 ♎ 47	10 55	10 51	4 01	22 01	19 44	9 04	29 01	15 47	21 17	9 47	16 14	29 51	4 29	0 33
29 Su	14 27 36	8 38 13	26 04	10 43	11 46	5 14	22 30	19 37	9 03	29 05	15 48	21 17	10 01	16 49	0 ♈ 19	4 34	0 36
30 M	14 31 33	9 36 30	9 ♏ 07	10 31	12 43	6 27	22 58	19 30	9 02	29 08	15 50	21 16	10 15	17 24	0 48	4 38	0 39

EPHEMERIS CALCULATED FOR 12 MIDNIGHT GREENWICH MEAN TIME. ALL OTHER DATA AND FACING ASPECTARIAN PAGE IN **EASTERN TIME (BOLD)** AND PACIFIC TIME (REGULAR).

MAY 2018

☽ Last Aspect day	ET	PT	asp	☽ Ingress sign	day	ET	PT
4/30	**10:56 pm**	7:56 pm	⚹♂	♐	1	**11:20 am**	8:20 am
3	**8:50 pm**	5:50 pm	△♅	♑	3	**10:06 pm**	7:06 pm
6	**9:48 am**	6:48 am	□♅	♒	6	**10:48 am**	7:48 am
8	**10:29 pm**	7:29 pm	⚹♅	♓	8	**11:11 pm**	8:11 pm
11	**5:02 am**	2:02 am	⚹♂	♈	11	**8:40 am**	5:40 am
13	**2:05 pm**	11:05 am	☌♅	♉	13	**2:15 pm**	11:15 am
15	**4:30 pm**	1:30 pm	△♂	♊	15	**4:43 pm**	1:43 pm
17	**2:18 pm**	11:18 am	☌♀	♋	17	**5:47 pm**	2:47 pm
19	**5:14 pm**	2:14 pm	⚹☉	♌	19	**7:11 pm**	4:11 pm
20	**11:30 pm**	8:30 pm	□♃	♍	21	**10:03 pm**	7:03 pm
23	**10:55 am**	7:55 am	△♇	♎	23		11:52 pm
23	**10:55 am**	7:55 am	△♇	♎	24	**2:52 am**	
25	**5:04 pm**	2:04 pm	□♇	♏	26	**9:39 am**	6:39 am
28	**1:25 pm**	10:25 am	☍☿	♐	28	**6:29 pm**	3:29 pm
29		11:26 pm	□♆	♑	31	**5:27 am**	2:27 am
30	**2:26 am**		□♆	♑	31	**5:27 am**	2:27 am

☽ Phases & Eclipses phase	day	ET	PT
4th Quarter	7	**10:09 pm**	7:09 pm
New Moon	15	**7:48 am**	4:48 am
2nd Quarter	21	**11:49 pm**	8:49 pm
Full Moon	29	**10:20 am**	7:20 am

Planet Ingress		day	ET	PT
☿	♉	13	**8:40 am**	5:40 am
♅	♉	15	**11:16 am**	8:16 am
♂	♒	15		9:55 pm
♂	♒	16	**12:55 am**	
♀	♋	19	**9:11 am**	6:11 am
☉	♊	20	**10:15 pm**	7:15 pm
⚳	♋	21	**9:09 am**	6:09 am
☿	♊	29	**7:49 pm**	4:49 pm

Planetary Motion		day	ET	PT
♇	℞	8	**3:48 am**	12:48 am

1 TUESDAY
☽ ⚻ ♅ **9:51 am** 6:51 am
♀ ⚻ ♄ **10:24 pm** 7:24 pm

2 WEDNESDAY
☽ ⚺ ♄ **4:39 am** 1:39 am
☽ ☍ ♀ **5:21 am** 2:21 am
☽ ⚻ ☉ **10:49 am** 7:49 am
☽ △ ☿ **5:58 pm** 2:58 pm
☽ □ ♆ **6:10 pm** 3:10 pm
☿ ⚺ ♆ **8:03 pm** 5:03 pm
☽ ⚺ ♃ 9:27 pm

3 THURSDAY
☽ ⚺ ♃ **12:27 am**
☽ ⚺ ♇ **4:43 am** 1:43 am
☽ ⚺ ♂ **11:27 am** 8:27 am
☽ △ ♅ **8:50 pm** 5:50 pm

4 FRIDAY
☽ ☌ ♄ **4:02 pm** 1:02 pm
☽ ⚻ ♀ **11:38 pm** 8:38 pm

5 SATURDAY
☽ △ ☉ **3:52 am** 12:52 am
☽ ⚹ ♆ **6:17 am** 3:17 am
☿ ⚻ ♃ **7:05 am** 4:05 am
☽ ⚹ ♃ **12:00 pm** 9:00 am
☽ □ ☿ **12:38 pm** 9:38 am
☽ ☌ ♇ **5:00 pm** 2:00 pm
☽ ☌ ♂ 11:20 pm

6 SUNDAY
☽ ☌ ♂ **2:20 am**
☽ □ ♅ **9:48 am** 6:48 am
☉ ⚹ ♆ **9:56 am** 6:56 am

7 MONDAY
☽ ⚺ ♄ **4:47 am** 1:47 am
☿ □ ♇ **4:52 am** 1:52 am
♀ □ ♆ **5:58 pm** 2:58 pm
☽ ⚺ ♆ **7:16 pm** 4:16 pm
☽ △ ♀ **7:25 pm** 4:25 pm
☽ □ ☉ **10:09 pm** 7:09 pm
☽ □ ♃ 9:11 pm

8 TUESDAY
☽ □ ♃ **12:11 am**
☽ ⚺ ♇ **5:43 am** 2:43 am
☽ ⚹ ☿ **8:50 am** 5:50 am
☽ ⚺ ♂ **5:12 pm** 2:12 pm
☉ ☍ ♃ **8:39 pm** 5:39 pm
☽ ⚹ ♅ **10:29 pm** 7:29 pm

9 WEDNESDAY
♀ ⚻ ♃ **2:36 pm** 11:36 am
☽ ⚹ ♄ **4:22 pm** 1:22 pm

10 THURSDAY
☽ ☌ ♆ **6:27 am** 3:27 am
☽ △ ♃ **10:26 am** 7:26 am
☽ □ ♀ **12:44 pm** 9:44 am
☽ ⚹ ☉ **1:58 pm** 10:58 am
☽ ⚹ ♇ **4:13 pm** 1:13 pm
☽ ⚺ ☿ 11:23 pm

11 FRIDAY
☽ ⚺ ☿ **2:23 am**
☽ ⚹ ♂ **5:02 am** 2:02 am
☽ ⚺ ♅ **8:15 am** 5:15 am
☉ △ ♇ **7:10 pm** 4:10 pm
☽ □ ♄ 9:35 pm
♀ ⚻ ♇ 10:05 pm

12 SATURDAY
☽ □ ♄ **12:35 am**
♀ ⚻ ♇ **1:05 am**
☿ □ ♂ **9:30 am** 6:30 am
☽ ⚺ ♆ **1:56 pm** 10:56 am
☽ ⚻ ♃ **5:02 pm** 2:02 pm
☽ □ ♇ **10:54 pm** 7:54 pm
☽ ⚹ ♀ 10:01 pm
☽ ⚺ ☉ 10:02 pm
☉ ⚺ ♀ 10:25 pm

13 SUNDAY
☽ ⚹ ♀ **1:01 am**
☽ ⚺ ☉ **1:02 am**
☉ ⚺ ♀ **1:25 am**
☿ ☌ ♅ **6:50 am** 3:50 am
☽ □ ♂ **12:31 pm** 9:31 am
☽ ☌ ♅ **2:05 pm** 11:05 am
☽ ☌ ☿ **2:57 pm** 11:57 am

14 MONDAY
☽ △ ♄ **4:58 am** 1:58 am
☽ ⚹ ♆ **5:44 pm** 2:44 pm
☽ ☍ ♃ **8:08 pm** 5:08 pm
☽ △ ♇ 11:05 pm

15 TUESDAY
☽ △ ♇ **2:05 am**
☽ ☌ ☉ **7:48 am** 4:48 am
☽ ⚺ ♀ **8:46 am** 5:46 am
☽ △ ♂ **4:30 pm** 1:30 pm
☽ ⚺ ♅ **4:44 pm** 1:44 pm
☽ ⚺ ☿ **11:32 pm** 8:32 pm

16 WEDNESDAY
♂ □ ♅ **3:04 am** 12:04 am
☽ ⚻ ♄ **6:42 am** 3:42 am
☽ □ ♆ **7:16 pm** 4:16 pm
☽ ⚻ ♃ **9:08 pm** 6:08 pm

17 THURSDAY
☽ ⚻ ♇ **3:20 am** 12:20 am
☽ ⚺ ☉ **12:26 pm** 9:26 am
☽ ☌ ♀ **2:18 pm** 11:18 am
☽ ⚹ ♅ **5:59 pm** 2:59 pm
☽ ⚻ ♂ **6:54 pm** 3:54 pm

18 FRIDAY
☽ ⚹ ☿ **6:51 am** 3:51 am
☽ ☍ ♄ **7:34 am** 4:34 am
☿ △ ♄ **12:49 pm** 9:49 am
☽ △ ♆ **8:23 pm** 5:23 pm
☽ △ ♃ **9:47 pm** 6:47 pm

19 SATURDAY
☽ ☍ ♇ **4:26 am** 1:26 am
♀ ⚹ ♅ **1:30 pm** 10:30 am
☽ ⚹ ☉ **5:14 pm** 2:14 pm
☽ □ ♅ **7:33 pm** 4:33 pm
☽ ⚺ ♀ **8:05 pm** 5:05 pm
☽ ☍ ♂ **9:37 pm** 6:37 pm

20 SUNDAY
☽ ⚻ ♄ **9:07 am** 6:07 am
☽ □ ☿ **3:31 pm** 12:31 pm
♀ ⚻ ♂ **10:06 pm** 7:06 pm
☽ ⚻ ♆ **10:32 pm** 7:32 pm
☽ □ ♃ **11:30 pm** 8:30 pm

21 MONDAY
☉ ⚺ ♅ **5:47 am** 2:47 am
☽ ⚻ ♇ **6:45 am** 3:45 am
☽ △ ♅ **10:38 pm** 7:38 pm
☽ □ ☉ **11:49 pm** 8:49 pm
☽ ⚻ ♂ 10:57 pm

22 TUESDAY
☽ ⚻ ♂ **1:57 am**
☽ ⚹ ♀ **3:47 am** 12:47 am
☽ △ ♄ **12:19 pm** 9:19 am
☿ ⚹ ♆ **10:13 pm** 7:13 pm
☿ ☍ ♃ 10:54 pm
☽ ☍ ♆ 11:30 pm
☽ ⚹ ♃ 11:59 pm

23 WEDNESDAY
☿ ☍ ♃ **1:54 am**
☽ ☍ ♆ **2:30 am**
☽ ⚹ ♃ **2:59 am**
☽ △ ☿ **3:10 am** 12:10 am
☽ △ ♇ **10:55 am** 7:55 am
☉ △ ♂ **10:39 pm** 7:39 pm

24 THURSDAY
☽ ⚻ ♅ **3:40 am** 12:40 am
☽ △ ♂ **8:19 am** 5:19 am
☽ △ ☉ **8:48 am** 5:48 am
☽ □ ♀ **2:03 pm** 11:03 am
☽ □ ♄ **5:28 pm** 2:28 pm

25 FRIDAY
♃ △ ♆ **5:52 am** 2:52 am
☽ ⚺ ♃ **8:25 am** 5:25 am
☽ ⚻ ♆ **8:27 am** 5:27 am
☿ △ ♇ **9:38 am** 6:38 am
☽ □ ♇ **5:04 pm** 2:04 pm
☽ ⚻ ☿ **6:23 pm** 3:23 pm
♀ ☍ ♄ 11:40 pm

26 SATURDAY
♀ ☍ ♄ **2:40 am**
☽ ☍ ♅ **10:43 am** 7:43 am
☽ □ ♂ **4:46 pm** 1:46 pm
☽ ⚻ ☉ **8:16 pm** 5:16 pm
☽ ⚹ ♄ 9:34 pm
☽ △ ♀ 11:55 pm

27 SUNDAY
☽ ⚹ ♄ **12:34 am**
☽ △ ♀ **2:55 am**
☽ ☌ ♃ **3:48 pm** 12:48 pm
☽ △ ♆ **4:23 pm** 1:23 pm
☽ ⚹ ♇ 10:12 pm

28 MONDAY
☽ ⚹ ♇ **1:12 am**
☽ ☍ ☿ **1:25 pm** 10:25 am
☽ ⚻ ♅ **7:48 pm** 4:48 pm
☉ ⚻ ♄ 11:36 pm

29 TUESDAY
☉ ⚻ ♄ **2:36 am**
☽ ⚹ ♂ **3:20 am** 12:20 am
☽ ⚺ ♄ **9:42 am** 6:42 am
☽ ☍ ☉ **10:20 am** 7:20 am
☽ ⚻ ♀ **6:33 pm** 3:33 pm
☽ ⚺ ♃ 10:15 pm
☽ □ ♆ 11:26 pm

30 WEDNESDAY
☽ ⚺ ♃ **1:15 am**
☽ □ ♆ **2:26 am**
☿ ⚺ ♅ **4:22 am** 1:22 am
☽ ⚺ ♇ **11:27 am** 8:27 am

31 THURSDAY
☽ △ ♅ **7:02 am** 4:02 am
☽ ⚻ ☿ **12:39 pm** 9:39 am
☽ ⚺ ♂ **4:06 pm** 1:06 pm
☽ ☌ ♄ **8:53 pm** 5:53 pm

Eastern time in bold type
Pacific time in medium type

MAY 2018

DATE	SID.TIME	SUN	MOON	NODE	MERCURY	VENUS	MARS	JUPITER	SATURN	URANUS	NEPTUNE	PLUTO	CERES	PALLAS	JUNO	VESTA	CHIRON
1 T	14 35 29	10 ♉ 34 45	21 ♏ 57	10 ♌ 18 ℞	13 ♈ 44	7 ♊ 39	23 ♑ 26	19 ♏ 22 ℞	9 ♑ 01 ℞	29 ♈ 12	15 ♓ 51	21 ♑ 16 ℞	10 ♌ 30	17 ♊ 59	1 ♈ 17	4 ♑ 42	0 ♈ 42
2 W	14 39 26	11 32 59	4 ♐ 31	10 05	14 48	8 52	23 54	19 15	9 00	29 15	15 53	21 16	10 45	18 33	1 45	4 45	0 45
3 Th	14 43 23	12 31 11	16 50	9 55	15 54	10 05	24 22	19 07	8 58	29 18	15 54	21 16	11 00	19 08	2 14	4 48	0 48
4 F	14 47 19	13 29 21	28 57	9 47	17 03	11 17	24 49	19 00	8 57	29 22	15 56	21 15	11 16	19 43	2 43	4 50	0 51
5 Sa	14 51 16	14 27 29	10 ♑ 53	9 42	18 15	12 30	25 16	18 52	8 55	29 25	15 57	21 15	11 31	20 18	3 11	4 52	0 54
6 Su	14 55 12	15 25 37	22 43	9 39	19 29	13 42	25 43	18 45	8 53	29 28	15 59	21 15	11 47	20 53	3 40	4 53	0 56
7 M	14 59 9	16 23 43	4 ♒ 31	9 38 D	20 45	14 55	26 10	18 37	8 52	29 32	16 00	21 14	12 03	21 28	4 08	4 54	0 59
8 T	15 3 5	17 21 47	16 23	9 38 ℞	22 04	16 07	26 36	18 29	8 50	29 35	16 01	21 14	12 19	22 03	4 37	4 55 ℞	1 02
9 W	15 7 2	18 19 50	28 24	9 38	23 25	17 20	27 02	18 22	8 48	29 38	16 03	21 13	12 36	22 38	5 06	4 55	1 05
10 Th	15 10 58	19 17 51	10 ♓ 39	9 37	24 48	18 32	27 28	18 14	8 46	29 42	16 04	21 13	12 53	23 13	5 34	4 54	1 07
11 F	15 14 55	20 15 52	23 13	9 33	26 14	19 44	27 53	18 06	8 44	29 45	16 05	21 12	13 10	23 48	6 03	4 53	1 10
12 Sa	15 18 52	21 13 50	6 ♈ 10	9 27	27 42	20 56	28 18	17 59	8 42	29 48	16 06	21 12	13 27	24 23	6 31	4 51	1 12
13 Su	15 22 48	22 11 48	19 33	9 18	29 12	22 09	28 43	17 51	8 39	29 52	16 07	21 11	13 44	24 59	7 00	4 49	1 15
14 M	15 26 45	23 09 44	3 ♉ 20	9 08	0 ♉ 44	23 21	29 07	17 43	8 37	29 55	16 09	21 11	14 02	25 34	7 29	4 47	1 17
15 T	15 30 41	24 07 39	17 31	8 56	2 18	24 33	29 31	17 36	8 35	29 58	16 10	21 10	14 19	26 09	7 57	4 44	1 20
16 W	15 34 38	25 05 32	1 ♊ 59	8 46	3 54	25 45	29 55	17 28	8 32	0 ♉ 01	16 11	21 09	14 37	26 44	8 26	4 40	1 22
17 Th	15 38 34	26 03 24	16 39	8 36	5 33	26 57	0 ♒ 19	17 21	8 29	0 04	16 12	21 09	14 56	27 19	8 54	4 36	1 25
18 F	15 42 31	27 01 15	1 ♋ 21	8 30	7 13	28 09	0 42	17 13	8 27	0 08	16 13	21 08	15 14	27 55	9 23	4 31	1 27
19 Sa	15 46 27	27 59 04	16 00	8 25	8 56	29 21	1 04	17 06	8 24	0 11	16 14	21 07	15 32	28 30	9 51	4 26	1 29
20 Su	15 50 24	28 56 51	0 ♌ 30	8 24 D	10 41	0 ♋ 32	1 27	16 58	8 21	0 14	16 15	21 07	15 51	29 05	10 20	4 21	1 31
21 M	15 54 21	29 54 36	14 46	8 24	12 27	1 44	1 48	16 51	8 18	0 17	16 16	21 06	16 10	29 41	10 48	4 15	1 34
22 T	15 58 17	0 ♊ 52 20	28 49	8 24 ℞	14 16	2 56	2 10	16 44	8 15	0 20	16 17	21 05	16 29	0 ♋ 16	11 17	4 08	1 36
23 W	16 2 14	1 50 02	12 ♍ 36	8 24	16 07	4 07	2 31	16 37	8 12	0 23	16 18	21 04	16 48	0 51	11 45	4 01	1 38
24 Th	16 6 10	2 47 42	26 10	8 21	18 00	5 19	2 52	16 30	8 09	0 26	16 19	21 03	17 08	1 27	12 13	3 54	1 40
25 F	16 10 7	3 45 21	9 ♎ 30	8 17	19 56	6 30	3 12	16 23	8 06	0 29	16 19	21 03	17 27	2 02	12 42	3 46	1 42
26 Sa	16 14 3	4 42 59	22 37	8 10	21 53	7 42	3 32	16 16	8 03	0 32	16 20	21 02	17 47	2 37	13 10	3 38	1 44
27 Su	16 18 0	5 40 35	5 ♏ 33	8 00	23 52	8 53	3 51	16 09	7 59	0 35	16 21	21 01	18 07	3 13	13 38	3 29	1 46
28 M	16 21 56	6 38 09	18 16	7 50	25 53	10 05	4 10	16 02	7 56	0 38	16 22	21 00	18 27	3 48	14 07	3 20	1 48
29 T	16 25 53	7 35 43	0 ♐ 47	7 39	27 56	11 16	4 29	15 55	7 53	0 41	16 22	20 59	18 47	4 23	14 35	3 11	1 50
30 W	16 29 50	8 33 15	13 07	7 29	0 ♊ 01	12 27	4 47	15 49	7 49	0 44	16 23	20 58	19 07	4 59	15 03	3 01	1 52
31 Th	16 33 46	9 30 47	25 16	7 20	2 07	13 38	5 05	15 42	7 45	0 47	16 24	20 57	19 28	5 34	15 32	2 50	1 54

EPHEMERIS CALCULATED FOR 12 MIDNIGHT GREENWICH MEAN TIME. ALL OTHER DATA AND FACING ASPECTARIAN PAGE IN **EASTERN TIME (BOLD)** AND PACIFIC TIME (REGULAR).

JUNE 2018

☽ Last Aspect day	ET / hr:mn / PT		asp	☽ Ingress sign	day	ET / hr:mn / PT	
1	**11:37 pm**	8:37 pm	☌ ♇	♒	2	**6:06 pm**	3:06 pm
3		10:10 pm	□ ♃	♓	5	**6:53 am**	3:53 am
4	**1:10 am**		□ ♃	♓	5	**6:53 am**	3:53 am
6		11:35 pm	△ ♀	♈	7	**5:26 pm**	2:26 pm
7	**2:35 am**		△ ♀	♈	7	**5:26 pm**	2:26 pm
9	**3:37 pm**	12:37 pm	□ ♀	♉	9		9:04 pm
9	**3:37 pm**	12:37 pm	□ ♀	♉	10	**12:04 am**	
11	**11:29 pm**	8:29 pm	✶ ♀	♊	11		11:53 pm
11	**11:29 pm**	8:29 pm	✶ ♀	♊	12	**2:53 am**	
13	**3:43 pm**	12:43 pm	☌ ☉	♋	14	**3:20 am**	12:20 am
15	**12:18 pm**	9:18 am	☍ ♇	♌	16	**3:21 am**	12:21 am
17	**11:26 pm**	8:26 pm	✶ ☉	♍	18	**4:41 am**	1:41 am
20	**6:51 am**	3:51 am	□ ☉	♎	20	**8:29 am**	5:29 am
21	**9:34 pm**	6:34 pm	□ ♇	♏	22	**3:11 pm**	12:11 pm
24	**10:00 am**	7:00 am	△ ☿	♐	24		9:29 pm
24	**10:00 am**	7:00 am	△ ☿	♐	25	**12:29 am**	
26	**8:53 am**	5:53 am	□ ♆	♑	27	**11:52 am**	8:52 am
29	**4:58 am**	1:58 am	☌ ♇	♒	29		9:37 pm
29	**4:58 am**	1:58 am	☌ ♇	♒	30	**12:37 am**	

☽ Phases & Eclipses phase	day	ET / hr:mn / PT	
4th Quarter	6	**2:32 pm**	11:32 am
New Moon	13	**3:43 pm**	12:43 pm
2nd Quarter	20	**6:51 am**	3:51 am
Full Moon	27		9:53 pm
Full Moon	28	**12:53 am**	

Planet Ingress		day	ET / hr:mn / PT	
☿	♋	12	**4:00 pm**	1:00 pm
⚵	♐	13	**9:15 am**	6:15 am
♀	♌	13	**5:54 pm**	2:54 pm
☉	♋	21	**6:07 am**	3:07 am
⚳	♍	28	**5:04 am**	2:04 am
☿	♌	28		10:16 pm
☿	♌	29	**1:16 am**	

Planetary Motion		day	ET / hr:mn / PT	
♆	℞	18	**7:26 pm**	4:26 pm
♂	℞	26	**5:04 pm**	2:04 pm

1 FRIDAY
☽ ⊼ ☉ **3:03 am** 12:03 am
☿ △ ♂ **10:13 am** 7:13 am
♀ △ ♃ **10:29 am** 7:29 am
☽ ✶ ♃ **12:41 pm** 9:41 am
☽ ☍ ♀ **12:57 pm** 9:57 am
☽ ✶ ♆ **2:29 pm** 11:29 am
☽ ☌ ♇ **11:37 pm** 8:37 pm

2 SATURDAY
♀ △ ♆ **4:26 am** 1:26 am
☿ ⊼ ♄ **9:16 am** 6:16 am
☽ □ ♅ **7:58 pm** 4:58 pm

3 SUNDAY
☽ ☌ ♂ **6:22 am** 3:22 am
☽ ⊻ ♄ **9:27 am** 6:27 am
☽ △ ☿ **3:06 pm** 12:06 pm
☽ △ ☉ **9:23 pm** 6:23 pm
☽ □ ♃ 10:10 pm

4 MONDAY
☽ □ ♃ **1:10 am**
☽ ⊻ ♆ **3:32 am** 12:32 am
☽ ⊼ ♀ **8:43 am** 5:43 am
☽ ⊻ ♇ **12:31 pm** 9:31 am

5 TUESDAY
☽ ✶ ♅ **8:58 am** 5:58 am
☉ ⊼ ♃ **4:10 pm** 1:10 pm
☿ ⊼ ♃ **7:21 pm** 4:21 pm
☽ ⊻ ♂ **8:09 pm** 5:09 pm
☽ ✶ ♄ **9:35 pm** 6:35 pm
☉ ☌ ☿ **10:02 pm** 7:02 pm
♀ ☍ ♇ **10:25 pm** 7:25 pm

6 WEDNESDAY
☿ □ ♆ **10:07 am** 7:07 am
☽ △ ♃ **12:38 pm** 9:38 am
☽ □ ☉ **2:32 pm** 11:32 am
☽ ☌ ♆ **3:25 pm** 12:25 pm
☽ □ ☿ **4:34 pm** 1:34 pm
☽ ✶ ♇ **11:53 pm** 8:53 pm
☉ □ ♆ 10:58 pm
☽ △ ♀ 11:35 pm

7 THURSDAY
☉ □ ♆ **1:58 am**
☽ △ ♀ **2:35 am**
☽ ⊻ ♅ **7:35 pm** 4:35 pm

8 FRIDAY
☽ ✶ ♂ **6:56 am** 3:56 am
☽ □ ♄ **6:57 am** 3:57 am
♂ ⊻ ♄ **8:22 am** 5:22 am
☿ ⊼ ♇ **9:32 am** 6:32 am
☽ ⊼ ♃ **8:55 pm** 5:55 pm
☽ ⊻ ♆ **11:56 pm** 8:56 pm

9 SATURDAY
☽ ✶ ☉ **3:29 am** 12:29 am
☽ □ ♇ **7:42 am** 4:42 am
☽ ✶ ☿ **12:03 pm** 9:03 am
☽ □ ♀ **3:37 pm** 12:37 pm
☽ ☌ ♅ 11:14 pm

10 SUNDAY
☽ ☌ ♅ **2:14 am**
☽ △ ♄ **12:20 pm** 9:20 am
☽ □ ♂ **1:21 pm** 10:21 am
☽ ☍ ♃ 10:14 pm

11 MONDAY
☽ ☍ ♃ **1:14 am**
☽ ✶ ♆ **4:22 am** 1:22 am
☿ ⊻ ♀ **8:23 am** 5:23 am
☽ ⊻ ☉ **11:23 am** 8:23 am
☽ △ ♇ **11:31 am** 8:31 am
☉ ⊼ ♇ **1:14 pm** 10:14 am
☽ ✶ ♀ **11:29 pm** 8:29 pm
☽ ⊻ ☿ 9:39 pm

12 TUESDAY
☽ ⊻ ☿ **12:39 am**
☽ ⊻ ♅ **5:04 am** 2:04 am
☽ ⊼ ♄ **2:12 pm** 11:12 am
☽ △ ♂ **4:00 pm** 1:00 pm
☽ ⊼ ♃ 11:24 pm

13 WEDNESDAY
☽ ⊼ ♃ **2:24 am**
☽ □ ♆ **5:40 am** 2:40 am
☿ ✶ ♅ **7:41 am** 4:41 am
☽ ⊼ ♇ **12:26 pm** 9:26 am
☽ ☌ ☉ **3:43 pm** 12:43 pm

14 THURSDAY
☽ ⊻ ♀ **4:07 am** 1:07 am
☽ ✶ ♅ **5:35 am** 2:35 am
☽ ☌ ☿ **9:02 am** 6:02 am
☽ ☍ ♄ **2:09 pm** 11:09 am
☽ ⊼ ♂ **4:39 pm** 1:39 pm
♀ □ ♅ **11:33 pm** 8:33 pm
☽ △ ♃ 11:10 pm

15 FRIDAY
☽ △ ♃ **2:10 am**
☽ △ ♆ **5:39 am** 2:39 am
☽ ☍ ♇ **12:18 pm** 9:18 am
☽ ⊻ ☉ **6:56 pm** 3:56 pm
☿ ☍ ♄ **9:47 pm** 6:47 pm

16 SATURDAY
☽ □ ♅ **5:45 am** 2:45 am
☽ ☌ ♀ **8:14 am** 5:14 am
☽ ⊼ ♄ **2:06 pm** 11:06 am
☽ ⊻ ☿ **4:45 pm** 1:45 pm
☽ ☍ ♂ **5:18 pm** 2:18 pm
☿ ⊼ ♂ **9:03 pm** 6:03 pm
☽ □ ♃ 11:23 pm

17 SUNDAY
☽ □ ♃ **2:23 am**
☽ ⊼ ♆ **6:12 am** 3:12 am
☽ ⊼ ♇ **1:00 pm** 10:00 am
☽ ✶ ☉ **11:26 pm** 8:26 pm

18 MONDAY
☽ △ ♅ **7:19 am** 4:19 am
☽ ⊻ ♀ **2:12 pm** 11:12 am
☽ △ ♄ **3:39 pm** 12:39 pm
☽ ⊼ ♂ **7:39 pm** 4:39 pm
☽ ✶ ☿ 11:44 pm

19 TUESDAY
☽ ✶ ☿ **2:44 am**
☽ ✶ ♃ **4:33 am** 1:33 am
♀ ⊼ ♄ **6:54 am** 3:54 am
☽ ☍ ♆ **8:49 am** 5:49 am
☿ △ ♃ **3:43 pm** 12:43 pm
☽ △ ♇ **3:52 pm** 12:52 pm

20 WEDNESDAY
☽ □ ☉ **6:51 am** 3:51 am
☽ ⊼ ♅ **11:25 am** 8:25 am
☽ □ ♄ **7:48 pm** 4:48 pm
☽ ✶ ♀ **11:32 pm** 8:32 pm
☿ △ ♆ **11:58 pm** 8:58 pm
☽ △ ♂ 9:38 pm

21 THURSDAY
☽ △ ♂ **12:38 am**
☽ ⊻ ♃ **9:28 am** 6:28 am
♀ ☍ ♂ **12:54 pm** 9:54 am
☽ ⊼ ♆ **2:12 pm** 11:12 am
☽ □ ☿ **4:29 pm** 1:29 pm
☽ □ ♇ **9:34 pm** 6:34 pm

22 FRIDAY
☽ △ ☉ **5:50 pm** 2:50 pm
☽ ☍ ♅ **6:25 pm** 3:25 pm
☉ ✶ ♅ 10:58 pm
☽ ✶ ♄ 11:46 pm

23 SATURDAY
☉ ✶ ♅ **1:58 am**
☽ ✶ ♄ **2:46 am**
☿ ☍ ♇ **5:26 am** 2:26 am
☽ □ ♂ **8:24 am** 5:24 am
☽ □ ♀ **12:34 pm** 9:34 am
☽ ☌ ♃ **5:11 pm** 2:11 pm
☽ △ ♆ **10:23 pm** 7:23 pm

24 SUNDAY
☽ ✶ ♇ **6:00 am** 3:00 am
☽ △ ☿ **10:00 am** 7:00 am

25 MONDAY
☽ ⊼ ♅ **4:01 am** 1:01 am
☽ ⊼ ☉ **8:05 am** 5:05 am
☽ ⊻ ♄ **12:12 pm** 9:12 am
♀ □ ♃ **1:19 pm** 10:19 am
☽ ✶ ♂ **6:32 pm** 3:32 pm

26 TUESDAY
☽ ⊻ ♃ **3:18 am** 12:18 am
☽ △ ♀ **4:49 am** 1:49 am
☽ □ ♆ **8:53 am** 5:53 am
☽ ⊻ ♇ **4:40 pm** 1:40 pm

27 WEDNESDAY
☽ ⊼ ☿ **6:17 am** 3:17 am
☉ ☍ ♄ **9:28 am** 6:28 am
☽ △ ♅ **3:41 pm** 12:41 pm
☽ ☌ ♄ **11:34 pm** 8:34 pm
♀ ⊼ ♆ **11:41 pm** 8:41 pm
☽ ☍ ☉ 9:53 pm

28 THURSDAY
☽ ☍ ☉ **12:53 am**
☽ ⊻ ♂ **6:24 am** 3:24 am
☽ ✶ ♃ **3:13 pm** 12:13 pm
☽ ✶ ♆ **9:06 pm** 6:06 pm
☽ ⊼ ♀ **11:24 pm** 8:24 pm

29 FRIDAY
☽ ☌ ♇ **4:58 am** 1:58 am

30 SATURDAY
☽ ☍ ☿ **4:01 am** 1:01 am
☽ □ ♅ **4:38 am** 1:38 am
☿ □ ♅ **9:01 am** 6:01 am
☽ ⊻ ♄ **12:04 pm** 9:04 am
☽ ⊼ ☉ **7:08 pm** 4:08 pm
☽ ☌ ♂ **7:10 pm** 4:10 pm
☉ ⊼ ♂ **7:29 pm** 4:29 pm

Eastern time in bold type
Pacific time in medium type

JUNE 2018

DATE	SID.TIME	SUN	MOON	NODE	MERCURY	VENUS	MARS	JUPITER	SATURN	URANUS	NEPTUNE	PLUTO	CERES	PALLAS	JUNO	VESTA	CHIRON
1 F	16 37 43	10♊28 17	7♑15	7♌14℞	4♊15	14♋49	5♒22	15♏36℞	7♑42℞	0♉50	16♓24	20♑56℞	19♌48	6♋09	16♈00	2♑40℞	1♈55
2 Sa	16 41 39	11 25 46	19 08	7 10	6 24	16 00	5 38	15 29	7 38	0 52	16 25	20 55	20 09	6 45	16 28	2 29	1 57
3 Su	16 45 36	12 23 15	0♒56	7 08 D	8 34	17 11	5 54	15 23	7 34	0 55	16 25	20 54	20 30	7 20	16 56	2 17	1 59
4 M	16 49 32	13 20 42	12 43	7 08	10 46	18 22	6 10	15 17	7 31	0 58	16 26	20 53	20 51	7 55	17 24	2 06	2 00
5 T	16 53 29	14 18 09	24 35	7 09	12 57	19 33	6 25	15 11	7 27	1 01	16 26	20 52	21 12	8 31	17 53	1 54	2 02
6 W	16 57 25	15 15 35	6♓35	7 10℞	15 09	20 43	6 39	15 06	7 23	1 03	16 27	20 50	21 34	9 06	18 21	1 41	2 03
7 Th	17 1 22	16 13 01	18 49	7 10	17 21	21 54	6 53	15 00	7 19	1 06	16 27	20 49	21 55	9 41	18 49	1 29	2 05
8 F	17 5 19	17 10 26	1♈22	7 09	19 33	23 04	7 06	14 54	7 15	1 09	16 28	20 48	22 16	10 17	19 17	1 16	2 06
9 Sa	17 9 15	18 07 50	14 18	7 06	21 45	24 15	7 19	14 49	7 11	1 11	16 28	20 47	22 38	10 52	19 45	1 02	2 08
10 Su	17 13 12	19 05 13	27 41	7 02	23 56	25 25	7 31	14 44	7 07	1 14	16 28	20 46	23 00	11 27	20 13	0 49	2 09
11 M	17 17 8	20 02 37	11♉32	6 55	26 05	26 36	7 43	14 38	7 03	1 16	16 28	20 45	23 22	12 02	20 41	0 36	2 10
12 T	17 21 5	20 59 59	25 50	6 48	28 14	27 46	7 53	14 33	6 59	1 19	16 29	20 43	23 44	12 38	21 09	0 22	2 11
13 W	17 25 1	21 57 21	10♊30	6 41	0♋21	28 56	8 03	14 29	6 55	1 21	16 29	20 42	24 06	13 13	21 36	0 08	2 13
14 Th	17 28 58	22 54 43	25 25	6 36	2 27	0♌06	8 13	14 24	6 50	1 24	16 29	20 41	24 28	13 48	22 04	29♐54	2 14
15 F	17 32 55	23 52 04	10♋27	6 32	4 31	1 16	8 22	14 19	6 46	1 26	16 29	20 40	24 51	14 23	22 32	29 39	2 15
16 Sa	17 36 51	24 49 24	25 26	6 29 D	6 33	2 26	8 30	14 15	6 42	1 28	16 29	20 38	25 13	14 58	23 00	29 25	2 16
17 Su	17 40 48	25 46 43	10♌16	6 29	8 33	3 36	8 37	14 11	6 38	1 31	16 29	20 37	25 36	15 34	23 28	29 11	2 17
18 M	17 44 44	26 44 01	24 49	6 30	10 30	4 46	8 44	14 07	6 33	1 33	16 30℞	20 36	25 59	16 09	23 55	28 56	2 18
19 T	17 48 41	27 41 19	9♍03	6 31	12 26	5 55	8 50	14 03	6 29	1 35	16 30	20 35	26 21	16 44	24 23	28 42	2 18
20 W	17 52 37	28 38 35	22 55	6 32℞	14 20	7 05	8 56	13 59	6 25	1 38	16 30	20 33	26 44	17 19	24 50	28 27	2 19
21 Th	17 56 34	29 35 51	6♎27	6 32	16 11	8 14	9 00	13 55	6 20	1 40	16 29	20 32	27 07	17 54	25 18	28 13	2 20
22 F	18 0 30	0♋33 06	19 39	6 30	18 00	9 24	9 04	13 52	6 16	1 42	16 29	20 31	27 30	18 29	25 45	27 58	2 21
23 Sa	18 4 27	1 30 21	2♏35	6 27	19 47	10 33	9 08	13 49	6 11	1 44	16 29	20 29	27 54	19 04	26 13	27 44	2 21
24 Su	18 8 24	2 27 35	15 15	6 23	21 32	11 42	9 10	13 46	6 07	1 46	16 29	20 28	28 17	19 39	26 40	27 30	2 22
25 M	18 12 20	3 24 48	27 42	6 18	23 14	12 51	9 12	13 43	6 03	1 48	16 29	20 26	28 40	20 14	27 07	27 15	2 23
26 T	18 16 17	4 22 01	9♐58	6 12	24 54	14 00	9 13℞	13 40	5 58	1 50	16 29	20 25	29 04	20 49	27 35	27 01	2 23
27 W	18 20 13	5 19 13	22 04	6 07	26 32	15 09	9 13	13 38	5 54	1 52	16 29	20 24	29 27	21 24	28 02	26 47	2 24
28 Th	18 24 10	6 16 25	4♑03	6 03	28 07	16 18	9 13	13 35	5 49	1 54	16 28	20 22	29 51	21 59	28 29	26 34	2 24
29 F	18 28 6	7 13 37	15 55	6 00	29 40	17 26	9 11	13 33	5 45	1 56	16 28	20 21	0♍15	22 34	28 56	26 20	2 24
30 Sa	18 32 3	8 10 49	27 44	5 58 D	1♌11	18 35	9 09	13 31	5 41	1 58	16 28	20 19	0 39	23 08	29 23	26 07	2 25

EPHEMERIS CALCULATED FOR 12 MIDNIGHT GREENWICH MEAN TIME. ALL OTHER DATA AND FACING ASPECTARIAN PAGE IN **EASTERN TIME (BOLD)** AND PACIFIC TIME (REGULAR).

JULY 2018

☽ Last Aspect day	ET / hr:mn / PT		asp	☽ Ingress sign	day	ET / hr:mn / PT	
1	**6:56 pm**	3:56 pm	☍♀	♓	2	**1:31 pm**	10:31 am
4	**5:47 am**	2:47 am	⚹♇	♈	4		9:50 pm
4	**5:47 am**	2:47 am	⚹♇	♈	5	**12:50 am**	
7	**3:09 am**	12:09 am	△♀	♉	7	**8:51 am**	5:51 am
9	**12:09 pm**	9:09 am	□♀	♊	9	**12:58 pm**	9:58 am
10	**4:00 pm**	1:00 pm	□♆	♋	11	**1:59 pm**	10:59 am
12	**10:48 pm**	7:48 pm	☌☉	♌	13	**1:31 pm**	10:31 am
14	**7:12 pm**	4:12 pm	☌☿	♍	15	**1:31 pm**	10:31 am
17	**6:50 am**	3:50 am	⚹☉	♎	17	**3:42 pm**	12:42 pm
19	**3:52 pm**	12:52 pm	□☉	♏	19	**9:13 pm**	6:13 pm

☽ Last Aspect day	ET / hr:mn / PT		asp	☽ Ingress sign	day	ET / hr:mn / PT	
22	5:18 am	**2:18 am**	△☉	♐	22	**6:12 am**	3:12 am
24	4:22 am	**1:22 am**	△☿	♑	24	**5:49 pm**	2:49 pm
26	9:41 am	**6:41 am**	☌♇	♒	27	**6:41 am**	3:41 am
29	5:25 am	**2:25 am**	☍☿	♓	29	**7:28 pm**	4:28 pm
31	6:42 pm	**3:42 pm**	☍♀	♈	8/1	**6:54 am**	3:54 am

☽ Phases & Eclipses phase	day	ET / hr:mn / PT	
4th Quarter	6	**3:51 am**	12:51 am
New Moon	12	**10:48 pm**	7:48 pm
●	13	20° ♋	41'
2nd Quarter	19	**3:52 pm**	12:52 pm
Full Moon	27	**4:20 pm**	1:20 pm
●●	27	4° ♒	45'

Planet Ingress	day	ET / hr:mn / PT	
⚵ ♉	1	**4:46 am**	1:46 am
♀ ♍	9	**10:32 pm**	7:32 pm
☿ ♌	11	**5:47 pm**	2:47 pm
☉ ♌	22	**5:00 pm**	2:00 pm

Planetary Motion	day	ET / hr:mn / PT	
⚷ ℞	4		9:46 pm
⚷ ℞	5	**12:46 am**	
♃ D	10	**1:02 pm**	10:02 am
☿ ℞	25		10:02 pm
☿ ℞	26	**1:02 am**	

1 SUNDAY
☽□♃ **4:03 am** 1:03 am
♀⚻♇ **7:59 am** 4:59 am
☽⚺♆ **10:05 am** 7:05 am
☽⚺♇ **5:52 pm** 2:52 pm
☽☍♀ **6:56 pm** 3:56 pm

2 MONDAY
☽⚹♅ **5:38 pm** 2:38 pm
☿⚻♄ **7:49 pm** 4:49 pm
☽⚹♄ 9:27 pm
☽⚻☿ 10:05 pm

3 TUESDAY
☽⚹♄ **12:27 am**
☽⚻☿ **1:05 am**
☽⚺♂ **7:27 am** 4:27 am
☽△☉ **12:58 pm** 9:58 am
☽△♃ **4:21 pm** 1:21 pm
☽☌♆ **10:19 pm** 7:19 pm

4 WEDNESDAY
☽⚹♇ **5:47 am** 2:47 am
☽⚻♀ **1:03 pm** 10:03 am

5 THURSDAY
☽⚺♅ **4:54 am** 1:54 am
☉△♃ **7:04 am** 4:04 am
☿☍♂ **7:48 am** 4:48 am
☽□♄ **10:56 am** 7:56 am
☽⚹♂ **5:29 pm** 2:29 pm
☽△☿ **6:38 pm** 3:38 pm
☽⚻♃ 11:17 pm

6 FRIDAY
☽⚻♃ **2:17 am**
☽□☉ **3:51 am** 12:51 am
☽⚺♆ **7:57 am** 4:57 am
☽□♇ **2:54 pm** 11:54 am

7 SATURDAY
☽△♀ **3:09 am** 12:09 am
☽☌♅ **12:45 pm** 9:45 am
☽△♄ **5:59 pm** 2:59 pm
☽□♂ **11:52 pm** 8:52 pm

8 SUNDAY
☽□☿ **6:40 am** 3:40 am
☽☍♃ **8:30 am** 5:30 am
☉△♆ **10:42 am** 7:42 am
☽⚹♆ **1:47 pm** 10:47 am
☽⚹☉ **2:01 pm** 11:01 am
☽△♇ **8:11 pm** 5:11 pm

9 MONDAY
☿□♃ **5:14 am** 2:14 am
☽□♀ **12:09 pm** 9:09 am
☽⚺♅ **4:42 pm** 1:42 pm
☽⚻♄ **9:14 pm** 6:14 pm
☽△♂ 11:27 pm

10 TUESDAY
☽△♂ **2:27 am**
☽⚻♃ **11:04 am** 8:04 am
☽⚹☿ **1:24 pm** 10:24 am
☽□♆ **4:00 pm** 1:00 pm
☽⚺☉ **7:43 pm** 4:43 pm
☽⚻♇ **9:59 pm** 6:59 pm

11 WEDNESDAY
☽⚹♀ **5:09 pm** 2:09 pm
☽⚹♅ **5:36 pm** 2:36 pm
☽☍♄ **9:38 pm** 6:38 pm
♀△♅ **11:26 pm** 8:26 pm
☽⚻♂ 11:19 pm

12 THURSDAY
☽⚻♂ **2:19 am**
☿⚻♆ **3:52 am** 12:52 am
☉☍♇ **6:04 am** 3:04 am
☽△♃ **11:12 am** 8:12 am
☽△♆ **3:56 pm** 12:56 pm
☽⚺☿ **4:44 pm** 1:44 pm
☽☍♇ **9:43 pm** 6:43 pm
☽☌☉ **10:48 pm** 7:48 pm

13 FRIDAY
☽□♅ **5:10 pm** 2:10 pm
☽⚺♀ **8:25 pm** 5:25 pm
☽⚻♄ **8:54 pm** 5:54 pm
☽☍♂ 10:12 pm
♀△♄ 11:44 pm

14 SATURDAY
☽☍♂ **1:12 am**
♀△♄ **2:44 am**
☽□♃ **10:44 am** 7:44 am
☽⚻♆ **3:27 pm** 12:27 pm
☽☌☿ **7:12 pm** 4:12 pm
☽⚻♇ **9:17 pm** 6:17 pm
☽⚺☉ 10:43 pm

15 SUNDAY
☽⚺☉ **1:43 am**
☽△♅ **5:21 pm** 2:21 pm
☽△♄ **8:55 pm** 5:55 pm
☽☌♀ 9:35 pm
☽⚻♂ 9:53 pm

16 MONDAY
☽☌♀ **12:35 am**
☽⚻♂ **12:53 am**
♀⚻♂ **3:56 am** 12:56 am
☿⚻♇ **11:24 am** 8:24 am
☽⚹♃ **11:34 am** 8:34 am
☽☍♆ **4:24 pm** 1:24 pm
☽△♇ **10:29 pm** 7:29 pm
☽⚺☿ **11:04 pm** 8:04 pm

17 TUESDAY
☽⚹☉ **6:50 am** 3:50 am
☽⚻♅ **7:50 pm** 4:50 pm
☽□♄ **11:19 pm** 8:19 pm
☽△♂ 11:56 pm

18 WEDNESDAY
☽△♂ **2:56 am**
☽⚺♀ **7:55 am** 4:55 am
☽⚺♃ **3:14 pm** 12:14 pm
☽⚻♆ **8:15 pm** 5:15 pm
☽□♇ 11:43 pm

19 THURSDAY
☽□♇ **2:43 am**
☽⚹☿ **5:54 am** 2:54 am
☽□☉ **3:52 pm** 12:52 pm
☽☍♅ 10:42 pm

20 FRIDAY
☽☍♅ **1:42 am**
☽⚹♄ **5:05 am** 2:05 am
☽□♂ **8:13 am** 5:13 am
☽⚹♀ **7:40 pm** 4:40 pm
☽☌♃ **10:29 pm** 7:29 pm

21 SATURDAY
☽△♆ **3:38 am** 12:38 am
☽⚹♇ **10:28 am** 7:28 am
☽□☿ **4:00 pm** 1:00 pm

22 SUNDAY
☽△☉ **5:18 am** 2:18 am
♀⚹♃ **5:21 am** 2:21 am
☽⚻♅ **11:00 am** 8:00 am
☽⚺♄ **2:13 pm** 11:13 am
☽⚹♂ **4:37 pm** 1:37 pm

23 MONDAY
☽⚺♃ **8:58 am** 5:58 am
☽□♀ **11:35 am** 8:35 am
☽□♆ **2:07 pm** 11:07 am
☽⚺♇ **9:13 pm** 6:13 pm

24 TUESDAY
☽△☿ **4:22 am** 1:22 am
♀☍♆ **3:22 pm** 12:22 pm
☽⚻☉ **10:04 pm** 7:04 pm
☽△♅ **10:49 pm** 7:49 pm
☽☌♄ 10:46 pm

25 WEDNESDAY
☽☌♄ **1:46 am**
☽⚺♂ **3:14 am** 12:14 am
☉□♅ **7:36 am** 4:36 am
☽⚹♃ **9:32 pm** 6:32 pm
☽⚹♆ 11:29 pm

26 THURSDAY
☽⚹♆ **2:29 am**
☽△♀ **6:03 am** 3:03 am
☽☌♇ **9:41 am** 6:41 am
☽⚻☿ **5:20 pm** 2:20 pm
☉⚻♄ **5:40 pm** 2:40 pm
☉☍♂ 10:13 pm

27 FRIDAY
☉☍♂ **1:13 am**
☽□♅ **11:47 am** 8:47 am
☽⚺♄ **2:24 pm** 11:24 am
☽☌♂ **2:48 pm** 11:48 am
☽☍☉ **4:20 pm** 1:20 pm
♀△♇ **9:26 pm** 6:26 pm

28 SATURDAY
☽□♃ **10:47 am** 7:47 am
♂⚺♄ **12:40 pm** 9:40 am
☽⚺♆ **3:22 pm** 12:22 pm
☽⚺♇ **10:31 pm** 7:31 pm
☽⚻♀ 10:03 pm

29 SUNDAY
☽⚻♀ **1:03 am**
☽☍☿ **5:25 am** 2:25 am
☽⚹♅ 9:33 pm
☽⚺♂ 11:07 pm
☽⚹♄ 11:48 pm

30 MONDAY
☽⚹♅ **12:33 am**
☽⚺♂ **2:07 am**
☽⚹♄ **2:48 am**
☽⚻☉ **10:15 am** 7:15 am
☿⚺♀ **3:35 pm** 12:35 pm
☽△♃ **11:23 pm** 8:23 pm

31 TUESDAY
☽☌♆ **3:29 am** 12:29 am
☽⚹♇ **10:27 am** 7:27 am
☽⚻☿ **3:32 pm** 12:32 pm
☽☍♀ **6:42 pm** 3:42 pm

Eastern time in bold type
Pacific time in medium type

JULY 2018

DATE	SID.TIME	SUN	MOON	NODE	MERCURY	VENUS	MARS	JUPITER	SATURN	URANUS	NEPTUNE	PLUTO	CERES	PALLAS	JUNO	VESTA	CHIRON
1 Su	18 35 59	9♋08 00	9♒31	5♌58	2♌39	19♌43	9♒07℞	13♏29℞	5♑36℞	2♉00	16♓27℞	20♑18℞	1♍03	23♋43	29♈50	25♐53℞	2♈25
2 M	18 39 56	10 05 12	21 20	5 59	4 05	20 51	9 03	13 28	5 32	2 01	16 27	20 17	1 27	24 18	0♉17	25 40	2 25
3 T	18 43 53	11 02 23	3♓13	6 00	5 28	22 00	8 59	13 26	5 27	2 03	16 26	20 15	1 51	24 52	0 44	25 28	2 25
4 W	18 47 49	11 59 35	15 15	6 02	6 49	23 08	8 54	13 25	5 23	2 05	16 26	20 14	2 15	25 27	1 11	25 15	2 25
5 Th	18 51 46	12 56 47	27 30	6 03	8 07	24 15	8 48	13 24	5 19	2 06	16 25	20 12	2 39	26 02	1 37	25 03	2 25℞
6 F	18 55 42	13 53 59	10♈02	6 04℞	9 23	25 23	8 42	13 23	5 14	2 08	16 25	20 11	3 03	26 36	2 04	24 51	2 25
7 Sa	18 59 39	14 51 11	22 56	6 04	10 37	26 31	8 35	13 22	5 10	2 09	16 24	20 09	3 28	27 11	2 31	24 40	2 25
8 Su	19 3 35	15 48 24	6♉14	6 03	11 47	27 38	8 27	13 21	5 06	2 11	16 24	20 08	3 52	27 45	2 57	24 29	2 25
9 M	19 7 32	16 45 37	20 00	6 01	12 55	28 46	8 18	13 21	5 01	2 12	16 23	20 06	4 17	28 20	3 24	24 18	2 25
10 T	19 11 28	17 42 51	4♊12	5 59	14 01	29 53	8 09	13 21D	4 57	2 14	16 23	20 05	4 41	28 54	3 50	24 07	2 25
11 W	19 15 25	18 40 05	18 50	5 56	15 03	1♍00	7 59	13 21	4 53	2 15	16 22	20 03	5 06	29 29	4 16	23 57	2 24
12 Th	19 19 22	19 37 19	3♋47	5 55	16 02	2 07	7 48	13 21	4 49	2 16	16 21	20 02	5 31	0♌03	4 42	23 48	2 24
13 F	19 23 18	20 34 34	18 55	5 53	16 58	3 14	7 37	13 21	4 44	2 18	16 20	20 00	5 55	0 38	5 09	23 38	2 24
14 Sa	19 27 15	21 31 49	4♌06	5 53D	17 51	4 20	7 25	13 22	4 40	2 19	16 20	19 59	6 20	1 12	5 35	23 29	2 23
15 Su	19 31 11	22 29 04	19 10	5 53	18 41	5 27	7 12	13 22	4 36	2 20	16 19	19 58	6 45	1 46	6 00	23 21	2 23
16 M	19 35 8	23 26 19	3♍58	5 54	19 27	6 33	7 00	13 23	4 32	2 21	16 18	19 56	7 10	2 20	6 26	23 13	2 22
17 T	19 39 4	24 23 34	18 26	5 55	20 10	7 39	6 46	13 24	4 28	2 22	16 17	19 55	7 35	2 54	6 52	23 05	2 22
18 W	19 43 1	25 20 49	2♎29	5 56	20 49	8 45	6 32	13 25	4 24	2 23	16 16	19 53	8 01	3 29	7 18	22 58	2 21
19 Th	19 46 57	26 18 05	16 07	5 56℞	21 24	9 51	6 18	13 27	4 20	2 24	16 15	19 52	8 26	4 03	7 43	22 52	2 20
20 F	19 50 54	27 15 20	29 20	5 56	21 55	10 57	6 03	13 28	4 16	2 25	16 15	19 50	8 51	4 37	8 09	22 45	2 20
21 Sa	19 54 51	28 12 36	12♏12	5 56	22 22	12 02	5 48	13 30	4 12	2 26	16 14	19 49	9 16	5 11	8 34	22 40	2 19
22 Su	19 58 47	29 09 52	24 45	5 56	22 44	13 08	5 33	13 32	4 09	2 27	16 13	19 47	9 42	5 45	8 59	22 34	2 18
23 M	20 2 44	0♌07 09	7♐02	5 55	23 02	14 13	5 17	13 34	4 05	2 28	16 12	19 46	10 07	6 18	9 24	22 30	2 17
24 T	20 6 40	1 04 26	19 08	5 54	23 15	15 18	5 01	13 37	4 01	2 28	16 11	19 44	10 33	6 52	9 49	22 25	2 16
25 W	20 10 37	2 01 43	1♑05	5 54	23 24	16 22	4 45	13 39	3 58	2 29	16 10	19 43	10 58	7 26	10 14	22 22	2 15
26 Th	20 14 33	2 59 01	12 57	5 53	23 27℞	17 27	4 29	13 42	3 54	2 30	16 09	19 42	11 24	8 00	10 39	22 18	2 14
27 F	20 18 30	3 56 19	24 45	5 53D	23 26	18 31	4 12	13 45	3 50	2 30	16 07	19 40	11 49	8 33	11 04	22 15	2 13
28 Sa	20 22 26	4 53 38	6♒33	5 53	23 19	19 35	3 56	13 47	3 47	2 31	16 06	19 39	12 15	9 07	11 28	22 13	2 12
29 Su	20 26 23	5 50 57	18 22	5 53℞	23 08	20 39	3 40	13 51	3 44	2 31	16 05	19 37	12 41	9 41	11 52	22 11	2 11
30 M	20 30 20	6 48 18	0♓16	5 53	22 51	21 42	3 23	13 54	3 40	2 32	16 04	19 36	13 06	10 14	12 17	22 10	2 10
31 T	20 34 16	7 45 39	12 16	5 53	22 30	22 46	3 07	13 57	3 37	2 32	16 03	19 35	13 32	10 48	12 41	22 09	2 08

EPHEMERIS CALCULATED FOR 12 MIDNIGHT GREENWICH MEAN TIME. ALL OTHER DATA AND FACING ASPECTARIAN PAGE IN **EASTERN TIME (BOLD)** AND PACIFIC TIME (REGULAR).

AUGUST 2018

☽ Last Aspect day	ET / hr:mn / PT	asp	☽ Ingress sign day	ET / hr:mn / PT
7/31	**6:42 pm** 3:42 pm	☍♀	♈ 1	**6:54 am** 3:54 am
2	**10:52 pm** 7:52 pm	△☿	♉ 3	**3:51 pm** 12:51 pm
5	**7:46 pm** 4:46 pm	△♀	♊ 5	**9:32 pm** 6:32 pm
7	**3:54 am** 12:54 am	⚹☿	♋ 7	9:01 pm
7	**3:54 am** 12:54 am	⚹☿	♋ 8	**12:01 am**
9	**7:21 am** 4:21 am	☍♇	♌ 9	9:18 pm
9	**7:21 am** 4:21 am	☍♇	♌ 10	**12:18 am**
11	**5:58 am** 2:58 am	☌☉	♍ 11	**11:59 pm** 8:59 pm
13	9:37 pm	△♂	♎ 13	9:57 pm
14	**12:37 am**	△♂	♎ 14	**12:57 am**
16	**3:56 am** 12:56 am	□♂	♏ 16	**4:54 am** 1:54 am
18	**11:07 am** 8:07 am	⚹♂	♐ 18	**12:45 pm** 9:45 am
20	**7:47 pm** 4:47 pm	△☉	♑ 20	9:00 pm
20	**7:47 pm** 4:47 pm	△☉	♑ 21	**12:00 am**
23	**10:19 am** 7:19 am	☌♂	♒ 23	**12:56 pm** 9:56 am
24	9:39 pm	△♀	♓ 25	10:32 pm
25	**12:39 am**	△♀	♓ 26	**1:32 am**
28	**9:54 am** 6:54 am	⚹♂	♈ 28	**12:35 pm** 9:35 am
30	**7:04 pm** 4:04 pm	□♂	♉ 30	**9:30 pm** 6:30 pm

☽ Phases & Eclipses phase	day	ET / hr:mn / PT
4th Quarter	4	**2:18 pm** 11:18 am
New Moon	11	**5:58 am** 2:58 am
●	11	18° ♌ 42'
2nd Quarter	18	**3:49 am** 12:49 am
Full Moon	26	**7:56 am** 4:56 am

Planet Ingress	day	ET / hr:mn / PT
♀ ♎	6	**7:27 pm** 4:27 pm
♂ ♑	12	**10:14 pm** 7:14 pm
☉ ♍	22	9:09 pm
☉ ♍	23	**12:09 am**

Planetary Motion	day	ET / hr:mn / PT
⚵ D	1	**6:39 am** 3:39 am
♅ R	7	**12:48 pm** 9:48 am
☿ D	18	9:25 pm
☿ D	19	**12:25 am**
♂ D	27	**10:05 am** 7:05 am

1 WEDNESDAY
☽ ⚺ ♅ **11:51 am** 8:51 am
☽ ⚹ ♂ **12:05 pm** 9:05 am
☽ □ ♄ **1:45 pm** 10:45 am
♂ □ ♅ **10:39 pm** 7:39 pm
☽ △ ☉ 11:03 pm

2 THURSDAY
☽ △ ☉ **2:03 am**
☽ ⚻ ♃ **10:05 am** 7:05 am
☽ ⚺ ♆ **1:38 pm** 10:38 am
☽ □ ♇ **8:17 pm** 5:17 pm
☽ △ ☿ **10:52 pm** 7:52 pm

3 FRIDAY
☽ ⚻ ♀ **9:19 am** 6:19 am
☽ □ ♂ **7:38 pm** 4:38 pm
☽ ☌ ♅ **8:33 pm** 5:33 pm
☽ △ ♄ **10:07 pm** 7:07 pm

4 SATURDAY
☽ □ ☉ **2:18 pm** 11:18 am
☽ ☍ ♃ **5:50 pm** 2:50 pm
☽ ⚹ ♆ **8:48 pm** 5:48 pm
☿ ⚻ ♇ 10:15 pm
☽ □ ☿ 11:58 pm

5 SUNDAY
☿ ⚻ ♇ **1:15 am**
☽ □ ☿ **2:58 am**
☽ △ ♇ **3:03 am** 12:03 am
☽ △ ♀ **7:46 pm** 4:46 pm
☽ △ ♂ 9:08 pm
☽ ⚺ ♅ 10:57 pm

6 MONDAY
☽ △ ♂ **12:08 am**
☽ ⚺ ♅ **1:57 am**
☽ ⚻ ♄ **3:13 am** 12:13 am
☉ □ ♃ **7:27 pm** 4:27 pm
☽ ⚻ ♃ **10:12 pm** 7:12 pm
☽ ⚹ ☉ **10:23 pm** 7:23 pm
☽ □ ♆ 9:38 pm

7 TUESDAY
☽ □ ♆ **12:38 am**
☽ ⚹ ☿ **3:54 am** 12:54 am
☽ ⚻ ♇ **6:31 am** 3:31 am
♀ △ ♂ **8:33 pm** 5:33 pm
☽ ⚻ ♂ 10:41 pm
☽ □ ♀ 11:09 pm

8 WEDNESDAY
☽ ⚻ ♂ **1:41 am**
☽ □ ♀ **2:09 am**
☽ ⚹ ♅ **4:12 am** 1:12 am
☽ ☍ ♄ **5:15 am** 2:15 am
☉ ⚻ ♆ **7:10 am** 4:10 am
☉ ☌ ☿ **10:06 pm** 7:06 pm
☽ △ ♃ **11:43 pm** 8:43 pm
☽ △ ♆ 10:42 pm
☽ ⚺ ☿ 11:27 pm

9 THURSDAY
☽ △ ♆ **1:42 am**
☽ ⚺ ☿ **2:27 am**
☽ ⚺ ☉ **3:00 am** 12:00 am
☽ ☍ ♇ **7:21 am** 4:21 am
♀ ⚻ ♅ **7:57 am** 4:57 am
☿ ⚻ ♆ **5:29 pm** 2:29 pm
♀ □ ♄ **9:34 pm** 6:34 pm
☽ ☍ ♂ 10:12 pm

10 FRIDAY
☽ ☍ ♂ **1:12 am**
☽ □ ♅ **4:21 am** 1:21 am
☽ ⚻ ♄ **5:15 am** 2:15 am
☽ ⚹ ♀ **5:49 am** 2:49 am
☽ □ ♃ **11:46 pm** 8:46 pm
☽ ☌ ☿ **11:54 pm** 8:54 pm
☽ ⚻ ♆ 10:22 pm
☿ □ ♃ 11:31 pm

11 SATURDAY
☽ ⚻ ♆ **1:22 am**
☿ □ ♃ **2:31 am**
☽ ☌ ☉ **5:58 am** 2:58 am
☽ ⚻ ♇ **6:58 am** 3:58 am
☉ ⚻ ♇ **9:28 pm** 6:28 pm
☽ ⚻ ♂ 9:16 pm

12 SUNDAY
☽ ⚻ ♂ **12:16 am**
☽ △ ♅ **4:04 am** 1:04 am
☽ △ ♄ **4:51 am** 1:51 am
☽ ⚺ ♀ **8:59 am** 5:59 am
☽ ⚺ ☿ **9:53 pm** 6:53 pm
☽ ⚹ ♃ 9:09 pm
☽ ☍ ♆ 10:25 pm

13 MONDAY
☽ ⚹ ♃ **12:09 am**
☽ ☍ ♆ **1:25 am**
☽ △ ♇ **7:12 am** 4:12 am
☽ ⚺ ☉ **9:38 am** 6:38 am
☽ △ ♂ 9:37 pm

14 TUESDAY
☽ △ ♂ **12:37 am**
☽ ⚻ ♅ **5:13 am** 2:13 am
☽ □ ♄ **5:56 am** 2:56 am
☽ ☌ ♀ **2:06 pm** 11:06 am
☽ ⚹ ☿ **10:09 pm** 7:09 pm
☽ ⚺ ♃ 11:47 pm

15 WEDNESDAY
☽ ⚺ ♃ **2:47 am**
☽ ⚻ ♆ **3:41 am** 12:41 am
☽ □ ♇ **9:51 am** 6:51 am
☽ ⚹ ☉ **4:22 pm** 1:22 pm

16 THURSDAY
☽ □ ♂ **3:56 am** 12:56 am
☽ ☍ ♅ **9:27 am** 6:27 am
☽ ⚹ ♄ **10:06 am** 7:06 am
☽ ⚺ ♀ **11:15 pm** 8:15 pm
☽ □ ☿ 11:18 pm

17 FRIDAY
☽ □ ☿ **2:18 am**
☽ ☌ ♃ **9:06 am** 6:06 am
☽ △ ♆ **9:32 am** 6:32 am
☽ ⚹ ♇ **4:12 pm** 1:12 pm

18 SATURDAY
☽ □ ☉ **3:49 am** 12:49 am
☽ ⚹ ♂ **11:07 am** 8:07 am
☿ ⚹ ♀ **11:35 am** 8:35 am
☽ ⚻ ♅ **5:36 pm** 2:36 pm
☽ ⚺ ♄ **6:11 pm** 3:11 pm

19 SUNDAY
♃ △ ♆ **3:44 am** 12:44 am
☽ △ ☿ **11:13 am** 8:13 am
☽ ⚹ ♀ **1:14 pm** 10:14 am
☽ □ ♆ **7:12 pm** 4:12 pm
☽ ⚺ ♃ **7:22 pm** 4:22 pm
☽ ⚺ ♇ 11:17 pm

20 MONDAY
☽ ⚺ ♇ **2:17 am**
☽ △ ☉ **7:47 pm** 4:47 pm
☽ ⚺ ♂ **9:47 pm** 6:47 pm

21 TUESDAY
☽ △ ♅ **5:01 am** 2:01 am
☽ ☌ ♄ **5:33 am** 2:33 am
☉ ⚻ ♂ **6:52 pm** 3:52 pm
☽ ⚻ ☿ 9:29 pm

22 WEDNESDAY
☽ ⚻ ☿ **12:29 am**
☽ □ ♀ **6:36 am** 3:36 am
☽ ⚹ ♆ **7:27 am** 4:27 am
☽ ⚹ ♃ **8:21 am** 5:21 am
☽ ☌ ♇ **2:46 pm** 11:46 am
♀ ⚻ ♆ **5:10 pm** 2:10 pm

23 THURSDAY
♀ ⚺ ♃ **8:04 am** 5:04 am
☽ ☌ ♂ **10:19 am** 7:19 am
☽ ⚻ ☉ **2:04 pm** 11:04 am
☽ □ ♅ **5:55 pm** 2:55 pm
☽ ⚺ ♄ **6:24 pm** 3:24 pm

24 FRIDAY
☽ ☍ ☿ **4:27 pm** 1:27 pm
☽ ⚺ ♆ **8:17 pm** 5:17 pm
☽ □ ♃ **9:56 pm** 6:56 pm
☽ △ ♀ 9:39 pm

25 SATURDAY
☽ △ ♀ **12:39 am**
☽ ⚺ ♇ **3:35 am** 12:35 am
☉ △ ♅ **12:38 pm** 9:38 am
☉ △ ♄ **6:07 pm** 3:07 pm
☽ ⚺ ♂ **10:47 pm** 7:47 pm

26 SUNDAY
☽ ⚹ ♅ **6:22 am** 3:22 am
☽ ⚹ ♄ **6:49 am** 3:49 am
☽ ☍ ☉ **7:56 am** 4:56 am
♀ □ ♇ **3:21 pm** 12:21 pm
☿ ⚻ ♆ **8:29 pm** 5:29 pm

27 MONDAY
☽ ☌ ♆ **8:04 am** 5:04 am
☽ ⚻ ☿ **9:08 am** 6:08 am
☽ △ ♃ **10:25 am** 7:25 am
☽ ⚹ ♇ **3:14 pm** 12:14 pm
☽ ⚻ ♀ **5:06 pm** 2:06 pm
☿ □ ♃ 10:32 pm

28 TUESDAY
☿ □ ♃ **1:32 am**
☽ ⚹ ♂ **9:54 am** 6:54 am
☽ ⚺ ♅ **5:11 pm** 2:11 pm
☽ □ ♄ **5:37 pm** 2:37 pm
☽ ⚻ ☉ **11:42 pm** 8:42 pm

29 WEDNESDAY
☽ ⚺ ♆ **5:56 pm** 2:56 pm
☽ ⚻ ♃ **8:56 pm** 5:56 pm
☿ ⚻ ♇ **11:40 pm** 8:40 pm
☽ □ ♇ 9:54 pm
☽ △ ☿ 10:02 pm

30 THURSDAY
☽ □ ♇ **12:54 am**
☽ △ ☿ **1:02 am**
☽ ☍ ♀ **6:56 am** 3:56 am
☽ □ ♂ **7:04 pm** 4:04 pm
☽ ☌ ♅ 10:50 pm
☽ △ ♄ 11:17 pm

31 FRIDAY
☽ ☌ ♅ **1:50 am**
☽ △ ♄ **2:17 am**
☽ △ ☉ **12:42 pm** 9:42 am
☽ ⚹ ♆ 10:33 pm

Eastern time in bold type
Pacific time in medium type

AUGUST 2018

DATE	SID.TIME	SUN	MOON	NODE	MERCURY	VENUS	MARS	JUPITER	SATURN	URANUS	NEPTUNE	PLUTO	CERES	PALLAS	JUNO	VESTA	CHIRON
1 W	20 38 13	8♌43 01	24♓25	5♌53Rx	22♌03Rx	23♍49	2♒51Rx	14♏01	3♑34Rx	2♉33	16♓02Rx	19♑33Rx	13♍58	11♌21	13♉05	22♐08D	2♈07Rx
2 Th	20 42 9	9 40 24	6♈46	5 52	21 32	24 51	2 35	14 05	3 31	2 33	16 00	19 32	14 24	11 55	13 29	22 08	2 06
3 F	20 46 6	10 37 48	19 22	5 52	20 58	25 54	2 19	14 09	3 27	2 33	15 59	19 31	14 50	12 28	13 52	22 09	2 04
4 Sa	20 50 2	11 35 14	2♉15	5 51D	20 19	26 56	2 03	14 13	3 24	2 33	15 58	19 29	15 16	13 01	14 16	22 10	2 03
5 Su	20 53 59	12 32 40	15 30	5 51	19 37	27 58	1 48	14 17	3 22	2 33	15 57	19 28	15 42	13 34	14 40	22 11	2 01
6 M	20 57 55	13 30 08	29 07	5 52	18 53	29 00	1 33	14 22	3 19	2 34	15 55	19 27	16 08	14 08	15 03	22 13	2 00
7 T	21 1 52	14 27 38	13♊09	5 52	18 07	0♎01	1 18	14 26	3 16	2 34Rx	15 54	19 25	16 34	14 41	15 26	22 16	1 58
8 W	21 5 49	15 25 08	27 33	5 53	17 19	1 03	1 04	14 31	3 13	2 34	15 53	19 24	17 00	15 14	15 49	22 18	1 56
9 Th	21 9 45	16 22 40	12♋18	5 54	16 32	2 03	0 51	14 36	3 11	2 34	15 51	19 23	17 27	15 47	16 12	22 22	1 55
10 F	21 13 42	17 20 13	27 18	5 54Rx	15 45	3 04	0 37	14 41	3 08	2 34	15 50	19 21	17 53	16 20	16 34	22 26	1 53
11 Sa	21 17 38	18 17 48	12♌25	5 54	15 00	4 04	0 25	14 47	3 06	2 33	15 48	19 20	18 19	16 53	16 57	22 30	1 51
12 Su	21 21 35	19 15 23	27 31	5 54	14 17	5 04	0 13	14 52	3 03	2 33	15 47	19 19	18 45	17 26	17 19	22 34	1 49
13 M	21 25 31	20 13 00	12♍25	5 52	13 38	6 04	0 01	14 57	3 01	2 33	15 46	19 18	19 12	17 59	17 41	22 40	1 48
14 T	21 29 28	21 10 37	27 02	5 51	13 03	7 03	29♑50	15 03	2 59	2 33	15 44	19 17	19 38	18 31	18 03	22 45	1 46
15 W	21 33 24	22 08 16	11♎15	5 49	12 32	8 02	29 40	15 09	2 57	2 32	15 43	19 15	20 05	19 04	18 25	22 51	1 44
16 Th	21 37 21	23 05 55	25 01	5 47	12 07	9 00	29 31	15 15	2 54	2 32	15 41	19 14	20 31	19 37	18 46	22 58	1 42
17 F	21 41 18	24 03 36	8♏19	5 45	11 49	9 58	29 22	15 21	2 53	2 32	15 40	19 13	20 58	20 09	19 07	23 05	1 40
18 Sa	21 45 14	25 01 17	21 13	5 45D	11 37	10 56	29 14	15 28	2 51	2 31	15 38	19 12	21 24	20 42	19 29	23 12	1 38
19 Su	21 49 11	25 59 00	3♐45	5 45	11 32D	11 53	29 06	15 34	2 49	2 30	15 37	19 11	21 51	21 14	19 49	23 20	1 36
20 M	21 53 7	26 56 43	15 59	5 46	11 34	12 50	29 00	15 41	2 47	2 30	15 35	19 10	22 17	21 47	20 10	23 28	1 34
21 T	21 57 4	27 54 28	28 01	5 47	11 44	13 46	28 54	15 47	2 46	2 29	15 33	19 09	22 44	22 19	20 31	23 36	1 32
22 W	22 1 0	28 52 14	9♑53	5 49	12 02	14 42	28 49	15 54	2 44	2 29	15 32	19 08	23 10	22 51	20 51	23 45	1 29
23 Th	22 4 57	29 50 01	21 41	5 50	12 27	15 37	28 45	16 01	2 43	2 28	15 30	19 07	23 37	23 24	21 11	23 54	1 27
24 F	22 8 53	0♍47 50	3♒29	5 51Rx	13 00	16 32	28 42	16 08	2 41	2 27	15 29	19 06	24 04	23 56	21 31	24 04	1 25
25 Sa	22 12 50	1 45 40	15 19	5 51	13 40	17 26	28 39	16 16	2 40	2 26	15 27	19 05	24 30	24 28	21 50	24 14	1 23
26 Su	22 16 47	2 43 31	27 14	5 49	14 28	18 20	28 38	16 23	2 39	2 25	15 26	19 04	24 57	25 00	22 09	24 25	1 20
27 M	22 20 43	3 41 23	9♓17	5 46	15 23	19 13	28 37D	16 30	2 38	2 25	15 24	19 03	25 24	25 32	22 28	24 36	1 18
28 T	22 24 40	4 39 17	21 28	5 42	16 25	20 06	28 37	16 38	2 37	2 24	15 22	19 02	25 51	26 04	22 47	24 47	1 16
29 W	22 28 36	5 37 13	3♈50	5 37	17 33	20 58	28 37	16 46	2 36	2 23	15 21	19 01	26 18	26 36	23 06	24 58	1 13
30 Th	22 32 33	6 35 10	16 24	5 32	18 48	21 49	28 39	16 54	2 35	2 22	15 19	19 00	26 44	27 08	23 24	25 10	1 11
31 F	22 36 29	7 33 10	29 11	5 27	20 08	22 40	28 41	17 02	2 35	2 21	15 18	18 59	27 11	27 39	23 42	25 23	1 09

EPHEMERIS CALCULATED FOR 12 MIDNIGHT GREENWICH MEAN TIME. ALL OTHER DATA AND FACING ASPECTARIAN PAGE IN **EASTERN TIME (BOLD)** AND PACIFIC TIME (REGULAR).

SEPTEMBER 2018

☽ Last Aspect day	ET / hr:mn / PT	asp	☽ Ingress sign	day	ET / hr:mn / PT
1	10:56 pm	△♂	♊	2	**4:02 am** 1:02 am
2	**1:56 am**	△♂	♊	2	**4:02 am** 1:02 am
3	11:37 pm	✶☿	♋	4	**8:03 am** 5:03 am
4	**2:37 am**	✶☿	♋	4	**8:03 am** 5:03 am
6	**8:43 am** 5:43 am	☍♂	♌	6	**9:54 am** 6:54 am
8	**9:31 am** 6:31 am	✶♀	♍	8	**10:29 am** 7:29 am
10	**11:12 am** 8:12 am	△♂	♎	10	**11:20 am** 8:20 am
11	**6:58 pm** 3:58 pm	□♇	♏	12	**2:15 pm** 11:15 am
14	**4:54 am** 1:54 am	✶☉	♐	14	**8:45 pm** 5:45 pm
16	**7:15 pm** 4:15 pm	□☉	♑	17	**7:07 am** 4:07 am

☽ Last Aspect day	ET / hr:mn / PT	asp	☽ Ingress sign	day	ET / hr:mn / PT
19	**1:10 pm** 10:10 am	△☉	♒	19	**7:52 pm** 4:52 pm
21	**1:13 pm** 10:13 am	□♃	♓	22	**8:27 am** 5:27 am
23	10:26 pm	△♃	♈	24	**7:04 pm** 4:04 pm
24	**1:26 am**	△♃	♈	24	**7:04 pm** 4:04 pm
26	**6:28 am** 3:28 am	□♇	♉	27	**3:16 am** 12:16 am
28	**6:36 pm** 3:36 pm	☍♃	♊	29	**9:26 am** 6:26 am
30	**11:38 am** 8:38 am	△☿	♋	10/1	**2:00 pm** 11:00 am

☽ Phases & Eclipses phase	day	ET / hr:mn / PT
4th Quarter	2	**10:37 pm** 7:37 pm
New Moon	9	**2:01 pm** 11:01 am
2nd Quarter	16	**7:15 pm** 4:15 pm
Full Moon	24	**10:52 pm** 7:52 pm

Planet Ingress		day	ET / hr:mn / PT
♀	♍	4	**6:52 am** 3:52 am
☿	♍	5	**10:39 pm** 7:39 pm
⚳	♎	5	11:26 pm
⚳	♎	6	**2:26 am**
♀	♏	9	**5:25 am** 2:25 am
♂	♒	10	**8:56 pm** 5:56 pm
⚶	♑	17	9:02 pm
⚶	♑	18	**12:02 am**
☿	♎	21	**11:39 pm** 8:39 pm
☉	♎	22	**9:54 pm** 6:54 pm
⚷	♓	25	**8:09 pm** 5:09 pm
⚵	♊	29	**7:39 pm** 4:39 pm

Planetary Motion		day	ET / hr:mn / PT
♄	D	6	**7:09 am** 4:09 am
♇	D	30	**10:03 pm** 7:03 pm

1 SATURDAY
☽✶♆ **1:33 am**
☽☍♃ **5:06 am** 2:06 am
☽△♇ **8:16 am** 5:16 am
☽□☿ **3:07 pm** 12:07 pm
☽⚻♀ **5:46 pm** 2:46 pm
☽△♂ 10:56 pm

2 SUNDAY
☽△♂ **1:56 am**
☽⚺♅ **8:05 am** 5:05 am
☽⚻♄ **8:33 am** 5:33 am
☽□☉ **10:37 pm** 7:37 pm

3 MONDAY
☽□♆ **6:41 am** 3:41 am
☿✶♀ **8:58 am** 5:58 am
☽⚻♃ **10:44 am** 7:44 am
☽⚻♇ **1:09 pm** 10:09 am
☽△♀ 10:27 pm
☽✶☿ 11:37 pm

4 TUESDAY
☽△♀ **1:27 am**
☽✶☿ **2:37 am**
☽⚻♂ **6:24 am** 3:24 am
☽✶♅ **11:52 am** 8:52 am
☽☍♄ **12:22 pm** 9:22 am

5 WEDNESDAY
☽✶☉ **5:31 am** 2:31 am
☽△♆ **9:27 am** 6:27 am

☿⚻♂ **11:18 am** 8:18 am
☽△♃ **1:55 pm** 10:55 am
☽☍♇ **3:41 pm** 12:41 pm

6 THURSDAY
☽□♀ **6:20 am** 3:20 am
☽☍♂ **8:43 am** 5:43 am
☽⚺☿ **11:28 am** 8:28 am
☽□♅ **1:30 pm** 10:30 am
☽⚻♄ **2:03 pm** 11:03 am

7 FRIDAY
☿△♅ **3:41 am** 12:41 am
☿△♄ **8:20 am** 5:20 am
☽⚺☉ **10:07 am** 7:07 am
☽⚻♆ **10:24 am** 7:24 am
☉☍♆ **2:27 pm** 11:27 am
☽□♃ **3:21 pm** 12:21 pm
☽⚻♇ **4:33 pm** 1:33 pm

8 SATURDAY
☽✶♀ **9:31 am** 6:31 am
☽⚻♂ **9:48 am** 6:48 am
☽△♅ **1:58 pm** 10:58 am
☽△♄ **2:36 pm** 11:36 am
♀□♂ **4:38 pm** 1:38 pm
☽☌☿ **6:54 pm** 3:54 pm

9 SUNDAY
☽☍♆ **10:49 am** 7:49 am
☽☌☉ **2:01 pm** 11:01 am
☽✶♃ **4:23 pm** 1:23 pm
☽△♇ **5:03 pm** 2:03 pm

10 MONDAY
☽△♂ **11:12 am** 8:12 am
☽⚺♀ **12:51 pm** 9:51 am
☽⚻♅ **2:49 pm** 11:49 am
☽□♄ **3:34 pm** 12:34 pm

11 TUESDAY
☽⚺☿ **3:25 am** 12:25 am
☉✶♃ **8:10 am** 5:10 am
☉△♇ **11:31 am** 8:31 am
☽⚻♆ **12:22 pm** 9:22 am
☽⚺♃ **6:51 pm** 3:51 pm
☽□♇ **6:58 pm** 3:58 pm
☽⚺☉ **7:31 pm** 4:31 pm

12 WEDNESDAY
♃✶♇ **3:55 am** 12:55 am
♀☍♅ **5:02 am** 2:02 am
☽□♂ **2:52 pm** 11:52 am
☽☍♅ **5:51 pm** 2:51 pm
☽☌♀ **6:31 pm** 3:31 pm
☽✶♄ **6:47 pm** 3:47 pm
♀✶♄ **11:58 pm** 8:58 pm

13 THURSDAY
☽✶☿ **4:02 pm** 1:02 pm
☽△♆ **4:50 pm** 1:50 pm
☿☍♆ **9:31 pm** 6:31 pm
☽✶♇ **11:59 pm** 8:59 pm
☽☌♃ 9:33 pm

14 FRIDAY
☽☌♃ **12:33 am**
☽✶☉ **4:54 am** 1:54 am
☽✶♂ **10:23 pm** 7:23 pm
☽⚻♅ 9:30 pm
☽⚺♄ 10:41 pm

15 SATURDAY
☽⚻♅ **12:30 am**
☽⚺♄ **1:41 am**
☽⚺♀ **4:14 am** 1:14 am
☿△♇ **10:54 pm** 7:54 pm
☽□♆ 10:12 pm

16 SUNDAY
☽□♆ **1:12 am**
☿✶♃ **7:51 am** 4:51 am
☽⚺♇ **8:57 am** 5:57 am
☽⚺♃ **10:23 am** 7:23 am
☽□☿ **10:48 am** 7:48 am
☽□☉ **7:15 pm** 4:15 pm

17 MONDAY
☽⚺♂ **10:07 am** 7:07 am
☽△♅ **10:57 am** 7:57 am
☽☌♄ **12:25 pm** 9:25 am
☽✶♀ **6:03 pm** 3:03 pm

18 TUESDAY
☽✶♆ **12:54 pm** 9:54 am
♂□♅ **7:01 pm** 4:01 pm
☽☌♇ **9:03 pm** 6:03 pm
☽✶♃ **11:25 pm** 8:25 pm

19 WEDNESDAY
☽△☿ **10:20 am** 7:20 am
☽△☉ **1:10 pm** 10:10 am
☽□♅ **11:36 pm** 8:36 pm
☽☌♂ 9:23 pm
☽⚺♄ 10:21 pm

20 THURSDAY
☽☌♂ **12:23 am**
☽⚺♄ **1:21 am**
☽□♀ **9:46 am** 6:46 am
☉☌☿ **9:52 pm** 6:52 pm
☽⚺♆ 10:44 pm

21 FRIDAY
☽⚺♆ **1:44 am**
☽⚺♇ **9:57 am** 6:57 am
☽□♃ **1:13 pm** 10:13 am
♂⚺♄ **5:20 pm** 2:20 pm

22 SATURDAY
☽⚻☉ **7:15 am** 4:15 am
☽⚻☿ **10:00 am** 7:00 am
☽✶♅ **11:56 am** 8:56 am
☽✶♄ **1:56 pm** 10:56 am
☽⚺♂ **2:26 pm** 11:26 am
☿⚻♅ **10:46 pm** 7:46 pm
☽△♀ 9:22 pm

23 SUNDAY
☽△♀ **12:22 am**
☿□♄ **12:46 pm** 9:46 am
☽☌♆ **1:22 pm** 10:22 am
☽✶♇ **9:24 pm** 6:24 pm
☿△♂ **9:30 pm** 6:30 pm
☽△♃ 10:26 pm

24 MONDAY
☽△♃ **1:26 am**
☉⚻♅ **3:09 pm** 12:09 pm
☽⚺♅ **10:15 pm** 7:15 pm
☽☍☉ **10:52 pm** 7:52 pm
☽□♄ 9:27 pm
☽✶♂ 11:23 pm

25 TUESDAY
☽□♄ **12:27 am**
☽✶♂ **2:23 am**
☽☍☿ **6:12 am** 3:12 am
☽⚻♀ **12:08 pm** 9:08 am
☉□♄ **7:50 pm** 4:50 pm
☽⚺♆ **10:40 pm** 7:40 pm

26 WEDNESDAY
☽□♇ **6:28 am** 3:28 am
☽⚻♃ **11:08 am** 8:08 am

27 THURSDAY
☽☌♅ **6:11 am** 3:11 am
☽△♄ **8:35 am** 5:35 am
☿⚺♀ **9:48 am** 6:48 am
☽⚻☉ **11:27 am** 8:27 am
☽□♂ **11:50 am** 8:50 am
☉△♂ **7:34 pm** 4:34 pm
☽☍♀ **9:02 pm** 6:02 pm
☽⚻☿ **10:26 pm** 7:26 pm

28 FRIDAY
☽✶♆ **5:43 am** 2:43 am
☽△♇ **1:20 pm** 10:20 am
☽☍♃ **6:36 pm** 3:36 pm

29 SATURDAY
☽⚺♅ **12:07 pm** 9:07 am
☽⚻♄ **2:44 pm** 11:44 am
☽△♂ **7:16 pm** 4:16 pm
☽△☉ **9:34 pm** 6:34 pm

30 SUNDAY
☽⚻♀ **3:37 am** 12:37 am
☿⚻♆ **6:22 am** 3:22 am
☽□♆ **10:58 am** 7:58 am
☽△☿ **11:38 am** 8:38 am
☽⚻♇ **6:28 pm** 3:28 pm
☽⚻♃ 9:19 pm

Eastern time in bold type
Pacific time in medium type

SEPTEMBER 2018

DATE	SID.TIME	SUN	MOON	NODE	MERCURY	VENUS	MARS	JUPITER	SATURN	URANUS	NEPTUNE	PLUTO	CERES	PALLAS	JUNO	VESTA	CHIRON
1 Sa	22 40 26	8 ♍ 31 11	12 ♉ 13	5 ♌ 23 ℞	21 ♌ 34	23 ♎ 30	28 ♑ 44	17 ♏ 10	2 ♑ 34 ℞	2 ♉ 19 ℞	15 ♓ 16 ℞	18 ♑ 58 ℞	27 ♍ 38	28 ♌ 11	24 ♉ 00	25 ♐ 35	1 ♈ 06 ℞
2 Su	22 44 22	9 29 14	25 30	5 21	23 05	24 19	28 48	17 18	2 34	2 18	15 14	18 57	28 05	28 43	24 17	25 48	1 04
3 M	22 48 19	10 27 18	9 ♊ 04	5 20 D	24 41	25 08	28 53	17 27	2 33	2 17	15 13	18 57	28 32	29 14	24 34	26 01	1 01
4 T	22 52 15	11 25 25	22 55	5 21	26 20	25 56	28 59	17 35	2 33	2 16	15 11	18 56	28 59	29 46	24 51	26 15	0 59
5 W	22 56 12	12 23 34	7 ♋ 05	5 22	28 03	26 43	29 05	17 44	2 33	2 14	15 09	18 55	29 26	0 ♍ 17	25 08	26 29	0 56
6 Th	23 0 9	13 21 45	21 31	5 23 ℞	29 48	27 29	29 12	17 53	2 33D	2 13	15 08	18 54	29 53	0 49	25 24	26 43	0 54
7 F	23 4 5	14 19 58	6 ♌ 12	5 24	1 ♍ 36	28 15	29 20	18 01	2 33	2 12	15 06	18 54	0 ♎ 20	1 20	25 40	26 58	0 51
8 Sa	23 8 2	15 18 13	21 01	5 23	3 26	28 59	29 29	18 10	2 33	2 10	15 04	18 53	0 47	1 51	25 55	27 13	0 48
9 Su	23 11 58	16 16 30	5 ♍ 53	5 20	5 18	29 43	29 38	18 19	2 33	2 09	15 03	18 52	1 14	2 22	26 10	27 28	0 46
10 M	23 15 55	17 14 48	20 40	5 15	7 11	0 ♏ 26	29 49	18 29	2 33	2 07	15 01	18 52	1 41	2 54	26 25	27 43	0 43
11 T	23 19 51	18 13 08	5 ♎ 14	5 09	9 04	1 08	0 ♒ 00	18 38	2 34	2 06	14 59	18 51	2 08	3 25	26 40	27 59	0 41
12 W	23 23 48	19 11 30	19 27	5 02	10 58	1 49	0 11	18 47	2 34	2 04	14 58	18 51	2 35	3 56	26 54	28 15	0 38
13 Th	23 27 44	20 09 54	3 ♏ 16	4 55	12 53	2 28	0 24	18 57	2 35	2 03	14 56	18 50	3 02	4 27	27 08	28 31	0 35
14 F	23 31 41	21 08 19	16 39	4 49	14 47	3 07	0 37	19 07	2 35	2 01	14 54	18 50	3 29	4 57	27 21	28 48	0 33
15 Sa	23 35 38	22 06 46	29 36	4 45	16 41	3 44	0 51	19 16	2 36	1 59	14 53	18 49	3 56	5 28	27 34	29 05	0 30
16 Su	23 39 34	23 05 15	12 ♐ 10	4 42 D	18 35	4 21	1 05	19 26	2 37	1 58	14 51	18 49	4 23	5 59	27 47	29 22	0 27
17 M	23 43 31	24 03 45	24 25	4 42	20 28	4 56	1 20	19 36	2 38	1 56	14 50	18 48	4 50	6 30	27 59	29 39	0 24
18 T	23 47 27	25 02 17	6 ♑ 25	4 42	22 21	5 30	1 36	19 46	2 39	1 54	14 48	18 48	5 18	7 00	28 11	29 57	0 22
19 W	23 51 24	26 00 50	18 17	4 44	24 13	6 02	1 53	19 56	2 40	1 52	14 46	18 48	5 45	7 31	28 22	0 ♑ 15	0 19
20 Th	23 55 20	26 59 25	0 ♒ 04	4 44 ℞	26 04	6 33	2 10	20 06	2 42	1 50	14 45	18 47	6 12	8 01	28 34	0 33	0 16
21 F	23 59 17	27 58 02	11 53	4 44	27 54	7 02	2 28	20 17	2 43	1 48	14 43	18 47	6 39	8 32	28 44	0 52	0 14
22 Sa	0 3 13	28 56 41	23 47	4 42	29 43	7 30	2 46	20 27	2 44	1 46	14 42	18 47	7 06	9 02	28 54	1 10	0 11
23 Su	0 7 10	29 55 21	5 ♓ 49	4 38	1 ♎ 32	7 57	3 05	20 38	2 46	1 45	14 40	18 46	7 33	9 32	29 04	1 29	0 08
24 M	0 11 7	0 ♎ 54 03	18 03	4 31	3 19	8 22	3 25	20 48	2 48	1 43	14 38	18 46	8 00	10 02	29 14	1 48	0 05
25 T	0 15 3	1 52 47	0 ♈ 30	4 22	5 06	8 45	3 45	20 59	2 49	1 41	14 37	18 46	8 28	10 32	29 22	2 07	0 03
26 W	0 19 0	2 51 33	13 10	4 12	6 52	9 06	4 06	21 10	2 51	1 38	14 35	18 46	8 55	11 02	29 31	2 27	0 00
27 Th	0 22 56	3 50 21	26 03	4 02	8 36	9 26	4 27	21 20	2 53	1 36	14 34	18 46	9 22	11 32	29 39	2 47	29 ♓ 57
28 F	0 26 53	4 49 11	9 ♉ 10	3 52	10 20	9 43	4 49	21 31	2 55	1 34	14 32	18 46	9 49	12 02	29 46	3 07	29 55
29 Sa	0 30 49	5 48 04	22 28	3 43	12 03	9 59	5 11	21 42	2 57	1 32	14 31	18 45	10 16	12 32	29 54	3 27	29 52
30 Su	0 34 46	6 46 58	5 ♊ 58	3 37	13 45	10 13	5 34	21 53	3 00	1 30	14 29	18 45	10 44	13 02	0 ♊ 00	3 47	29 49

EPHEMERIS CALCULATED FOR 12 MIDNIGHT GREENWICH MEAN TIME. ALL OTHER DATA AND FACING ASPECTARIAN PAGE IN **EASTERN TIME (BOLD)** AND PACIFIC TIME (REGULAR).

OCTOBER 2018

☽ Last Aspect day	ET / hr:mn / PT		asp	☽ Ingress sign	day	ET / hr:mn / PT	
9/30	**11:38 am**	8:38 am	△ ☿	♋	1	**2:00 pm**	11:00 am
3	**4:33 am**	1:33 am	△ ♃	♌	3	**5:12 pm**	2:12 pm
5	**7:34 am**	4:34 am	□ ♃	♍	5	**7:19 pm**	4:19 pm
7	**10:03 am**	7:03 am	⚹ ♃	♎	7	**9:10 pm**	6:10 pm
9	**4:50 am**	1:50 am	□ ♇	♏	9		9:09 pm
9	**4:50 am**	1:50 am	□ ♇	♏	10	**12:09 am**	
11	**7:12 pm**	4:12 pm	☌ ♃	♐	12	**5:53 am**	2:53 am
13	**8:58 pm**	5:58 pm	⚹ ☉	♑	14	**3:17 pm**	12:17 pm
16	**5:49 pm**	2:49 pm	⚹ ♃	♒	17	**3:36 am**	12:36 am
19	**8:27 am**	5:27 am	△ ☉	♓	19	**4:20 pm**	1:20 pm
21	**7:47 pm**	4:47 pm	△ ♃	♈	21		11:58 pm
21	**7:47 pm**	4:47 pm	△ ♃	♈	22	**2:58 am**	
23	**2:18 pm**	11:18 am	□ ♇	♉	24	**10:33 am**	7:33 am
26	**10:49 am**	7:49 am	☍ ♃	♊	26	**3:41 pm**	12:41 pm
27		9:37 pm	△ ♂	♋	28	**7:27 pm**	4:27 pm
28	**12:37 am**		△ ♂	♋	28	**7:27 pm**	4:27 pm
30	**10:31 pm**	7:31 pm	△ ☿	♌	30	**10:42 pm**	7:42 pm

☽ Phases & Eclipses phase	day	ET / hr:mn / PT	
4th Quarter	2	**5:45 am**	2:45 am
New Moon	8	**11:47 pm**	8:47 pm
2nd Quarter	16	**2:02 pm**	11:02 am
Full Moon	24	**12:45 pm**	9:45 am
4th Quarter	31	**12:40 pm**	9:40 am

Planet Ingress		day	ET / hr:mn / PT	
☿	♏	9	**8:40 pm**	5:40 pm
☉	♏	23	**7:22 am**	4:22 am
⚵	♉	24	**3:56 am**	12:56 am
☿	♐	30		9:38 pm
☿	♐	31	**12:38 am**	
♀	♎	31	**3:42 pm**	12:42 pm

Planetary Motion		day	ET / hr:mn / PT	
♀	℞	5	**3:04 pm**	12:04 pm
⚵	℞	11		9:05 pm
⚵	℞	12	**12:05 am**	

1 MONDAY
☽ ⚻ ♃ **12:19 am**
☽ ⚹ ♅ **4:29 pm** 1:29 pm
☽ ☍ ♄ **7:18 pm** 4:18 pm
☽ ⚻ ♂ 10:05 pm

2 TUESDAY
☽ ⚻ ♂ **1:05 am**
☽ □ ☉ **5:45 am** 2:45 am
☽ △ ♀ **8:18 am** 5:18 am
☽ △ ♆ **2:46 pm** 11:46 am
☿ □ ♇ **8:03 pm** 5:03 pm
☽ ☍ ♇ **10:10 pm** 7:10 pm
☽ □ ☿ **10:27 pm** 7:27 pm

3 WEDNESDAY
☽ △ ♃ **4:33 am** 1:33 am
☽ □ ♅ **7:29 pm** 4:29 pm
☉ ⚺ ♀ **9:36 pm** 6:36 pm
☽ ⚻ ♄ **10:31 pm** 7:31 pm

4 THURSDAY
☽ ☍ ♂ **5:31 am** 2:31 am
☽ □ ♀ **11:22 am** 8:22 am
☽ ⚹ ☉ **12:19 pm** 9:19 am
☽ ⚻ ♆ **5:18 pm** 2:18 pm
☽ ⚻ ♇ 9:38 pm

5 FRIDAY
☽ ⚻ ♇ **12:38 am**
☽ ⚹ ☿ **7:20 am** 4:20 am
☽ □ ♃ **7:34 am** 4:34 am
☿ ⚺ ♃ **9:39 am** 6:39 am
☽ △ ♅ **9:26 pm** 6:26 pm
☽ △ ♄ 9:43 pm

6 SATURDAY
☽ △ ♄ **12:43 am**
☽ ⚻ ♂ **8:59 am** 5:59 am
☽ ⚹ ♀ **1:16 pm** 10:16 am
☽ ⚺ ☉ **5:51 pm** 2:51 pm
☽ ☍ ♆ **7:04 pm** 4:04 pm
☽ △ ♇ 11:27 pm

7 SUNDAY
☽ △ ♇ **2:27 am**
☽ ⚹ ♃ **10:03 am** 7:03 am
☉ ⚻ ♆ **11:17 am** 8:17 am
☽ ⚺ ☿ **3:21 pm** 12:21 pm
☽ ⚻ ♅ **11:10 pm** 8:10 pm
☽ □ ♄ 11:47 pm

8 MONDAY
☽ □ ♄ **2:47 am**
☽ △ ♂ **12:35 pm** 9:35 am
☽ ⚺ ♀ **3:04 pm** 12:04 pm
☽ ⚻ ♆ **9:11 pm** 6:11 pm
☽ ☌ ☉ **11:47 pm** 8:47 pm

9 TUESDAY
☽ □ ♇ **4:50 am** 1:50 am
☽ ⚺ ♃ **1:21 pm** 10:21 am
☽ ☌ ☿ 9:36 pm
☽ ☍ ♅ 11:05 pm

10 WEDNESDAY
☽ ☌ ☿ **12:36 am**
☽ ☍ ♅ **2:05 am**
☽ ⚹ ♄ **6:12 am** 3:12 am
☿ ☍ ♅ **1:36 pm** 10:36 am
☽ □ ♂ **6:02 pm** 3:02 pm
☽ ☌ ♀ **6:15 pm** 3:15 pm
♀ □ ♂ **10:29 pm** 7:29 pm
☽ △ ♆ 10:12 pm

11 THURSDAY
☽ △ ♆ **1:12 am**
☽ ⚺ ☉ **8:12 am** 5:12 am
☽ ⚹ ♇ **9:23 am** 6:23 am
☽ ☌ ♃ **7:12 pm** 4:12 pm
☉ □ ♇ 9:11 pm

12 FRIDAY
☉ □ ♇ **12:11 am**
☿ ⚹ ♄ **4:20 am** 1:20 am
☽ ⚻ ♅ **7:47 am** 4:47 am
☽ ⚺ ♄ **12:34 pm** 9:34 am
☽ ⚺ ☿ **1:38 pm** 10:38 am
☽ ⚺ ♀ 9:09 pm

13 SATURDAY
☽ ⚺ ♀ **12:09 am**
☽ ⚹ ♂ **3:06 am** 12:06 am
☽ □ ♆ **8:32 am** 5:32 am
☽ ⚺ ♇ **5:25 pm** 2:25 pm
☽ ⚹ ☉ **8:58 pm** 5:58 pm

14 SUNDAY
☽ ⚺ ♃ **4:50 am** 1:50 am
☽ △ ♅ **5:07 pm** 2:07 pm
☽ ☌ ♄ **10:40 pm** 7:40 pm

15 MONDAY
☽ ⚹ ☿ **7:48 am** 4:48 am
☽ ⚹ ♀ **9:05 am** 6:05 am
☽ ⚺ ♂ **4:17 pm** 1:17 pm
☿ ☌ ♀ **4:21 pm** 1:21 pm
☽ ⚹ ♆ **7:26 pm** 4:26 pm

16 TUESDAY
☽ ☌ ♇ **4:54 am** 1:54 am
☽ □ ☉ **2:02 pm** 11:02 am
☽ ⚹ ♃ **5:49 pm** 2:49 pm

17 WEDNESDAY
☽ □ ♅ **5:17 am** 2:17 am
☽ ⚺ ♄ **11:31 am** 8:31 am
☽ □ ♀ **7:44 pm** 4:44 pm

18 THURSDAY
☽ □ ☿ **5:10 am** 2:10 am
☽ ☌ ♂ **7:50 am** 4:50 am
☽ ⚺ ♆ **8:13 am** 5:13 am
♂ ⚺ ♆ **4:30 pm** 1:30 pm
☽ ⚺ ♇ **5:52 pm** 2:52 pm
☉ ⚺ ♃ **10:01 pm** 7:01 pm

19 FRIDAY
☿ △ ♆ **5:47 am** 2:47 am
☽ □ ♃ **7:45 am** 4:45 am
☽ △ ☉ **8:27 am** 5:27 am
☿ □ ♂ **1:23 pm** 10:23 am
☽ ⚹ ♅ **5:47 pm** 2:47 pm
☽ ⚹ ♄ 9:26 pm

20 SATURDAY
☽ ⚹ ♄ **12:26 am**
☽ △ ♀ **5:44 am** 2:44 am
☽ ☌ ♆ **8:07 pm** 5:07 pm
☽ ⚺ ♂ **10:28 pm** 7:28 pm
☽ △ ☿ 10:14 pm

21 SUNDAY
☽ △ ☿ **1:14 am**
☽ ⚹ ♇ **5:33 am** 2:33 am
☽ △ ♃ **7:47 pm** 4:47 pm
☽ ⚻ ☉ 9:32 pm

22 MONDAY
☽ ⚻ ☉ **12:32 am**
☽ ⚺ ♅ **4:10 am** 1:10 am
☽ □ ♄ **10:59 am** 7:59 am
☽ ⚻ ♀ **1:16 pm** 10:16 am
☿ ⚹ ♇ **3:14 pm** 12:14 pm

23 TUESDAY
☽ ⚺ ♆ **5:15 am** 2:15 am
☽ ⚹ ♂ **9:58 am** 6:58 am
☽ □ ♇ **2:18 pm** 11:18 am
☽ ⚻ ☿ **5:01 pm** 2:01 pm
☉ ☍ ♅ **8:47 pm** 5:47 pm

24 WEDNESDAY
☽ ⚻ ♃ **4:39 am** 1:39 am
♀ ⚹ ♄ **8:52 am** 5:52 am
☽ ☌ ♅ **11:31 am** 8:31 am
☽ ☍ ☉ **12:45 pm** 9:45 am
☽ ☍ ♀ **6:00 pm** 3:00 pm
☽ △ ♄ **6:27 pm** 3:27 pm

25 THURSDAY
☽ ⚹ ♆ **11:30 am** 8:30 am
☽ □ ♂ **6:18 pm** 3:18 pm
☽ △ ♇ **8:15 pm** 5:15 pm

26 FRIDAY
☽ ☍ ☿ **4:46 am** 1:46 am
☉ ☌ ♀ **10:16 am** 7:16 am
☽ ☍ ♃ **10:49 am** 7:49 am
☽ ⚺ ♅ **4:27 pm** 1:27 pm
☽ ⚻ ♀ **8:38 pm** 5:38 pm
☽ ⚻ ☉ **9:56 pm** 6:56 pm
☽ ⚻ ♄ **11:36 pm** 8:36 pm

27 SATURDAY
☽ □ ♆ **3:48 pm** 12:48 pm
♂ ⚺ ♇ **8:19 pm** 5:19 pm
☉ ⚹ ♄ **10:52 pm** 7:52 pm
☽ ⚻ ♇ 9:27 pm
☽ △ ♂ 9:37 pm

28 SUNDAY
☽ ⚻ ♇ **12:27 am**
☽ △ ♂ **12:37 am**
☽ ⚻ ☿ **2:09 pm** 11:09 am
☽ ⚻ ♃ **3:28 pm** 12:28 pm
☽ ⚹ ♅ **8:03 pm** 5:03 pm
☽ △ ♀ **10:10 pm** 7:10 pm

29 MONDAY
☽ ☍ ♄ **3:32 am** 12:32 am
☽ △ ☉ **5:34 am** 2:34 am
☿ ☌ ♃ **7:05 am** 4:05 am
☽ △ ♆ **7:12 pm** 4:12 pm

30 TUESDAY
☽ ☍ ♇ **3:53 am** 12:53 am
☽ ⚻ ♂ **6:07 am** 3:07 am
☽ △ ♃ **7:32 pm** 4:32 pm
☽ △ ☿ **10:31 pm** 7:31 pm
☽ □ ♅ **11:09 pm** 8:09 pm
☽ □ ♀ **11:21 pm** 8:21 pm

31 WEDNESDAY
♀ ☍ ♅ **4:45 am** 1:45 am
☿ ⚺ ♀ **5:21 am** 2:21 am
☿ ⚻ ♅ **5:36 am** 2:36 am
☽ ⚻ ♄ **7:02 am** 4:02 am
☽ □ ☉ **12:40 pm** 9:40 am
☽ ⚻ ♆ **10:18 pm** 7:18 pm

Eastern time in bold type
Pacific time in medium type

OCTOBER 2018

DATE	SID.TIME	SUN	MOON	NODE	MERCURY	VENUS	MARS	JUPITER	SATURN	URANUS	NEPTUNE	PLUTO	CERES	PALLAS	JUNO	VESTA	CHIRON
1 M	0 38 42	7 ♎ 45 55	19 ♊ 38	3 ♌ 33 ℞	15 ♎ 26	10 ♏ 24	5 ♒ 57	22 ♏ 04	3 ♑ 02	1 ♉ 28 ℞	14 ♓ 28 ℞	18 ♑ 45 D	11 ♎ 11	13 ♍ 32	0 ♊ 06	4 ♑ 08	29 ♓ 46 ℞
2 T	0 42 39	8 44 55	3 ♋ 28	3 32 D	17 06	10 34	6 20	22 16	3 04	1 26	14 26	18 45	11 38	14 01	0 12	4 29	29 44
3 W	0 46 36	9 43 56	17 29	3 32	18 45	10 41	6 45	22 27	3 07	1 23	14 25	18 45	12 05	14 31	0 17	4 50	29 41
4 Th	0 50 32	10 43 00	1 ♌ 40	3 32 ℞	20 24	10 47	7 09	22 38	3 09	1 21	14 23	18 46	12 32	15 00	0 21	5 11	29 38
5 F	0 54 29	11 42 07	15 59	3 32	22 01	10 50 ℞	7 34	22 50	3 12	1 19	14 22	18 46	12 59	15 30	0 26	5 32	29 36
6 Sa	0 58 25	12 41 15	0 ♍ 25	3 29	23 38	10 50	8 00	23 01	3 15	1 17	14 20	18 46	13 27	15 59	0 29	5 54	29 33
7 Su	1 2 22	13 40 26	14 53	3 24	25 14	10 49	8 26	23 13	3 18	1 14	14 19	18 46	13 54	16 28	0 32	6 16	29 31
8 M	1 6 18	14 39 39	29 18	3 16	26 49	10 45	8 52	23 25	3 21	1 12	14 18	18 46	14 21	16 57	0 35	6 38	29 28
9 T	1 10 15	15 38 54	13 ♎ 35	3 06	28 24	10 38	9 19	23 36	3 24	1 10	14 16	18 46	14 48	17 26	0 37	7 00	29 25
10 W	1 14 11	16 38 11	27 36	2 54	29 57	10 29	9 46	23 48	3 27	1 07	14 15	18 47	15 15	17 55	0 38	7 22	29 23
11 Th	1 18 8	17 37 30	11 ♏ 18	2 42	1 ♏ 30	10 18	10 14	24 00	3 30	1 05	14 14	18 47	15 42	18 24	0 39	7 45	29 20
12 F	1 22 4	18 36 51	24 38	2 32	3 03	10 05	10 42	24 12	3 33	1 03	14 12	18 47	16 10	18 53	0 39 ℞	8 07	29 18
13 Sa	1 26 1	19 36 14	7 ♐ 34	2 23	4 34	9 49	11 11	24 24	3 37	1 00	14 11	18 47	16 37	19 22	0 39	8 30	29 15
14 Su	1 29 58	20 35 39	20 08	2 17	6 05	9 30	11 39	24 36	3 40	0 58	14 10	18 48	17 04	19 50	0 38	8 53	29 13
15 M	1 33 54	21 35 06	2 ♑ 23	2 13	7 35	9 10	12 08	24 48	3 44	0 55	14 09	18 48	17 31	20 19	0 37	9 16	29 10
16 T	1 37 51	22 34 34	14 24	2 12 D	9 04	8 47	12 38	25 00	3 47	0 53	14 07	18 49	17 58	20 47	0 35	9 39	29 08
17 W	1 41 47	23 34 04	26 16	2 12 ℞	10 33	8 22	13 08	25 13	3 51	0 51	14 06	18 49	18 25	21 16	0 33	10 03	29 05
18 Th	1 45 44	24 33 36	8 ♒ 04	2 12	12 01	7 55	13 38	25 25	3 55	0 48	14 05	18 50	18 52	21 44	0 30	10 26	29 03
19 F	1 49 40	25 33 10	19 53	2 11	13 28	7 27	14 08	25 37	3 59	0 46	14 04	18 50	19 19	22 12	0 27	10 50	29 01
20 Sa	1 53 37	26 32 46	1 ♓ 50	2 08	14 54	6 56	14 39	25 50	4 03	0 43	14 03	18 51	19 46	22 41	0 23	11 14	28 58
21 Su	1 57 33	27 32 23	13 58	2 02	16 20	6 24	15 10	26 02	4 07	0 41	14 02	18 51	20 13	23 09	0 18	11 38	28 56
22 M	2 1 30	28 32 02	26 21	1 54	17 45	5 51	15 42	26 14	4 11	0 38	14 01	18 52	20 40	23 37	0 14	12 02	28 54
23 T	2 5 27	29 31 42	9 ♈ 01	1 43	19 09	5 16	16 13	26 27	4 15	0 36	14 00	18 53	21 07	24 04	0 08	12 26	28 51
24 W	2 9 23	0 ♏ 31 25	22 00	1 30	20 32	4 41	16 45	26 40	4 19	0 33	13 58	18 53	21 34	24 32	0 02	12 51	28 49
25 Th	2 13 20	1 31 10	5 ♉ 15	1 17	21 55	4 05	17 18	26 52	4 24	0 31	13 57	18 54	22 01	25 00	29 ♉ 56	13 15	28 47
26 F	2 17 16	2 30 57	18 46	1 04	23 16	3 28	17 50	27 05	4 28	0 29	13 57	18 55	22 28	25 28	29 49	13 40	28 45
27 Sa	2 21 13	3 30 45	2 ♊ 29	0 54	24 36	2 52	18 23	27 18	4 33	0 26	13 56	18 55	22 55	25 55	29 41	14 05	28 43
28 Su	2 25 9	4 30 36	16 21	0 46	25 55	2 15	18 56	27 30	4 37	0 24	13 55	18 56	23 22	26 22	29 33	14 30	28 41
29 M	2 29 6	5 30 29	0 ♋ 19	0 40	27 13	1 39	19 29	27 43	4 42	0 21	13 54	18 57	23 49	26 50	29 25	14 55	28 39
30 T	2 33 2	6 30 25	14 21	0 38	28 30	1 03	20 02	27 56	4 47	0 19	13 53	18 58	24 16	27 17	29 16	15 20	28 37
31 W	2 36 59	7 30 22	28 25	0 37	29 46	0 28	20 36	28 09	4 51	0 16	13 52	18 59	24 43	27 44	29 07	15 45	28 35

EPHEMERIS CALCULATED FOR 12 MIDNIGHT GREENWICH MEAN TIME. ALL OTHER DATA AND FACING ASPECTARIAN PAGE IN **EASTERN TIME (BOLD)** AND PACIFIC TIME (REGULAR).

NOVEMBER 2018

☽ Last Aspect day	ET / hr:mn / PT		asp	☽ Ingress sign	day	ET / hr:mn / PT	
1		9:32 pm	✶♀	♍	1		10:48 pm
2	**12:32 am**		✶♀	♍	2	**1:48 am**	
4	**2:26 am**	12:26 am	✶♃	♎	4	**4:01 am**	1:01 am
6	**3:19 am**	12:19 am	☌♀	♏	6	**8:02 am**	5:02 am
8	**5:42 am**	2:42 am	□♂	♐	8	**1:59 pm**	10:59 am
10	**10:35 pm**	7:35 pm	△♅	♑	10	**10:55 pm**	7:55 pm
13	**10:13 am**	7:13 am	□♅	♒	13	**10:45 am**	7:45 am
15	**10:58 pm**	7:58 pm	✶♅	♓	15	**11:41 pm**	8:41 pm
18	**3:04 am**	12:04 am	△☉	♈	18	**10:56 am**	7:56 am
20	**5:46 pm**	2:46 pm	☌♅	♉	20	**6:43 pm**	3:43 pm
22	**4:59 am**	1:59 am	△♇	♊	22	**11:10 pm**	8:10 pm
24		9:31 pm	✶♅	♋	24		10:38 pm
25	**12:31 am**		✶♅	♋	25	**1:38 am**	
26		11:22 pm	□♅	♌	27	**3:35 am**	12:35 am
27	**2:22 am**		□♅	♌	27	**3:35 am**	12:35 am
29	**4:47 am**	1:47 am	△♅	♍	29	**6:08 am**	3:08 am

☽ Phases & Eclipses phase	day	ET / hr:mn / PT	
New Moon	7	**11:02 am**	8:02 am
2nd Quarter	15	**9:54 am**	6:54 am
Full Moon	22		9:39 pm
Full Moon	23	**12:39 am**	
4th Quarter	29	**7:19 pm**	4:19 pm

Planet Ingress		day	ET / hr:mn / PT	
♀	♎	4	**8:30 pm**	5:30 pm
♅	♈	6	**2:00 pm**	11:00 am
♃	♐	8	**7:38 am**	4:38 am
⚷	♏	11	**4:37 pm**	1:37 pm
♂	♓	15	**5:21 pm**	2:21 pm
☉	♐	22	**4:01 am**	1:01 am

Planetary Motion		day	ET / hr:mn / PT	
♀	D	16	**5:51 am**	2:51 am
☿	℞	16	**8:33 pm**	5:33 pm
♆	D	24	**8:08 pm**	5:08 pm

1 THURSDAY
☽ ⚻ ♇ **7:04 am** 4:04 am
☽ ☍ ♂ **11:22 am** 8:22 am
☽ □ ♃ **11:25 pm** 8:25 pm
☽ ✶ ♀ 9:32 pm
☽ △ ♅ 11:06 pm

2 FRIDAY
☽ ✶ ♀ **12:32 am**
☽ △ ♅ **2:06 am**
☽ □ ☿ **6:24 am** 3:24 am
☽ △ ♄ **10:26 am** 7:26 am
☽ ✶ ☉ **7:40 pm** 4:40 pm
♀ ⚺ ♃ **9:22 pm** 6:22 pm
☽ ☍ ♆ 10:21 pm

3 SATURDAY
☽ ☍ ♆ **1:21 am**
☽ △ ♇ **10:15 am** 7:15 am
☽ ⚻ ♂ **4:41 pm** 1:41 pm
☽ ⚺ ♀ 10:58 pm

4 SUNDAY
☽ ⚺ ♀ **1:58 am**
☽ ✶ ♃ **2:26 am** 12:26 am
☽ ⚻ ♅ **4:11 am** 1:11 am
☿ ⚺ ♄ **11:01 am** 8:01 am
☽ □ ♄ **1:02 pm** 10:02 am
☽ ✶ ☿ **1:12 pm** 10:12 am
☽ ⚺ ☉ 11:04 pm

5 MONDAY
☽ ⚺ ☉ **2:04 am**
☽ ⚻ ♆ **3:47 am** 12:47 am
☽ □ ♇ **12:56 pm** 9:56 am
☽ △ ♂ **9:43 pm** 6:43 pm
☉ △ ♆ 10:40 pm

6 TUESDAY
☉ △ ♆ **1:40 am**
☽ ☌ ♀ **3:19 am** 12:19 am
☽ ⚺ ♃ **7:16 am** 4:16 am
☽ ☍ ♅ **8:03 am** 5:03 am
☽ ✶ ♄ **5:39 pm** 2:39 pm
☽ ⚺ ☿ **9:48 pm** 6:48 pm

7 WEDNESDAY
☽ △ ♆ **8:30 am** 5:30 am
☽ ☌ ☉ **11:02 am** 8:02 am
☽ ✶ ♇ **6:06 pm** 3:06 pm
♃ ⚻ ♅ 10:20 pm

8 THURSDAY
♃ ⚻ ♅ **1:20 am**
☽ □ ♂ **5:42 am** 2:42 am
☽ ⚺ ♀ **7:36 am** 4:36 am
☽ ⚻ ♅ **1:51 pm** 10:51 am
☽ ☌ ♃ **2:06 pm** 11:06 am
☽ ⚺ ♄ 9:27 pm

9 FRIDAY
☽ ⚺ ♄ **12:27 am**
☽ ☌ ☿ **8:37 am** 5:37 am
♀ △ ♂ **10:12 am** 7:12 am
☽ □ ♆ **3:42 pm** 12:42 pm
☽ ⚺ ☉ **11:11 pm** 8:11 pm
☽ ⚺ ♇ 10:57 pm

10 SATURDAY
☽ ⚺ ♇ **1:57 am**
☽ ✶ ♀ **2:55 pm** 11:55 am
☽ ✶ ♂ **4:59 pm** 1:59 pm
☽ △ ♅ **10:35 pm** 7:35 pm
☽ ⚺ ♃ 9:04 pm

11 SUNDAY
☽ ⚺ ♃ **12:04 am**
☉ ✶ ♇ **10:22 am** 7:22 am
☽ ☌ ♄ **10:25 am** 7:25 am
☽ ⚺ ☿ **10:17 pm** 7:17 pm
☽ ✶ ♆ 11:01 pm

12 MONDAY
☽ ✶ ♆ **2:01 am**
☽ ☌ ♇ **12:57 pm** 9:57 am
☽ ✶ ☉ **3:21 pm** 12:21 pm
☽ □ ♀ 10:32 pm

13 TUESDAY
☽ □ ♀ **1:32 am**
☽ ⚺ ♂ **7:47 am** 4:47 am
☽ □ ♅ **10:13 am** 7:13 am
☽ ✶ ♃ **1:05 pm** 10:05 am
☽ ⚺ ♄ **11:09 pm** 8:09 pm

14 WEDNESDAY
☽ ✶ ☿ **1:25 pm** 10:25 am
☽ ⚺ ♆ **2:40 pm** 11:40 am
☽ ⚺ ♇ 10:55 pm

15 THURSDAY
☽ ⚺ ♇ **1:55 am**
♂ ✶ ♅ **4:31 am** 1:31 am
☽ □ ☉ **9:54 am** 6:54 am
☽ △ ♀ **2:05 pm** 11:05 am
☽ ✶ ♅ **10:58 pm** 7:58 pm
☽ ☌ ♂ 9:02 pm

16 FRIDAY
☽ ☌ ♂ **12:02 am**
☽ □ ♃ **3:10 am** 12:10 am
☽ ✶ ♄ **12:27 pm** 9:27 am
☽ □ ☿ 11:41 pm

17 SATURDAY
☽ □ ☿ **2:41 am**
☽ ☌ ♆ **3:07 am** 12:07 am
☉ ⚺ ♀ **11:35 am** 8:35 am
☽ ✶ ♇ **2:10 pm** 11:10 am
☽ ⚻ ♀ 10:52 pm

18 SUNDAY
☽ ⚻ ♀ **1:52 am**
☽ △ ☉ **3:04 am** 12:04 am
☽ ⚺ ♅ **10:05 am** 7:05 am
☽ ⚺ ♂ **2:20 pm** 11:20 am
☽ △ ♃ **3:18 pm** 12:18 pm
☽ □ ♄ **11:30 pm** 8:30 pm

19 MONDAY
☽ △ ☿ **11:26 am** 8:26 am
☽ ⚺ ♆ **12:52 pm** 9:52 am
♂ □ ♃ **8:30 pm** 5:30 pm
☽ □ ♇ **11:22 pm** 8:22 pm

20 TUESDAY
☽ ☍ ♀ **10:45 am** 7:45 am
☽ ⚻ ☉ **3:59 pm** 12:59 pm
☽ ☌ ♅ **5:46 pm** 2:46 pm
☽ ⚻ ♃ **11:45 pm** 8:45 pm
☽ ✶ ♂ 9:36 pm

21 WEDNESDAY
☽ ✶ ♂ **12:36 am**
☽ △ ♄ **6:54 am** 3:54 am
☉ ⚻ ♅ **2:51 pm** 11:51 am
☽ ⚻ ☿ **3:18 pm** 12:18 pm
☽ ✶ ♆ **7:01 pm** 4:01 pm

22 THURSDAY
☽ △ ♇ **4:59 am** 1:59 am
☽ ⚻ ♀ **4:25 pm** 1:25 pm
☽ ⚺ ♅ **10:09 pm** 7:09 pm
☽ ☍ ☉ 9:39 pm

23 FRIDAY
☽ ☍ ☉ **12:39 am**
☽ ☍ ♃ **4:47 am** 1:47 am
☽ □ ♂ **7:11 am** 4:11 am
☽ ⚻ ♄ **11:09 am** 8:09 am
☽ ☍ ☿ **3:30 pm** 12:30 pm
☽ □ ♆ **10:21 pm** 7:21 pm

24 SATURDAY
☽ ⚻ ♇ **8:03 am** 5:03 am
☽ △ ♀ **8:03 pm** 5:03 pm
☽ ✶ ♅ 9:31 pm

25 SUNDAY
☽ ✶ ♅ **12:31 am**
☽ ⚻ ☉ **6:53 am** 3:53 am
☽ ⚻ ♃ **7:55 am** 4:55 am
☽ △ ♂ **11:46 am** 8:46 am
☿ ⚺ ♄ **1:22 pm** 10:22 am
☽ ⚻ ☿ **1:41 pm** 10:41 am
☽ ☍ ♄ **1:43 pm** 10:43 am
☽ △ ♆ 9:25 pm
☉ ☌ ♃ 10:33 pm

26 MONDAY
☽ △ ♆ **12:25 am**
☉ ☌ ♃ **1:33 am**
☿ □ ♂ **3:06 am** 12:06 am
☽ ☍ ♇ **10:07 am** 7:07 am
☽ □ ♀ **11:16 pm** 8:16 pm
☽ □ ♅ 11:22 pm

27 TUESDAY
☽ □ ♅ **2:22 am**
☉ ☌ ☿ **4:15 am** 1:15 am
☽ △ ♃ **10:41 am** 7:41 am
☽ △ ☿ **11:22 am** 8:22 am
☽ △ ☉ **12:39 pm** 9:39 am
☽ ⚻ ♂ **4:06 pm** 1:06 pm
☽ ⚻ ♄ **4:07 pm** 1:07 pm
♂ ✶ ♄ **4:31 pm** 1:31 pm
☿ ☌ ♃ **5:27 pm** 2:27 pm
☽ ⚻ ♆ 11:33 pm

28 WEDNESDAY
☽ ⚻ ♆ **2:33 am**
☽ ⚻ ♇ **12:27 pm** 9:27 am

29 THURSDAY
☽ ✶ ♀ **3:17 am** 12:17 am
☽ △ ♅ **4:47 am** 1:47 am
☽ □ ☿ **9:42 am** 6:42 am
☽ □ ♃ **2:11 pm** 11:11 am
☉ ⚺ ♄ **7:03 pm** 4:03 pm
☽ △ ♄ **7:18 pm** 4:18 pm
☽ □ ☉ **7:19 pm** 4:19 pm
☽ ☍ ♂ **9:19 pm** 6:19 pm

30 FRIDAY
☽ ☍ ♆ **5:34 am** 2:34 am
☽ △ ♇ **3:48 pm** 12:48 pm
♀ ☍ ♅ **9:13 pm** 6:13 pm

Eastern time in bold type
Pacific time in medium type

NOVEMBER 2018

DATE	SID.TIME	SUN	MOON	NODE	MERCURY	VENUS	MARS	JUPITER	SATURN	URANUS	NEPTUNE	PLUTO	CERES	PALLAS	JUNO	VESTA	CHIRON
1 Th	2 40 56	8 ♏ 30 22	12 ♌ 30	0 ♌ 37 R	0 ♐ 59	29 ♎ 54 R	21 ♒ 10	28 ♏ 22	4 ♑ 56	0 ♉ 14 R	13 ♓ 51 R	19 ♑ 00	25 ♎ 09	28 ♍ 11	28 ♉ 57 R	16 ♑ 10	28 ♓ 33 R
2 F	2 44 52	9 30 24	26 36	0 37	2 12	29 21	21 44	28 35	5 01	0 11	13 51	19 01	25 36	28 38	28 47	16 36	28 31
3 Sa	2 48 49	10 30 28	10 ♍ 41	0 34	3 22	28 50	22 18	28 48	5 06	0 09	13 50	19 01	26 03	29 05	28 37	17 01	28 29
4 Su	2 52 45	11 30 34	24 44	0 28	4 30	28 21	22 53	29 01	5 11	0 07	13 49	19 02	26 30	29 32	28 26	17 27	28 27
5 M	2 56 42	12 30 42	8 ♎ 43	0 20	5 36	27 53	23 28	29 14	5 16	0 04	13 48	19 03	26 56	29 58	28 15	17 53	28 25
6 T	3 0 38	13 30 52	22 33	0 09	6 40	27 27	24 03	29 27	5 21	0 02	13 48	19 04	27 23	0 ♎ 25	28 03	18 19	28 24
7 W	3 4 35	14 31 04	6 ♏ 12	29 ♋ 57	7 40	27 03	24 38	29 40	5 27	0 00	13 47	19 06	27 50	0 51	27 51	18 45	28 22
8 Th	3 8 31	15 31 18	19 36	29 44	8 38	26 42	25 13	29 53	5 32	29 ♈ 57	13 47	19 07	28 16	1 18	27 39	19 11	28 20
9 F	3 12 28	16 31 34	2 ♐ 43	29 32	9 32	26 22	25 49	0 ♐ 06	5 37	29 55	13 46	19 08	28 43	1 44	27 27	19 37	28 19
10 Sa	3 16 25	17 31 51	15 30	29 23	10 21	26 05	26 25	0 19	5 43	29 53	13 45	19 09	29 10	2 10	27 14	20 04	28 17
11 Su	3 20 21	18 32 10	28 00	29 16	11 07	25 51	27 00	0 33	5 48	29 50	13 45	19 10	29 36	2 36	27 01	20 30	28 16
12 M	3 24 18	19 32 31	10 ♑ 13	29 12	11 47	25 39	27 37	0 46	5 54	29 48	13 45	19 11	0 ♏ 03	3 02	26 48	20 57	28 14
13 T	3 28 14	20 32 53	22 12	29 10 D	12 21	25 29	28 13	0 59	6 00	29 46	13 44	19 12	0 29	3 28	26 35	21 23	28 13
14 W	3 32 11	21 33 17	4 ♒ 04	29 10	12 50	25 22	28 49	1 12	6 05	29 43	13 44	19 14	0 56	3 53	26 22	21 50	28 11
15 Th	3 36 7	22 33 42	15 51	29 10 R	13 11	25 17	29 26	1 26	6 11	29 41	13 43	19 15	1 22	4 19	26 08	22 17	28 10
16 F	3 40 4	23 34 08	27 41	29 10	13 24	25 15 D	0 ♓ 03	1 39	6 17	29 39	13 43	19 16	1 48	4 44	25 55	22 44	28 09
17 Sa	3 44 0	24 34 36	9 ♓ 37	29 09	13 29 R	25 15	0 39	1 52	6 23	29 37	13 43	19 18	2 15	5 09	25 41	23 11	28 08
18 Su	3 47 57	25 35 04	21 47	29 06	13 25	25 17	1 16	2 06	6 28	29 35	13 42	19 19	2 41	5 35	25 28	23 38	28 06
19 M	3 51 54	26 35 35	4 ♈ 13	29 00	13 11	25 22	1 54	2 19	6 34	29 33	13 42	19 20	3 07	6 00	25 14	24 05	28 05
20 T	3 55 50	27 36 06	17 00	28 52	12 47	25 29	2 31	2 32	6 40	29 31	13 42	19 22	3 33	6 25	25 01	24 32	28 04
21 W	3 59 47	28 36 39	0 ♉ 10	28 42	12 13	25 39	3 08	2 46	6 46	29 28	13 42	19 23	3 59	6 49	24 47	24 59	28 03
22 Th	4 3 43	29 37 13	13 41	28 31	11 27	25 51	3 46	2 59	6 53	29 26	13 42	19 24	4 25	7 14	24 34	25 27	28 02
23 F	4 7 40	0 ♐ 37 49	27 34	28 21	10 32	26 05	4 23	3 12	6 59	29 24	13 42	19 26	4 52	7 39	24 21	25 54	28 01
24 Sa	4 11 36	1 38 26	11 ♊ 42	28 13	9 27	26 21	5 01	3 26	7 05	29 22	13 42	19 27	5 18	8 03	24 07	26 21	28 00
25 Su	4 15 33	2 39 04	26 01	28 06	8 15	26 39	5 39	3 39	7 11	29 20	13 42 D	19 29	5 44	8 27	23 54	26 49	28 00
26 M	4 19 29	3 39 45	10 ♋ 26	28 03	6 57	26 59	6 17	3 53	7 17	29 19	13 42	19 30	6 09	8 51	23 42	27 17	27 59
27 T	4 23 26	4 40 26	24 51	28 01 D	5 36	27 21	6 55	4 06	7 24	29 17	13 42	19 32	6 35	9 15	23 29	27 44	27 58
28 W	4 27 23	5 41 10	9 ♌ 12	28 02	4 13	27 44	7 33	4 19	7 30	29 15	13 42	19 33	7 01	9 39	23 17	28 12	27 57
29 Th	4 31 19	6 41 54	23 27	28 03	2 53	28 10	8 12	4 33	7 36	29 13	13 42	19 35	7 27	10 03	23 05	28 40	27 57
30 F	4 35 16	7 42 41	7 ♍ 32	28 03 R	1 38	28 38	8 50	4 46	7 43	29 11	13 42	19 37	7 53	10 27	22 53	29 08	27 56

EPHEMERIS CALCULATED FOR 12 MIDNIGHT GREENWICH MEAN TIME. ALL OTHER DATA AND FACING ASPECTARIAN PAGE IN **EASTERN TIME (BOLD)** AND PACIFIC TIME (REGULAR).

DECEMBER 2018

☽ Last Aspect day	ET / hr:mn / PT	asp	☽ Ingress sign	day	ET / hr:mn / PT
1	**9:34 am** 6:34 am	⚹ ☿	♎	1	**9:49 am** 6:49 am
3	**1:16 pm** 10:16 am	☍ ♅	♏	3	**2:55 pm** 11:55 am
5	**4:53 pm** 1:53 pm	☌ ☿	♐	5	**9:49 pm** 6:49 pm
8	**5:00 am** 2:00 am	△ ♅	♑	8	**7:01 am** 4:01 am
10	**4:27 pm** 1:27 pm	□ ♅	♒	10	**6:39 pm** 3:39 pm
13	**5:20 am** 2:20 am	⚹ ♅	♓	13	**7:40 am** 4:40 am
15	**6:49 am** 3:49 am	□ ☉	♈	15	**7:44 pm** 4:44 pm
17	11:21 pm	☌ ♅	♉	18	**4:37 am** 1:37 am
18	**2:21 am**	☌ ♅	♉	18	**4:37 am** 1:37 am
19	**7:42 pm** 4:42 pm	⚹ ♂	♊	20	**9:34 am** 6:34 am

☽ Last Aspect day	ET / hr:mn / PT	asp	☽ Ingress sign	day	ET / hr:mn / PT
22	**9:21 am** 6:21 am	⚹ ♅	♋	22	**11:28 am** 8:28 am
24	**9:50 am** 6:50 am	□ ♅	♌	24	**11:59 am** 8:59 am
26	**10:37 am** 7:37 am	△ ♅	♍	26	**12:50 pm** 9:50 am
28	**11:27 am** 8:27 am	☍ ♂	♎	28	**3:23 pm** 12:23 pm
30	**5:53 pm** 2:53 pm	☍ ♅	♏	30	**8:23 pm** 5:23 pm

☽ Phases & Eclipses phase	day	ET / hr:mn / PT
New Moon	6	11:20 pm
New Moon	7	**2:20 am**
2nd Quarter	15	**6:49 am** 3:49 am
Full Moon	22	**12:49 pm** 9:49 am
4th Quarter	29	**4:34 am** 1:34 am

Planet Ingress		day	ET / hr:mn / PT
☿	♏	1	**6:12 am** 3:12 am
⚶	♒	1	**3:42 pm** 12:42 pm
♀	♏	2	**12:02 pm** 9:02 am
☿	♐	12	**6:43 pm** 3:43 pm
☉	♑	21	**5:23 pm** 2:23 pm
♂	♈	31	**9:20 pm** 6:20 pm

Planetary Motion		day	ET / hr:mn / PT
☿	D	6	**4:22 pm** 1:22 pm
⚷	D	8	11:52 pm
⚷	D	9	**2:52 am**
⚵	D	23	**9:56 pm** 6:56 pm

1 SATURDAY
☽ ⊼ ♅ **8:19 am** 5:19 am
☽ ⊻ ♀ **8:46 am** 5:46 am
☽ ⚹ ☿ **9:34 am** 6:34 am
☿ ⊻ ♀ **4:50 pm** 1:50 pm
☽ ⚹ ♃ **6:56 pm** 3:56 pm
☽ □ ♄ **11:44 pm** 8:44 pm

2 SUNDAY
☽ ⚹ ☉ **3:31 am** 12:31 am
☽ ⊼ ♂ **3:58 am** 12:58 am
☿ ⊼ ♅ **5:16 am** 2:16 am
☽ ⊼ ♆ **9:53 am** 6:53 am
☉ □ ♂ **7:34 pm** 4:34 pm
☽ □ ♇ **8:30 pm** 5:30 pm

3 MONDAY
☽ ⊻ ☿ **11:42 am** 8:42 am
☽ ☍ ♅ **1:16 pm** 10:16 am
☽ ☌ ♀ **4:05 pm** 1:05 pm
☽ ⊻ ♃ 10:14 pm

4 TUESDAY
☽ ⊻ ♃ **1:14 am**
☽ ⚹ ♄ **5:43 am** 2:43 am
☽ △ ♂ **12:24 pm** 9:24 am
☽ ⊻ ☉ **1:38 pm** 10:38 am
☽ △ ♆ **3:46 pm** 12:46 pm
☽ ⚹ ♇ 11:50 pm

5 WEDNESDAY
☽ ⚹ ♇ **2:50 am**
☽ ☌ ☿ **4:53 pm** 1:53 pm
☉ □ ♆ **5:22 pm** 2:22 pm
☽ ⊼ ♅ **7:59 pm** 4:59 pm
☽ ⊻ ♀ 10:43 pm

6 THURSDAY
☽ ⊻ ♀ **1:43 am**
☽ ☌ ♃ **9:31 am** 6:31 am
☽ ⊻ ♄ **1:41 pm** 10:41 am
☽ □ ♂ **11:11 pm** 8:11 pm
☽ □ ♆ **11:42 pm** 8:42 pm
☽ ☌ ☉ 11:20 pm

7 FRIDAY
☽ ☌ ☉ **2:20 am**
♂ ☌ ♆ **9:11 am** 6:11 am
☽ ⊻ ♇ **11:20 am** 8:20 am
☽ ⊻ ☿ 11:02 pm

8 SATURDAY
☽ ⊻ ☿ **2:02 am**
☽ △ ♅ **5:00 am** 2:00 am
☽ ⚹ ♀ **2:20 pm** 11:20 am
☽ ⊻ ♃ **8:19 pm** 5:19 pm
☽ ☌ ♄ 9:09 pm

9 SUNDAY
☽ ☌ ♄ **12:09 am**
☽ ⚹ ♆ **10:06 am** 7:06 am
☽ ⚹ ♂ **12:52 pm** 9:52 am
☽ ⊻ ☉ **6:12 pm** 3:12 pm
☽ ☌ ♇ **10:20 pm** 7:20 pm

10 MONDAY
☽ ⚹ ☿ **3:38 pm** 12:38 pm
☽ □ ♅ **4:27 pm** 1:27 pm

11 TUESDAY
☽ □ ♀ **6:01 am** 3:01 am
☿ ⊼ ♅ **6:38 am** 3:38 am
☽ ⚹ ♃ **9:34 am** 6:34 am
☽ ⊻ ♄ **12:56 pm** 9:56 am
☉ ⊻ ♇ **8:26 pm** 5:26 pm
☽ ⊻ ♆ **10:37 pm** 7:37 pm

12 WEDNESDAY
☽ ⊻ ♂ **4:59 am** 1:59 am
☽ ⊻ ♇ **11:15 am** 8:15 am
☽ ⚹ ☉ **12:36 pm** 9:36 am

13 THURSDAY
☽ ⚹ ♅ **5:20 am** 2:20 am
☽ □ ☿ **8:39 am** 5:39 am
☽ △ ♀ **11:10 pm** 8:10 pm
☽ □ ♃ **11:44 pm** 8:44 pm
☽ ⚹ ♄ 11:31 pm

14 FRIDAY
☽ ⚹ ♄ **2:31 am**
♀ ⊻ ♃ **10:59 am** 7:59 am
☽ ☌ ♆ **11:35 am** 8:35 am
☽ ☌ ♂ **9:19 pm** 6:19 pm
☽ ⚹ ♇ 9:05 pm

15 SATURDAY
☽ ⚹ ♇ **12:05 am**
☽ □ ☉ **6:49 am** 3:49 am
☽ ⊻ ♅ **5:23 pm** 2:23 pm
☽ △ ☿ 10:48 pm

16 SUNDAY
☽ △ ☿ **1:48 am**
♀ ⚹ ♄ **9:26 am** 6:26 am
☽ △ ♃ **12:12 pm** 9:12 am
☽ □ ♄ **2:21 pm** 11:21 am
☽ ⊼ ♀ **2:39 pm** 11:39 am
☽ ⊻ ♆ **10:27 pm** 7:27 pm
♂ ⚹ ♇ 10:57 pm

17 MONDAY
♂ ⚹ ♇ **1:57 am**
☽ □ ♇ **10:20 am** 7:20 am
☽ ⊻ ♂ **10:46 am** 7:46 am
☽ △ ☉ **9:27 pm** 6:27 pm
☽ ☌ ♅ 11:21 pm

18 TUESDAY
☽ ☌ ♅ **2:21 am**
☽ ⊼ ☿ **3:31 pm** 12:31 pm
☽ ⊼ ♃ **8:54 pm** 5:54 pm
☽ △ ♄ **10:27 pm** 7:27 pm
☽ ☍ ♀ 10:54 pm

19 WEDNESDAY
☽ ☍ ♀ **1:54 am**
☽ ⚹ ♆ **5:33 am** 2:33 am
☽ △ ♇ **4:41 pm** 1:41 pm
☽ ⚹ ♂ **7:42 pm** 4:42 pm

20 THURSDAY
☽ ⊼ ☉ **7:05 am** 4:05 am
☽ ⊻ ♅ **7:24 am** 4:24 am
☉ △ ♅ **11:22 am** 8:22 am
☽ ☍ ☿ 9:41 pm
☽ ☍ ♃ 10:35 pm
☽ ⊼ ♄ 11:40 pm

21 FRIDAY
☽ ☍ ☿ **12:41 am**
☽ ☍ ♃ **1:35 am**
☽ ⊼ ♄ **2:40 am**
☽ ⊼ ♀ **8:46 am** 5:46 am
☽ □ ♆ **8:58 am** 5:58 am
♀ △ ♆ **12:11 pm** 9:11 am
☿ ☌ ♃ **12:37 pm** 9:37 am
☽ ⊼ ♇ **7:31 pm** 4:31 pm
☽ □ ♂ 9:41 pm
☿ ⊻ ♄ 9:41 pm

22 SATURDAY
☽ □ ♂ **12:41 am**
☿ ⊻ ♄ **12:41 am**
☽ ⚹ ♅ **9:21 am** 6:21 am
☽ ☍ ☉ **12:49 pm** 9:49 am

23 SUNDAY
☽ ⊼ ♃ **3:35 am** 12:35 am
☽ ☍ ♄ **4:17 am** 1:17 am
☽ ⊼ ☿ **6:44 am** 3:44 am
☽ △ ♆ **10:03 am** 7:03 am
☽ △ ♀ **12:55 pm** 9:55 am
☽ ☍ ♇ **8:23 pm** 5:23 pm

24 MONDAY
☽ △ ♂ **3:37 am** 12:37 am
☽ □ ♅ **9:50 am** 6:50 am
☽ ⊼ ☉ **4:52 pm** 1:52 pm
☿ □ ♆ **7:32 pm** 4:32 pm

25 TUESDAY
☽ △ ♃ **4:44 am** 1:44 am
☽ ⊼ ♄ **5:07 am** 2:07 am
☽ ⊼ ♆ **10:34 am** 7:34 am
☽ △ ☿ **12:06 pm** 9:06 am
☽ □ ♀ **4:37 pm** 1:37 pm
☽ ⊼ ♇ **9:04 pm** 6:04 pm

26 WEDNESDAY
☽ ⊼ ♂ **6:38 am** 3:38 am
☽ △ ♅ **10:37 am** 7:37 am
☽ △ ☉ **9:33 pm** 6:33 pm

27 THURSDAY
☽ □ ♃ **6:48 am** 3:48 am
☽ △ ♄ **6:51 am** 3:51 am
☽ ☍ ♆ **12:09 pm** 9:09 am
♃ ⊻ ♄ **2:18 pm** 11:18 am
☽ □ ☿ **7:04 pm** 4:04 pm
☽ ⚹ ♀ **9:52 pm** 6:52 pm
☽ △ ♇ **11:04 pm** 8:04 pm

28 FRIDAY
☽ ☍ ♂ **11:27 am** 8:27 am
☽ ⊼ ♅ **1:02 pm** 10:02 am
♀ ⚹ ♇ **4:31 pm** 1:31 pm

29 SATURDAY
☽ □ ☉ **4:34 am** 1:34 am
☽ □ ♄ **10:41 am** 7:41 am
☽ ⚹ ♃ **11:00 am** 8:00 am
☿ ⊻ ♇ **11:44 am** 8:44 am
☽ ⊼ ♆ **3:52 pm** 12:52 pm
♂ ⊻ ♅ **8:14 pm** 5:14 pm

30 SUNDAY
☽ □ ♇ **3:23 am** 12:23 am
☽ ⚹ ☿ **5:13 am** 2:13 am
☽ ⊻ ♀ **5:59 am** 2:59 am
☽ ☍ ♅ **5:53 pm** 2:53 pm
☽ ⊼ ♂ **7:03 pm** 4:03 pm
☿ ⊻ ♀ 10:00 pm

31 MONDAY
☿ ⊻ ♀ **1:00 am**
☽ ⚹ ☉ **2:46 pm** 11:46 am
☽ ⚹ ♄ **5:09 pm** 2:09 pm
☽ ⊻ ♃ **5:52 pm** 2:52 pm
☽ △ ♆ **10:10 pm** 7:10 pm

Eastern time in bold type
Pacific time in medium type

DECEMBER 2018

DATE	SID.TIME	SUN	MOON	NODE	MERCURY	VENUS	MARS	JUPITER	SATURN	URANUS	NEPTUNE	PLUTO	CERES	PALLAS	JUNO	VESTA	CHIRON
1 Sa	4 39 12	8 ♐ 43 28	21 ♍ 29	28 ♋ 03 ℞	0 ♐ 29 ℞	29 ♎ 07	9 ♓ 28	5 ♐ 00	7 ♑ 49	29 ♈ 10 ℞	13 ♓ 42	19 ♑ 38	8 ♏ 18	10 ♎ 50	22 ♉ 41 ℞	29 ♑ 36	27 ♓ 56 ℞
2 Su	4 43 9	9 44 18	5 ♎ 15	28 00	29 ♏ 29	29 37	10 07	5 13	7 56	29 08	13 42	19 40	8 44	11 13	22 30	0 ♒ 04	27 55
3 M	4 47 5	10 45 08	18 51	27 55	28 40	0 ♏ 10	10 46	5 26	8 02	29 06	13 43	19 42	9 09	11 37	22 19	0 32	27 55
4 T	4 51 2	11 46 01	2 ♏ 16	27 48	28 02	0 43	11 24	5 40	8 09	29 05	13 43	19 43	9 35	12 00	22 09	1 00	27 55
5 W	4 54 58	12 46 54	15 29	27 40	27 36	1 18	12 03	5 53	8 16	29 03	13 43	19 45	10 00	12 22	21 59	1 28	27 54
6 Th	4 58 55	13 47 49	28 29	27 31	27 20 D	1 55	12 42	6 07	8 22	29 01	13 44	19 47	10 26	12 45	21 49	1 57	27 54
7 F	5 2 52	14 48 45	11 ♐ 16	27 24	27 16	2 33	13 21	6 20	8 29	29 00	13 44	19 48	10 51	13 08	21 40	2 25	27 54
8 Sa	5 6 48	15 49 42	23 48	27 17	27 23	3 12	14 00	6 33	8 36	28 58	13 45	19 50	11 16	13 30	21 31	2 53	27 54
9 Su	5 10 45	16 50 40	6 ♑ 07	27 13	27 38	3 52	14 40	6 47	8 42	28 57	13 45	19 52	11 42	13 52	21 22	3 22	27 54 D
10 M	5 14 41	17 51 39	18 14	27 11D	28 03	4 34	15 19	7 00	8 49	28 56	13 45	19 54	12 07	14 14	21 15	3 50	27 54
11 T	5 18 38	18 52 38	0 ♒ 10	27 10	28 35	5 17	15 58	7 13	8 56	28 54	13 46	19 55	12 32	14 36	21 07	4 19	27 54
12 W	5 22 34	19 53 38	12 00	27 11	29 15	6 00	16 37	7 27	9 03	28 53	13 47	19 57	12 57	14 58	21 00	4 47	27 54
13 Th	5 26 31	20 54 39	23 47	27 13	0 ♐ 01	6 45	17 17	7 40	9 09	28 52	13 47	19 59	13 22	15 19	20 54	5 16	27 54
14 F	5 30 27	21 55 41	5 ♓ 35	27 15	0 52	7 31	17 56	7 53	9 16	28 50	13 48	20 01	13 46	15 41	20 48	5 45	27 54
15 Sa	5 34 24	22 56 42	17 30	27 16 ℞	1 48	8 18	18 36	8 06	9 23	28 49	13 48	20 03	14 11	16 02	20 43	6 13	27 55
16 Su	5 38 21	23 57 45	29 38	27 16	2 49	9 05	19 16	8 19	9 30	28 48	13 49	20 05	14 36	16 23	20 38	6 42	27 55
17 M	5 42 17	24 58 48	12 ♈ 01	27 15	3 53	9 54	19 55	8 33	9 37	28 47	13 50	20 06	15 01	16 44	20 34	7 11	27 56
18 T	5 46 14	25 59 51	24 47	27 12	5 00	10 43	20 35	8 46	9 44	28 46	13 51	20 08	15 25	17 04	20 30	7 40	27 56
19 W	5 50 10	27 00 54	7 ♉ 56	27 08	6 10	11 33	21 15	8 59	9 51	28 45	13 51	20 10	15 50	17 25	20 27	8 09	27 56
20 Th	5 54 7	28 01 58	21 32	27 03	7 23	12 24	21 55	9 12	9 58	28 44	13 52	20 12	16 14	17 45	20 24	8 38	27 57
21 F	5 58 3	29 03 03	5 ♊ 33	26 58	8 38	13 16	22 35	9 25	10 05	28 43	13 53	20 14	16 38	18 05	20 22	9 07	27 58
22 Sa	6 2 0	0 ♑ 04 08	19 57	26 55	9 55	14 09	23 15	9 38	10 12	28 42	13 54	20 16	17 02	18 25	20 21	9 36	27 58
23 Su	6 5 56	1 05 13	4 ♋ 38	26 52	11 14	15 02	23 55	9 51	10 19	28 42	13 55	20 18	17 27	18 45	20 20	10 05	27 59
24 M	6 9 53	2 06 19	19 28	26 51D	12 34	15 56	24 35	10 04	10 26	28 41	13 56	20 20	17 51	19 04	20 19D	10 34	28 00
25 T	6 13 50	3 07 25	4 ♌ 21	26 51	13 55	16 51	25 15	10 17	10 33	28 40	13 57	20 22	18 15	19 23	20 20	11 03	28 01
26 W	6 17 46	4 08 32	19 08	26 52	15 18	17 46	25 55	10 30	10 40	28 40	13 58	20 24	18 39	19 42	20 20	11 32	28 02
27 Th	6 21 43	5 09 39	3 ♍ 44	26 53	16 41	18 42	26 35	10 43	10 47	28 39	13 59	20 26	19 02	20 01	20 22	12 01	28 03
28 F	6 25 39	6 10 47	18 04	26 54	18 06	19 38	27 15	10 55	10 54	28 39	14 00	20 28	19 26	20 20	20 24	12 30	28 04
29 Sa	6 29 36	7 11 55	2 ♎ 06	26 55 ℞	19 31	20 35	27 55	11 08	11 01	28 38	14 01	20 30	19 50	20 38	20 26	13 00	28 05
30 Su	6 33 32	8 13 04	15 49	26 55	20 57	21 33	28 36	11 21	11 08	28 38	14 02	20 32	20 13	20 56	20 29	13 29	28 06
31 M	6 37 29	9 14 14	29 14	26 54	22 24	22 31	29 16	11 34	11 16	28 37	14 04	20 34	20 37	21 14	20 33	13 58	28 07

EPHEMERIS CALCULATED FOR 12 MIDNIGHT GREENWICH MEAN TIME. ALL OTHER DATA AND FACING ASPECTARIAN PAGE IN **EASTERN TIME (BOLD)** AND PACIFIC TIME (REGULAR).

Notes

Notes

Notes